# Church and
# Community
# in Crisis

# THE NEW TESTAMENT IN CONTEXT

Friendship and Finances in Philippi
THE LETTER OF PAUL TO THE PHILIPPIANS
*Ben Witherington III*

Walking in the Truth: Perseverers and Deserters
THE FIRST, SECOND, AND THIRD LETTERS OF JOHN
*Gerard S. Sloyan*

Church and Community in Crisis
THE GOSPEL ACCORDING TO MATTHEW
*J. Andrew Overman*

# Church and Community in Crisis

## THE GOSPEL ACCORDING TO MATTHEW

## J. Andrew Overman

THE NEW TESTAMENT IN CONTEXT

Howard Clark Kee and J. Andrew Overman, editors

TRINITY PRESS INTERNATIONAL

Valley Forge, Pennsylvania

*# 3441/1/5*

Trinity Press International, P.O. Box 851, Valley Forge, PA 19482-0851

**Library of Congress Cataloging-in-Publication Data**
Overman, J. Andrew, 1955-
    Church and community in crisis : the Gospel according to Matthew /
J. Andrew Overman.
        p.    cm. – (The New Testament in context)
    Includes bibliographical references and index.
    ISBN 1-56338-101-X (pbk. : alk. paper)
    1. Bible. N.T. Matthew–Commentaries.    I. Title.    II. Series.
BS2575.3.O94  1996
226.2'07–dc20                                                              96-12471
                                                                                       CIP

Printed in the United States of America

96   97   98   99        10   9   8   7   6   5   4   3   2   1

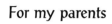

For my parents

# Contents

# Abbreviations

| | |
|---|---|
| *ANRW* | *Aufstieg und Niedergang der römischen Welt* |
| *ARN* | *Avot Rabbi Nathan* |
| *ATR* | *Anglican Theological Review* |
| *BA* | *Biblical Archaeologist* |
| *BASOR* | *Bulletin of the American Schools of Oriental Research* |
| BHTh | Beiträge zur historischen Theologie |
| *BTB* | *Biblical Theology Bulletin* |
| *BZ* | *Biblische Zeitschrift* |
| *CBQ* | *Catholic Biblical Quarterly* |
| CIJ | Corpus inscriptionum judaicarum |
| EKKNT | Evangelisch-Katholischer Kommentar zum Neuen Testament |
| *EvTh* | *Evangelische Theologie* |
| HTKNT | Herders theologischer Kommentar zum Neuen Testament |
| *HTR* | *Harvard Theological Review* |
| *JAAR* | *Journal of the American Academy of Religion* |
| *JBL* | *Journal of Biblical Literature* |
| *JJS* | *Journal of Jewish Studies* |
| *JRS* | *Journal of Roman Studies* |

| | |
|---|---|
| *JSNT* | *Journal for the Study of the New Testament* |
| *JSOT* | *Journal for the Study of the Old Testament* |
| *JTS* | *Journal of Theological Studies* |
| *NovT* | *Novum Testamentum* |
| NovTSup | Novum Testamentum, Supplements |
| *NTS* | *New Testament Studies* |
| SBLDS | Society of Biblical Literature Dissertation Series |
| SBLSP | Society of Biblical Literature Seminar Papers |
| SNTSMS | Studiorum Novi Testamenti Societas Monograph Series |
| *SNTU* | *Studien zum Neuen Testament und Umvelt* |
| *TS* | *Theological Studies* |
| ZDPV | *Zeitschrift des deutschen Palästina-Vereins* |
| ZNW | *Zeitschrift für die neutestamentliche Wissenschaft und die Kunde der älteren Kirche* |
| ZTK | *Zeitschrift für Theologie und Kirche* |

# Introduction

## The Aim and Approach of This Commentary

This commentary on Matthew's Gospel is part of a series entitled "The New Testament in Context." The term "context," however, can have numerous definitions. For one writer "context" may refer to a narrative context; that is, the place at which a particular saying, parable, or event appears in the context of the larger story helps determine the meaning. How might a saying or vignette, or the sequence in which each appears in the entire narrative, affect features of the story? This is the context that matters most to some readers and writers. For other writers, the contemporary context in which the ancient text is read is the context that matters most. This interpretive approach has a long history within the church and within biblical interpretation. The meaning of the Gospel or part thereof is determined mostly by the larger and immediate social and political context in which it is *read,* not written. The modern context helps illumine and interpret the meaning and message of the text. This approach and understanding of context has been recently revived and applied to the text with profound significance by so-called liberation theologians, though this application of context is by no means restricted to the later twentieth century and to liberation theologians.

These understandings of context will be in evidence in this commentary. The whole story of Matthew is a crucial context and, in fact, an absolute necessity for understanding smaller parts or units of the Gospel. It is impossible, for example, to understand the Sermon on the Mount in Matthew (chaps. 5-7) in isolation from the rest of the Gospel. The story itself, written by the author as best we can reconstruct it, is the first place a sensible reader will look for clues and for a context that will help supply meaning to words, instruction, and stories in the Gospel. And there is little doubt that cross-cultural analogies, and stories and events from our own time, can indeed help to shed more light on the Gospel texts, their meanings, and their application. This, too, will be in evidence in this commentary.

The dominant meaning and use of the notion of context in this commentary is what has been referred to as the *social context* in which the ancient text was written. This is the context that most informs my reading and interpretation of Matthew. I stress this is not to the exclusion of other *contexts*. But the Gospel of Matthew is a very short work coming out of the Greek-speaking East toward the end of the first century C.E. Scholars, readers, and preachers of the Gospel need all the help they can get while trying to understand the meanings and impact of a Gospel that is short, at many points oblique, and part of a larger conversation, much of which has been lost to us.

The author wants to tell a story about the life, death and resurrection, and teachings of Jesus. The author believes his own understanding of the story of Jesus can inform the issues and problems that characterize the lives of many of the members of his group. Matthew is telling a story about Jesus. But it is important to remember that his story of Jesus has been influenced and shaped by the situation in which his community lives. Throughout the commentary I will refer to Matthew as the author and mind behind the text. Although he is reporting Jesus' words or actions, "Matthew" is deciding what belongs in his story. In this sense, the Jesus we read about in this Gospel is "Matthew's Jesus." That is, the author Matthew has described Jesus and his meaning for his church consciously and carefully so that Jesus will address the Matthean community and their predicament at the close of the first century C.E. in Palestine. Why did Matthew write his story in the manner he did? Why did he include the things he did? Why did he omit some other things he knew to be included in Mark's earlier Gospel? The answers to these questions can be found through an examination of the broader social context and setting of Matthew's own community. This social context will help us better understand the nature and meaning of Matthew's Jesus. Jesus is presented in certain ways in Matthew's Gospel for certain reasons. The broader social, cultural, and political context in which this Gospel was written will help us understand particular passages and parts of the Gospel better, and it will help amplify the meanings of Matthew's "book of Jesus Christ, son of David, son of Abraham" (Matt. 1:1).

Much from this first-century document can be confounding to many modern readers. This is because Matthew's story is part of a larger conversation, what we may call the "taken-for-granted knowledge" for Matthew and his church. The background and context for the things being said in the Gospel are more-or-less clear to Matthew's readers or hearers. People in Matthew's church and world simply tend to know what the author means by these words and stories, and they know the issues and problems that provoked his address to them in the first place. We contemporary readers do not possess this knowledge. We do not inhabit the world and setting of Matthew's congregation. Much of what might have been clear to Matthew's community is elliptical and elusive to us. How can sense be made of a text written in a time so different from ours in space and substance? This is not simply a theoretical question for arcane academics. Matthew's Gospel is among a set of texts to which Christian culture certainly, and most of Western culture generally, has afforded unusual authority and voice. Matthew's Gospel has helped serve as the ground for the formation of belief systems, ethical convictions, and social behavior throughout Western history. This is an unusually long shadow for such a short work. That this Gospel — because it is a Gospel — carries so much weight and authority in many parts of the world behooves the student and expounder of this text to attempt to gather as much information as possible about it in the hope that this may actually help explicate Matthew's meanings and intentions.

The social context or world of Matthew's Gospel involves reconstructing the political and cultural developments in Matthew's setting. This helps scholars and students to better understand what is being said and why. Matthew's Gospel was written in a period of time, and in a local or parochial setting, which helped shape the message and nature of the Gospel. The broader social world, setting, or context must be supplied if it is Matthew's meaning and message we are after in reading the Gospel. The social context is the background and taken-for-granted knowledge that was evident to Matthew's group, but that we must acquire if we want to know what this Gospel may have meant to the author and its first hearers. In this introductory section we will briefly treat the salient features of Matthew's context in order to help frame our reading of his story.

In this commentary I have not tried to offer an analysis of every word or phrase in Matthew's Gospel. Instead, I have tried to look at the Gospel in terms of the sections, pericopae, or structure I believe Matthew devised. His Gospel is well ordered. He thoughtfully gathered his material according to certain themes, he carefully accepted, amended, or edited the material he received from Mark's Gospel written a generation earlier, and he set out his story of Jesus in a way that would address issues and crises effecting his congregation. I have commented on the text according to what I take to be the author's own thematic and structural divisions. The table of contents reflects these divisions.

The reader will recognize quickly that I, like the overwhelming majority of scholars, take Mark's Gospel to be the earliest Gospel. In fact, Matthew had Mark's Gospel in front of him while writing his Gospel. It is very instructive for the reader to notice when Matthew follows Mark precisely, when he introduces nuanced changes, and when Matthew completely deletes material from that earlier source. Matthew also had access to or had been exposed to another source, which he seems to share with the author of Luke's Gospel. This source is usually referred to as "Q," from the German word for "source," *Quelle*. The Sermon on the Mount, for example, contains some Q material. One may compare Matthew 5 and 6 with Luke 6. This will highlight the two authors' treatment of the earlier Q material. This source or document has never been found, but a careful analysis of Matthew and Luke will reveal a common source. Q, however, is a source less defined and obvious in Matthew than Mark. All but roughly sixty verses of Mark's Gospel can be found in Matthew. Matthew's utilization and conversation with his earlier sources have been favorite subjects of Matthean scholars for most of this century, and continue to be subjects of considerable interest that can still yield some important insights. I have also introduced some parallels between certain Matthean material and the so-called Gnostic *Gospel of Thomas* when appropriate. This, too, is another voice and view of Jesus. Matthew almost certainly did not have *Thomas* available to him, but *Thomas* represents a set of Jesus traditions that, when compared and contrasted with Matthew, can help further define his message. I have tried to hold the use of Greek terms to a minimum. If I suspect the term may hold some significance for the informed reader, then I have included it.

Fundamental to this commentary is the question of how Matthew's Gospel relates to and is informed by the developments occurring in his community's environment. The author at points explicitly, and at other points more generally, addresses these developments. The Gospel of Matthew was written with a view toward, if not prompted by, the question of how the author's community should react to developments in their setting. It is the presupposition of the author that the life and teachings of Jesus, as recalled by the community, will instruct and guide the group through a period of transition and even crisis. Let us briefly describe those aspects of Matthew's social context which most inform his Gospel and the day-to-day issues of his community.

## Matthew in the Roman World

First we need to realize the larger historical and political context in which Matthew's Gospel should be read. This book was written toward the end of the first century of the Roman Empire. Augustus (formerly Octavian), the adopted son of Julius Caesar, became Rome's first emperor following the collapse of the Roman republic and the putative cessation of civil wars that dominated Roman life and politics for at least the last half of the first century B.C.E. Jesus was born during the reign of Augustus, Rome's first emperor.

From the point of view of Rome and the few first-century Roman officials who would have heard of this group, Jesus and the subsequent movements gathered around him were Jewish groups from the East (Anatolia). For Rome, Jesus movements were part of the Eastern Empire. They were among the diverse people, languages, and cultures that Rome had encountered from the late second century B.C.E. forward. Followers of Jesus and communities gathered around him lived out on the edge of the empire. They were part of a curious and perhaps exotic culture that was increasingly having an influence in more central parts and places in the empire. The East was becoming economically and politically important to Rome. This can be seen in the career and accomplishments of Pompey the Great whom, it was said, pacified the East, reorganized it administratively, made it safe and suitable for trade and tours, and brought these eastern lands as far away as the Euphrates River into Rome's orbit and control. In the midst of these political and economic developments lies Matthew's community, tucked away somewhere in Palestine.

By the time of the writing of Matthew's Gospel the empire had gone through at least twelve or thirteen emperors. Syria, Palestine, and Jordan had seen governors and procurators too numerous to mention. But the empire was well established in Matthew's world. By this time Palestine, and perhaps Galilee in particular, had become more of a thoroughfare in the empire than a mere cultural or economic backwater. The eastern end of the Mediterranean Sea had become crucial for Rome's military and economic security. For good or for ill the East had received the attention and affections of the empire and its officials for some time. Matthew's community was part of the larger Roman world for good reason and they would have known it.

Issues that were part and parcel of the Roman world would have, therefore, been part of Matthew's world. Should one pay taxes to Rome? Who locally works with the Roman administration? And how does being Jewish square with being a participant in the broader Roman world? These questions were part of Matthew's community and part of his Gospel precisely because the community obviously lived within, and recognized themselves to be a part of, the Roman Empire in the Greek-speaking East. The political developments and cultural pressures that came as part of being under the sway of Rome informed the life of the Matthean community and helped shape the Gospel.

Perhaps most significantly in this regard is the role of colonialism in reading and interpreting the Gospel. To recognize that Matthew's Gospel is also a document rooted in and partially shaped by the currents and realities of the broader Roman world is to recognize at the same time that the Matthean community lived and developed within a colonial context. Someone else controlled the land of Matthew's foreparents. Foreigners held ultimate control over the cities in the region in which Matthew lived. And this foreign power selectively worked with local elite and others whom they deemed necessary to maintain control. This colonial reality then divided the local population. Division and tension are predictable features of any colonial reality and, as we shall see, Matthew's Gospel betrays great division and tension. That tension was not with the Romans so much as it was with other local leaders whom the author believed would mislead and destroy the people.

Matthew's Gospel is first a document that came out of the Roman world. For Matthew and his church this meant most immediately that they were not in charge of certain aspects of their lives. For some the empire may have meant opportunity, for others it may have meant terror and death. But to all living in Roman Palestine, the empire meant a loss of control. Someone else was in charge, and if one meant to survive, one had to find a way to work with this political reality. Matthew's Gospel deals with this reality rather directly, and the author offers some clear advice to his community about living in the Roman world. What readers today think of as Christianity and as Judaism both developed within this colonial context of the Roman Empire. This feature of Matthew's context should not be overlooked by the reader and interpreter.

## Matthew within Second-Temple Judaism

One of the most important advances in the last twenty years
in the study of Judaism around the time of Jesus has been the
realization that Judaism in this formative period was fluid and
diverse. From at least the time of the advance of hellenistic
culture, religion, and language in Palestine, Jewish society and
religion reflected dramatic diversity and even fragmentation.
The hellenization of the East has been traditionally associated
with Alexander the Great, who brought Greek language and
beliefs to all the regions he conquered. Palestine, too, was
conquered and became part of Alexander's kingdom around
330 B.C.E. At Alexander's death Palestine, like Egypt and Syria,
became a land disputed between Alexander's surviving gener-
als. Ptolemaic and Seleucid families who had served Alexander
now fought over Palestine, the small strip of land that separated
them. Being "a land in between" put Israel in the midst of a host
of military, economic, and cultural pressures that boiled over in
the Maccabean revolt in 165 B.C.E. This revolt, the legends of
which are described in the books of 1 and 2 Maccabees, captured the deep divisions these pressures provoked *within* Israel.
The influences of other cultures, other worldviews, and new political personae created tensions that finally boiled over in Israel
during the rule of the Seleucid tyrant Antiochus Epiphanies in
165 B.C.E. The Maccabean rebels, known usually by their family
name of the Hasmoneans, won independence for Israel, which
would then officially be lost to the Roman general Pompey in the
year 63 B.C.E., a mere 100 years after the revolt. The fragmentation and tensions between various Jewish groups continued, and
even picked up speed, during Roman rule in Palestine.

The first-century C.E. Jewish historian Josephus, roughly a
contemporary of Matthew's, describes several of the more popular schools within Judaism during his day: the Essenes, usually
associated with the famous Dead Sea Scrolls, the Pharisees, the
Sadducees, and a revolutionary group called the Fourth Philosophy (*J.W.* 2.119–66; *Ant.* 18.11–17). In addition to these
groups, Josephus describes a number of other less-official groups,
popular groups that also laid claim to traditions, heroes, and,

above all, expectations in Israel. These groups were variously referred to as bandits, rebels, popular movements, Sicarii, or even Zealots. But there were more than even these — a number of groups associated with the temple in Jerusalem, Samaritans who laid claim to many of Israel's traditions and institutions, numerous apocalyptic groups not mentioned by Josephus but whose texts have survived, and the groups gathered around Jesus of Nazareth. These, too, were popular Jewish groups who must be viewed within their original setting within second-temple Judaism. So varied was Jewish society in the land of Israel in this period, and so varied were the Jewish groups, that scholars no longer speak of Judaism in the singular when discussing this formative and fertile period in Jewish history. Instead, we speak about Judaisms. In this time and place, there existed a number of competing, even rival Judaisms. At stake were fundamental issues of identity, authority, and the future of God's covenant people. Among the Judaisms of Jesus' day, who truly spoke for the God of Israel? Who understood and accurately interpreted Torah? And who was best suited to interpret the past and lead God's people into the future? These were the salient questions that defined and distinguished the various second-temple Judaisms, and these issues and questions set certain Jewish groups against one another in the colonial context in which they lived at the turn of the eras in Roman Palestine.

Because of the work of J. Neusner and other scholars of this formative period in Jewish history we are able to step back and see how some of the documents from the New Testament fit squarely into this lively and fragmented period in Jewish history. Matthew's Gospel is also a Judaism. The author took up issues important and potent among his second-temple contemporaries. Matthew claims, like so many others in his time and place, to speak about and for Israel and its God.

Matthew thought of himself as a Jew. His Gospel indicates nothing to the contrary. His community seems by every indication to be a Jewish community, centered around Jesus of Nazareth. While it may come as a surprise to some readers to think of Matthew and his church as Jewish, to others it may seem obvious. "Christianity" as a term and even more as an identifiable entity distinct from Judaism had not emerged by the time of the writing of Matthew's Gospel. To speak of Christians or Christianity with respect to the Gospels, historically speaking, is anachronistic. I recognize that the Gospels are now Christian books and belong in a Christian canon. But when viewed and studied in its historical and social context, Matthew's Gospel appears quite clearly as a Jewish document, addressed to Jews who thought that they were living out Judaism in its truest sense. This book was later claimed by Christianity and the church. When one views Matthew within the context in which it was written, we see that this book takes up the issues both common and crucial among Judaisms of the second-temple period. When we think about the context in which to place Matthew historically, we must think most immediately of the fragmented and yet formative context of competing forms of Judaism in Roman Palestine in the first century C.E. This is the setting against which the Gospel should be read and interpreted. The members of Matthew's church practiced and believed themselves to be part of what we may refer to as *Matthean Judaism.*

This directs our reading and understanding of Matthew dramatically. Matthew is not a book that details the split and enmity between "Christians" and "Jews." This book details the tensions and issues that existed between different Judaisms at the close of the first century C.E. in Palestine. When we read about "synagogues" in Matthew, this is not the place "where Jews gather," as opposed to a church "where Christians gather." No, more important and more precisely, this is a place where some Jews, representing a type of Judaism, meet. The split and the tensions in Matthew are typical and predictable, though no less painful, when viewed within the larger context of the diverse and divided setting of Jewish society in this period.

Matthew wrote at a particularly poignant time in Jewish history, in the wake of the first Jewish revolt against Rome (66–70 C.E.). The Gospel dates to little more than a generation after this watershed event. A number of Judaisms seem to have disappeared after the first Jewish revolt. Except for Pliny (c. 110 C.E.), we never hear of Essenes again. The Fourth Philosophy, along with the Qumran community, and a number of messianic and popular movements dissolved around 70 C.E. because the truly transforming event of the first Jewish revolt was the destruction of the temple in Jerusalem. The country's religious and cultural center, and perhaps the institution that most provided continuity and leadership for Israel, was destroyed by the general and eventual emperor Titus, son of Vespasian. This event and humiliation was celebrated on the so-called Judea Capta coins, which depicted Judea bound and kneeling at the base of a tree; Nike, the goddess of victory, stands over Judea. And in the Arch of Titus Rome's victory over the Jews was carved in stone for all of Rome and its visitors to see.

The arch erected in Rome depicted the treasures of the temple in Jerusalem paraded through the city, along with prisoners and other spoils of war. Leading the parade was the emperor Vespasian with his victorious general son Titus, followed at a distance by Titus's younger brother Domitian. The result of the first Jewish revolt was proclaimed for Jews and Romans alike to see and remember. The events of 66–70 were disastrous for Jews, but the memory and the lessons of the revolt continued and were cultivated for some time by Roman leaders and officials.

It is hard to underestimate the impact of this event. While certain forms of Judaism seem to have disappeared along with the temple's spoils, remaining forms of Judaism found themselves in the precarious position of living in a context where the traditional leadership had been profoundly disrupted, if not destroyed, and the organizing symbol and institution for the religion lay in ruin. The problems and issues this raised were manifold. Matthew lived and wrote in a time when there was a crisis of leadership and identity. The questions about how to relate to Rome, and who would do it, remained strong after 70. Who was in charge, and how would they order their lives in the wake of the temple's destruction? The author believed he had the answers to many of these questions that plagued his and other communities in the post-70 period. It stands to reason, however, and it is indeed the case, that Matthew was not alone in claiming the right to teach, lead, work with Rome, and, in short, fill the void left with the failure of the revolt and the destruction of the temple. Matthew's Gospel depicts Matthean Jews contending with another Jewish group, whom Matthew refers to as "scribes and Pharisees," for voice, influence, and control in the years of uncertainty. This competition and contention shape the Gospel.

## Matthew's Opponents

A dramatic and defining strain in Matthew's story is the on-going conflict with the scribes and Pharisees. Matthew attacks these groups with surprising vitriol and vigor from 3:7 forward. R. Hummel and many others have noted how Matthew has a tendency to import the Pharisees into his story. When-ever possible, Matthew makes this Jewish leadership group the embodiment of what is wrong with Israel. Matthew is exces-sive and stereotypical in his characterization of this group. His attack upon their actions and motives reaches its climax in chapter 23 where he describes these opponents as hypocrites, ar-rogant, bad teachers and blind guides, "whitewashed tombs full of dead men's bones," and murderers. This rhetoric and embit-tered name-calling is typical of a deeply divided colonial setting and points to the competition and rivalry that existed on a lo-cal level between various Jewish leadership groups. In Matthew's view, as we shall see, this group was responsible for most of what had gone wrong recently in Israel. Matthew believed his group had been called by God to replace the scribes and Pharisees as heirs of the mantle of authority and carriers of God's promise to God's people (cf. 21:43). Matthew shared with Josephus the view that the ills that had befallen Israel were a result of poor, divided, and faithless leaders (cf. *Ant.* 14.77). Matthew believed that God had acted, and was acting, to replace the inept lead-ers in his setting with the true and faithful leaders, which he believed was the Matthean community.

   This was a real life conflict within Matthew's church. He felt under attack by the current leadership. The scribes and Pharisees had some understandable questions about Matthean Jews and Judaism. They were clearly raising questions locally about the Matthean community. Time and again throughout Matthew's

Gospel the scribes and Pharisees emerge as the debate partners in the conflicts that arise. The "scribes and Pharisees" represent the local leadership group that had questions about Matthean Judaism's treatment of the law (cf. 5:17–20; 15:1–20); they become the standard against which Matthew defines justice and right behavior (5:18; 23:4–36); and they are the group who began the plot to do Jesus in (12:14). A similar coalition of leaders appears at the birth and death of Jesus.

Matthew wanted his audience to believe that local leaders, described variously as scribes, Pharisees, elders of the people, or chief priests, were responsible for the uncertainty and the struggles that characterized life in Matthew's setting. Yet Matthew himself concedes that these people are in charge locally (23:2–3). Matthean Jews were put in the precarious position of having to "practice and observe whatever they [the scribes and Pharisees] tell them," but they should not do what they practice (23:3). This group "sits in the seat of Moses," an unofficial symbol of authority associated with Jewish gathering places and civic centers. This group of leaders possessed sufficient authority to make it difficult for Matthean Jews should they fall out with the scribes and Pharisees. These two groups — "scribes and Pharisees" and Matthean Judaism — were squaring off in a struggle for voice and influence in Matthew's setting. The harsh and strident tone of Matthew's treatment of his competition suggests he may have believed he was losing that struggle.

Who were these so-called scribes and Pharisees? I am not sure if this was their literal name in Matthew's context toward the end of the first century. I do believe, though, that J. Neusner has shown the high probability of both scribal and Pharisaic elements in the leadership coalition that emerged in Israel after the fall of the temple. So, while this group may not have literally been called "scribes and Pharisees," there is a very good chance that there was a fair amount of both in the dominant post-70 group(s) in Matthew's world. Matthew did not make up these terms or names. His predecessor Mark used them in his story as well. But for Matthew this leadership coalition had sharper contours, had a much greater presence, and was decidedly bad. Marcan Pharisees, in this respect, are a pale reflection of later Matthean Pharisees, who were real threats and were in charge. Matthean Jews believed the Pharisees were making life very difficult for them. The Pharisees were, of course, literate. They were legal experts. They seem to have controlled the local courts. They were able to work with other imperial authorities in their Palestinian setting, something Matthew believed his group, not the scribes and Pharisees, should be doing. And they possessed influence and a clear measure of authority with the people. Matthew's Pharisees look and sound a lot like Josephus's description of the Pharisees. Writing at some time between 75 and 90 C.E., Josephus says that the Pharisees were famous for their legal expertise, that they tended to work well with those in power, and they were popular with the people. A. Baumgarten has shown also that the Pharisees were associated with a set of popular traditions they encouraged among the people. One can see Matthean Judaism and the Pharisees clashing over these popular traditions in several places in Matthew's Gospel, such as the dispute about clean and unclean hands in 15:1–20. Josephus's description of the Pharisees and their role in Judean and Galilean society has been fully analyzed recently by A. J. Saldarini. Saldarini describes the Pharisees as retainers, that is, something like mid-level officials in the agrarian society and colonial setting of second-temple Palestine. They vied for position and influence with those in power, who used them to understand and have influence with the people. The ground of Pharisaic power was their legal expertise and their influence and popularity with the people. Matthew explicitly took up these two issues with the Pharisees. He tried to make the argument to his group that in fact the Pharisees really did not understand the law. He instructed the congregation not to be taken in by what they said and, above all, not to do what the scribes and Pharisees did.

Matthew's group was very similar to the competition. Both had "scribes" (cf. 7:28; 13:52). Both had their gathering places or "synagogues." This is captured in the characteristic Matthean addition of the pronoun "their" (*auton*) to the word "synagogue" (12:9; 13:54). Matthean Jews possessed their own gathering place. They did not refer to theirs as a *synagoge,* but an *ecclesia.*

Etymologically the terms are different, but socially they performed similar functions for these two kindred but competing groups. Also, each of these two groups had a following or disciples. The respective leaders looked and sounded like teachers, and both claimed to speak with inspired authority. Both groups seemed to claim they were capable of negotiating the space and tension between the local people and the regional imperial officials in Palestine. To an outsider these two groups so opposed to one another, if one listens to Matthew, would actually look quite similar. It is this proximity, both ideologically as well as physically, that helped spawn the harsh words and the negative debates that characterize so much of Matthew's story.

The so-called scribes and Pharisees of Matthew's Gospel had begun to fill the vacuum of leadership and authority in post-70 Palestine. They were probably located up north away from Jerusalem. Jerusalem, perhaps more so after than before 70, was the place of official Roman imperial rule. These retainers with modest followings might have been found in the outlying cities of the Galilee or northern Judea. In Matthew's setting the "scribes and Pharisees" had started to take over. They became the judges, the interpreters, and go-betweens in the post-70 years. They emerged as the people who would describe what constituted true Judaism in the strange in-between years of 70–100 C.E. In many respects, and I have argued this elsewhere, these Matthean opponents represented a nascent form of the coalition that finally brought some order to the chaos of the post-revolt years: rabbinic Judaism. Rabbinic Judaism, too, was concentrated in the north in Israel — it was largely a Galilean movement at the outset — and rabbinic Judaism retained many of the features of post-70 Judaism we hear debated in the pages of Matthew's Gospel. Historically speaking, then, Matthew's opponents ultimately prevailed. Matthean opponents dramatically influenced the Judaism that would speak for the majority of Jews in Palestine by the year 250 C.E. and, ultimately, speak for most Jews around the world even today. Matthean Judaism had little direct influence on the shape of the coalition that finally took charge out of the fluid period of 70 and after. But Matthew may have had a hand in shaping his opponents indirectly through their debates and conflict. If so, then a legacy left by Matthean Judaism was faintly etched in the margins of the texts of rabbinic Judaism.

## The Date and Location of Matthew's Gospel

Matthew was written sometime during or between the reigns of Domitian (81–96), the last Flavian ruler, and the emperor Trajan (98–117). I have suggested elsewhere that the Gospel was written in or around a Galilean city. I have been followed in this suggestion by several others, including D. Harrington, A. J. Saldarini, and A. Segal. Most New Testament handbooks will suggest Antioch in western Syria as the place of origin for the Gospel. There is little outside of scholarly tradition and convention to commend this hypothesis. It may be the case that Ignatius of Antioch (beginning of the second century C.E.) quotes Matthew. If this is so, Ignatius's allusions to and citations of Matthew are few and indirect. I am not convinced that it is even the Gospel of Matthew to which Ignatius refers. However, it is true that by the early second century Matthew was being quoted by at least a few other writers. The *Didache* and the first two chapters of 4 Ezra, which were added later and called 5 Ezra, are two examples of early-second-century documents that quote Matthew. Ignatius may have known Matthew's Gospel, but this in no way suggests Antioch as a place of origin for the Gospel.

There have been other suggestions for the place of formation of the Gospel. S. van Tilborg has suggested Alexandria in Egypt. This is a novel suggestion and not impossible. However, a sizable body of literature survives from ancient Alexandria and Matthew's Gospel reads like no other text with a putative Alexandrian origin that I am aware of. H. D. Slingerland has suggested a city east of the Jordan, perhaps one of the Decapolis cities. And B. T. Viviano has put forth the crown jewel in Herod the Great's building projects, Caesarea Maritima, as a possibility. None of these suggestions, were they ever to be confirmed, would greatly affect our reading of Matthew. A Decapolis city or Caesarea would have been similar settings to one of the Galilean cities or larger towns, which I think makes the most sense. Alexandria is a setting only vaguely effected by the destruction of the temple, and there is little evidence of Pharisaic-like Judaisms in this city.

Two reasons might point toward a Galilean location for the Gospel. First, Matthew rather strikingly did not allow Jesus to leave Galilee. W. Trilling and others took note of this some time ago. No sufficient rationale has been provided for this Matthean tendency. There have been some unsuccessful attempts to explain this feature through appeal to Matthean theology. Some have suggested that Matthew viewed Galilee as a land of salvation, which is not supported in Matthew's text. It is true, however, that Jesus remains in Galilee until his ill-fated trip south to Jerusalem and his death. I have suggested that this feature of the Gospel points not so much to Matthean theology but to Matthew's own social setting. To him Jesus was a Galilean and the community Jesus now addresses through Matthew's Gospel is also Galilean.

The most plausible locale would be in or near a large Galilean city or town. Matthew placed Jesus and his movement in Capernaum. Jesus and his disciples are far less itinerant in Matthew than they are in Mark. Capernaum is their home base. It is not out of the question that Matthew's church was located in Capernaum, and the city of Tiberias (built c. 18 C.E.) was the large center nearby where authorities, courts, legal experts, and imperial officials resided.

Another Galilean possibility could be the city of Sepphoris, located a few kilometers northwest of Nazareth. In Sepphoris, or the region of this "ornament of Galilee," all the people, institutions, and tensions referenced in the Gospel would have been present. Also, as F. Manns and S. Miller have shown, Sepphoris was a center for the development of early rabbinic Judaism. There are distinct traces of this later form of Judaism present in some nascent form in the Matthean opponents.

This brings up the second reason for a possible Galilean provenance for the Gospel. Rabbinic Judaism took shape in the Galilee. This movement's early heroes, Yohan ben Zakkai and Rabbi Judah the Prince, were basically Galileans. The term "rabbi" as a technical term for an office within Judaism is first attested in the material culture in Galilee, as E. Meyers has shown, and the first authoritative work of rabbinic Judaism, the Mishna, was edited in Galilee, probably in Sepphoris. It is some early form of this movement that is contesting with Matthean Judaism. Issues of ritual purity and legal interpretation, followers and disciples depicted as teachers, struggles over authority, who will work with the imperial powers, and how to structure the community in the post-destruction years are examples of the issues found both in Matthew and early rabbinic literature. These conversations and developments were taking place largely in the north in Israel after 70. We must add Matthew's voice and interpretation to this debate.

Matthew's Galilean setting was near a court, as chapter 5 suggests. The community lived in close proximity to officials who were able to make life difficult for Matthean Jews. Legal debate characterizes much of the give and take in Matthew's context. The competition for authority and leadership in Matthew is reflective of the vacuum that would have existed in the areas outside of Jerusalem after 70. Prior to 70 the temple and the temple system helped coordinate and control the regions beyond Jerusalem for Rome. With the destruction of the temple, regions such as Galilee, formerly controlled through the temple system, experienced a crisis in leadership and structure. Matthew's Gospel is part of the struggle for leadership and structure in such a Galilean setting.

I would suggest, then, that this Gospel was written in or near the Galilean cities of Sepphoris or Tiberias. A village on the outskirts of these thriving cities would also remain a possibility. The cities of Sepphoris and Tiberias were important first-century cities. They were centers of trade, they both possessed courts, were home to numerous officials and imperial personnel, and they were large enough to contain sizable but diverse Judaisms. Both of these Galilean cities were large enough to contain several gathering places for different Jewish communities. Also, these cities would have possessed the necessary cultural and civic institutions to provide for the relatively high level of learning reflected in Matthew, as well as in the Mishna, which was codified about 100 years after the Gospel, though it obviously contains traditions that are much earlier than 200 C.E.

Recent excavations at ancient Sepphoris, for example, have placed in broad relief the cultural and intellectual vitality of the Galilee in the Roman period. A thoughtful and provocative piece like Matthew's Gospel, informed by the Septuagint and nuanced legal debates, reflecting competing groups of elites and literati trying to work out the tensions inherent in a time of dramatic transition, could quite easily have been produced in the Galilee.

Within this setting in the land of Israel at the close of the first century one Jewish community, gathered in large measure around the memory and acts of Jesus, was large enough and engaged enough in the religious and political events of the day, that one member of the community, whom we will refer to as Matthew, believed he could reasonably raise his voice amid the clamor of many rival Judaisms and claim that his group held the key to the future of God's people. For at least a time Matthean Judaism was in this fray during a brief period that was surely one of the most fertile and formative in all of Jewish history.

## A Book for a Church and Community in Crisis

Matthew's Gospel quite transparently seeks to address a range of issues that have emerged in the life of this Jesus-centered Jewish community in the years following the first revolt and the destruction of the temple. These issues and troubles have been around for Matthean Judaism, in all likelihood, for some time. But the tenor and tone of Matthew's Gospel suggests some problems had escalated to a crisis point. What were the crises that precipitated the writing of the Gospel? Of course we cannot be absolutely sure, but certain dominant themes in the book provide clues that point to the issues that had begun to put the future of the church in peril.

The leadership and cultural vacuum caused by the temple's destruction prompted the contention between various Judaisms in Roman Palestine. This competition had characterized the Matthean setting for some time. The so-called scribes and Pharisees were the legendary bad boys in Matthew's world. Matthew's church viewed these people not just as rivals, but as threats to their safety and way of life. Matthew's community vied with the scribes and Pharisees for position and voice in Matthew's city or town. The Gospel reveals that Matthew believed these opponents possessed the upper hand. This group's influence and authority cast a long shadow of doubt over Matthew's community. Some in Matthew's church seemed to believe the criticism leveled at them by these authorities. Perhaps even some had started to desert the Matthean church for the way of life and belief promoted by these leaders. The competition and threat from these local authorities seems to have escalated to a crisis point in Matthew's context. He had to stake out his group's claims in the face of what he believed was a very serious threat to their identity and future. The debate and contention with these more powerful and influential leaders had provoked a crisis in Matthew's church. Among the things Matthew's story of Jesus had to address, paramount perhaps was the nature of the current leadership, why their charges against Matthean Judaism were wrong, and why Matthew's community should aspire to assume the leadership in their setting. How does he accomplish these tasks?

Jesus is depicted in Matthew as constantly critiquing the current leadership and extolling the authority and insight of the Matthean church. This theme, which runs throughout the Gospel, was intended to cast further doubts about the dominant leadership and cultivate the hope that someday soon Matthew's community would assume their rightful place as the true leaders in their setting. The disciples in Matthew are depicted as the true leaders who, unlike the disciples in Mark, really understand what authority and leadership are all about. Jesus is an extremely effective teacher in Matthew and his followers become very well-trained students. Most notable in this regard is Peter, who becomes the paradigm for an understanding faith in Matthew. Jesus nurtured a generation of teacher/leaders and Matthew saw his community as standing in that train of tradition within Jesus-centered Judaism. In short, the current local leaders are described repeatedly by Jesus as unfit, while the Matthean disciples are the true authorities in their setting. They possess this authority because God gave it to them. The conflict between these two groups has reached a point of no return. In Matthew's setting one must choose between allegiance to Matthean Judaism or the Judaism represented by the scribes and Pharisees. In chapter 23 Matthew shrewdly counsels his church to keep their noses clean, but he cautions the group not to actually do what these leaders do. He tells them that to emulate these leaders is to put their own lives in peril. So the crisis of leadership and authority is one clear issue which is transparent in the Gospel.

A related issue that emerges with force in the Gospel is the dispute about the law and legal interpretation. This is where Matthew defines most of the differences and disputes between these two groups. The Matthean opponents clearly found the Matthean interpretation and application of the law wanting. Matthew repeatedly defends the community's view of the law. The local leaders viewed Matthean Jews as anomic. In the view of the scribes and Pharisees, Matthean Jews played fast and loose with the law. They inherited this mode of legal interpretation from Jesus. Matthew, though, claimed that in fact his community was the only one that truly understood and fulfilled the law. Matthew was trying to make his case in the face of the attacks by the local leaders. But at the same time, and perhaps even more important, he was trying to convince the troubled and the doubtful in his church that theirs was the right way to live out Torah. Jesus came to fulfill the law completely, Matthew's Jesus claims, and the author would have the beleaguered community believe that they should still continue to do the same, despite harsh criticism, and perhaps even punishment, from the local authorities.

In this time of transition Matthew had to confront issues relating to community order and structure. The uncertainty and the crises of their day had fostered some disorder. Issues of discipline, community structure and authority, and instructions for church liturgy and worship are examples of the order Matthew sought to supply for the group. Chapters 18, 16, and, above all, the Sermon on the Mount are where Matthew concentrated his instruction about how to structure the life of the community so it could survive, if not flourish.

Questions about authority and leadership, law, order, and community structure were long-time issues that took on a new urgency in Matthew's day and setting. All these themes emerge repeatedly in the Gospel. Along with these is the issue fundamental to community life, particularly in times of uncertainty, change, and crisis — the question of identity; in light of the struggles and questions that surround us, who are we? Matthew's church faced this vital question of identity and self-definition.

Once again, it is in Matthew's literary tour de force, the Sermon on the Mount, where the issue of the community's identity is dealt with most directly. The famous Beatitudes, which have been canonized within much of Western culture as desired attributes and actions, are really an epitome of the characteristics that should mark off Matthean Jews in their local setting from other groups and leaders. The Beatitudes, or *makarioi* as they are called in Greek, laid out for Matthew's audience the values that should guide their day-to-day decisions and relationships. The behavior and disposition Matthew encouraged were primarily intended for the group. That is, Matthew's attempts at responding to the identity question, "who are we?" really do focus on "we," and not those outside of the group. Matthew was not describing the identity and ideal nature of all people in the world, and he was not describing the identity and nature of all people who follow Jesus. Remember, Matthew had Mark's Gospel in front of him while he wrote and Matthew was aware that he and Mark disagreed on some important points concerning discipleship. No, Matthew was describing the ideal nature and identity of his group, of his church. The Sermon articulates the character of a follower and their relationships within the Matthean community, no more and no less.

Along with the Beatitudes, other famous Matthean admonitions from the Sermon on the Mount that echo through Western culture, such as "Turn the other cheek," "Love your enemies and pray for those who persecute you," "If someone asks for your cloak give them also your shirt," and the so-called Golden Rule, are all instructions from Jesus in Matthew intended to shore up the collective self-understanding of the church that has so dramatically come under scrutiny of late. The turmoil and uncertainty that punctuated Matthew's world understandably provoked doubts and questions about "who are we?" and "where are we headed?" More than any other section of the Gospel, the Sermon speaks to the issue of Matthean identity. This famous section focuses above all on the values and marks of the community and its members, and it describes for Matthean Jews the nature and contours of the relationships within their group and their immediate setting.

The strain of the crises and questions that characterize the Matthean setting had taken a toll on relationships within the church. The Matthean Jesus addresses these tensions and provides advice for this divided community. The crises within and around the Matthean community led the author to discuss issues of leadership and authority, of law, order, and structure in the church, and he had to speak to the pivotal questions about Matthean identity. These issues and themes reoccur throughout the Gospel and assume a transparency that, in fact, reveal a great deal about Matthew's own church.

The final theme, which is part of the life of this church and community in crisis, and one that clearly informs the message and shape of the Gospel, is the crisis about the future. Such angst was surely prompted by the prospect of the group's marginalization, if not disappearance. What would happen to them and when, if ever, would the things come to pass they had heard and believed for too long? These questions are hardly below the surface in this Gospel. Matthew's Jesus must address the questions pertaining to the future of the community.

Although Matthew supplied order, structure, and routine for his community, thereby giving the distinct impression he was planning for the long haul, he nevertheless retained a form of apocalypticism that maintains God's intervention at some point in the history of the community. Matthew argues that his community is in utter continuity with the history and eschatological drama of Israel, that what has happened to the great heroes of Israel, and the faithful people of Israel, is happening and will happen to Matthew's church. As Israel's heroes and prophets of

old were ignored and persecuted, so Matthean Jews also are persecuted for righteousness' sake. But as the prophets and sages of
old are now Israel's heroes and hallmarks, so faithful Matthean
Jews who live according to Jesus' teachings will one day be vindicated. They, too, will be numbered among Israel's heroes and
faithful for they will have played a role in saving Israel from
corrupt days and leaders.

Conversely, the current leaders who typologically appear as
the villains and wicked leaders of Israel's past will be judged by
God. They will be exposed for what the author believes they
truly are. On that day the righteous will stand out and the
wicked will take their appropriate place with the evil-doers of
Israel's history. This scenario is played out in chapters 23–26.
This apocalyptic hope is by no means unique to Matthean Judaism. Many other apocalyptic groups and apocalypses existed
in Matthew's day. In many respects Matthew's is a toned-down
apocalypticism. But this scenario would have made sense to
many in his group, it would have sounded familiar, and it would
have supplied hope to at least some in the Matthean church.

But Matthew also believed that if his community would fully
embrace the teachings of Jesus as presented in the Gospel, the
future of the community would take care of itself. That is, the
more the group fully reiterated the teaching and behavior put
forth by Jesus, the more the community would become "the
kingdom of heaven." This distinctly Matthean phrase symbolizes
the goal of the community's life together. The author believed
Jesus taught his followers how to actually mimic, if not embody, the kingdom of heaven on earth. This hope for the future
is captured in the now-familiar Matthean phrase from the so-
called Lord's Prayer, "on earth as it is in heaven" (6:10). If the
group would fully live out the law and the values, attributes, and
disposition Jesus promoted, and if they structured their communal relations according to his instructions, then they would be
whole, or complete (*teleios*), as their father in heaven is whole
(5:48).

Also, if the church truly lived out the life to which the Matthean Jesus gave expression, then they would not really have to
worry about tomorrow. Like the apocalyptic material, one won-

ders if this would have provided solace to everyone. Probably not. But it most certainly did to some. Matthew taught his community in crisis and doubt that if they put God's kingdom first, all the other issues and worries about life here and now could be resolved (6:33). This familiar verse about the primacy of the kingdom of heaven must be balanced with Matthew's other instructions about the future and how to approach it. Taken out of context 6:33 can provide the license for irresponsibility and the abandonment of this world. This would be very far from Matthew's counsel indeed. But this advice does play a role in coping with the future. There were things that were out of control for Matthean Jews. As we noted above, the loss of control is a defining characteristic of a colonial context like Matthew's. They had to keep their eyes on the prize and the promise they heard, which was still unfulfilled in their setting. If they continued to do this, then many of the worries and struggles going on within their lives and in the community could be overcome or resolved.

Did Matthew's Gospel finally succeed in supplying the hope and guidance necessary amid the crises of faith and communal life we have outlined? In the short term it would seem so. There is a Matthean circle of sorts that appears on the literary horizon by the early second century. Matthew's perspectives did seem to enjoy some resonance for a generation or so after the writing of the Gospel. One cannot argue that his story was an early-second-century bestseller. But parts of the story were copied and reiterated by some for their communities going through similar struggles in their settings. To this extent Matthew's story was effective. But in the long run Matthew's advice to his community in crisis did not seem to prevail. Matthean Judaism was eclipsed by the end of the second century in Palestine. It is difficult to find traces of his voice in Palestine past the first third of the second century C.E. Some may count this, finally, as a failure of his priorities and perspectives on Jesus and Judaism.

Matthew's Gospel did flourish in another context and in another time. When something called Christianity emerged, distinct from its progenitor Judaism, Matthew emerged as an important Christian text. But for most of Christian history, Matthew's original setting, situation, and even message have been obscured. The crises and questions that provoked the Gospel in the first place — the struggles and tensions within and among competing Judaisms in Palestine in the late first century — have been lost on most interpreters. This has contributed to Christian misrepresentations and occasional abuses of Matthew. This is more obviously the case with Christian anti-Judaism. In this regard Matthew has erroneously and impishly been marshaled as evidence of God's rejection of the Jews and God's election of Christians. (This issue will be discussed at some length in chapter 14, "The Passion and Death.") Matthew's original intent and message are to be found behind the layers of subsequent church history, and within the setting that formed and prompted his story. This commentary aims to take that original setting seriously, and in so doing lay bare Matthew's first meanings and messages to his Jewish church gathered around Jesus. In so doing, the import and significance of this early Gospel may be heard in a manner most of subsequent Western and Christian history has been unable to hear for far too long.

## Further Reading

Balch, D., ed. *Social History of the Matthean Community: Cross-Disciplinary Approaches.* Minneapolis: Fortress, 1991.

Baumgarten, A. I. "The Pharisaic Paradosis." *HTR* 80 (1987): 63–78.

Davies, W. D., and D. C. Allison. *A Critical and Exegetical Commentary on the Gospel According to Saint Matthew.* 2 vols. International Critical Commentary Series. Edinburgh: T. & T. Clark, 1988–91.

Harrington, D. *The Gospel of Matthew.* Sacra Pagina 1. Collegeville, Minn.: Michael Glazier/Liturgical Press, 1991.

———. "Matthean Studies Since Joachim Rohde." *Heythrop Journal* 16 (1975): 375–88.

Hummel, R. *Die Auseinandersetzung zwischen Kirche und Judentum im Matthäusevangelium.* Munich: Chr. Kaiser, 1963.

Kingsbury, J. *Matthew as Story.* Philadelphia: Fortress, 1987.

Levine, L. I., ed. *The Galilee in Late Antiquity.* Cambridge: Harvard University Press; New York: KTAV, 1992.

Manns, F. "Un centre judeo-chrétien important: Sepphoris." In *Essais sur le Judeo-Christianisme,* 165–90. Jerusalem: Franciscan Press, 1977.

Meyers, E. M., and A. T. Kraabel. "Archaeology, Iconography, and Non-literary Remains." In *Early Judaism and Its Modern Interpreters*, ed. R. Kraft and G. Nickelsburg, 175–210. Atlanta: Scholars Press, 1986.

Miller, S. *Studies in the History and Traditions of Sepphoris*. Leiden: Brill, 1984.

Neusner, J. "First Cleanse the Inside." *NTS* 22 (1976): 486–95.

———. "The Formation of Rabbinic Judaism: Yavneh from A.D. 70–100." *ANRW* II.19.2 (1979): 3–42.

———. *From Politics to Piety: The Emergence of Pharisaic Judaism*. Englewood Cliffs: Prentice-Hall, 1973.

Overman, J. A. "Heroes and Villains in Palestinian Lore: Matthew's Use of Traditional Jewish Polemic in the Passion Narrative." SBLSP 29 (1990): 592–602.

———. *Matthew's Gospel and Formative Judaism: The Social World of the Matthean Community*. Minneapolis: Fortress, 1990.

Saldarini, A. J. *Matthew's Christian-Jewish Community*. Chicago Studies in the History of Judaism. Chicago: University of Chicago Press, 1994.

———. *Pharisees, Scribes, and Sadducees in Palestinian Society: A Sociological Approach*. Wilmington, Del.: Michael Glazier, 1988.

Schoedel, W. R. "Ignatius and the Reception of the Gospel of Matthew in Antioch." In *Social History of the Matthean Community*, ed. Balch, 129–77.

Segal, A. "Matthew's Jewish Voice." In *Social History of the Matthean Community*, ed. Balch, 3–37.

Slingerland, H. D. "The Transjordan Origin of St. Matthew's Gospel." *JSNT* 3 (1979): 18–28.

Stanton, G. "The Origin and Purpose of Matthew's Gospel: Matthean Scholarship from 1945–1980." *ANRW* II.25.3 (1889–1951).

Tilborg, S. van. *The Jewish Leaders in Matthew*. Leiden: Brill, 1972.

Trilling, W. *Das Wahre Israel: Studien zur Theologie des Matthäus-Evangeliums*. Munich: Kösel, 1964.

Viviano, B. T. "Where Was the Gospel of Matthew Written?" *CBQ* 41 (1979): 533–46.

# Chapter One

# The Book of Jesus' Origin and Birth — 1:1–2:23

## Christ, Son of David, Son of Abraham

Matthew begins his Gospel with the use of the term "book" (*biblos*) to describe the record of Jesus' family history and birth. The second term here (*genesis*) might best be rendered "origin," rather than "birth" or "genealogy" as some translations do. In 1:17 the term is used in a more limited sense of Jesus' actual birth. The same construction (*biblos genesis*) can be found in the Septuagint (LXX: the Greek translation of the Hebrew Bible) in Genesis 2:4 and 5:1. This is not necessarily to be understood as Matthew's description of his entire work. Rather, this is a record, or book, of Jesus' origin. In the ancient world especially, one's lineage, or to whom one was connected, was of great importance. Naturally, as the early communities of Jesus' followers gathered, there were questions about who Jesus really was, about his family, and, of course, about the provocative nature of the early traditions about his birth. Did Jesus have a family? If so, who were they? Who were Jesus' relatives, what was his background? Matthew 1:1–17 is an attempt to anticipate or respond to such questions from both those within the community and those outside looking in, who were perhaps leveling charges against the group's beliefs. Matthew's opening chapter addresses profound questions about Jesus' identity and heritage and, thereby, those who found themselves aligned with him.

The Hebrew Bible reflects this interest in origins and foundation stories as well as the more limited question of how and where one was born. Matthew's double use of the Greek term *gennao,* translated as "origin" in 1:1 and "birth" in 1:17, parallels the double use and meaning of the term in the LXX in Genesis 2:4 and 5:1. This demonstrates his familiarity with LXX Genesis, as well as the fact that his audience would have been interested in how Jesus was born, but even more in where he came from, to whom he was connected, and God's role in his birth. However, these were not concerns to be identified only with Jewish literature and culture in antiquity.

The ancient world more generally reflected an acute concern with questions of origin and identity. While Jews all over the Roman world would have known the story of Genesis, both genealogy and creation, Greeks knew the stories of the *Iliad* and the *Odyssey* and saw in those stories information about who they were, their people, their relation to the gods, and their fate or destiny. The Romans told their myth of origin in the story of Romulus and Remus. And, in the form of Virgil's *Aeneid,* Romans around the time of the birth of Jesus and the beginning of the reign of Caesar Augustus would have been listening to yet another story about the founding of Rome, their heroic forbearers, and the divinely inspired fate of the Roman Empire under Augustus.

Matthew's book of origin, then, should not be viewed as simply a perfunctory list of names that serves as a prologue to the real story. This is his answer to questions about Jesus' identity, origin, and place within the history of Israel. These claims for Jesus bolster also the claims made by communities formed around him and his message. They help legitimate the community's own claim to authority and true interpretation. The author Matthew believes his community bears the message of Jesus and his interpretation of the history and future of the people Israel. If one believes God really did orchestrate the lineage, background, and birth of Jesus, then the claims and interpretation of the community gathered around Jesus are obviously viewed as possessing greater veracity and authority. The questions of just who possesses authority, who has the accurate interpretation of scripture and Israel's history, and who has the right to speak for the local community are themes that run throughout Matthew's Gospel. The book of Jesus' origin and birth plays an important initial role in the claims made about Jesus and his heirs by Matthew's church.

Matthew associates two hallowed names in Jewish tradition with Jesus when he makes both David and Abraham virtually part of Jesus' own title or name in 1:1. Prior to the beginning of the genealogy Matthew links Jesus to David and Abraham with a series of genitive associations: "the book of the origin of Jesus Christ, the son of David, the son of Abraham." By this time the term "Christ" may well be on its way to being Jesus' last name within the circle of believers. In first-century Palestinian parlance this term meant "anointed," or someone empowered or sent by God. This is not a claim or term Matthew employs lightly.

The vital personae and events in Israel's history are met in Jesus' lineage and biography. His identity can be traced back through the great kings of Israel to the very progenitor of the people Israel, Abraham. As is widely recognized, Luke's Gospel traces Jesus' roots back to Adam, who was "the son of God" (Luke 3:38). Luke does not begin his story with the familial and titular claims so prominent in Matthew. Unmistakably, in Matthew Jesus is ensconced within the history of Israel's divinely driven story. He is Jesus the messiah, the son of David, the son of Abraham. These two heroes of Israel's story are signaled out again as the touchstones of the genealogy in 1:17. There are fourteen generations, Matthew writes, from Abraham to David, fourteen from David to the Babylonian exile (in 587 B.C.E.), and fourteen from the exile to the birth of Jesus (1:17). By Matthew's peculiar reckoning, at the birth of Jesus Israel was due another anointed agent. Jesus is in the same family and in the same league with these two great figures and reformers in Israel's grand story. This sets a tone for Matthew's own story about Jesus and sets a series of expectations for the informed reader.

## The Genealogy

Matthew's genealogy has several curious aspects. The names included in the list have received considerable attention. Of particular interest to commentators has been the mention of the four mothers Tamar, Rahab, Ruth, and Bathsheba. Some have suggested that these women were non-Jews and this accounts for their inclusion in the genealogy. Their presence signals God's intention to incorporate non-Jews into Matthew's understanding of Israel. A second theory involves the sexual exploits of some or all of the women, something scholars have referred to oddly as "divine irregularity." This is intended to accent God's unexpected, or surprising *modus operandi*. Related to this is the interpretation that the women represent God's use of sinners or scarlet persons to accomplish God's purposes. Let us briefly address these interpretations.

Concerning the first suggestion, there is little indication outside of 10:5 that Matthew would be opposed to non-Jews joining his community. As we shall see, his Gospel is not particularly concerned with what might be called *mission*. Matthew's primary concern is his understanding and interpretation of Jesus' message as it relates to and instructs his community. Matthew provides some indication that he or others have been worrying about the place of non-Jews in the "kingdom of heaven," which is his double entendre for his faithful community and for those who comprise God's elect at the last judgment. In response to the centurion who asked for help for his paralyzed servant Jesus says, "Nowhere in Israel have I found such faith" (8:10). Because this takes place in Capernaum, we assume Jesus must be referring to the fact that the centurion is not an Israelite. At the close of the book Jesus commands his followers to go to all people, make disciples, baptize them, and "teach them to observe all I have commanded you" (28:19). There is then some suggestion that Matthew has in mind non-Jews and Jews in the kingdom of heaven. There is no doubt, however, that he is addressing primarily Jews and those who understand themselves as placed within the history of Israel. Gentiles were probably around and may have been welcome in Matthew's church. However, these, like any other participant in the group, would have had to abide by the interpretation, structure, and requirements that characterized the community.

It is very important for modern interpreters and readers to understand that Judaism in the second-temple period was well established and deeply involved in many aspects and parts of the broader Roman world. Judaism was a venerable and popular religion within the empire. The involvement and inclusion of Gentiles was by no means novel or unusual. A number of ancient authors attest to the attraction of Judaism to non-Jews. The Jewish communities in Antioch, Sardis, Alexandria, and Rome, to name a few, were clearly sizable, deeply involved in the broader civic life of their cities, and were an influential minority among many of the non-Jewish members of their cities. Indeed, as the Acts of the Apostles suggests in its highly stylized narrative, Jewish communities in the Greco-Roman diaspora had many gentile sympathizers and devotees and were continually attracting them to their gathering places, called *synagogues*. While Gentiles may have been more of a minority in Roman Palestine, some nevertheless also would have found aspects of Jewish religion and life attractive and advantageous, as was the case in the diaspora. The extensive talk about Jesus, Jews, and Gentiles in scholarly literature on the Gospels forgets this point. Modern interpreters tend to be far more fixated on the relationship and gulf between Jews and non-Jews than someone like Matthew. There were non-Jews around the synagogues and some were deeply involved in these Jewish communities — some to the point of conversion to Judaism through circumcision. A supposed non-Jew in one of Matthew's stories may not be the point of the story for Matthew at all, but it certainly catches the eye of most modern interpreters and many instantly assume therein lies the point of the story. Such interpretations fail to take into account the broader setting and situation of Judaism within the Roman world. I think there were Gentiles in and around many Jewish communities in antiquity and they were not necessarily the least bit unusual to Matthew or many other ancient Jewish authors.

More insidious than the failure to take seriously the involvement of non-Jews in Jewish communities throughout the Roman

Empire is the desire on the part of many twentieth-century interpreters to pass through earliest Christianity's "Jewish phase" as quickly as possible. This tendency quickly dismisses Judaism, its contribution in the ancient world, and the unavoidable and essential fact that Jesus of Nazareth and the author of the Gospel of Matthew were Jews thoroughly grounded in the realities and issues that characterized Judaism in all its variety in the first century. Modern interpreters have assumed Matthew was distancing himself — if he was not already utterly distanced — from Jews and Judaism and told his story of Jesus in large measure to capture the rejection of Judaism and Israel and to make clear the movement of the Gospel to the Gentiles. The suggestion that the point of the women in the genealogy is to foreshadow the movement to the Gentiles by the church reflects such an imposition. Every putative Gentile who appears in Matthew's story should not be read as a vindication of non-Jews and the rejection of historic Israel due to its obduracy and apparent rejection of Jesus. Much of Gospel scholarship over the last few generations has suffered from such flawed assumptions and has helped nurture expressions of Christian anti-Semitism from the pulpit and other points within Christian communities.

The suggestion that the women are there because of some sexual misdeed or scarlet act also is flawed. The notion of "divine irregularity" mentioned above claims that Matthew included these four women to emphasize God's inclusion of sinners into the kingdom of heaven. First, these women are not portrayed as sinners in the stories that make them relatively famous in Israelite history. On the contrary, Ruth, Tamar, and Rahab are heroines. And surely if he was looking for dramatic sins and sinners Matthew could have done better. And why, if we think Matthew has this on his mind, have interpreters offered this thesis about the women in the genealogy but not David, clearly a sinner of fairly high order? As far as the women being non-Jews, Tamar does not seem to have been a Gentile, we are given no indication with Bathsheba, the wife of Uriah, and only in the case of Ruth does one sense that her being a "foreigner" is even an important point.

What is common among these women is that all except Rahab had unusual births or birth stories associated with them. Also, these women through their actions kept the royal line of Israel alive. Bathsheba gave birth to Solomon after the trauma of the death of her first child by David. Ruth gave birth to Obed, "who became the father of Jesse, the father of David" (Ruth 4:17). Tamar slept with Onan, the second son of Judah, after her first husband and son of Judah, Er, had died because "he was found wicked in the Lord's sight" (Gen. 38:7). The Book of Ruth makes explicit that Ruth and Tamar also helped save Israel by preserving the line (4:12, 18).

The case of Rahab does not involve an unusual birth. She is credited with saving the spies sent by Joshua to reconnoiter the land and prepare for the taking of Jericho. Rahab hid the spies, denied knowledge of their whereabouts, and enabled Joshua and his troops to take both Jericho and the Land. As a result her family was spared and they were allowed to settle permanently among the Israelites (Josh. 7:25). She is said by Matthew to have been the mother of Boaz whom Ruth married (Ruth 4:13). She then also insures the perpetuation of the Davidic line.

All these women, one could say, saved Israel. The first three did so through rather unusual births, and the fourth did so quite literally through her deception of Israel's enemies, in this case her own people. All play important roles in the continuation of the royal line of David. This is not a certain interpretation, but it is the most reasonable explanation for the presence of the names of the women in the genealogy. The birth of Jesus and the introduction of Mary then fit into this interpretation of the other four women in the genealogy. Mary plays a similar role in the history of Israel and in the birth of Jesus. In a pregnancy that appears illegitimate, provokes fear and doubt on Joseph's part, and requires divine intervention, the line or heritage that will save Israel is perpetuated. The mention of the women culminating in Mary is probably less a scandal and more a potent reminder to Matthew's audience of the lengths to which God has gone to save the people of God in the past and has recently acted similarly in the person and story of Jesus, messiah, son of David, son of Abraham.

## The Name "Jesus"

The name of Jesus, as interpreted by Matthew, highlights the early communities' belief that God has acted through Jesus on behalf of Israel. It was important to keep alive the royal line of descendants, which included such notables as Abraham, Isaac, Jacob, and David, because the birth of Jesus signaled the arrival of a true king of the Jews who would save Israel. In Matthew's view there was nothing new in the story he was telling. Rather, he stressed the continuity in Israel's story from Abraham to Jesus. Jesus represented a fulfillment or fruition of God's relationship with Israel. The line traced from Abraham through David to Jesus highlights this continuity and the orderly nature of the events surrounding Jesus' birth, life, and death. In Matthew's view there is an inherent logic in believing in Jesus and he tried to lay out that rationale and defense.

In 1:20–21 Joseph is instructed by an angel to take the pregnant Mary home, make her his wife, and name the child Jesus "for he will save his people from their sins." As is widely known, the name "Jesus" is the Greek form for the Hebrew name *Yeshua*. This is a form of the name "Joshua," which means something like "Yahweh helps/saves." The interpretation and meaning Matthew supplied to the name of the child highlights the mission the community believed Jesus was called to undertake. Jesus was on a mission from the God of Israel to save them. The term "sin" (*hamartia*) cannot be construed from the Hebrew or Greek name for Jesus. The name says only but significantly that "God saves." Matthew supplied "from their sins" in his rendering of the name.

The Gospel of Luke (1:31), of course, knows the child's name is Jesus, but provides no such interpretation of the name and its deeper significance. Luke writes only, "You are to give him the name Jesus. He will be great, and will be called the son of the most high God." The name "Jesus" in Luke does not anticipate or denote anything about the ministry and fate of Jesus.

Matthew had a second name for Jesus, which appears in 1:23. He cites a text from Isaiah saying that a young woman will be with child and she will bear a son called Emmanuel. This is a very common convention for Matthew. He frequently quotes from the LXX, or some variant of it, to support aspects of his story or validate an event in the life of Jesus. Many of these citations are concentrated in the first two chapters of the Gospel. Here Matthew found a passage from Isaiah 7:14 which in the LXX reads, "The virgin [*parthenos*] will conceive and bear a son, and they will call his name 'Emmanuel' [which is interpreted 'God with us']." The Hebrew text reads "young woman" (Heb. *alma*), which the LXX rendered *parthenos,* or "virgin." In both the Hebrew and Greek of Isaiah the woman is understood to be young and a virgin and there is no indication that the birth of the child in Isaiah 7:14 should occur in any way other than the usual fashion. Matthew, though, seems to have interpreted this in a way that attempts to deal with Mary's troubled pregnancy. At the time of Jesus' birth Matthew says Joseph and Mary had not had intercourse. He sees the LXX passage from Isaiah as possible support for the assertion in 1:18 and 1:20 that the Holy Spirit has caused Mary to be with child. In Matthew's mind this is the import of the citation from LXX Isaiah 7:14. He is not opposed to the theological freight of the name "Emmanuel," but he hardly seems to notice the child already has a name and that the significance of it has been explicated.

## Joseph

Matthew is unique among the Gospels where Joseph is concerned. Only Matthew made Joseph a pivotal figure in the book of the origin and birth of Jesus. Joseph is the primary source of revelation in the first two chapters. He receives four dreams in two chapters (1:20; 2:13, 19, 22) which guide the family, help them fulfill the prophecies that are so important to Matthew, and keep the family out of harm's way. Dreams were a standard way in which the gods spoke to people in antiquity. The receiver of the dreams, or seer, was considered a particularly anointed, spiritual, or powerful person. The one who could determine what the future augured was one who could go where only angels and other anointed ones dared to tread. In Luke's

Gospel the women are the agents through which the story is told and interpreted. The women are the ones who understand what is going on in Luke's birth narrative. However, in Matthew it is Joseph who receives the dreams, obeys instructions, and fulfills what is necessary to make sure the birth happens in the right place and at the right time, and that the child remains safe from the political figures who threaten him.

In 1:19 Joseph is described as a "righteous" man (*dikaios*), Matthew's highest acclamation and the goal of the faithful person. He is obedient, apparently understands the highly unusual circumstances following the intervention of the angels, and is the prominent human agent through whom the entire story of the origin and birth of Jesus is fulfilled.

Why did Matthew so accentuate Joseph's role compared to the other Gospels? At the time Judaism in Israel was patrilineal. That one is determined to be a Jew by the identity of the mother (matrilineal) emerged later in Judaism, which is one reason why the mention of the women in the genealogy garners the attention it does. The women break the pattern of "so and so the father of so and so . . . ," and they are not particularly relevant to the question of the child's identity and tribe. This is why the women's inclusion begs some sort of explanation. In Matthew it is Joseph who determines finally Jesus' identity and heritage. He is of the line of David.

The Christmas story is ingrained in the collective memory of Western culture, particularly for those who have some acquaintance with Christianity. Yet the version of the Christmas story in most people's memory is a hybrid of Matthew and Luke's stories. For example, only Luke, not Matthew, makes *explicit* the connection between Bethlehem and the house and line of David. If one were familiar with the Hebrew Bible or LXX texts dealing with Ruth, as Matthew seems to have been, then one would know that Ruth, Boaz, Jesse, and David are associated with Bethlehem. Yet Matthew does not mention that Bethlehem is "the city of David." This is Luke's phrase. It is, however, as 2:6 shows, the city that will give rise to a new ruler in Israel.

Matthew offers no explanation of why the family arrives in Bethlehem. He characteristically provides scriptural support for the significance of the place for producing a leader or ruler (*hege-menos;* "arkonta" in the citation from LXX Mic. 5:1) who will "shepherd my people Israel." The confirmation that the messiah is born in Bethlehem comes ironically from some of the antagonists in Matthew's story, that is, the chief priests and scribes who form a coalition that dogs Jesus throughout the story. They are the ones who provide the scriptural proof for Bethlehem being the place of the anointed ruler's birth. This coalition emerges again at the time of Jesus' trial.

Joseph, then, is the person who provides for Jesus belonging to the line of David. Jesus' heredity and his being "Son of David" are not as pronounced a concern in Luke as in Matthew. Joseph anchors Jesus' identity within the family of both Abraham and David. For Matthew this is essential and accounts for some of the emphasis on Joseph in the first two chapters of the Gospel.

Also, within the extremely diverse and fascinating religious world of the Roman Empire women were rather prominent as interpreters and divine channels. While the Roman world was both extremely hierarchical and patriarchal, some of the most popular cults of this period focused on goddesses. The cults of Isis and Diana or Artemis of Ephesus, for example, whose central figures were women, were very popular. In Rome itself the Vestal Virgins were an important part of institutionalized Roman religion and politics, and women were quite popular and prominent in the nearly ubiquitous cult of Dionysus. Some inscriptions from synagogues in the Greco-Roman world indicate some prominent women may have held leadership roles in these synagogues. These cults and institutions that fostered roles for women, however qualified, did not flourish in Palestine, the place of the writing of Matthew's Gospel. Unlike Luke, Matthew was not part of a setting that tended to afford these sorts of roles for women. Women do not figure as prominently in Matthew's story as they do in Luke's. While women are the vehicles for dreams and revelation in the Lucan birth story, it would be surprising to find them playing the same role in Matthew. Indeed, they do not. Joseph is the interpreter and agent through whom the story of the birth of Jesus is guided and fulfilled. This seems consistent with what we can recover about the broader cultural and religious milieu of Matthew's setting.

## Jesus and Herod

Chapter 2 initiates the conflict between Jesus and the local client political system that ultimately does him in. We are told Jesus was born at the time of Herod the King. Here the conflict between one king and another is inaugurated. The Magi who pay a visit to Judea in 2:2 punctuate this tension by asking about a king who has been born whom they would like to honor. It is clear they do not mean Herod, the current king, and the Magi are granted an audience with Herod to provide more information about the new king. Herod summons the Magi secretly (*lathra*) to a meeting where he tries to find out the exact time of the star's appearance.

The men from the East had followed the sign of the star, which led them to Judea. In much of the ancient world the births of great or auspicious personae were frequently accompanied by astrological signs or natural wonders. Early in the second century Tacitus quipped, "A comet means a change of Emperors" (*Ann.* 14.22).

Many even believed around this time some anointed person would arise from the East to rule the world. This legend was mentioned by Tacitus (*Hist.* 5.13), and found also in Josephus in support of Vespasian's emperorship (*J.W.* 6.313; see Suetonius, *Vesp.* 4), that a portent would come from the East indicating the rise of a new world ruler from Judea. Josephus explained that some Jewish revolutionaries at the time of the first Jewish revolt against Rome (66–70 C.E.) erroneously believed this referred to a liberator from Judea to rule them. "The oracle, however, in reality signified the sovereignty of Vespasian, who was proclaimed Emperor on Judean soil," says Josephus (*J.W.* 6.314).

Did Matthew intend such seditious meanings with his heavenly signs, the title "King of the Jews" for the young ruler, and the delegation from the East to pay homage to the one born king? Was Jesus understood by Matthew as a political and religious revolutionary who would destroy the status quo and institute a new rule and kingdom based on the priorities of the God of Israel? Some clearly took it this way. In chapter 2 Herod becomes aware of the threat the child poses and begins to plot his demise. Through the help of angels and dreams, the Magi and Joseph's family stay one step ahead of the political authorities wishing to do them in.

By announcing the birth in this fashion in 2:1 ("during the period of Herod the King"), Matthew makes plain the larger political picture into which the birth scene must be placed. Jesus was "born a king," and therefore in the eyes of Matthew is a legitimate king. We have seen the important role of the genealogy in stressing this. Jesus was the rightful heir to the throne of Israel, not Herod or his offspring. This thinly veiled claim sets off the competition and contention that runs throughout the story.

Herod the Great reigned from 38 B.C.E. to 4 B.C.E. in Palestine. He was from a family of political survivors and insiders. His father, Antipater, was deeply involved in the politics of the Near East before his son, and dealt successfully with rulers in Judea, Galilee, Jordan, and Egypt. Antipater, and consequently his son Herod, were allied with Mark Antony of Cleopatra fame during a period of civil war and political intrigue at the end of the Roman Republic. In a battle between Mark Antony and Octavian (Caesar Augustus) at Actium off the west coast of modern Greece in 31 B.C.E. toward the end of what is called the second Triumvirate (43–31 B.C.E.), Octavian defeated Anthony. The following year Octavian annexed Egypt to the Roman Empire. Octavian was honored and granted the title "Augustus" by the Senate in 27 B.C.E.

Augustus consolidated his power through military might and facility with the Senate and others in power in Rome and was henceforth known as Emperor Caesar Augustus. Augustus is associated with the so-called Golden Age of the early empire. A number of Rome's most famous writers flourished during this period, some with Augustus's explicit support. Also, this was the period of the *Pax Romana,* or peace of Rome, which Augustus and his supporters believed he accomplished through his reign.

Augustus, it is said, "found a Rome made of brick and left it marble."

Augustus was an astute politician, an accomplished military leader, and used his reign to promote Roman identity, power, and imperium through decree and such public displays as temples, statuary, and inscriptions. He built an empire out of a series of local client-lords and fiefdoms. Judea and Galilee were such regions under Augustus. He expected tribute and a firm hand through a local lord or elite he could trust. In return the region enjoyed security, support, and largess from the emperor. Augustus died in the year 14 C.E. He was succeeded by Tiberius.

Herod backed Mark Antony in the civil war between Augustus and Mark Antony. He sent troops and fought on Mark Antony's behalf. How would Herod remain a viable political force in the East after such a political miscue? In one of the most notable stories associated with Herod he traveled to Rhodes and gained an audience with Augustus. There Herod did not ask Augustus's forgiveness, pay undue homage, or recant his earlier alliance with Augustus's enemy. Instead Herod described the greatness of his loyalty to Antony. True friends, he said, share in danger and benefit. Herod's affections did not shift even when Antony's fortunes fell. He, so Herod's argument before Augustus went, would be just that kind of friend and ally to Augustus if he would serve as Herod's new patron and benefactor. "Examine my behavior toward my benefactors," said Herod, "and what kind of friend I am" (*Ant.* 15.193).

Herod's argument prevailed and Caesar Augustus awarded him honors, restored the diadem to Herod (the sign of kingship), and granted him reign over additional territory beyond Judea and Galilee. Herod's power and influence in the East continued to grow. He was careful also to court Caesar's favor at every turn, welcoming him in Egypt and Syria. He gave gifts to Caesar and to his army. He helped insure their victory and safe passage. But most notable among Herod's relationship with Caesar were the many building projects Herod undertook in Judea and Galilee. From Banias/Caesarea Philippi on the Lebanese border, to Samaria Sebaste outside of Jerusalem, to the magnificent port city Caesarea Maritima, to the grand expansion of the temple in Jerusalem, Herod further ingratiated himself with Augustus and boasted to the local leaders and population of his affection for and influence with Caesar. These great cities still stand today as reminders of Herod's political finesse, and the burden such programs necessarily constituted for the people of his realm.

Consequently Herod's power was virtually unrivaled in the East. He was known on coins and in inscriptions as "King," "friend of Caesar," and "friend and ally of Rome." Matthew explicitly places his story of Jesus into this political setting in Judea and Galilee, and at the outset has the one *born* "King of the Jews" both engage and outsmart (2:16) this notorious king and savvy political ruler Herod the Great. This master of local politics and survivor of Roman in-fighting and intrigue is the one who hears of another king born just outside of Jerusalem in Bethlehem. He must endure the embarrassment of foreign dignitaries coming to see the new king and not Herod. Such a seasoned veteran of political and military battles would not relinquish either his reputation or realm very easily. Here Matthew sets in bold relief the broader political context and consequences of Jesus' program.

## The Magi

The Magi emerge as important indicators of the political subtext that is initiated in the birth story and runs throughout the Gospel. The Magi are not so much astrologers as political figures. They are representatives from an eastern kingdom to bring gifts and signs of friendship and cooperation to the new king. They are part of a royal delegation carrying with them the message of detente and stronger relations between the two realms. Their visit can easily be viewed as a statement on Matthew's (and others') part about Herod's poor administration and the tension his rule has brought to Palestine and to the region. Indeed, Herod had ruled with an iron hand. At his death there were numerous revolts, and Judea and Galilee were straining under the burden of increased taxation and tribute under Herod. Someone had to pay for all the building projects and munificence Herod showed toward Rome and Caesar, and the people of Palestine were the ones. In the Magi we see another eastern political realm throwing its support behind the new king and distancing itself from Herod. This point is highlighted through the irony of the Magi visiting with Herod (2:7) and inquiring about the "King of the Jews." By this they do not mean Herod, but Jesus.

The Magi are a celebrated feature of the Christmas story, and are enshrined in Western culture through art and in the literature of no less a name than T. S. Eliot in his "Journey of the Magi." Yet the romance of this part of Matthew's story (the Magi do not appear in Luke's version of the birth) has obscured some of the significance of the Magi's visit. These men are part of a political institution in the Roman Empire known as embassy, or official political visits to a ruler or authority. Judea and Galilee were particularly aware of this institution and attempted to employ it often in arguing their case and needs before authorities, very often Caesar himself.

Around the time of the first century a contingent from Gadara (on the eastern shore of the Sea of Galilee) petitioned Augustus to be released from Herod's realm and added to Syria (*Ant.* 15.354ff.). This group was not successful and ultimately committed suicide rather than return to Herod. An embassy of Jews and Samaritans went to Augustus to bring charges against Archelaus, the ruler mentioned in Matthew 2:22. Augustus heard their complaints and exiled Archelaus to Vienna (*Ant.* 17.355). In a separate incident, a group of Samaritans petitioned not Caesar in Rome, but a governor named Vitellius in charge of Tiberius's eastern policy (Tacitus, *Ann.* 6.32), "not as rebels, but as refugees from the persecution of Pilate" (*Ant.* 18.88ff.). They, too, were successful, and Pontius Pilate was recalled to Rome. We have spoken already of Herod's embassy to Augustus on Rhodes. The first-century historian Josephus boasts of having made successful embassies to Rome and that he personally made one to Vespasian at Jotopata, the center of the first Jewish revolt against Rome in the Galilee, where he predicted the general would soon become emperor (*J.W.* 3.400). In a similar story, Yohan ben Zakkai, a famous figure in the formation of early rabbinic Judaism, legend has it, in the wake of the destruction of Jerusalem at the close of the first revolt also approached Vespasian and pleaded with him to save Yavneh/Jamnia, modern-day Yaffo/Joppa, in order to start a school. Of the four later rabbinic traditions about Yohan, *Lamentations Rabbah* 1:5, 31 asks that Jerusalem, not Yavneh, be saved. In both instances involving Josephus and Yohan we see appeal to a power figure or ruler to work out a *modus vivendi* between the ruler and the people of Judea and Galilee.

The people and rulers of Galilee and Judea were familiar with the political institution of embassy and knew how to use it to their advantage. It is interesting to note another story about an embassy that occurred during the reign of Nero around 65 C.E. In this story, the sons of three Parthians rulers made a visit to the emperor. These three sons were called "Magi" by the late-first/early-second-century author Pliny (*N.H.* 30.6.16–17). These three came with a king from Armenia to pay homage to Nero. Incidentally, in the account of this written by Dio they took leave of Nero "by another way" (Dio 63.7; see also Suetonius, *Nero* 13), which is reminiscent of Matthew 2:12. In their embassy the entourage asked Nero to rebuild the city Artaxata, which had been destroyed in the year 58 C.E. Nero granted their request and gave them money and artisans for the construction. The city, when completed, was renamed Neronia.

Our Magi in Matthew 2 are very much in the tradition of embassy. This was a significant political moment in the Magi's view, and they took the appropriate political steps to make the most out of it. They wanted to court the favor of this new king, and this was probably their opportunity to put some distance between their eastern realm and Herod's power and influence. So viewed, the stakes were raised and the drama surrounding the arrival of the new king increased. The embassy of the Magi to Jesus reinforces his kingship and punctuates Herod's maladministration. He has been a poor client-lord. The new king, whom other powers and officials welcome, will displace the current destructive and illegitimate king of the Jews. These provocative suggestions set the scene for conflict and crisis.

## Jesus and Judean Politics:
## The Start and Finish of Matthew's Story

Chapter 2 has been viewed appropriately as a foreshadowing of the passion and death of Jesus. There are many parallels between this chapter and the trial and death scenes. The challenge Jesus and his followers represent to the local king Herod continues throughout the story. In chapter 2 Herod enlists some local leaders to assist him in finding the child. The chief priests and scribes of the people work with Herod to find the child and kill him. This alienation of certain local leaders continues throughout the Gospel. A similar coalition appears in 26:5, 57 (along with Caiaphas), 59, and 27:1, 41, 62 (with Pharisees also). The chief priests and elders pay off the guards in the resurrection scene and promise to protect the guards through their influence with the governor if need be (28:11-14). The passion and trial is the other place where the provocative title "King of the Jews" appears (27:11, 29, 57), and there are some important verbal connections between the birth and the passion in Matthew. The verb "to assemble" (*synagein*) appears frequently in chapters 2 and 27, "to be deceived," mocked or toyed with (*enepaixthe*), occurs at 2:16, 27:29, 31, 34. "To destroy" (*apolesai*) at 2:13 suggests 27:20 and 12:14, where the Pharisees take counsel as to how they might destroy Jesus.

Matthew took this confrontation between rulers and leaders seriously. The conflict presaged in the birth and early history of Jesus continued in the life and setting of Matthew's church. Indeed, the tension and crisis between Matthew's community and local leaders was really a continuation of the conflict initiated at Jesus' birth. Two generations after the death of Jesus the relations between local political leaders, as well as the ubiquitous international force of the Roman Empire, remained a salient issue for the Matthean community. In trying to figure out their relationship with local leaders and the leaders of the empire Matthew's church looked back to the early history of the life of Jesus for help and guidance.

Matthew connected the imperial political reality of Judea and Galilee in the first century with both the start and conclusion of his story. Matthew believed local leaders had successfully enlisted the power of Rome to inhibit or destroy the movement gathered around Jesus. Roman power and the realities that it posited locally serve as bookends to this Gospel and cast a shadow over the entire book. Most commentaries on Matthew make virtually no mention of this important factor. Matthew's story about Jesus and the author's own community are sandwiched between these explicit and potent narratives — the birth and the death of Jesus — which emphasize the contours of the day-to-day political realities of Matthew and his church. When one takes seriously the birth and passion narratives as symbols of Roman power and its local manifestations, the material *in between* in the Gospel takes on a different hue. The entire Gospel is played out within this abiding reality of Roman political power and local division and contention around those political realities.

Matthew's understanding of Jesus and his meaning for Israel not only took place within this political reality and under its shadow. He believed Jesus and his community's interpretation of him represented a response to the political situation of late-first-century Judea-Galilee. In Matthew Jesus offers interpretations of the law, a critique of the local leaders, a scenario of Israel's history from his point of view, and holds out his remedy for what he believes are the salient ills of his moment in time. Jesus emerges as a rival of the prevailing order in Matthew. The birth narrative announces Jesus' arrival on the scene of Judean politics. That political and civil struggle did not cease with Jesus' death. Matthew believed his community stood in the tradition of Jesus and his understanding of law and society. Matthean Jews were engaged in some of the same struggles that emerge initially in chapter 2 but run throughout the Gospel. Jesus' story as told by Matthew provides instruction for Matthew's church concerning their response and strategy in the post-70 period in Roman Palestine.

## Matthew, Jesus, and Moses

In the book of Jesus' origin and birth Matthew associates Jesus with Moses in several significant ways. Of course, Jesus is depicted as a liberator like Moses in that, like Moses, he was "called out of Egypt" (2:15). Jesus' own miraculous birth in certain respects parallels that of Moses'. Josephus (in *Ant.* 2.9–10) tells the story of the birth of Moses in ways similar to Matthew's version of Jesus' birth. First, of course, the birth is miraculous. The giving and meaning of the name is highly significant, as in Matthew. And in Josephus Moses' birth, like Jesus', is the fulfillment of prophecy.

The parallels in Matthew between Jesus and Moses continue. As Pharaoh sought to do away with Moses, so Herod seeks to destroy Jesus. Herod massacres all the boys under 2 in Bethlehem in the same manner Pharaoh killed every male born to the Hebrews (Exod. 1:22). Both remarkable children are divinely guided to and from Israel, safely eluding their enemies and allowing for the fulfillment of the mission set for them by the God of Israel.

That Jesus is in some manner Moses *redivivus* in Matthew is seen elsewhere in the Gospel as well. As we shall see, Jesus appears much like Moses in Matthew's literary tour de force, the Sermon on the Mount. Jesus' words and explication of the law look and sound very much like a reiteration and interpretation of the Ten Commandments. In fact, in the Sermon Jesus offers his *true* interpretation of the commandments. Jesus looks so much like Moses in Matthew that he is accused of trying to surpass Moses in authority. This was not Matthew's meaning, however. To the contrary, Matthew wished to portray Jesus as a new or true Moses, but not one who supersedes Moses. The force of Matthew's claim about the law, Israel's history, and the current life of his community is that all are in consonance with one another. That is, Matthew's community and their interpretation of Israel's law and history and, in particular, their beliefs in Jesus, are supported by the history of Israel and by the great figures in Israel's past, in particular, in this instance, Moses. The Matthean antagonists, the scribes and Phar-

isees, falsely lay claim to the mantle and authority of Moses
(23.1ff.). Matthew attempts to portray Jesus and his followers
as Moses' people carrying on the traditions and interpretation
started with Moses.

## Matthew and the Bible: The Fulfillment Citations

Much has been made of Matthew's use of a Greek translation of
the Hebrew Bible or so-called Old Testament. There are fourteen
citations in the first two chapters of his Gospel where Matthew
explicitly cites a version of the LXX. Half of these come from
the prophet Isaiah. Matthew supplied them to help explain to
the reader why something occurred. Matthew is alone among
the Gospel writers where this concern to ground explicitly the
events of Jesus' life in scripture is concerned. Seemingly trivial
events in Jesus' life are supported through appeal to a Matthean proof-text. Mark's Gospel, for example, seems comfortable
with allusions to scripture. This is not the case with Matthew.
The connections between Jesus' life and ministry and the scripture and history of Israel are made absolutely clear. In a prosaic
manner Matthew makes the connections for the audience and
does not risk leaving it up to the reader or interpreter. This feature of the author has been described by Matthean scholars as
"scribal-like" activity.

The operative word in these citations is "fulfill" ⁻(*pleroma*).
Something has taken place "in order to fulfill" the words of an
earlier Israelite prophet. Within his world and setting Matthew
is not alone in this type of scriptural application. The Dead
Sea Scrolls discovered along Wadi Qumran in 1948 contain a
use of scripture and scriptural citations that bear some resem-
blance to Matthew. In the case of the scrolls, citations from
scripture support or legitimate the actions and beliefs of the
Qumran community. This particular style of scriptural exegesis
at Qumran has been called *pesher*. Qumran understood scriptural
passages as applying solely to the community, its future and fate,
and to the leader of the community, the so-called Teacher of
Righteousness. J. Fitzmyer has called this type of scriptural inter-

pretation at Qumran, which so closely parallels Matthew's own use of scripture, "modernization" of ancient biblical texts; that is, the community, whether Qumran or Matthean, saw only in these older texts the events and issues unfolding in their own setting.

Events and quotations from the prophets of the Hebrew Bible are interpreted as thinly veiled references to the life of Jesus and the beliefs of the Matthean community. Why did the author utilize scripture in this arbitrary and selective manner? First, Matthew's use of scripture suggests the authority the LXX carries in the Matthean setting. That Matthew should quote the LXX in his community—just as the Scrolls cite Hebrew and Aramaic versions of the same—is a demonstration of the *a priori* authority the scriptures of Israel possessed in the settings of Matthew and Qumran. A moment's reflection on this, however, will also signal that there was surely difference of interpretation and meaning where these texts are concerned. Otherwise, there would be little need for the authors to assert *a* particular interpretation. In fact, both Matthew and Qumran provide evidence of other interpretations of scripture in their settings, which they subsequently vigorously reject. We will treat Matthew's debate over the law and his distinctive interpretation of the law later.

Second, Matthew utilizes scripture to legitimate and to strengthen the views of his community or, at the very least, his view as reflected in his Gospel within the community. As Matthew marshals scriptural "proof" for his version of the story of Jesus and the subsequent Matthean community, his case is made stronger. If people, whether outsiders or insiders, can be convinced that the story of Jesus as Matthew tells it is prefigured in the words of the Israelite Prophets, then his version of the story of Jesus, and the present course of the Matthean community patterned on that, gain significant weight and merit. Without the support and confirmation of the acknowledged authority of scripture, Matthew's interpretation of past events and his view of the future carry significantly less force.

Citing the LXX lends a veneer of antiquity to Matthew's claims. With the help of the fulfillment citations the beliefs of the Matthean community in Jesus do not emerge as radical or *de novo.* Rather, they appear as the culmination of the hopes and expectations of Israel from long ago. The Matthean peppering of the book of Jesus' origin and birth with isolated scriptural passages is, above all, an attempt to legitimate Matthew's version and interpretation of the Gospel and it putatively confirms his followers in their present course, no matter how difficult that may be at present.

## Further Reading

Brooten, B. *Women Leaders in the Ancient Synagogue: Inscriptional Evidence and Background Issues.* Brown Judaic Studies 36. Chico, Calif.: Scholars Press, 1982.

Brown, R. E. *The Birth of the Messiah.* Garden City, N.Y.: Doubleday, 1977.

Fitzmyer, J. A. "The Use of Explicit Old Testament Quotations in the Qumran Literature and in the New Testament." In *Essays in the Semitic Background of the New Testament,* 3–58. Missoula, Mont.: Scholars Press, 1974.

Harrington, D. *The Gospel of Matthew.* Sacra Pagina 1. Collegeville, Minn.: Michael Glazier/Liturgical Press, 1991.

Overman, J. A. *Matthew's Gospel and Formative Judaism: The Social World of the Matthean Community.* Minneapolis: Fortress, 1990.

Rothfuchs, W. *Die Erfüllungszitate des Matthäus-Evangeliums.* Stuttgart: Kohlhammer, 1969.

Stendahl, K. "Quis et Unde? An Analysis of Matthew 1–2." In *The Interpretation of Matthew,* ed. G. Stanton. Philadelphia: Fortress, 1983.

———. *The School of St. Matthew and Its Use of the Old Testament.* 2nd ed. Philadelphia: Fortress, 1968.

Strecker, G. *Der Weg der Gerechtigkeit: Untersuchung zur Theologie des Matthäus.* Göttingen: Vandenhoeck und Ruprecht, 1962.

# Chapter Two

# The Preparation for Jesus' Ministry — 3:1–4:25

## John the Baptist

In preparing for Jesus' ministry in the early chapters of his Gospel Matthew followed a combination of the Marcan and Q (from the German *Quelle* — a source that Matthew and Luke have in common but not Mark) material. John the Baptist is portrayed as one who prepares people for Jesus' coming through his preaching and ministry of baptism. Mark, Luke, and Matthew each cite Isaiah 40 as the scriptural and prophetic backdrop for John's ministry. Luke provides the longest quotation from Isaiah 40, and Matthew follows Mark in citing only Isaiah 40:3. This is John's mission in the divinely driven story of Jesus according to Matthew. John was the precursor and signal of what was to come.

The connection between John's ministry and Isaiah's predictions is made explicit again in chapter 11 when Jesus hears of John's imprisonment. In 11:14 John is even called Elijah, the prophet of Israel whose return is traditionally associated with the imminent arrival of the messianic age.

John announces judgment. In this regard the synoptic writers (Matthew, Mark, and Luke) depict John as an apocalypticist after a fashion. That is, John preaches an impending judgment, the destruction of those opposed to the plan and will of God, and he offers forgiveness for those who seek his particular way. John's message strikes a note of apocalyptic urgency. In the Gospel John symbolizes a pregnant moment. There is an eschatologically quickened pace to his ministry and message. His preaching suggests something awesome is about to happen quickly.

In Matthew 11 John is described as a pivotal figure in Israel's history. He is the greatest among those born of women, yet even the least in the kingdom of heaven is greater than John. And in a perplexing verse unique to Matthew it is said that "from the days of John the Baptist until now [*eos arti* — a favorite Matthean redactional conjunction] the kingdom of heaven has suffered violence, and violent people take it by force." I take Matthew's meaning to be this: In his view, the opposition to his movement, and to the form of Jesus-centered Judaism he represents, really began with John. John, if you will, was the first martyr of the movement. He was imprisoned and killed even before Jesus. His message of apocalyptic judgment, imminent end, the vindication of a minority group and its interpretation of scripture, and, perhaps most important, the denunciation of local political leaders, led to his demise. John, like Jesus after him, was killed for sedition. His voice and his interpretation of the times — much like that of Jesus — were viewed as too hostile by those in power to be allowed. Matthew understood his beleaguered church as standing in a tradition of opposition to local client-lords which actually started with John, not Jesus. John represents the beginning of open hostilities between those who possess de jure power locally and the Jesus movement in Matthew's setting. Matthew understood the crisis and conflict that the Matthean church was experiencing as that same violence the kingdom of heaven has suffered ever since John, roughly two or three generations prior to the writing of Matthew's Gospel.

Of course John is portrayed by the writers as one who prepares the way for Jesus' coming and his ministry. This is done primarily through the citation from Isaiah 40 familiar to us in the West because of the Christmas story and Handel's *Messiah*. However, this citation does not appear in the mouth of John. In all the Gospels, including Matthew, this is an interpretation of John and his ministry by the writers, an interpretation that appears to have started with the Gospel of Mark. Whether, historically speaking, John would have understood himself as simply a precursor for Jesus is a fair question. There is some indication of competition between those gathered around the Baptist and those gathered around Jesus in John's Gospel. In John's Gospel Jesus and the Baptist are at the same time attracting followers and baptizing. Some competition between the two groups is given voice by the crowds in John 3. Also in John, and in the ancient manuscript evidence of Mark's Gospel, there seems to have been some confusion over whether Jesus actually baptized people, and precisely when John was baptizing. Again, here we can see faint traces of two popular first-century Jewish groups with charismatic figures as their leaders competing and occasionally coming into conflict.

However, by the time of Matthew's Gospel such faint traces have been obscured. John is clearly one who prepares for Jesus' coming and ministry and eagerly defers to him. The use of Isaiah 40:3 by Matthew and Mark codifies this role for John in relation to Jesus. As far as the Jesus movements reflected by the synoptic Gospels are concerned, by the post-70 period John's purpose and the nature of his ministry were clear and defined. If there were any bona fide followers of the Baptist in the post-70 period they have left no record, or they were reabsorbed into a form of Judaism that would have been sympathetic to their worldview. Certain forms of Jesus-centered Judaism might have been receptive to followers of the Baptist (though other forms less so), perhaps revolutionary/apocalyptic groups that ultimately coalesced on the eve of the Bar Kochba revolt (133–135 C.E.) would have found alliance with such followers, or perhaps these followers found a home within the broad coalition of rabbinic Judaism after 135. These are hypotheses. The fate of the followers of John the Baptist following his execution at the hands of Herod Antipas remains an unanswered question.

In 3:7–10 Matthew follows Q (Luke 3:7–9) quoting John's speech about the end and the wrath to come. The passage contains a favorite Matthean logism, "bearing fruit," or "a tree that bears fruit." It is those who, in Matthew's terminology, "bear fruit" who will inherit the kingdom of heaven and serve as God's clients in the new age. The Q passage contains the saying, "Do not begin to say to yourselves, 'We have Abraham for our father'; I tell you, God is able from these stones to raise up children to Abraham. Even now the axe is laid to the root of the trees; every tree therefore that does not bear fruit is cut down and thrown into the fire." This view about the impending judgment and right behavior in the here and now from Q suited Matthew's ethics and theology quite well. There are plenty who think they are sons of God but, in his view, are not. "Do not presume to say, 'We have Abraham for our father.'" It is those who bear fruit — the righteous (*dikios*) —who will inherit the kingdom.

The Q passage affirms Matthew's understanding of the nature of the kingdom of heaven as well as his interpretation of at least one aspect of Jesus' teaching. However, such a conviction on Matthew's part sets the stage for conflict and crisis between his community and the local leaders whom Matthew believes are not righteous and are not "bearing fruit." Indeed, Matthew departs from the Q wording in 3:7 and supplies "Pharisees and Sadducees" for the Q term "crowds" (*ochlois*) found in Luke 3:7. Here is an early indication of something that becomes painfully evident throughout the course of the Gospel. That is, Matthew's primary issue is with local leaders who claim to speak for the God of Israel but, Matthew believes, do not. They are false guides and teachers, they are not *dikaios,* and they do not "bear fruit." At every opportunity Matthew inserts the titles for these leaders into the Q or Marcan material he inherits. This passage involving the Baptist is one such incident of many. The impending judgment and wrath are intended for these false leaders. Of course, this sets up enmity and crisis between the Matthean community and the local leaders Matthew refers to as Pharisees in conjunction usually with some other authoritative title (scribes, Sadducees, or elders of the people). Matthew wastes no time drawing out these lines of conflict and crisis. He places in the mouth of the Baptist an unprovoked attack on these local leaders. Matthew's church is in a crisis involving local political and religious leaders which ultimately will be its undoing. It is not a faceless, nameless "multitude" that is called "a broad of vipers" in Matthew 3:7. Matthew has the Baptist name these "vipers," and they are unmistakably the leadership groups with which the Matthean community means to contend. And so they do, throughout the length of his Gospel.

The Baptist goes on to praise Jesus in his speech. Jesus is mightier than the Baptist. The Baptist is not worthy to carry Jesus' sandals. While John baptizes with water, Jesus will baptize with the Holy Spirit and fire. In the words of the Baptist, Jesus has come to judge — to clear the threshing floor, to gather the wheat and burn the chaff in unquenchable fire.

Jesus then comes to John for baptism. John protests the inappropriateness of this act but acquiesces after Jesus utters the distinctly Matthean phrase, "It is necessary to fulfill all righteousness" (*dikaiosyne* — another favorite Matthean term). When Jesus comes out of the water following his baptism the heavens open up, the Spirit of God descends like a dove upon him, and a voice from heaven announces, "This is my beloved son with whom I am well pleased."

One notable feature in the voice from heaven following Jesus' baptism is that the voice in Matthew makes a public pronouncement. In the other Gospels the voice speaks to Jesus, saying, "You are [*su ei*] my son." In Matthew the voice says, "This is [*outos estin*] my beloved son." Matthew suggests that this was not an interior, mystical experience at the baptism for Jesus' knowledge alone. To the contrary, the confirmation of Jesus' role at his baptism is for everyone to hear. This accomplishes two things. First, it helps to substantiate this unusual claim through possible other witnesses. Matthew, one assumes, believes that others heard the voice that day and, in so far as orality can provide such a confirmation, that fact is a matter of public record.

Second, however, the public proclamation relates to an ongoing theme one can observe throughout Matthew's Gospel. Matthew was deeply concerned with, for want of a better term, education. He wanted people to know and understand. He believed there was information that people should be aware of. He believed one could reason one's way to his position concerning his community and the crisis they were experiencing with the local leaders, the so-called scribes and Pharisees. Leaders in the Matthean church were primarily teachers. Also, Matthew rejected secret and esoteric knowledge, something in which the author of Mark tends to revel. And, according to Matthew, one can get it wrong. Knowledge is a good thing, it can be abused (see chapter 23), but it is necessary for those who wish to enter the kingdom of heaven. It is in keeping with these Matthean concerns and precepts that the voice at the baptism is moved from the personal and mystical realm to the public arena and is intended for general consumption and debate.

## Jesus and the Devil

Following the baptism Jesus is led into the wilderness to be tempted by the devil (*tou diabolou*). Matthew follows the outline of the temptations and dialogue with the devil found in Q. Luke and Matthew both utilize the series of temptations to offer a litany of biblical passages for a besieged individual or community. The collage of passages in the temptation scene is a short catechesis for those having second thoughts about the political and material cost of membership in the community. Jesus was offered all the things the devil had to give. Jesus only had to relinquish his vision of the kingdom of heaven. Similarly, the Matthean community in many respects felt it, too, was under siege. Right or not, the Matthean church understood itself as a persecuted minority. Matthew develops this theme further in the Gospel. The temptation scene, and the biblical responses to the temptations Matthew inherited from Q, constitute important support and instruction for the struggling members of the Matthean community.

Homiletically, there have been many attempts to make sense out of the three temptations: turning the stones into bread, throwing himself off the temple, and possessing all the kingdoms of the world. In truth there does not seem to be any logical progression to these temptations and they do not seem to function allegorically for Matthew either. The temptations reveal simply that Jesus was confronted with choices about success in the world and submission to the prevailing powers. Jesus rejected such a *modus vivendi* with the political powers that be and so too, apparently, did the faithful within the Matthean community.

As with the other synoptic Gospels, there are a number

of other scenes involving "diabolization" or demon possession.
There are some charges made against Jesus involving the devil.
Jesus himself is charged with having a demon (11:18; Q7:33).
There are a handful of cases where the devil is mentioned with
the definite article in Matthew. The struggle with the devil and
demonic forces does not seem as central a feature in Matthew
when compared to Mark's Gospel. There is evil and corruption,
and the threat of damnation and Ghenna, in Matthew's worldview. But, as we shall see, the peril in Matthew that garners the
most attention is the wickedness of the authorities in Matthew's
setting, and the cost of not living up to true membership in the
kingdom of heaven, that is, Matthew's community.

## Capernaum and the Lower Galilean Setting
for Jesus' Mission

In 4:12, following the conclusion to the temptation scene, Jesus'
ministry actually begins. Jesus hears that John is in prison and
therefore begins his ministry in earnest. There is no overlap or
obvious competition between Jesus and John in Matthew. Following Mark (1:14), Matthew understands John's arrest as the
start of Jesus' preaching and teaching. Matthew records that
Jesus "withdrew" into Galilee from the Judean desert to the
south where the temptations putatively took place. Matthew records Jesus left Nazareth — Jesus' *patria* or hometown — and dwelt
(*katokasen*) in Capernaum.

Jesus' movement in Matthew is almost strictly Galilean. Matthew is careful, as W. Trilling and others have noted, not to have
Jesus leave Galilee save his one ill-fated trip to Jerusalem. The
movement was located in Lower Galilee and housed or centered
on the western shore of the Sea of Galilee in Capernaum. There
are very few place names in the Gospel outside of Lower Galilee. Caesarea Philippi, modern Banias on the Galilean-Lebanese
border, is one exception. In Matthew, unlike Mark, people came
from the coastal towns of Tyre and Sidon, and from the Decapolis region east and south of Galilee across the Kinneret Lake to
see Jesus. He did not travel to them or their areas.

Lower Galilee is a small area bordered by the Esdraelon Plain and Nazareth rift on the south and the Meiron range to the north. To the west is the Plain of Acco and on the east the Sea of Galilee or Kinneret. Movement east and west is far easier in the Galilee than north or south. The steep mountains make north/south travel difficult on foot or even by car. Lower Galilee can be traversed by foot west/east in a day. It is a very small and compact geographical region that gave birth to what we now call Christianity and played a crucial role in the development of rabbinic Judaism sometime after the Bar Kochba revolt.

Although small, Lower Galilee was no backwater or isolated chain of undeveloped villages. A major trade route and thoroughfare came from the port city of Acco-Ptolemais on the Mediterranean Sea going east along the Bet Natopha Valley past Sepphoris, Shikhin, Nazareth, Cana, Jotopata, Nain, onto the Sea of Galilee, and beyond to the Decapolis region and Damascus in Syria. A major Roman troop road that ran through the floor of the Bet Natopha Valley is still visible today. Lower Galilee was the scene of some significant urban development around the time of Jesus' ministry. The city of Sepphoris was a major administrative, cultural, and political center from the first century B.C.E. Sepphoris is approximately three miles from Nazareth. Excavations currently going on in Sepphoris have revealed a bustling, ornate, and large urban center in the middle of Lower Galilee.

At the eastern end of Lower Galilee, along the sea, the city of Tiberias was built sometime around 18–20 C.E. This large city rivaled Sepphoris in size and influence. Built in honor of the emperor's birthday, this city boasted a hippodrome, a forum, fortress, and palace. According to Josephus the city possessed an *archon* (ruler), a Senate of 600, and a town *boule,* or council of ten (*Life* 69, 296). There were other urban areas in and around Lower Galilee. Bet Shean, or Scythopolis, both the largest city and capital of the Decapolis region, was situated just south of the Galilee, and Magdala (most likely referenced by Matthew only among the Gospel writers in 15:39), a city along the Sea of Galilee, and Gabara are other cities in the Lower Galilean region.

The picture of Jesus and his movement as rural, uneducated, bucolic backwoodsmen owes much more to the romanticism of

Sunday school and nineteenth-century hymns than it does to the reality of Galilee in the early Roman period. A close analysis of the ancient texts and history, and in particular the archaeological discoveries in the Galilee over the last twenty years, reveals a much different context and setting in which Jesus engaged in his work, Matthew wrote his Gospel, and the rabbis shaped rabbinic Judaism.

Matthew quotes Isaiah 9 in 4:15ff., saying Galilee is the traditional land belonging to the tribes of Naphtali and Zebulun. Matthew uses the citation to support Jesus making Galilee his home base. The original context of the quote in Isaiah is a promise about a period when the gloom and anguish of the people will be transformed into glory. Galilee in particular is mentioned as a place formerly of contempt, which will be made glorious. After this promise begins the famous poem, "The people who walked in darkness have seen a great light...." Here Matthew offers a loose rendering of LXX Isaiah. Galilee is described as "Galilee of the gentiles." The Hebrew text of Isaiah describes Galilee similarly (*Ha Galil goyim*), and Matthew reiterates LXX Isaiah's translation of the same (*Galilaia ton ethnon*), "Galilee of the gentiles." While the force of the quotation in Matthew has to do with the region Galilee and not so-called Gentiles, an explanation should be offered here about this phrase.

The Hebrew term for so-called Gentiles is *goyim,* which basically means those who are not Jews. So a literal rendering of this phrase from Hebrew Isaiah 8:23 would be "Galilee of the non-Jews." The second-century B.C.E. document 1 Maccabees describes Galilee in similar terms (1 Macc. 5:9ff.). In Greek the term used to render the Hebrew *goyim* is *ethnon* (from which the term "ethnic," for example, is derived). This Greek term is notoriously ambiguous. This can mean simply "nations" or "the rest of the world." The term can also mean "common people" and in certain select passages can mean "Gentiles," that is, non-Jews. Which sense(s) does Matthew intend with his use of this term? Matthew utilizes *ethnon,* and other forms from this family of terms in a number of places, so this is not an unimportant question for understanding the Gospel. We will return to this question again, and the question is far more pertinent when treating other Matthean passages like the so-called final commission in chapter 28.

The original meaning in Isaiah 9 most likely refers to Galilee being taken over by Assyrians in the eighth century B.C.E. Perhaps from that time forward Galilee was ethnically mixed. The geographer Strabo describes Galilee thusly around the turn of the eras, as does 1 Maccabees a century before. Of course, by Matthew's time, in no small part as a result of Rome's urbanization program and the vital commerce around the Galilee, this region would have been even more diverse and cosmopolitan. Such cultural realities and currents no doubt made the Galilee of the early Roman period a vigorous and interesting but at times highly charged environment. Once again, however, it should come as no surprise to genuine students of this period that Jews and Gentiles should be engaging one another throughout the Roman east. Galilee, in this regard, was surely no exception.

The cities and fair-sized villages of Galilee brought extensive trade, commerce, cultural contact, and interaction to the region. The benefit such trade and cultural intercourse may have represented for Galilee must be balanced by the burden that this clearly placed on the indigenous population. Someone had to build these cities and pay for them. Taxes were high in Galilee and Judea during the reign of Herod the Great and his sons. Galilee was on a cultural and economic thoroughfare in the eastern end of the Roman Empire, but there was also a price to this important and strategic location. Galilee and Judea were under the watchful eye of Rome and Roman client-lords. There were soldiers to house and feed, taxes to be paid, and tax-gatherers to be paid off. Galilee was in a colonial situation. There was always division among people over how much — or to what extent — they should cooperate with the occupying forces. Some believed Roman rule and occupation were beneficial, or at least unavoidable. A Galilean figure no less than Flavius Josephus believed Roman rule was ordained by God. Many popular leaders in Galilee felt differently. These were various revolutionaries who believed the God of Israel would have them throw off the oppressive cloak of Roman rule. At the same time, those who helped Rome — Judean and Galilean client-lords and collaborators — would be punished and killed. The so-called Fourth Philosophy, various bandit groups (*lestai*), and probably branches of the Baptist's followers and some followers of Jesus believed they were called to resist and rebel against Rome. There were some popular and messianic groups led by John of Gischala, or Theudas the Egyptian, and others who also represented the revolutionary spirit in the Galilee. Indeed, in the year 67 C.E. such disparate revolutionary groups coalesced and together at Jotopata/Yodefat in the Galilee made their first attempt at resistance against Rome at the outbreak of the first Jewish revolt against Rome which lasted until 70–72 C.E. Matthew was writing his Gospel not too terribly long after the smoke had settled from the devastation of the first revolt.

The urbanization and development referenced above played a significant role in dividing Galilean and Judean society. These cities were potent and obstinate symbols of Roman presence, influence, power, and control. To some these symbols were attractive. To others they were daily reminders of God's call to do away with the foreign imperialists. Also, in a practical way, these cities were the centers for political and military personnel. If one was going to run amuck with the authorities — whether regional or imperial — it would most likely be in one of these cities. Here were the courts, the judges, the soldiers, banks, and arsenals, and all the other accoutrements of the broader Greco-Roman world. These were places that may have stood as symbols of a colonial life to many, but were at the same time places that the would-be rebel should avoid if at all possible.

It is interesting to note that these larger cities referenced above are not mentioned in the Gospel tradition. To archaeologists, historians, and anyone familiar with the landscape of the Galilee, the absence of Tiberias, Sepphoris, Magdala, or Scythopolis in the Gospels is deafening. It is astonishing that one could write a story about a wandering figure in first-century Galilee and not mention these prominent and unavoidable places. Yet, the Gospel writers, including Matthew with the exception of 15:39, do not. Instead, we hear about the villages on the outskirts, or within earshot of these larger urban centers. Chorazin, Bethsaida, Nazareth, Capernaum are familiar names within the Gospel tradition. It is the latter of these, Capernaum, or Kefar Nahum (the village of Nahum), which Matthew chose as Jesus' center.

Capernaum in the first century was a fair-size village. Population is notoriously difficult to predict in antiquity, but the size of the town has been estimated at around 10,000–15,000. Archaeological excavations of this mid-sized village reveal evidence of town planning with residential areas laid out in forty-by-forty-meter blocks. This would have allowed three to four dwellings per block. There are remains of a substantial first-century building that provide the foundation for the later fourth-century synagogue. Across the street from the synagogue is a later Basilica, which rests upon an early Roman house which was transformed into modest public space prior to the building of the Basilica. Some early graffiti from Capernaum has been the subject of considerable study and debate published by the Franciscans, who have guided most of the excavations at Capernaum this century. A lively fishing industry has been reflected in some of the finds from Capernaum. Also, resting as it does between Galilee on the western shore of the sea, and Gaulanitis (the present-day Golan Heights) at the northern extent of the sea, Capernaum may well have been a town where taxes and tolls were levied as merchants moved from one political region or realm to another as they passed through Capernaum.

Matthew alone among the Gospel writers makes Capernaum Jesus' base. Only Matthew says Jesus actually lived, or "dwelt," in Capernaum. Jesus and the movement seem so settled in Capernaum in Matthew that the group is depicted as using "the house" belonging to Peter as their gathering place (cf. 8:14). This focus on Capernaum and the use of Peter's house has led at least one contemporary interpreter to say that Matthew has blunted ostensibly the synoptic logion that "the Son of Man has nowhere to lay his head." The Jesus movement in the hands of Matthew does not emerge as an itinerant, charismatic group. Rather, the movement is focused, both geographically and in content, there is an order and system to Matthew's thought (even "lapidary," according to one commentator), and he is very much concerned with community building and construction, not in eschewing community and the potential impediments of community life. In some important respects this is a difference in Matthew's interpretation of Jesus and his movement when compared to the earliest Gospel, Mark.

## Jesus and the Proclamation of the Kingdom of Heaven

The substance of Jesus' message is described as the proclamation of the arrival of the kingdom of heaven (4:17). What does this phrase "kingdom of heaven" mean to Matthew? This is Matthew's own phrase. He supplies "heaven" for the more familiar kingdom of *God*. It has been suggested over the years that for some reason use of the term "God" offended Matthew. However, Matthew uses "God" in some other important places in the Gospel. This is not a satisfactory answer. The phrase "kingdom of heaven" in Matthew has at least two senses. First, the phrase represents a hope in the future. It is a reward for righteous living and the right disposition among Jesus' followers. The Beatitudes at the start of the Sermon on the Mount have this sense for the phrase "kingdom of heaven." Those who live a certain way, possess certain traits, or have a certain set of values (desire righteousness, turn the other cheek, are "poor in spirit," and so on) will inherit the kingdom of heaven. A second sense for this phrase involves a description of Matthew's own ideal community.

Matthew at points speaks in an almost realized sense about the kingdom of heaven. He speaks freely about who is least and greatest in the kingdom as more of a realization than an anticipation (5:19; 11:11). In Matthew's language and imagery, and in the phrase "kingdom of heaven" in particular, we see a coalescing of the then and now, or here and there. Whatever is represented by the symbol "kingdom of heaven," in terms of a reward at a better time or in a better place, seems at points to be met in, or at least projected onto the Matthean church. In the words of sociologist P. L. Berger, the author understands the Matthean community as a mimetic reiteration of values, life, and authority of a kingdom in heaven. The idealized realm of the hereafter is being enacted within the Matthean community. This conviction on the part of Matthew is captured in several key places.

As noted above, Matthew's knowledge of the hierarchy within the kingdom and his ability to rank putative members is an expression of the merging of his community and the kingdom that is in heaven. But this conviction is given even more potent expression elsewhere in the Gospel. It is Matthew's community that recites — probably with regularity — in its collective prayer, "Thy will be done, *on earth as it is in heaven*" (6:10). Further, the disciples and leaders in the community through Peter in 16:19, and the entire church in 18:18, are granted the authority to effect in the here and now what is effected in heaven. "Truly I say to you, whatever you bind on earth shall be bound in heaven, and whatever you loose in on earth shall be loosed in heaven." And more broadly, as we shall see, in the Sermon on the Mount Matthew describes the nature and contours of the kingdom of heaven in real terms and demands for his community. His community is called to embody now the priorities, disposition, and relationships that characterize God's kingdom in heaven. In this distinct sense the phrase "kingdom of heaven" also stands for Matthew's own community, the church of the kingdom of heaven. So while this phrase has eschatological freight for Matthew (that is, there is a hope connected with it), "kingdom of heaven" also carries a sense of Matthew's own community here and now and the life and choices in which they should be engaged. The phrase "kingdom of heaven" is both a signification of a future reward for the faithful in the community and an appellation for Matthew's very own church.

## Calling Followers

One of the more memorable vignettes in the Gospel tradition is Jesus' calling the fishermen by the sea to drop their nets and follow him. Matthew follows Mark in this scene with very little change. The first four followers of Jesus (they are not called disciples or apostles at this point) are two sets of brothers. Simon (Matthew adds, "who is called Peter," so there is no missing this crucial person in the story) and his brother Andrew are the first to be called, though Simon Peter is mentioned first. The brothers Zebedee, James and John, are the next to be called. They apparently own a boat and leave it and their father to follow after Jesus. In Mark's version of the call of James and John they also have hired servants (*misthos* in Mark 1:20 is the common Greek term for "pay" or "being hired out"), which Matthew skips or deletes.

The term employed here for "following" (*akoluthein*) has been the subject of considerable study and debate. M. Hengel, in particular, devoted a short monograph to this phrase with the aim of showing the call to follow after goes back to Jesus himself, and that there is basically no ancient parallel to this call found in chapter 4 and repeated in chapter 8 in Matthew. Hengel appears to be responding primarily to H. D. Betz. Much of this particular debate can be attributed to German theological infighting. While trying to determine what really goes back to the mouth of Jesus in the Gospels is a favorite pastime of New Testament scholarship, over 100 years of this pursuit have clearly demonstrated our inability to answer this fundamental historical question. While what scholars refer to as "the quest for the historical Jesus" is a question that exhibits amazing resilience, its import rests not in what it reveals historically, but in what such quests reveal about the authors and the culture and period in which they were written. The autobiographical and self-critical value of such quest-like questions, despite their failure in a historical sense, should not be diminished. Such historical questions usually reveal more about us than they do the subjects of the inquiry, as no less a thinker than Albert Schweitzer noted much earlier in this century. For this reason Hengel's (and many others') question about the historicity of certain words in the Gospel, such as Jesus' call, though fraught with presuppositions and biases, remains important. Such historically unanswerable questions constitute an important mirror for scholars and the popular cultures they vaguely reflect. It is important for cultures and communities of faith in each epoch to be able to take stock of who they are, what questions emerge as critical to them, and how their answers to critical questions change as they journey forward. The favorite biblical conundrum of the quest for the historical Jesus is in effect a mirror that can serve as a gauge for the priorities and predilections of a particular culture or community and in this respect is extremely important.

Given the relatively small size of Lower Galilee and close proximity of the Galilean places named in the Gospel, there is no need to assume that those who supposedly followed Jesus never returned home again. In fact, that is quite implausible. A far more likely scenario is the group gathered around Jesus, being out on the road for a day or two, and then returning back to their homes and town. This is exactly the scene in chapter 8 when Jesus and his followers come to Capernaum. They reside in Peter's house (8:14). The putative itinerancy of the Jesus movement and the stark nature of the call to follow after Jesus must be understood in context. One could easily travel with Jesus for several days, or even one day, get to a Galilean town, engage in an argument with local leaders, and be home by nightfall. Such a modification of the call to follow Jesus is evidenced even within Matthew. I doubt the extent to which traditional, familial, and village ties were utterly severed within the Jesus movement. Those ties may have been strained, but this would have been much more a result of one's allegiance to the Jesus movement and not that these followers had forever left home. According to the narrative, Jesus retained ties with his mother and his village, Peter did the same with his home and village, and the group was never more than a half-day to a day's walk from their traditional homes. This, I think, provides a different picture of the relationship between the Jesus movement — especially as depicted by Matthew —and their *patria,* or native region, Lower Galilee.

## The *Synagogues* as Center Stage

The close of chapter 4 provides a narrative summary of the beginning of Jesus' ministry. Jesus went around all the Galilee, preaching the gospel of the kingdom and healing every dis-

ease among the people. His fame spread throughout Syria to the
north and east, and people followed him from Galilee, from the
Decapolis (the region of ten cities originally founded by Alexander the Great), from Jerusalem and Judea. Matthew infers that
these people came to Jesus and followed him in Galilee. Jesus is
portrayed in Matthew 4:23–25 as a preacher and healer. His notoriety begins to spread throughout the whole region and not
just Galilee.

In 4:23 Matthew says that Jesus was also teaching in *their* synagogues. In many respects the synagogues are center stage in the
Matthean drama. How should we understand this term, what
were *synagoge,* and how did they function in the early Roman
period?

*Synagogue* is a Greek term. Like the legal term "Sanhedrin"
(*synedrion*), Jews took this term over eventually to describe a developing central institution within their corporate life. In fact,
today most people would associate both of these terms almost
exclusively with Jewish institutions. But originally these were
common generic terms within the broader Greek world. That
these two common Greeks terms became so ensconced within
Jewish religious and cultural life is a reminder of the degree
of cultural engagement, broadly speaking, between hellenistic
and Jewish worlds. Such a facile distinction between these two
worlds, which is still commonplace among some second-temple
scholars, is no longer viable. Jews and Greeks had significant influence on one another from the time of Alexander the Great
forward and, indeed, aspects of each held considerable appeal
for the other.

"Synagogue" literally means "to gather with," or "gather together." I have rendered this term "gathering place." This, I
think, captures the function of the synagogue in the early
Roman period (c. 37 B.C.E.–135 C.E.). *Synagoge* were common,
simple, public or semi-public spaces where groups could gather
to engage in a variety of necessary and spontaneous activities.
Synagogues in this period were something like town halls. These
halls probably functioned in a number of ways. In such gathering places people could debate, hear a pronouncement, law,
or new inscription read aloud, vote if their political structure

allowed for such activity, and probably engage in the religious activities that were so closely bound up with the political and civic life of the ancient city. In certain respects the early synagogue was like a smaller, and covered, *agora,* or mall, that great Greek institution that was the center and heart of Greek intellectual and cultural life.

Such early Roman gathering places have been found in Israel, at Gamala in the Golan Heights, Herodium and Masada (though there are some extenuating features in these two places), and the first-century building that supports the fourth/fifth-century synagogue at Capernaum referenced above is suggestive of just such a public gathering place. There are probably many such spaces in Israel and in the diaspora which have yet to be discovered by archaeologists. These buildings were not particularly large or ornate. They were simple, cheaply made, and functional. In time, these simple buildings gave way to far more splendid structures in Israel with obvious religious, political, and economic significance, as in the case of Hammat Tiberias, Bet Alpha, and Capernaum. The development of these later, impressive buildings (Synagogues) corresponds to the formation and development of a dominant religious structure and party within Israel in the third–fifth century, so-called rabbinic Judaism. Prior to the third or late-second century of the common era there was no such dominant group within Israel. The early Roman period in Israel was a fluid, fragmented, and often conflicting period. A measure of stability and the semblance of a dominant coalition or party did not begin to emerge until after the Bar Kochba revolt in 133 C.E. Matthew was writing between the two revolts against Rome and arguably at the height of domestic tension and division within Israel.

It is extremely important then to realize that the term "synagogue" should not be read as a code word for "Jews." "Synagogue" in the Gospel does not stand for "the place where Jews meet." To the contrary, most of the people we meet in Matthew's story are Jews. The synagogues are civic buildings where the townspeople meet. To forget this and read the story as if Jesus enters the synagogues to argue with Jews and demonstrate their rejection of his message is to foster historically erroneous and potentially anti-Semitic interpretations of the text. Synagogues in this period were common buildings found throughout Israel and belonged, more or less, to the community in which they were built. In Matthew the disputes that arise in the synagogues are over questions of interpretation and leadership between the Matthean "leaders" and those who are currently having the most impact and enjoying the most control over the rank and file in Lower Galilee and, eventually, Judea.

Matthew's use of the qualifying pronoun "their" (*auton*) in association with the synagogue in 4:23 is important to note. Matthew views the gathering places Jesus frequents as associated with and under the sway of the Matthean opponents. The qualifying pronoun occurs throughout the Gospel in 4:23, 9;35, 10:17, 12:9, 13:54, and 23:34, as many commentators have noted. Only in Matthew 6:2, 5; 23:6 is *synagoge* not followed by the pronominal genitive. The leadership in Matthew's setting has started to develop their own roles and offices, their own scribes (Matthew uses the same convention of the pronominal genitive when talking about scribes as in 7:29). There are two instances when Mark refers to "their synagogues," but the text is corrupt at both points. Here we have two instances of later scribes trying to bring Mark into harmony with the later Gospel Matthew. Also, as J. Kilpatrick observed, Luke's lone use of the genitive with *synagoge* has the same manuscript problems.

This manner of describing gathering places in terms of "us and them" is a Matthean trait. There are places where the local leaders control and hold forth. In Matthew Jesus ventures into these places and begins to offer his message and his interpretation of the law, Israel's past, and the fate of those living in this age. In so doing, a conflict is cultivated and provoked. It is interesting to note that Matthew has seized upon a similar, if not synonymous term to describe his community and gathering. His community is an *ekklesia*. This also is a common Greek term for a place of meeting. Only in time, like *synagoge* within Jewish parlance, does *ekklesia* become a technical term for the Christian gathering place, that is, a church. Matthew selected a stock term from Greek language and culture to describe his group, quite obviously in this instance, as over against *their* gathering place, the synagogue of the local leaders. Early in the Gospel the synagogue emerges as the setting where the issues dividing the Matthean community from others are delineated, and it is the venue where the conflict and opposition toward the Jesus movement emerges.

## Further Reading

Berger, P. L. *The Sacred Canopy: Elements of a Sociological Theory of Religion.* Garden City, N.Y.: Doubleday, 1969.

Betz, H. D. *Nachfolge und Nachahmung Jesu Christi im Neuen Testament.* BHTh 37. Tübingen: J. C. B. Mohr (Paul Siebeck), 1967.

Bornkamm, G. "The Authority to 'Bind' and to 'Loose' in the Church of Matthew's Gospel: The Problem of Sources in Matthew's Gospel." In *The Interpretation of Matthew,* ed. G. Stanton, 85–97. Philadelphia: Fortress, 1983.

Cohen, S. "Respect for Judaism by Gentiles According to Josephus." *HTR* 80 (1987): 409–30.

Hengel, M. *The Charismatic Leader and His Followers.* Trans. J. Greig. New York: Crossroad, 1981.

Horsley, R. H., and J. S. Hanson. *Bandits, Prophets, and Messiahs: Popular Movements at the Time of Jesus.* Minneapolis: Winston, 1985.

Kilpatrick, J. *The Origins of the Gospel According to St. Matthew.* Oxford: Clarendon, 1946.

Kingsbury, J. D. "The Verb 'Akolouthein' as an Index of Matthew's View of His Community." *JBL* 97 (1978): 67–87.

Levine, L., ed. *Ancient Synagogues Revealed.* Detroit: Wayne State University, 1982.

———, ed. *Galilee in Late Antiquity.* Cambridge: Harvard University Press; New York: KTAV, 1992.

Overman, J. A. "Who Were the First Urban Christians? Urbanization in Galilee in the First Century." *SBLSP* 27 (1988): 160–68.

Przybylski, B. "The Role of Matt. 3:13–4:11 in the Structure and Theology of the Gospel of Matthew." *BTB* 4 (1974): 222–35.

Schweitzer, A. *The Quest for the Historical Jesus.* 3rd ed. New York: Macmillan, 1968.

Strange, J. "Archaeology and the Religion of Judaism in Palestine." *ANRW* II.19.1 (1979): 646–85.

———. "Review Article: The Capernaum and Herodium Publications." *BASOR* 226 (1977): 65–73.

Trilling, W. *Das Wahre Israel: Studien zur Theologie des Matthäus-Evangelium.* Munich: Kösel, 1964.

Wink, W. *John the Baptist in the Gospel Tradition.* SNTSMS 7. Cambridge: Cambridge University Press, 1968.

Witherington, B. "Jesus and the Baptist — Two of a Kind?" SBLSP 27 (1988): 225–44.

Wuellner, W. *The Meaning of "Fishers of Men."* Philadelphia: Fortress, 1968.

*Chapter Three* _____

# Jesus as Teacher — 5:1–7:29

## THE SERMON ON THE MOUNT

---

## The Beatitudes

Matthew moves from the beginning of Jesus' ministry in Galilee to the longest and most significant discourse in the Gospel. The Sermon on the Mount comprises chapters 5 through 7 in Matthew's Gospel. A good deal of the material is taken from Q, found also in Luke's so-called Sermon on the Plain. Yet Matthew's hand is clearly evident in the language and themes that the Sermon puts forward. The suggestion has been made by one or two scholars over the years that perhaps the Sermon on the Mount is pre-Matthean; that is, it existed in its present form prior to the writing of Matthew's Gospel and he took it over as it was. This theory owes more to the desire for scholastic novelty than it does to logic, and virtually no one other than the authors of the theory themselves subscribe to it. There is pre-Matthean material in the Sermon, unmistakably, but Matthew shaped the Sermon to address the issues that characterized his setting and context.

The Sermon begins with Jesus seeing the crowds and getting to a high place from which to teach. Here Matthew has taken up the Hebrew Bible tradition of having good or momentous things occur on a mountain. Here also we see Matthew's Jesus looking and sounding much like a modern-day Moses. But it is the disciples who gather around Jesus to receive instruction. The crowds (*oxlous*) have receded and for the first time the disciples come forward as the focus of Matthew's teaching and story.

73

The term "disciples" in 5:1 (*mathetai*) means literally "learners" or "students." "Disciple" is one of Matthew's preferred terms for followers of Jesus and members of his community. The teaching and experiences directed toward the disciples in the Gospel constitute thinly veiled instructional material for the Matthean community. U. Luz and others have demonstrated this transparent function of the notion of "disciple" in Matthew. While there may well be historical traces of the first followers of Jesus embedded within the stories of Peter and the others, it is clear that when we have disciples on the scene in Matthew we are also engaging in issues and concerns that occupy the Matthean church at present. The Sermon on the Mount is just such an occasion.

There are some other clear indications from the Sermon itself that this is a sermon intended for the ears of the Matthean church and shaped by the realities of this late-first-century congregation. The Matthean concern for and concentration on the law is inserted into the middle of chapter 5 in verses 17–20. The legal terminology and concern with the courts which we associate with Matthew, and which reflect again his concern with local political and legal authorities, emerge throughout the Sermon. Even the casual reader can see the thrust of the Sermon, especially in chapter 5, is relationships within the community, seen particularly in the so-called antithesis in 5:21–48. And Matthew regularly employs the term "brother" (*adelphos*) throughout the Sermon (5:22, 23, 24, 47; 7:3, 4, 5). Matthew continues this convention elsewhere in the Gospel. The Matthean community has been described by J. Gnilka as a "brotherhood." This is a communal term of endearment which Matthew employs with regularity to address and describe his church. Matthew is alone among the synoptic writers in using *adelphos* in this manner. When Mark and Luke use this term they tend to mean it in a literal sense. Some exceptions to this can be found in Mark 3:34 and Luke 6:42 and 8:21, but in the main for Mark and Luke this term denotes literal, biological family members. Matthew's use of this term suggests his community is a fictive family. The metaphor of family, and *adelphoi* in particular, captures the ideal nature of the relationships and commitment which Matthew sought to engender within his church. Matthew, through his instruction, encouragement, and his particular presentation of Jesus and his message, hoped to foster a family that withstands the competition and conflict with those powers and leaders opposed to the community. The Sermon on the Mount plays a pivotal role in Matthew's attempt to achieve these ends.

Matthew begins the Sermon with nine beatitudes, blessings or, in Greek, *makarioi*. In classical Greek this term denoted happiness, good fortune, or well-being. Pindar, Plato, and Aristotle, for example, all regularly used the term in greetings, in sending wishes, or in describing the well-born, educated, or content person. Matthew's use of the term carries this same general sense of completeness, joy, and reward for living in the manner the beatitudes encourage.

The Q source contains several beatitudes and a set of corresponding woes. Matthew added some of his own beatitudes as well as amending Q's. One well-known emendation is Matthew's first beatitude, "Blessed are the poor in spirit, for theirs is the kingdom of heaven." The Lucan version simply states, "Blessed are the poor, for yours is the kingdom of God" (Luke 6:20). There is no clear explanation for this particular Matthean change. It is true, however, that most of the beatitudes aim at a disposition or attitude on the part of the community member. Literal, material, or corporeal needs and issues do not emerge as crucial elements in the beatitudes. These do emerge at other points in the Gospel, but here Matthew is trying to highlight the attitude or spirit of the disciple. Matthew makes a similar change in 5:6 when he alters Luke 6:21 from "Blessed are you that hunger now," to "Blessed are those who hunger and thirst *for righteousness.*" Here Matthew is attempting to sketch the *disposition* of the righteous community member and this is probably best summed up in the favorite Matthean term *dikiosyne,* or "righteousness." The literal and corporeal thrust of Luke 6:20 and 21 would appear as apples among oranges in this part of the Sermon. In Matthew's own words, the beatitudes are attempting to express in various ways what constitutes a "pure heart" for a Matthean Jew (5:8). The slight addition of "spirit" (*pneuma*) in 5:3 and "righteousness" (*dikiosyne*) in 5:6, while perhaps finally obfuscating, do bring the first and fourth beatitudes into the realm of one's attitude and begin to accomplish Matthew's goal in the early part of the Sermon, that is, to paint a portrait of the ideal Matthean community member.

The eighth and ninth beatitudes possess a concreteness the others seem to lack. Here Matthew introduces his theme of the persecution of the faithful person and community. Persecution seems to be the plight of the righteous. They will not be without their reward for enduring such persecution. In 5:11 Matthew claims that the persecuted Matthean minority stand in the tradition of the great Israelite prophets of old who also were rejected. An important German monograph by R. Hummel has stressed that Matthew's message is developed over against (*Ausein-andersetzung*) those authorities whom Matthew believed had it out for his community, and, he thought, would also lead the covenant people astray. The Sermon offers instruction to the church both about true community and about the characteristics of what Matthew held to be false relationships and corrupt leadership.

Matthew 5:13–16 are the well-known verses about being the salt of the earth and the light of the world. The audience of the Sermon is compared to a city set on a hill which cannot be hidden. Let your light shine before people, the Matthean Jesus counsels, "so that they may see your good works and give glory to your father who is in heaven." These verses, along with being beautifully crafted, also seem to say that Matthew plans to make his case in the public square. In Matthew's view the argument they are having over legal interpretation, over the nature of true leadership and teaching, and over Israel's shape and fate is too important to duck. He and his church plan to make their case in broad daylight. He plans to persuade and to allow those within earshot to see and hear what's good about the Matthean version and interpretation of Judaism. The disciples are to have a public presence, and so should the Matthean community. As we will see, it may be that by the time of the writing of the Gospel the Matthean church was losing much of that public face and was losing ground politically in terms of their reputation beyond the walls of their gathering place. The church members' "good works" (5:16) would speak much louder than words in making the Matthean case among the people.

## Jesus, Matthew's Church, and the Law

There is a possible indication of the public perception of Matthean Judaism in 5:17–20. These few short distinctly Matthean verses pertaining to the "law and the prophets" and concluding with a gratuitous reference to the "scribes and Pharisees" have spawned endless monographs and dissertations. The reason these few verses have caught the eye of Christian interpreters is that they seem to say followers of Jesus must keep the law. The law and prophets that carried so much authority from the second-temple period forward, in the view of Matthew's Jesus, still abide. This seems to many to fly in the face of traditional Christian teaching about grace, and especially Paul — or perhaps Paul as refracted through sixteenth-century Protestant reformers — who insisted Jesus did away with the law and requirements of any kind and brought people into the kingdom of heaven solely through grace, not, to quote Martin Luther quoting the Apostle Paul, "works."

A host of monographs have been devoted to these four verses attempting to show that Jesus did not mean that the law must be fulfilled when he seemed to have said the law must be fulfilled. For example, some interpreters have found an escape clause in 5:18b which concludes with the phrase "until all is accomplished" (*an panta genatai*). Some have claimed that Jesus "fulfilled all," and therefore the law and the prophets were in force during Jesus' lifetime, but not after his death since, at that point, "all was accomplished." Such hermeneutical gymnastics seem excessive, if not tortured. Such contrived interpretations of 5:17–20 are also a result of isolating these verses from the rest of the Gospel. Indeed, throughout the Gospel Matthew demonstrates a sophisticated knowledge of the law, its interpretation, and the abiding validity of the law as he interprets it.

It was the Tübingen New Testament scholar E. Käsemann who finally said we must allow for the possibility that this Matthean *crux interpretum* actually means what it appears to be saying. Although this passage is the subject of lively controversy, it is unambiguous and does indeed command obedience to the whole Torah. Of course, we would not expect anything less from a faithful, apparently well-trained, late-first-century Palestinian Jew. The Qumran scrolls, the first-century B.C.E. Psalms of Solomon, or the post-70 works of 2 Baruch or 4 Ezra all make the validity and interpretation of the law a vital and central issue. For these authors, like Matthew, when it comes to issues of the law, the stakes were very high. Of course Matthew, like his other second-temple colleagues, would assert the importance and abiding authority of the law and prophets. Attempts to see in Matthew 5:17-20 something other than this have required reading Matthew and lifting him altogether out of the social and cultural context that shaped his thinking and his Gospel. The law, how to interpret it, and its potency were crucial issues among the Judaisms of the late second-temple period. Debate and harsh charges concerning the law in documents like Matthew and many others only serve to highlight this point. We cannot hold Matthew responsible for Paul or, more accurately, later enlightenment and early modern interpretations of Paul and the Gospel. For a Jew like Matthew the law was both the common ground and the battleground among and between competing Judaisms in the post-70 period.

If fulfilling the law and the prophets and understanding them correctly were integral parts and *a priori* assumptions for most Jews in the first and second century of the common era — especially one with the scribal and legal inclinations of a Matthew — why then has he bothered to mention it in 5:17-20? Is this not stating the obvious? In fact, this reference to the law and the prophets in Matthew comes out of the blue. There has been no reference made to the law up to this point, and no one has leveled any charges even vaguely related to the law. The author sounds defensive. Who is thinking, "I have come to abolish the law"? This question is part of the "taken for granted" knowledge of the Matthean community. This charge is part of the background noise of the Matthean crisis. Beyond the boundaries of the Matthean community the view is held by some that they,

Matthew's church, play fast and loose with issues of the law. Their interpretations and overall hermeneutical scheme (the way they understand the whole law and prophets now in light of the life and teachings of Jesus) are viewed as weak or reductionistic by some in the broader community. This charge is common knowledge within the Matthean church. Here Jesus is reiterating a well-known critique of Jesus and Matthean Judaism by other authorities in the Matthean setting.

Matthew must also be concerned about these charges against the church making in-roads into the community. No doubt members of the church hear these views in the marketplace, at the theater, in public debate, or at home at a meal. Perhaps some Matthean Jews, especially newer or younger, more vulnerable members (like Matthew's *mikroi,* or "little ones"?), are beginning to believe the arguments of those outside the group. Is the Matthean treatment of the law beginning to divide a town, a community, or family? This seems quite probable. Matthew 5:17–20 repeats an acknowledged charge against the church and offers a rebuttal as much for the members as for those outside the church leveling the claims and repeating the rumors.

Why was this issue of the law so important to Matthew and many of his contemporaries? In late second-temple parlance the term "law" (*nomos* in Greek, *Torah* in Hebrew) was an expansive and fluid notion which, while possessing discrete and very specific connotations in certain contexts, tended to stand for the traditions, divine injunctions, and authoritative corpus pertaining to historic Israel. The law contained instruction about living, ordering life, and helped to guide relations within Israel and between Israel and the nations. Further, in the recitation and study of the law Jews heard and read *their own* story. The history, adversity, judgments, and promises written in the law was a story about them. The proper rendering and interpretation of the law was really, then, an argument about them, who they were, where they had come from and where they were headed. Some modern interpretations to the contrary, and notwithstanding trivial dichotomies between so-called law and Gospel, the arguments about the law we see in Matthew and other second-temple documents are not simply arguments about arcane and casuistic points of scripture. They are fundamental arguments about personal and corporate identity. How one renders, understands, and enacts the law places them on the spectrum of late-first-century Judaisms, but also places them within the history, traditions, and future of God's Israel. To argue about the law and its interpretation is to argue about myself, my community, and to engage in the profound process of self-understanding and identification. To ask and argue about the law is to ask and argue ultimately about who we are and our place within God's people. All Jews would have understood themselves incorporated in this story. No one wanted to see themselves or their community written out of the story. Therefore, charges flew back and forth concerning the law and points of interpretation. Emotions, the cost, and the stakes were very high. Matthew was well aware of this, and in 5:20 overtly set his community's interpretation of the law, and the living out of it as summed up in his word "righteousness" (*dikaiosyne*), over against the interpretation of the scribes and Pharisees. Unless one's righteousness does not exceed that of the scribes and Pharisees (that is, those who embrace the interpretation and enactment of the law championed by these leaders), one will never enter the kingdom of heaven. These are severe words and potent charges about the law. In employing such rhetoric and denouncing his legal opponents in such dramatic terms Matthew placed himself squarely within the conflicted setting of late-first-century Palestinian society.

## Relationships within the Community

Matthew moves on from his sketch of the disposition and attitude of community members in the beatitudes, and his brief defense of his church's understanding of the law in 5:17–20, to the subject of relationships within the group. Verses 21ff. take up behavior and interaction within the *brotherhood*. This section of the Sermon has been referred to as the *Antitheses*. It is so named because people have tended to see these verses as the Matthean Jesus contrasting his understanding of the law, and the Ten Commandments in particular, with the prevailing interpretation of the law within Judaism. Matthew has here been frequently viewed as "one-upping" the Torah or even abrogating it in light of his new demands. Therefore, the term "antitheses" has often been used with the intention of juxtaposing the Matthean Jesus' view of the law with the traditional Jewish interpretation of the same, though of course there is no such thing. The variety of Judaisms in the late first century did not possess a monolithic view of anything, and certainly not the combustible subject of the law.

In these verses, however, Matthew is not juxtaposing Jesus' interpretation of the law with that of Moses' and the decalogue. The usual English translation of "You have heard it said of old, *but* I say to you . . . " is potentially misleading. One need not read this "but" in the strongly adversative sense the English tends to carry. There is a common and older copulative sense to *de* (the Greek particle usually rendered "but"), which suggests more coordination or continuity. In fact, one exhaustive Greek grammar makes this comment, "However we take it, there is in the word no essential notion of antithesis or contrast" (p. 1184 in Robertson). Such an interpretation would not abide for every instance of *de,* surely, but this should caution us against reading Jesus' words in Matthew 5:21ff. as simply antithetical to what has come before him and, in fact, the grammatical construction does not warrant such an interpretation.

As we have seen already in the fulfillment citations, in the birth story, and in 5:17–20, Matthew is at pains to demonstrate continuity and resonance with the history, heroes, and scriptural traditions of Israel. One senses that Matthew sees himself and his community as the guardians of the right understanding of the law and the prophets. His interpretation and that of Jesus' reflected in the Gospel is not radical, dismissive, or *de novo* where the law and Israel's traditions are concerned. To the contrary, they fulfill and embody those laws and traditions. This section of the Sermon connects the decalogue with his beatitudes. The laws that have governed relationships and judgment within Israel traditionally are really grounded in attitudes and attributes like those given expression in the beatitudes by Matthew. In 5:21ff. these attitudes are applied to specific instances in the experience of the community. Anger, insults, and harboring ill-will against a brother are also viewed as violations of the law.

The internal motives and attitudes of the followers and disciples emerge again as a central focus in Matthew's hermeneutic. There is a direct correlation between what is inside and what is outside. This is a key to correctly understanding and interpreting the law. To lust after a woman is the same as committing adultery in one's heart. Of course, there has to be a difference between actually committing adultery and doing so in one's heart. And Matthew seems to be aware of this distinction despite 5:28. Matthew is the only Gospel writer when discussing divorce to allow for the exception of adultery or *porneia,* as does the Hebrew Bible in Deuteronomy 24:1. Whereas Mark says no divorce (Mark 10:2ff.), Matthew says no divorce except for *porneia* or some sort of adulterous activity or "indecency." In this instance, in keeping with Mosaic law the woman is to be given a document of divorce (5:31). Matthew was very much a part of the first-century debate about divorce in Palestine. Hillel and Shammai also debated this issue (*b. Git.* 9.10). Matthew discusses this very subject again in a dispute with the Pharisees in chapter 19.

What Matthew is trying to accomplish in 5:21ff. — and the issue of adultery is a good case in point — is the connection that exists between characteristics and attitudes on the one hand and behavior and community well-being on the other. The point is not only the actions the laws take up, but the internal disposition of the actors. Matthew believes the law has always made this clear and he means to emphasize this over against the convenient interpretation which overlooks internal matters when taking up the law. While anger is not the same as murder, and lust is not literally the same as adultery, both actions and attitudes in their own way disrupt community and finally make a joke out of the laws that are to define and guide the people of God. From 5:21–48 Matthew gives specific instances of how the law should really work in concrete, communal settings.

In 5:38–48 Matthew unveils what he believes to be the hermeneutical key to all the laws and the prophets. These verses begin with perhaps the most famous of Sermon sayings and counsel. "Do not resist one who is evil. But if anyone strikes you on the right cheek, turn to him the other also; and if anyone would sue you and take your coat, let them have your shirt as well; and if anyone forces you to go one mile, go with them two miles." These famous verses have inspired many people to live a selfless life, to fashion a new ethic for their country or community, or to reflect seriously on their own priorities and values. Here Matthew lays bare his interpretive strategy where the whole of the law is concerned. "Love your enemies and pray for those who persecute you," he says. "This is how you will be complete [teleioi; not accurately rendered as "perfect" in 5:48], as your heavenly father is complete." The fulfillment of the law and the goal of reiterating within the Matthean community the fullness and righteousness of the heavenly kingdom are accomplished through the enactment of the love command in the relationships and conflict the community encounters.

This command to love is prominently placed throughout the Gospel in 5:43ff., 7:12, 19:19, 24:12, and 27:34ff. Matthew expands on this important notion about love and the law in chapter 22. Jesus is asked quite pointedly what is the greatest commandment? Matthew's Jesus answers, "You shall love the Lord your God with all your heart, and with all your soul, and all your mind. This is the great and first commandment. And the second is like it. You shall love your neighbor as yourself." And Matthew is careful to add here, "On these two commandments depend all the law and the prophets" (compare Mark 12:31). Significantly, two other legendary first-century Palestinian leaders and teachers, Hillel and Yohan ben Zakkai, are said to have summarized the whole of the law similarly (b. Šabb. 31a; m. 'Abot 2.9). In chapter 5 of the Sermon and in other places throughout the Gospel, notably chapter 22, Matthew makes sure the love command stands out as the controlling force in the community's understanding of the law, in contrast, Matthew believes, to that of the so-called scribes and Pharisees. This interpretive tool and precis of the law in no way dismisses the law or parts thereof for Matthew's church. It does make clear, though, that one's understanding and enactment of the law are shaped by this greatest command and legal summation. Community harmony and the right relationships between community members can be main-

tained if the legal principle of loving one's neighbor is provided
a central place in the church's thought and actions.

## Civil Disputes and the Courts in Matthew

When thinking about Matthew's legal interpretation and his advice about the law in 5:38–48, we should recall the colonial
setting of the Gospel and the loss of control and influence Matthew sensed locally. The prominence of the love command and
his counsel not to resist those who would do harm also has
a practical and strategic edge to it. There are apparently some
harsh political and civil realities that Matthew and his church
had to face. The section that brings the love command and non-
retaliation to the fore is also a section that reflects the colonial
situation of the Matthean community.

For example, 5:41 recalls the legal right of Roman soldiers
to enlist the service of a civilian in carrying their packs or
other burden for a roman mile. As has often been noted, Matthew specifies the right cheek is the one being slapped in 5:39.
Based on the assumption that the assailant is right-handed, interpreters have understood this as an insult; that is, the assailant
has slapped the hypothetical Matthean Jew with the back of his
right hand. This, then, is a picture of public humiliation inflicted
on the subject by a putative person of authority. And not unrelated to this, verse 40 constructs the scene of the Matthean
follower losing his shirt in court. All these form a composite
portrait of an environment that was out of the control of the
Matthean community. They were at the mercy of those who
commanded political and civil authority. This colonial or imperial setting helped fashion the strategy for dealing with insults,
threats, and force which we encounter in 5:38–48. Matthew's
counsel of passive resistance and turning the other cheek, love
your neighbors, and do not resist the one who seeks to do you ill
was shaped within the volatile context of Roman imperial rule
where there was a supreme cost to overt resistance and the decision to meet force with force. The dashed hopes and destruction
related to the first revolt against Rome in 66–70 were most likely

fresh in the memories of Matthew and many within his community. Matthew's ethics and interpretation of the law offers a *modus vivendi* with his colonial situation and the political realities of his context. Such a strategy might allow Matthew and his community to survive and continue in their debate with local leaders which, hopefully for Matthew's church, was too parochial and too indigenous to catch the eye of those who possessed the power to imprison, to harm, or kill.

It is for this reason that Matthew repeatedly urges his audience to avoid the courts at all costs. The courts and other military venues (like certain institutions in the big cities of Sepphoris and Tiberias, as mentioned above) were where the Matthean community member ran the clear risk of encountering the imperial presence and the punishment they could legally dole out for any form of deviance. Chapter 5 of the Sermon counsels the church members to stay away from the courts. Verses 25–26 offer the shrewd advice to "make friends quickly with your accuser while you are going to court." You will be handed over to the judge, and the judge to the guard, and the guard will throw you in jail. You will not get out of the jail until you have handed over every last penny, Matthew's Jesus reports. It sounds as though this community was accustomed to paying bribes to get people out of jail, and understood the courts as a place hostile and alien to the group. Matthew's term for the court in 5:22 is *synedrion* (transliterated, "Sanhedrin"). (Despite most English translations, the term for court or council does not appear in 5:25.) This is the common Greek term for the Roman courts established in the Greek-speaking East. Synedria were first established in Palestine around 60 B.C.E. by Pompey the Great and his general Gabinius. Pompey officially took Judea and Galilee for Rome in 63 B.C.E. through intervening in a civil war between two warring heirs of the Hasmonean kingdom. Rome had been involved in Judean affairs and controlling that region of the Greek East for fifty or one hundred years before that. Pompey was given a hero's welcome back in Rome because he brought stability to the Greek East and he administratively reorganized Galilee and Judea. General Gabinius reorganized Palestine into five *synedria*, or courts and judicial

regions (*J.W.* 1.170; *Ant.* 14.91). The five courts were in Jerusalem, Gadara, Amathus, Jericho, and Sepphoris in Galilee. This
restructuring, which occurred around 55 B.C.E., signaled the
permanent presence of Roman officials and their hirelings —
the troops and other personnel needed to support such institutions — in Judea and Galilee. This historical development within
Palestine introduced a new level of political power and legal
authority. Matthew was warning his community to beware of
the *synedrion* and stay away from the clutches of Roman troops
and officials.

The occupation and usurpation of the courts and other central civic institutions is characteristic of a colonial environment
where the legal and political institutions have been taken over
by the occupying forces. Only a skeletal crew of local elites
and officials worked within the imperial political structure in
such places. While one could debate with and even harangue
the scribes and Pharisees, the courts and large cities constituted
the den of those forces and people associated with foreign, occupying forces. Matthew could have a serious debate with local
Jewish leaders and compete for the allegiance of the local population. Arguments about the law, who correctly interpreted the
history and events of historic Israel, and who were the qualified
teachers and leaders of the people Israel had been going on for a
long time. But people tended not to come back from the courts,
and when they lost their cool in the presence of a Roman legion-
naire there was a very high cost to be paid. Therefore, they knew
to carry his pack without protest and do whatever they could to
stay out of court. This is one reason why the assertion that getting angry or insulting another was cause for a visit to the court
is such a serious charge in 5:21–22. The struggle for control was
going on at least at two levels in Matthew's setting. And Matthew
strongly encouraged his audience to avoid those Roman imperial
forces present in the courts, political arenas, and urban centers
of the Galilee. His struggle and conflict were aimed at a more
local level and at a more traditional group of Jewish leaders. A
very serious concern for Matthew, however, would be his rather
local group of opponents finding a way to make common cause
or form a coalition with the imperial political forces in Galilee

and Judea. This scenario would have very serious repercussions for the life and fate of the Matthean church.

Matthew 5:21–48 provides instruction, then, in at least two important respects. First, Matthew demonstrates how attitudes and emotions are an important part of understanding and living out the law. As we will see (cf. chap. 23), Matthew believed the current local leadership neglected this vital aspect of life and law. The external manifestations of a lawful life are inextricably bound to internal motives and attitudes. Neglecting this truism results in the disruption of community. The concrete examples provided by Matthew formed instruction to his church about the attitudes and actions that should guide their interaction and life together.

Matthew's advice, however, has some very practical ramifications as well. His teaching about how to deal with hostility, enemies, and those who would do you harm is also important advice for survival in a colonial context. Matthew felt free to have a serious and highly charged debate with traditional local officials and religious leaders. The so-called scribes and Pharisees represented such a group of traditional leaders. But Matthew counsels his community to steer clear of the institutions obviously in the control of occupying forces and those plainly in league with Roman power, to keep their noses clean around soldiers and do whatever they had to in order to stay out of court, or it would cost them every last cent.

## Piety in the Kingdom of Heaven

In 6:1ff. Jesus teaches about how to practice one's righteousness. The now-familiar Matthean term *dikiosyne* is used in 6:1. This term is usually rendered "piety" here, though elsewhere in the Gospel it is translated "righteousness." The specific content of *dikiosyne* in this section of the Sermon is giving alms, praying, fasting, money, possessions, and priorities in one's day-to-day affairs. Perhaps "piety" is not an inappropriate term to capture this range of Matthean concerns in 6:1ff.

Matthew's instruction in chapter 6 alternates between *via neg-*

*ativa,* or teaching through a negative example, and offering a constructive suggestion. The negative example is supposed to be emblematic of the "false" piety of the opponents. "Beware," Jesus begins, "of practicing your righteousness before people in order to be seen by them" (6:1). This is, of course, what Matthew believes his church's opponents do. They will have no reward in heaven (6:1b). Do not make a lot of noise about the money you give. Again, this is behavior, and more an attitude, that Matthew associates with his debate partners. In 6:2 Matthew uses the term "hypocrite" (*hupocritai*), which is a favorite Matthean slang term for his opponents. Indeed, Matthew is almost single-handedly responsible for the term "Pharisee" being a synonym in English parlance for "hypocrite." Looking up the term "Pharisee" in just about any dictionary will confirm this. This passage, and several others in Matthew's Gospel, are the reasons why. When the writer says "hypocrite," he means the so-called scribes and Pharisees.

In classical Greek the term "hypocrite" refers to an expounder, interpreter, or one who plays a part on the stage. Plato, Aristophanes X, Lucian, and the Zenon Papyri (71), for example, all use the term in this manner. In language similar to Matthew, chapter 4 of the highly polemical first-century B.C.E. Psalms of Solomon uses the term to describe the Jerusalem leadership who live in hypocrisy, make false oaths, deceitfully quote the law, try to impress people, and let the Romans into their city during the time of Pompey (c. 63 B.C.E.).

Matthew's Galilean contemporary Josephus, in an interesting verse, uses this term to describe John of Gischala, one of his chief rivals and opponents around the time of the outbreak of the Jewish War in Galilee. In this passage (*J.W.* 1.585ff.), Josephus attacks this rival in the most personal of terms. John is unscrupulous, his craftiness knows no end, he is an intriguer, liar, a brigand (*lestes*), and one who practices deceit among his most intimate friends. John always pretends (*hupocrites*) to be a friend, or philanthropic, toward others (*philanthropias*), but in fact his love of money makes him bloodthirsty (*J.W.* 1.587).

Josephus's polemical and personal tone here should make the reader suspicious. Why is Josephus so vitriolic concerning

John? As R. Horsley and other students of popular resistance in Palestine have pointed out, John was Josephus's chief rival for leadership in Galilee at the outbreak of the revolt (*Life* 13.71). John emerges again during the siege of Jerusalem as a leader in the Zealot party (a coalition of bandit groups who came together at the end of the revolt to defend Jerusalem against Rome). Yet even this coalition experienced some of the same in-fighting and fragmentation we can see emerging in Josephus's own rhetoric when discussing John of Gischala. Inside the walls of Jerusalem during the siege there was a struggle for control. Rebel groups competed and fought with one another even while the Romans laid in wait outside the walls of the city (*J.W.* 4.566–78). John was very much involved in this in-fighting within Jerusalem and he showed himself to be both a popular leader and a shrewd political survivor (*J.W.* 4.389–97).

The term *hupocrites* then emerges in the early Roman period as a word that suggests a critical, highly charged atmosphere where competing groups and factions are engaging in quite personal attacks and rivalries. Chapter 4 of the Psalms of Solomon, Josephus's concern about John of Gischala, and Matthew's concerns about the scribes and Pharisees are excellent examples of this. The relationship between the term's common meaning in the earlier classical period and its use in later second-temple Jewish texts is this. Those who are called this name are viewed by the authors as pretenders, impostors, false leaders, and liars. Like actors in a play they assume a role, their actions are disingenuous, their words are not to be believed, they are supposedly motivated by personal gain and greed, and they are viewed as people who perform duplicitous roles where the larger powers are concerned.

It is important to recognize the theme of local division, rivalry, competition, and personal and highly emotional conflict this term suggests. Josephus, Matthew, and other second-temple authors, in their selection and use of this term, reveal a considerable amount about the political and social context in which they are doing their work and making their case.

It is important to note that the Matthean community engages in the same acts of piety as the so-called hypocrites do. The key, however, as we have already seen in the Sermon, is the motivation and attitude behind acts of righteousness. Those who are motivated by attention and personal gain practice their righteousness in the public arena, in the synagogues and main streets (*plateion* in 6:5, literally, "broad-street"). In the public and civic space (the *synagoge,* or public gathering space and in the biggest street in town), the hypocrites practice their piety. This is a sign of corrupt motives and goals. This behavior and the motives it signals render the acts of righteousness — or here, piety — null and void.

In this portion of Jesus' teaching at least, and quite in contrast to other parts of the Gospel, what we are calling piety is a private matter. This is a bit surprising in light of the emphasis Matthew tends to put on community and the *brotherhood.* But in chapter 6 alms are given in secret (vv. 3–4). Prayer is not done in public but in a closet, with the door closed, "in secret" (6:6). Also, fasting is an act of piety, not done with overt signs, like the made-up sullen faces of the hypocrites so others will know they are fasting (6:16). No, do not let people see you fast, but only God who sees "in secret" (6:18). Piety in this portion of the Sermon is most clearly depicted as a private, personal, even secret matter between the disciple and God. Acts done in public, and in particular done with the obvious intention of gaining others' approval and attention, are spent and useless piety. Those people have already received their reward, so Matthew claims.

From 6:19 through the end of the chapter is about material possessions and their relation to members' piety. The community is strongly encouraged not to store up possessions and wealth on earth. The mention of the pernicious eye (*opthalmos sou poneros*), followed by 6:24 and the tension between God and mammon, makes it clear that Matthew is actively discouraging the members from focusing on or devoting energy to the concern for money. The notion of the evil eye is present in a number of passages in Matthew, and at least once in Mark (Mark 7:22). Matthew 20:15 has this same sense as 6:24, and 12:35 and 15:19 make the connection between *poneros* and undue focus on money and possessions. In these passages, Matthew's view of *things* and money emerges. Things can be distractions. They tend to catch people's eye in a literal and metaphorical sense, and they draw away energy and enthusiasm from the things he believes are really important and enduring in life. In this portion of the Sermon Jesus is depicted as teaching the disciples to look beyond, and in other places than, those arenas of life where wealth, acquisition, and things in the here and now are the focus.

"Do not store up treasures on earth, but store up your treasure in heaven." As D. Harrington has observed, the notion of a treasure in heaven was not uncommon in second-temple, and particularly post-70 Palestinian writers such as 4 Ezra 7:77; 8:33, 36; 2 Bar. 14:12; 24:1; Tob. 4:8–9. Your treasure, so says Matthew, is where your heart is. This portion of the Sermon is derived ostensibly from Q (Luke 11:34–36; 12:22–34; 16:33). Matthew has made some slight alterations, but the force of this portion of the Gospel, and why these passages are so often associated with Matthew, is the context in which he has placed this material in his story. This is a central piece in his most extended teaching about discipleship and the true nature of membership in the kingdom of heaven, remembering that this phrase has the dual meaning of both his church and the kingdom that is to come. Matthew has skillfully edited this Q material on possessions and their place in the life of the disciple. One's disposition about *things* and *stuff* is a distinguishing factor within the kingdom of heaven. Based on where he has placed this material in his story it is clear that someone's position vis-à-vis money and possessions is a fundamental aspect of their piety or righteousness. Matthew cautions his congregation about maintaining the appropriate perspective and not being distracted by treasures on earth.

The conflict between God and stuff seems almost inevitable in 6:24. The Semitic word for money or riches, *Mammon,* is used in 6:24 and is juxtaposed with devotion to God. Within the Matthean setting it would seem you cannot have it both ways. God or money will take priority in your life. Both of these controlling forces tend to demand your all. A choice usually has to be made. So, counsels the Matthean Jesus, do not worry about food and drink, about clothes, or about your life. Verse 25b seems to suggest you already have more than enough by virtue of your life and your health. Here Matthew employs the Q argument from nature. There is a lesson to be learned in studying the created order. Yet among all creatures humans seem to be that species preoccupied with the *stuff* of life. The rewards and treasures of this earth take our focus off the lesson the rest of nature can teach. "Look [*emblepsate*] at the birds of the heavens; they do not sow or reap, or gather into barns, and yet God feeds them" (6:26). How can you live even a moment longer by worrying about life or death? Do not be anxious (*merimnao;* a common term from Greek tragedies; e.g., Sophocles, *Oedipus Rex* 1124) about food, life, or clothes.

Matthew seizes upon this notion still current in the Greco-Roman period (*Ep. Arist.* 296; *Sib. Or.* 3.222, 234; 1 Pet. 5:7; 2 Cor. 11:28), and repeats it several times. Worries, both political and material, confront the members of the Matthean church. They feel persecuted, they feel threatened, and with the loss of control they observe and sense comes also economic and financial pressures and worries. Much of this they cannot change, and much of the rest serves only to take their eye and focus off the goal of true righteousness and full participation in the kingdom of heaven. The priority for the Matthean community member in life is clarified and punctuated in 6:33. The tandem goals and strongly related notions of "kingdom" (*basileian*), and "righteousness" (*dikiosyne*) are the foci of the disciple. In this latter half of chapter 6 anxiety about the daily needs of the church has emerged as a prominent issue (vv. 25, 27, 28, 31, 34a, 34b). It is mentioned also in 10:19 concerning anxieties about being dragged into courts before governors and kings, and in 13:22, which references once again worrying about the things of this age and this world. Such anxiety and undue focus on *things* subverts the piety Matthew is promoting. He responds to these anxieties by reasserting what he believes were the twin pillars of Jesus' ethical instruction, namely the notion of the kingdom (of heaven) and righteousness (6:33). Recalling these two crucial ethical and conceptual anchors may help the community endure their crises.

# The Lord's Prayer

Matthew's version of the Lord's Prayer is know virtually world-wide, and was adopted by most of the Christian church in subsequent centuries. A simpler and earlier form of the prayer from Q survives in Luke 11:1-4, but it has been Matthew's later emended version that is recognized and recited around the world as the so-called Lord's Prayer. In certain respects the prayer may be viewed as an epitome of the life and hope of the Matthean community. This prayer was quickly adapted within certain streams of the early church as the prayer Jesus taught his disciples to pray, as in the case of the *Didache* 8:2-3 where it is said the prayer should be said three times daily. The prayer has six petitions, three "you" and three "we." The passive voice is utilized in the three "you" petitions, where in effect God is enjoined to "make God's name holy," "make God's kingdom come," and "cause God's will to be done," then adding the distinctive Matthean view of his own setting, "on earth as it is in heaven" (6:10). Matthew again asserts his belief that much of what passes for heaven "up there" can be effected "down here" within the Matthean setting and community. The second three petitions are direct addresses to God for the provision of bread, forgiveness of sins, and protection from temptation. It is worth recognizing that the provision of bread and forgiveness of sins constitute the center of the prayer. Here material and supposed personal needs are met at the heart of the Lord's Prayer.

The inclusion of the prayer roughly in the center of the Sermon is itself very significant. This later form of the prayer signals some important developments within the Matthean community and probably within the broader setting of Matthew's environment. This rather sophisticated liturgical expression represents an important stage socially within Matthew's church. Sociologically speaking, Matthew's community has developed some structure, there are now rather refined rituals the community reiterates together, and an epitome, or brief outline, of the hopes and beliefs of the group has been codified. These are important steps in terms of the social life and self-definition of the Matthean church. The routinization and codification of a prayer/

liturgy such as this provides an important means of education within the community. To borrow P. Berger's phrase, the prayer, like the Gospel itself, is vital "second-generation" literature. That is to say, the second generation (as any parent readily recognizes) at some point or another posits a problem of compliance. Routinized, stock, and reiterated material such as a liturgy teaches, explains, and reminds people about the nature, identity, goals, and priorities of the group. The development and presence of the Lord's Prayer at the heart of the Sermon on the Mount indicates the Matthean community has arrived at that important sociological and theological stage. There is now a brief recitation the community can regularly share which facilitates their cohesion, educates new or younger members, and reminds older or struggling members of their nature and purpose.

Matthew intends to contrast the Lord's Prayer with the ostentatious piety and prayers of his opponents, the *hypocrites,* who stand on the main streets and in the synagogues and practice their righteousness for all to see. The Lord's Prayer is a brief outline for the Matthean Jews to pray properly or "as the Lord has taught them." The Matthean church has developed a liturgy that can be contrasted and compared with their opponents, the scribes and Pharisees. This polemical context of even the Lord's Prayer in Matthew can hardly be missed.

A number of scholars have observed that there were some other significant institutional developments within other Jewish communities and types of Judaism during this period. There are some suggestive parallels between Matthew's Prayer and one of the most significant liturgical developments in the history of post-biblical Judaism, the *Amidah,* or Eighteen Benedictions. Recently P. Schäfer and K. Kohler have both analyzed the development of the *Amidah.* This prayer of eighteen benedictions (to be said standing) had a protracted and complicated developmental process. Certain parts of the Eighteen Benedictions were established before others. In its present form this may not have been codified until the later third century. But surely parts of the *Amidah* had been developing from the early Roman period forward. Some aspects of the *Amidah* may have been developing or in force within some forms of Judaism in the immediate post-

70 period. This could well bring early portions of the *Amidah* into competition with Matthean Judaism and its liturgical developments and the learned authorities who stand behind these liturgies.

One particular development, which has been postulated as being relatively earlier within the development of the *Amidah,* is the twelfth benediction, the so-called *Birkat Ha Minim,* or Blessing Upon Dissenters. This is actually no blessing at all but a curse on those excluded from the community for their dissident or deviant beliefs and behavior. The act of banning, like other liturgical developments, always represents an important stage in the development of a community. For a community to be able to decide who to kick out, why, and how, as brutal as such a process can be, does in fact signal a significant stage in a community's self-definition. The erection of such boundaries and guidelines distinguish the community from those outside. The act of banning is an attempt on the part of the community to say, "Here is where we stop, and they begin." As we will see in treating Matthew 18, the Matthean community, too, had developed its own process of exclusion and community banning. The rabbinic version of the twelfth benediction is given final expression in the much later Babylonian Talmud in *b. Berakot* 28a.

Some scholars believe that the Hebrew term *Minim* actually is a code word for "Christians." This is incorrect and anachronistic. Christians did not become acknowledged by or an issue for rabbinic Judaism for a long, long time, if ever. But the broad coalition that was struggling to take shape and bring some order to otherwise chaotic Judea and Galilee in the wake of the destruction of the first revolt in time would have formed boundaries and sanctions that would have excluded some Jews and forms of Judaism. For example, later rabbinic Judaism was never very enthusiastic, according to A. J. Saldarini, about apocalypticists and apocalyptic groups. Such groups might have felt the pressure of a slowly developing consensus and coalition hostile to such a worldview. R. Kimelman has shown definitively that any facile juxtaposition between Christians and Jews using the *Birkat Ha Minim* as the basis is completely anachronistic and seriously flawed in many other ways.

But some people and groups could have started to sense the reality of an emerging leadership or authoritative body and coalition, as J. Neusner has suggested for some time, which was beginning to bring some order in thought and behavior to Jewish society in Palestine in the post-70 period. Matthew's Lord's Prayer could have been a response to the prayer, liturgy, or developing quasi-institutionalism of his opponents. The Q Sermon on the Plain does talk about getting thrown out (*ekballo*) and utilizes the common word for exclusion (*aphorizo*) when speaking of the rejection of the disciples on account of the Son of man (Luke 6:22). And Matthew 10:17 talks about being flogged and persecuted in the court or council (*synedria*), and in their (*auton*) synagogues. Remember, though, that here "synagogue" does not mean the place of the Jews. It means only the central, common public gathering space. The rejection, exclusion, or punishment of some varieties or members of Jesus-centered Jewish groups may have been sanctioned by local officials, or simply rejected on a popular level by the townsfolk or crowd. Matthew, I believe, sees their rejection or imminent rejection coming from local, recognized officials. Matthew 10:17, in fact, makes that quite clear.

One more rather celebrated case bears on this discussion of the early institutional and liturgical developments within the Jesus movements and their potential parallel with the same developments in other forms of post-70 Judaism. In John's Gospel 9:22 (cf. 12:42; 16:2), we read where a blind man who had been healed by Jesus was "put out of the synagogue" because he confessed Jesus to be the Christ. Such a specific and overt christological issue is not given expression in Matthew. But the highly stylized story in John 9 is an example of the sort of thing that might have been happening sporadically or in an ad hoc manner in Judea and Galilee. G. Forkman has discussed the number of Jewish and so-called early Christian groups that developed some form of expulsion, including Qumran and the Corinthian church. Some members of the Johannine community had heard or had experienced such a sanction in their setting. In no way should the story from John be read as the beginning of Jewish expulsion and persecution of Christians. First, the notion and identity of "Christian" is still a long way off from a Matthew or John, but also there is finally no real indication of Jewish persecution or expulsion of would-be Christians.

There is ample evidence, however, of different Jewish groups, of which Matthew would have been one, developing their own identities, rules, and authoritative bodies, and competing for a voice and for an opportunity to put in place their particular interpretations, regulations, and leaders. The Lord's Prayer may well reflect Matthean liturgical developments that rival or replace prayers, guidelines and instructions emanating from other circles and groups within the diverse and divided world of post-70 Palestine. In addition, as we have noted, Matthew's version of the prayer seemed to obtain an audience rather quickly, based on the *Didache.*

Matthew's petition to "forgive us our debts" represents an interesting modification from the Lucan version of the prayer. Luke 11:4a uses the usual New Testament word for "sins" (*hamartia*). Matthew, however, uses another, and rather different word *opheilamata,* or "debts." Luke 11:4b uses this term also. Here Luke should be using the same term twice (whichever one), as Matthew does, because the verse represents a couplet. In 11:4 Luke has disrupted the parallelism. The possibility exists, of course, that this petition in the prayer did not originally circulate as a couplet. I doubt this, however. Why after all that familiarity, if not training, in Hebrew poetry and hellenistic-Jewish prayers would the earliest recorders of this prayer not be able to reproduce or fashion rather typical Hebrew or hellenistic-Jewish parallelism or couplets? This was a stock feature of Jewish poetry and religious literature from the Psalms forward. I suspect here we have Luke, in 11:4a, supplying what was by then a more common word for "sin" (*hamartia*) into the prayer. It seems to me quite likely that *opheilamata,* in Matthew 6:12 and Luke 11:4b, represents the more original wording of this petition, although we will never know with certainty.

The force of this perhaps more original term in the fifth petition of the prayer draws attention to real, material debts. This

word, from Homer forward, referred to owing a debt of money—
something is due a person. Matthew uses the term again in chapter 18 in the parable of the corrupt servant who owes his master
money, is forgiven, but then refuses to forgive those who owe
him (18:24ff.). This petition, in the selection of this term, suggests that issues pertaining to real debts, things that are owed,
and contracts that have gone unfulfilled are part of the life
of the community. Of course the material debts owed one another serve as metaphors for Matthew for the debts from which
God has released God's faithful. However, at an early strata of
the prayer attention is drawn to the exchange of goods and the
unfulfilled promises and unmet debts that could easily have
characterized life together, and potential division, within the
church.

Such a scenario is not at all surprising, given what we know
about the realities of debt, loans, and, ultimately, loss of land
and indentured service in early Roman Palestine. M. Goodman,
along with others, has demonstrated the vicious cycle of debt
that was part of many people's lives in Judea and Galilee during
this period. Rome's urbanization policy, the building projects
that started with Herod but continued through the middle Roman period at least, resulted in larger tax burdens for most
people. The colonial system also involved the seizure of land by
imperial right, or by force for failure to pay one's rising taxes.
The Gospel tradition reflects this social and economic reality
(cf. Matt. 18:23-34; Luke 16:1-7), and early forms of the Lord's
Prayer sought to encourage benevolence and forgiveness within
the community in the face of these harsh realities. Such realities would have continued to prevail after the revolt and during
the writing of Matthew's Gospel. Chapter 18 and Matthew's
form of the fifth petition offer instruction and a thoughtful
response to what was for some difficult economic times. Here
material concerns and piety have clearly coalesced in the Matthean community's concern for those who have or are slipping
into debt.

The disciples' response to those who owe them parallels, and
in fact effects, God's response to them and their own debts
(6:15).

## Judgment, Discernment, and True Membership

In the opening of chapter 7 and the final section of the Sermon Matthew comes out strongly against judging others within the community. One must live by the standard of judgment one imposes on others. Yet 7:1 and 7:5 compose an interesting contrast. "Do not judge," says 7:1, but 7:5 says after taking the log out of your own eye you can see clearly enough to take the speck out of another's eye. It is important not to overly romanticize this portion of the Sermon. Matthew is not afraid of judgments within the community. Chapter 18 is a rather detailed description of how that judgment takes place. Also, whatever the Matthean leadership decides or "binds" in their community is putatively bound also in heaven. The same corollary is mentioned in 6:15 at the conclusion of the Lord's Prayer where the community reminds itself that what they do not forgive others God in heaven will also not forgive. There is order, some structure, and decisions within the group about their corporate life. In reality, even within the Gospel itself, one sees judgments being made. And Matthew makes clear other judgments are forthcoming.

What Matthew is promoting in the prayer, and elsewhere in the Gospel, is circumspect, very thoughtful judgments. This process must first begin with thorough, and probably rather agonizing, self-assessment, as 7:1–5 shows. The judgments of chapter 18 are couched carefully and repeatedly in the broader context of forgiveness. And a parable in 13:24–30 counsels caution and patience in rooting out the alien or destructive forces within the community. Such judgments are best left to God. However, Matthew did not completely abdicate in this regard. Indeed, he makes the very bold claim that the judgments of the community at important points parallel the judgments in heaven. Such heightened confidence is provocative but, in Matthew's mind, provides license for judgments that from time to time are necessary within the corporate life of the group. Those judgments are probably quite painful to make and are arrived at slowly and always informed by the principles of forgiveness. It is in this sense that in 7:12 he offers again another version of the Golden Rule as a reminder of how life and relations should be guided in the church. This rule is the central principle employed by ideal Matthean members when working out disputes, legal struggles, or dealing with aberrant behavior within the community.

Matthew's church has been described as a *corpus mixtum*. That is, Matthew was aware that there was clearly good and bad within the community. I take the strange and offensive lone verse in Matthew 7:6, which is neither in Mark or Q, to be advice about avoiding those people from whom Matthew believed little or no good could come. In this one verse Matthew combines two traditional, deeply offensive Middle Eastern images of the dog and the pig. These people, of whom we are told virtually nothing, are likened to both — a deeply offensive logion indeed. Matthew's Jesus seems to be saying, don't waste your time, stay away, your breath and efforts are simply wasted. I do not believe Matthew had an unrealistic or too highly idealized view of the nature and composition of his church. Such language does not lend itself to internal harmony and may seem to be at odds with his advice in 7:12. But the presence of such elements within the group, assuming Matthew is correct, would be a reality they had to face and address. Matthew here seems to offer instruction to the disciples about such people coming in and, perhaps, out of the church.

This reality necessitated discernment on the part of the Matthean Jews. Who were those in their setting who represented a virtual waste of their time? Also, many followed an easy and wide way that would lead to destruction. Many were susceptible to a certain siren call that looked, and may well have been, much easier and simpler than the life sketched out by Matthew's Gospel. Apparently few followed the way Matthew articulated, which was hard but would lead to life.

There were false prophets within the community ("they come to you in sheep's clothing") who, Matthew believed, posed a threat to members (7:15). How would Matthew's audience be able to recognize and defend themselves against such threats? In Matthew's setting, which included persecution and conflict with those in power locally, one had to be aware, cautious, and keep a vigilant eye out. Again, such concerns and worries are not surprising within the colonial setting of Matthew's Gospel. One thing we know definitely about colonial settings is that they tend to divide the indigenous population against one another. Some support the alien force and influence. Others would rather die than do that. Deep divisions, traitors and turncoats, paranoia, false accusations, and betrayal are always elements in a colonial setting. There is always the possibility that in your midst is someone who could squeal, tell stories about you, or make it so you and/or the group would be paying a visit to the court and, as we know (5:26), you may never get out of there. Such deep divisions and enmity were characteristic of Galilee and Judea before and after the first Jewish revolt. Such internal intrigue and division was as responsible for the fall of Jerusalem as the Romans themselves. This atmosphere continued at least through the second revolt against Rome in 133–135 C.E. It is very hard to believe that for some reason Matthew and his community should have been spared these widespread social divisions. On the contrary, and as should be expected, Matthew's community also had to be aware of and deal with the colonial reality of even small or intimate groups and communities turning on one another. Matthew 7:13–23 says to the Matthean church "beware."

How would they know who to trust and listen to in this dangerous setting? Matthew says to watch the behavior and actions of others carefully. This is also the advice he offers in chapter 23. There is a direct correlation in Matthew's portrayal of Jesus' teaching in these passages between piety and actions. Remember, so-called hypocrites and Matthean Jews in good standing engage in the same forms of piety and religious behavior. How should they distinguish between those who are in truth members and those who would lead them astray? Watch them, says Matthew. In time their behavior and actions will give them away. In some distinctive and favorite Matthean terminology he says, "you will know them by their fruits" (7:16, 20). Really rotten trees cannot bear good fruit; this language is reminiscent of John the Baptist's words earlier in the Gospel. Conversely, in time the people who can be trusted, who are true and reliable members, will emerge through their actions and behavior. One's true attitudes and motives ultimately become manifest in one's actions.

Watch closely, don't rush to judgment, and in time you will recognize the difference between the sheep and wolves. This ability
and power of discernment are very important attributes of true
Matthean members. In fact, the cost is quite high, in Matthew's
view, for not obtaining this attribute. Beware, be circumspect,
and watch others' actions closely. This will disclose the true
nature of their piety, plans, and priorities.

There are some who seemed to be Matthean members and
engaged in the confessions and rituals that would ordinarily
denote full participation in the group. However, in 7:21 Matthew substantially reworks a Q saying about allegiance to explain
the eschatological fate of such false brethren. Matthew's edition
says, "Not everyone who says to me, 'Lord, Lord,' will enter the
kingdom of heaven, but he who does the will of my father who
is in heaven." Again, true piety, confession, and membership are
related to true action, or *doing* the will of God in heaven. These
false members performed mighty works — prophesy, exorcisms,
and other powerful works — but these did not translate into "doing God's will." Here membership, allegiance, and attitude as it
relates to one's actions distinguished these from other Matthean
members.

Hearing and doing are the foundation of true and full participation in Matthew's church. To hear the words of the Sermon
and really do them (*poiei*) is likened to a parable about someone who built their home on a rock (*petran;* 7:25). Associations
with the famous Matthean verse to come later in 16:18 are unavoidable here. As much for the Matthean audience as for most
modern readers, Peter, and whomever or whatever Peter represents within the Matthean community, comes to mind when
Matthew speaks about a rock. Much is made in chapter 16 about
the meaning and importance of this term. These passages about
Peter as the rock and foundation of the church in 16:18 are
unique to Matthew. While the parable about the house built on
a rock is found also in Q, when Matthew uses this term a series
of unmistakable associations comes to mind for the reader.

The teaching in the Sermon is like a foundation for the
follower. Peter, his understanding and leadership among the
disciples, personifies the sure ground of Matthean Judaism. De-

pendence on the teaching and leadership that is in place within the Matthean church is a key to survival amid the storms of Matthew's political and social context. Those who do not attend to these two features of Matthean life are fixing for a great fall, the author claims (7:27). Matthew concludes the Sermon on the Mount with a narrative insertion about the amazement of those listening and the authority of Jesus' words. The crowds are mentioned again in 7:28. They are astonished at his teaching (*didache*). "For he taught as one who had authority [*exousian*], and not like one of *their scribes*" (7:29). Even at the end of this finely crafted Sermon Matthew inserts another comparison and putative qualitative distinction between the Matthean teaching and the teaching and leadership of the opposition. These local leaders who may be making in-roads into the Matthean community possess no real authority as teachers and leaders. In fact, they do and they don't. They do possess some measure of de jure authority based on 23:1ff. But Matthew hopes to establish that they do not possess de facto authority. He claims the words of Jesus as they are interpreted and lived out within the Matthean community constitute the only corpus of instruction and guidance that can be counted on as true and reliable.

## The Sermon as Constitution for Matthew's Church

Matthew's Sermon on the Mount is arguably the central piece of instruction within the Gospel. The Sermon is a distillation of the ethics, expectations, and relationships that should characterize life within the Matthean church. At points the teaching is ideal. That is, it aims high in terms of the traits, attitudes, and motives of the ideal Matthean member. Matthew, however, though at points ideal, was not, I would say, overly romantic or out of touch with some of the hard realities of life in his setting. He offers some practical if not shrewd advice about the courts and local councils. He was aware that not all Matthean Jews were of the same ilk. Some even within the Matthean community were not to be trusted or minimally did not understand the true nature of Matthean discipleship. This is a concrete indication of the in-roads other perspectives, worldviews, or allegiances were making into the Matthean community.

In the Sermon Matthew provides some in-depth instruction on substantive matters of Matthean self-definition. In particular, the law receives the weight Matthew believes it deserves in describing his community's view and interpretation of the same.

Despite claims and rumors to the contrary, the Matthean church took the law and the prophets, and all matters of the law, with extreme seriousness. The law was understood and interpreted in light of the Matthean interpretation of the teaching of Jesus, but in no way did Matthew believe his community violated, bent, or abrogated any aspect of the law of Moses. And any members guilty of this are least in the kingdom of heaven. Matthew believed that in any full and true interpretation of the law attitudes and acts must coalesce and reinforce one another. The failure to have actions and attitudes in consonance is the first and foremost sign of failure to fulfill the law and, therefore, the will of the God who is in heaven.

This combination of right attitude and action is summed up in the notion of *dikiosyne*. Righteousness in Matthew is that all-embracing notion that sums up the character of a Matthean disciple. As B. Przybylski has reminded us, *dikiosyne* emerges as the demand placed upon humans and the response expected from the true members of the Matthean community. Righteousness is both an attitude and an action (*praxis*). Matthew stresses this important notion because within the Sermon it becomes a primary means of defining community membership and it serves to delineate between Matthew's church and his opponents.

The Sermon on the Mount can rightly be called a constitution for the Matthean community. Like a constitution the Sermon provides in broad outline the nature of membership and life in the community. It also supplies answers to vital questions that will resurface among subsequent generations, and that were most likely surfacing during the drafting of the Gospel. Who are we? What are the contours of life within the group? What are our goals and reason-for-being as a community? How are we different from *them?* What is or will be our fate? These and other questions are given expression in the Sermon. And very important for the Matthean church, the responses to these questions are invested with great authority because they were uttered by Jesus. The Sermon highlights the assertion that the priorities and judgments of the Matthean community are really a mimetic reiteration of the priorities and judgments of the kingdom which is in heaven. These are, ideally speaking, parallel kingdoms. What is forgiven here is forgiven there. What is bound here is bound there. The traits of the ideal members as captured in the beatitudes are those traits characteristic of the kingdom in heaven. The parallelism between community and kingdom in Matthew is summarized in the distinctly Matthean phrase from the Lord's Prayer, "on earth as it is in heaven." Matthew has invested his constitution — as any constitution must be — with a cosmic authority. Matthew, or the current leaders of the church, did not make this up in light of the tensions and issues that confronted them. These instructions and precepts have come to the community as if from heaven. Such convictions and authority are important pieces in the process of community building and in fending off anomic or lawless forces that inevitably will challenge or threaten the church's life.

The Sermon is a potent, superbly written epitome of what Matthean Judaism is or should be all about. Goals and ideals for the community are blended with practical advice and concrete, daily concerns. The institutionalization evidenced in the liturgical developments — especially the Lord's Prayer, legal instruction, and a codified outline of members' actions and attitudes — reflect both a community responding to issues and questions from people, as well as one preparing for the long haul. How will relationships within the church survive the inevitable conflicts and division that happen within communities? Will the economic and political turmoil in Matthew's environment finally destroy the community? Matthew's instruction about relationships, about forgiving, about being ever slow to judgment, and above all the primacy of the love command and Golden Rule all show his concern for the future and longevity of Matthean Judaism.

## Concerning the Legacy of the Sermon

The legacy and extreme popularity of the Sermon on the Mount, and its impact on significant figures in history, serve as testimony to Matthew, in one sense, achieving his goals for the Sermon. The Sermon is such a succinct and highly effective interpretation and *precis* of Jesus' teaching. It is viewed by many as the apex of his teaching ministry. It is portions of the Sermon that most people recall when forced to provide a summary or sense of Jesus' teaching. The Beatitudes, Matthew's teaching on nonretaliation, or his version of the Lord's Prayer are the passages most people recall when thinking of Jesus or what a follower of his would believe. It is in this sense that Matthew has fulfilled his aim of providing an unforgettable, *a priori* authoritative summation of the words and will of Jesus. Even though, as we have indicated at numerous points, Matthew shaped the Sermon in light of the particular issues in his immediate setting, this is no longer seen when looking at the Sermon. Indeed, this is the way Matthew wanted it and, I suspect, believed it to be. That is, though we can see Matthew was responding to some very specific issues in his setting (like arguments about the law, competition with the "scribes and Pharisees," or dissension within his church), the Sermon has obtained a far great currency and authority than that. The Sermon is looked to, even though it is at odds with other Gospels at some important points, as the quintessential expression of the teachings of Jesus and, ultimately, of Christianity.

The Sermon has played an important role in a number of twentieth-century movements and has significantly influenced several pivotal twentieth-century figures. The Sermon on the Mount was extremely important in the thought of Leo Tolstoy. Tolstoy even wrote a short monograph on the Sermon. His writing and the social experiment he advocated for Russian society — if not beyond — owed much to the Sermon. His utopian Christian socialism was fashioned largely out of a selective reading and interpretation of the Sermon. Around the mid-point of the century Mahatma Gandhi fashioned a nonviolent revolution indebted, in part, to Matthew's Sermon. Louis Fischer has reported the lone decoration on the walls of Gandhi's hut was a black and white print of Jesus. While he of course was not a Christian, and the exclusivity and narrowness of salvation only through the Christian Gospel was untenable to him, he did say, "If I had to face only the Sermon on the Mount and my own interpretation of it I should not hesitate to say, 'Oh yes, I am a Christian. . . . ' But," he added, "negatively I can tell you that much of what passes as Christianity is a negation of the Sermon on the Mount."

The influence and importance of the Sermon in the thought and actions of Martin Luther King Jr. and the beginnings of the civil rights movement in America are well documented. In large part as a result of the influence of Gandhi, King says in *Stride Toward Freedom,* he began to see Jesus' teachings, especially in the Sermon, as more than just individual ethics. It was Gandhi who taught him that the Sermon, as we have been saying, is really community-forming literature. Prior to this King did not see the collective force of Jesus' love ethic. Remember that Matthew's Gospel was written in a colonial setting, and so his teaching about resistance, survival, and corporate ethics should have some resonance in English-dominated India or in the black South in the United States teeming with and dominated by white bigotry.

Martin Luther King Jr. studied American social gospel theologians like Walter Rauschenbusch, studied with Reinhold Niebuhr at Union Theological Seminary and Walter Muelder at Boston University. The Sermon on the Mount had tremendous influence on the work of these earlier twentieth-century theologians, as well as other social gospel theorists like S. J. Case and S. Mathews. But King had to overcome some aspects of this teaching, too. Niebuhr finally rejected the position of nonretaliation as expressed in the Sermon because, he thought, it was soft on collective or corporate evil. King continued to struggle with this and finally determined that Niebuhr had overstated the fallenness of humanity in *Moral Man and Immoral Society.* When King was confronted with the crisis and challenge of the dawning civil rights movement, and the protests it involved, back in the parish in Montgomery, he appealed to the Sermon and its teaching on love and nonviolent strategy.

Did Matthew intend to offer a manifesto and strategy for nonviolent revolution within the Sermon? Or did Jesus himself intend this and its force is still present in the Sermon, though obscured by Matthew's redaction? One short answer to this question is yes, the Sermon does offer a manifesto and strategy for nonviolent resistance because it has been so used, and effectively so in this century. The Sermon has obtained a life of its own and has been interpreted in a wide range of ways. The text is now on its own across history and it will be used, and occasionally abused, as various interpreters cultivate it for their own meaning and message. But let us inquire briefly about Matthew's intention with the Sermon. In his view is this a manifesto for resistance or revolution?

There is little overt indication that Matthew intended to overthrow Roman rule. The synoptic saying and concern over the question of whether it is right to pay taxes occurs twice in Matthew, which reveals that this is a salient issue in this colonial setting. Matthew 17:24ff. and 22:15ff. both treat the loaded question of paying tax to the lords. Yet, in both instances Jesus' response is so oblique that it could hardly be viewed as a call to revolution. In 17:27 Jesus and Peter do pay the tax. This in and of itself, I think, would have been instructive to the Matthean community, although the miraculous form of the payment could be construed as casting some doubt on the community's commitment to the tax (which, by the way, was about the only thing, along with absence of civil strife, that Rome insisted upon). Also, Matthew's apocalyptic sections, for example, 24:5ff., could be viewed by Rome as disturbing and provocative literature. Apocalyptic literature does call for the end of this age and the dawn of another, almost always with someone new in charge. Matthew's apocalyptic material, however, is by no means unique to him. Apocalypticism was widespread during the Roman period and his material is, relatively speaking, somewhat tame when compared to other apocalypticists. In short, Matthew does not seem to call explicitly for the overthrow of Rome. If he did, his message is too subtle for us to divine, or he simply is not consistent on this issue. Some of his contemporaries pushed for Rome's demise. One of the more notable examples is the New Testament Apocalypse or Book of Revelation, which is openly defiant of Rome and envisions its destruction. Such a hope does not seem to me to appear on Matthew's agenda, though admittedly one could come away with this impression by focusing selectively on a few Matthean passages.

On the other hand, Matthew does seem to be counseling resistance to and rejection of the people in power and control in a regional or local sense. We have already seen how the birth narrative sets the stage for the conflict between the newly born "King of the Jews" and Herod, Rome's client-, or puppet-king. In the birth narrative Matthew did show his hand concerning his awareness of and distaste for the colonial setting in which they lived. And no reader could be unaware that both John and Jesus had been killed as a result of this imperial reality.

Matthew's teaching was so often aimed at his local opponents, even or especially within the Sermon, that one could argue Matthew was looking for a reversal of fortune within his own parochial setting soon. Those who were in control in his backyard were those whom God would judge, who had no authority, and yet falsely exercised power in Matthew's setting. This is the reversal the Matthean church seemed to look for and a change Matthew appeared to relish. Rome might ultimately become embroiled in this regional dispute if it appeared as though it might lead to widespread instability, which happened during the Hasmonean civil war under Pompey. He and his troops came down from Damascus to put an end to the civil unrest. Some of the Matthean parables we will treat later in this commentary seem to suggest Matthew was aware of this possibility. So he had to walk a fine line or, in his own words, "be as shrewd as serpents, but as innocent as doves" (10:16).

Matthew's issue was not directly with Rome, but rather with the local leaders and powers-that-be. A change there would be good news for his community and, Matthew believed, for Israel. His teaching challenged their authority, and did so openly. He would not replace them by force, his strategy seemed to be to remove them, more or less, through popular opinion and support.

Enemies will be won over through the love ethic and Golden Rule (5:43–44). The positive and constructive works of Matthean members are on display as if a city set on a hill (5:14–16). The good works of the community will amaze people and they will thank God for them. And, Matthew asserts, against some impressions to the contrary, his disciples are good citizens. They keep all facets of the law, fulfilling it completely, they do not end up in court, and they do not equivocate in discussions or contracts (5:37). With God's help (quite soon), and if the Matthean community stays the course that Jesus has laid out for them in the Sermon, the false and destructive leaders with whom Matthew and his church contend may be history. If a revolutionary strategy in the advice and ethic emerges in Matthew's mind and in his Sermon on the Mount I suspect this is it.

This, of course, in no way limits the meanings and potential impact of the Sermon. It will doubtless continue to inspire audiences, leaders, and movements in ways Matthew could not have fully imagined. The breadth and potency of the Sermon, and the vision of life and human relationships it espouses, however ideal, remain an end toward which people and societies will aspire.

## Further Reading

Berger, P., and T. Luckmann. *The Social Construction of Reality.* Garden City, N.Y.: Doubleday, 1967.

Davies, W. D. *The Setting of the Sermon on the Mount.* Cambridge: Cambridge University Press, 1964.

Dupont, J. *Les Béatitudes: Le probléme littéraire. Les deux versions du Sermon sur la Montagne et des Béatitudes.* Bruges: Abbaye de Saint-André, 1958.

Fischer, L. *Gandhi: His Life and Message.* New York: Mentor, 1954.

Forkman, G. *The Limits of Religious Community: Expulsion from the Religious Community within the Qumran Sect, within Rabbinic Judaism, and within Primitive Christianity.* Lund: Gleerup, 1972.

Gnilka, J. "Matthäusgemeinde und Qumran." *BZ* 7 (1963): 43–63.

Goodman, M. "The First Jewish Revolt: Social Conflict and the Problem of Debt." *JJS* 33 (1982): 418–27.

Guelich, R. "Interpreting the Sermon on the Mount." *Interpretation* 41 (1987): 117–30.

————. *The Sermon on the Mount: A Foundation for Understanding.* Waco, Tex.: Word, 1982.

Harrington, D. *The Gospel of Matthew.* Sacra Pagina 1. Collegeville, Minn.: Michael Glazier/Liturgical Press, 1991.

Horsley, R. "Ancient Jewish Banditry and the Revolt against Rome, A.D. 66–70." *CBQ* 43 (1981): 409–32.

————. "Ethics and Exegesis: 'Love Your Enemies' and the Doctrine of Non-Retaliation." *JAAR* 54 (1986): 3–31.

Hummel, R. *Die Auseinandersetzung zwischen Kirche und Judentum im Matthäusevangelium.* Munich: Chr. Kaiser, 1963.

Käsemann, E. "Die Anfange christlichen Theologie." *ZTK* 57 (1960): 158–79.

Kimelman, R. "*Birkat Ha-Minim* and the Lack of Evidence for an Anti-Christian Jewish Prayer in Antiquity." In *Jewish and Christian Self-Definition,* ed. E. P. Sanders, 2:226–44. Philadelphia: Fortress, 1981.

King, M. L., Jr. *A Stride toward Freedom: The Montgomery Story.* New York: Harper, 1958.

Kissinger, W. S. *The Sermon on the Mount: A History of Interpretation and Bibliography.* Metuchen, N.J.: Scarecrow, 1975.

Kohler, K. "The Origin and Composition of the Eighteen Benedictions." In *Contributions to the Scientific Study of the Jewish Liturgy,* ed. J. Petuchowski. New York: KTAV, 1970.

Luz, U. "The Disciples in the Gospel According to Matthew." In *The Interpretation of Matthew,* ed. G. Stanton, 98–128. Philadelphia: Fortress, 1983.

Neusner, J. "The Formation of Rabbinic Judaism: Yavneh from A.D. 70–100." *ANRW* II.19.2 (1979): 3–42.

Overman, J. A. *Matthew's Gospel and Formative Judaism: The Social World of the Matthean Community.* Minneapolis: Fortress, 1990.

Przybylski, B. *Righteousness in Matthew and His World of Thought.* Cambridge: Cambridge University Press, 1980.

Robertson, A. T. *A Grammar of the Greek New Testament in the Light of Historical Research.* Nashville: Broadman Press, 1934.

Saldarini, A. J. "Apocalyptic and Rabbinic Literature." *CBQ* 37 (1975): 348–58.

Schäfer, P. "Die sogenannte Synode von Jabne." In *Studien zur Geschichte und Theologie des rabbinischen Judentums,* 45–64. Leiden: Brill, 1978.

# Chapter Four

# Mighty Deeds and Seeds of Doubt – 8:1–9:32

## HEALING, SOCIAL RELATIONS, AND CONFLICT

### The Power to Heal: Palestinian Politics, Diaspora Patronage, and the Source of Jesus' Authority

With the conclusion of the Sermon on the Mount begins a section that seems to be devoted to the works of Jesus. Frequently chapters 5 through 7 have been described as the Gospel of Jesus the teacher and chapters 8 through 9 the Gospel of Jesus the healer. Matthew has a tendency to lump similar materials together. Teaching tends to be concentrated in discrete discourses throughout the Gospel. Parables are as well, and, to a certain extent, the actions of Jesus. There are exceptions to Matthew's ordering principles, but in broad outline one can see how he went about gathering and structuring the material he used for his story.

After three chapters of teaching we see Jesus in action in Matthew. The first miracle is a cleansing of a leper that appears to be a story from Mark (Mark 1:40–45). Luke has also included the story in 5:12–16. Matthew has not made substantial changes in the story. The leper shows belief in Jesus' authority and power. "If you are willing you are able to make me clean" (Matt. 8:2). Neither Matthew or Luke report Jesus being "moved with pity," as Mark does in 1:41. He is healed, of course, in all three Gospels and told by Jesus to "show yourself to the priest, and offer the gift that Moses commanded, for a proof to the people" (8:4).

The term for "proof" (*marturion*, from which the term "martyr" is derived) really means witness, or testimony. The notion of the healed person "proving" something is not really the sense this term carries. Rather, he is providing a testimony or message about what has happened to him. In light of what Matthew has already said about fulfilling the law and the prophets, Jesus' command to the person to fulfill what Moses has commanded takes on additional force. The regulations pertaining to cleansing of leprosy are found in Leviticus 14:48ff. The guideline, "to show [any leprosy], when it is clean and when it is unclean" (Lev. 14:57), has as its ground the safety and concern of the community. This is not a trivial law from which Jesus, or certainly Matthew, would seek to "free" anyone. On the contrary, this law in Leviticus has as its focus the health and safety of the entire community. There could be a temptation to keep a problem like leprosy to oneself or family. But this decision imperils the community. If the community is informed, then steps can be taken to curb the spread of the disease. Therefore, one must inform the priest both when infected and when one is clean. Jesus here demonstrates the importance and validity of this communal statute.

In 8:5ff. is another miracle involving a centurion asking for help for his "servant" (*pais*) who is paralyzed and in great distress. The tradition history of this miracle story is interesting, but somewhat vexing. This appears initially to be a Q story found also in Luke 7:1–10. However, a very similar story occurs in John 4:46ff. In Matthew and in John the centurion comes on his own to Jesus for help. In Luke, or Q, if in fact his version is earlier, the centurion sends "elders of the Jews" (Luke 7:3) to plead with Jesus on his behalf. In Matthew and John, (in John he is not a centurion but a high-ranking official or king, *basilikos*), he goes to Jesus himself.

In John the healed person is clearly the centurion's "son" (*uios*). In Luke the one healed is clearly a servant or slave (*doulos*) of the centurion. Only Matthew uses the ambiguous *pais* in this story. This term can mean either "child" or "servant." It is true that in New Testament or *Koine* Greek the far more common term for son is *uios*. Yet, in classical Greek *pais* is not an overwhelmingly common term for servant and more often tends to suggest relation or offspring. Matthew uses *uios,* his usual term for son, many, many times. *Pais,* on the other hand, is a rare term for Matthew. I doubt he came up with it. He uses it three times in this story, once when quoting Isaiah in 12:10, and one more time in reference to the servants of Herod Antipas in 14:2. The ambiguity cannot be done away with. This term of double meaning may have been used purposefully to suggest that this person is as much or more a "son" of the kingdom in a metaphorical sense than those "sons" (*uioi*) who ultimately will be thrown into outer darkness (8:12). This, after all, is the message or point of the miracle in Matthew's view. "Servant," not "slave" or "son," is the best translation of this term in this context. There is, incidentally, an interesting rabbinic parallel to this story involving a first-century figure, R. Hanina b. Dosa, who also healed the son of a prominent figure (R. Gamaliel), by prayer from a distance (*b. Ber.* 34b).

I believe here Matthew retains the version closest to the original. The outline of the original story can be seen in Matthew, Luke, and perhaps John. It may be a Q tradition then, or a very basic, rather widespread healing story about Jesus and a centurion from Capernaum repeated by Q and, later, by John in a varied form. This story, though, would have reached John through a different route, or branch of the tradition, and not through Q, as was the case with Matthew and Luke. But Luke in 7:4–5 fills this story out considerably. He adds what would have been a very important story for those Jews living in the diaspora (that is, Jews living outside of Palestine).

Jews in the diaspora were a well-established, and generally well-regarded, significant minority. Jewish communities were venerable and sizable in Alexandria in Egypt, Rome, Sardis in modern-day western Turkey (ancient Asia Minor), and, it seems, along the North Coast of the Black Sea, as recent excavations are beginning to show. These Jewish communities made significant contributions to the cultural and civic life of their diaspora settings. There was a lively give-and-take between these important diaspora communities and the surrounding, dominant, non-Jewish cultures. As A. T. Kraabel and others have pointed out, the story of Greco-Roman diaspora communities is one of the great, though sadly neglected, stories of all Jewish history.

One prime example of flourishing diaspora Jewish communities is the Jewish community from Sardis. This large community, probably dating from the sixth century B.C.E., made an ongoing and substantial contribution to their city. As Kraabel notes, "By the first century B.C.E. these Jews were an influential group in the gentile city." They enjoyed considerable autonomy, and also, according to Josephus, controlled their own place, designated area, or building within the city (*topos idios; Ant.* 14.235). In the passage from *Antiquities* Josephus is quoting an official Roman decree pertaining to rights of the Jewish community in Sardis. The Jews of Sardis were important members of and maintained an important presence in the city, so much so in fact that the city gave the Jewish community the largest synagogue ever discovered, located in the heart of the ancient city and adjacent to a Roman bath complex.

Here we begin to see where the story in Luke 7 and the Jews of Sardis begin to connect. These diaspora communities, though large and venerable, like any other even sizable minority in a Greco-Roman city would necessarily depend on the largess and benefaction of the broader city. They were, nevertheless, a minority and, as Kraabel says, always in some measure "immigrants, exiles, and expatriates." They would always require the patronage and benefaction of significant individuals to secure their place in a world that at least politically, if not culturally and religiously, was not theirs. Here Luke's story of the good Gentile who "loves our nation and built us our synagogue" (Luke 7:5) interacting with Jesus begins to make more sense. As F. Danker, G. Rogers, and many others have demonstrated, most public buildings in the ancient world were erected as a result of the patronage system and some specific benefaction. The Sardis synagogue in one of its phases seems to be a prime example of this. In addition to the synagogue in Sardis there is also mention in an inscription (CIJ 751) of the "fountain of the synagogue," which was municipally licensed and open to all. Luke's additions to the story of the centurion in Capernaum capture this important aspect of his diaspora reality. The community is working well with those non-Jews who possess influence and power in their diaspora context. Involvement of these people in some manner in their life is usual, necessary, and important, and their interest and appreciation of the Jewish community is reflected in their financial support. The author of Luke is probably a diaspora Jew like those Jewish leaders from Sardis or maybe Aphrodisias, also in Asia Minor. He is not embroiled in the same social and political malaise that characterizes the Matthean Palestinian setting. I believe the political, and therefore also social lives of the Jews in Palestine were quite different, on the whole, from Jews in the diaspora. The two revolts against Rome so close together, the series of tensions and uprisings throughout the first century in Palestine, and the lack of a protracted, positive relationship between Jewish communities and the powers-that-be such as existed in the diaspora generally, made Palestine a very different place for Jewish communities around the time of Matthew. Luke 7:3–5 is Luke's addition to the earlier (perhaps) Q story that focuses on the authority a gentile authority or ruler ascribes to Jesus. Like so much of Matthew's Gospel in its own way, this brief but important addition is also a reflection of Luke's own cultural and political context placed within his story of Jesus.

Matthew reports the earlier version of the miracle of the healing of the centurion's servant, but not because he is bashful about shaping a story in a way he feels is most applicable to his community. In his view it probably really happened this way. This form of constructive revisionism is common among teachers, preachers, and pastors, and Matthew is all of these. The words of Jesus and the forms of the stories Matthew reports are those he believes address most powerfully and fruitfully the issues and people of his own congregation. This earlier version of the healing of the centurion accomplishes these ends for Matthew. Luke's diaspora concern about making room for gentile supporters and benefactors is miles away from Matthew's paramount concerns.

What Matthew highlights in the healing of the centurion's servant is the acknowledgment of Jesus' authority. The centurion defers to and honors Jesus. "I am not worthy to have you come under my roof," he says (8:8). He sees Jesus as a man of power or authority. Even more precisely, he sees Jesus as a man *exercising* power or authority (*exousian;* 8:9). The centurion says to Jesus, "For I [too] am a man *under* authority with soldiers under me; and I say to one 'Go,' and he goes, and to another, 'Come,' and he comes, and to my slave, 'Do this,' and he does it." The Greek *kai* in 8:9 carries the sense of "too" or "also." The term "under" is the Greek preposition *upo* with the accusative case meaning "under." The centurion understands how authority works. He understands that both he and Jesus receive their power and authority from somewhere or someone. In the case of the centurion it is Caesar or the regional imperial lord or governor, and, it seems he recognizes, in the case of Jesus it is God. Jesus, amazed by the centurion, says, " 'Go, be it done for you as you have believed.' And the servant was healed at that very moment" (8:13).

There is palpable irony in this conversation with the centurion. That someone entrenched within the imperial power structure should understand so deeply, almost intrinsically, the nature of Jesus, how and why he does what he does, is certainly poignant. "Not even in Israel have I found such faith," says Jesus (8:10). One would not expect someone so much a part of the colonial system to receive such a commendation from Jesus. In fact, he is the first person so praised in the Gospel. The man is able to see something in the way Jesus acts, or is able to act, that others hitherto have been unable to see. There is something analogous in their lives that enables the centurion to make this connection with Jesus (cf. 8:9). Local leaders have not been able to see this, but the authority from the imperial system has.

Following Jesus' exclamation in 8:10 Matthew adds this verse, "Many will come from east and west and sit at table with Abraham, Isaac, and Jacob in the kingdom of heaven, while the sons of the kingdom will be thrown into outer darkness" (8:12). This is somewhat reminiscent of the Baptist's announcement about judgment to the Pharisees and Sadducees in 3:9, "Do not presume to say, 'We have Abraham as our father.' For I tell you, God is able from these stones to raise up children of Abraham." The focus of this story is the authority Jesus possesses. It is that much more persuasive that the testimony about Jesus' authority should come from such an obvious and ubiquitous symbol of authority: the centurion. The centurion as Gentile seems secondary. Still, Matthew 8:11–12 claims the content and contours of the kingdom of heaven will be different from what has been previously assumed. Many will come from east and west and sit at the table. The putative sons of the kingdom will be cast out. This is consistent with John's theme in 3:9 that something is happening now. Changes are in the offing and expectations and definitions that have held up to now must be reevaluated and modified.

Does this mean Gentiles will be in the kingdom of heaven, that is, Matthew's community as well as the hereafter? The answer to this, based on 8:11ff. and some other important passages in the Gospel, seems to be yes. I would only hasten to add that this does not mean for Matthew that therefore traditional Jews and historic Israel are out. He nowhere says this. There will be some insiders who on that day will be outsiders, and the readers of Matthew's Gospel are well aware of who those outsiders will be.

Also, that Israel is changing in some manner to include also Gentiles is not really new. Israel has always seen itself as involving non-Jews. The extensive legislation concerning the *Gerim*, or resident aliens in the Hebrew Bible, is a reflection of this concern. Exodus 22:21, 23:9, Deuteronomy 10:18, 24:19, and Numbers 15:13–16 contain rules for the inclusion and protection of the *Ger*. Also, others of Matthew's contemporaries would have seen Gentiles as significant players in the life of their community. We just discussed Luke's version of this very story and his additions aimed at highlighting the importance of gentile involvement and support. It may have been that by the first century or so, with the increased Roman presence in the Greek East, the issue of gentile involvement had become more pressing. I am not sure that Matthew here is saying anything particularly radical. He is punctuating the possible presence of Gentiles in the kingdom of heaven, and that would include too, very likely, their presence in his community.

One must say, however, that there is little internal evidence from the Gospel to suggest Gentiles in Matthew's church. If they are present, their numbers are few. The statements about potential gentile involvement here, in 3:9, and perhaps the end of the Gospel seem to point more toward the future and less toward a current situation or problem. What is most striking in this story, when read in context, is that a person so closely associated with the occupying forces should be celebrated as a potential "son of the kingdom of heaven." This only goes to underscore the point that Matthew, and perhaps Jesus himself, did not ultimately seek to reject Rome, but instead challenged and competed with traditional local leaders and teachers. These are the insiders whom Matthew anticipates will soon be outsiders. The story of the centurion from Capernaum in chapter 8 serves to highlight this. Both the healing of the leper in 8:1–4 and the centurion's servant in 8:5ff. stress the authority and power Jesus possesses. In these stories Matthew draws attention to the fact that, in his view, there is no other authority the community should revere but him.

The brief story in 8:14–19 of the healing of Peter's mother-in-law in Peter's house in Capernaum appears also in Mark (1:29) and Luke (4:38), though curtailed by Matthew. The story virtually serves as a narrative summary for the first fifteen verses of chapter 8. Matthew reports that Peter's mother-in-law serves only Jesus (*auto*), not all of them (*autois*), as is the case in Mark 1:31 and Luke 4:39, following her healing. Matthew deletes the note about Jesus' popularity reported in Mark and Luke. Also, the struggle over the demons' speech, so much a concern in Mark's Gospel, is missing in Matthew. The story serves to summarize Jesus' healing activity up to this point. The Matthean narrative summary leads us to believe Jesus engaged in this work on a widespread basis helping and healing many people. This is reinforced by a Matthean fulfillment citation from Isaiah 53:4. "This was to fulfill what was spoken by the prophet Isaiah, 'He took our infirmities and bore our diseases'" (8:17). The *precis* of healing activity provided in 8:16–17 inserted by Matthew is another opportunity for him to highlight the correspondence between Jesus' ministry and the prophets and promises of ancient Israel. For the Matthean community the Isaiah citation reinforces the authority, power, and trustworthiness of Jesus' teaching and actions as interpreted by Matthew. The assertion here is that the authority for Jesus' ministry is deeply rooted in the plans and promises of the God of Israel. His authority is unrivaled. This appears to have been recognized by the leper (8:2), the centurion (8:6–8), and in the Isaiah citation from 8:17.

Two other healing stories appear in this narrative unit. They are the healing of the Gadarene demoniacs in Matthew 8:28–34, and the paralytic child in 9:1–8 at Capernaum. These two stories come after the section on discipleship. These Matthean miracles also emphasize Jesus' authority. First this is seen in the demoniacs, who offer a confession to Jesus as "son of God" (8:29), and as menacing as they seem (though far less so in Matthew than in Mark or Luke), they instantly submit themselves to Jesus and his authority. The demons are cast into a herd of pigs and rush down a slope into the Sea of Galilee. News that Jesus has done this spreads into the nearby city. The people come out to see Jesus and the healed demoniacs who were, no doubt, rather well known throughout the area. The people then ask Jesus to leave their neighborhood (*orion*). The demoniacs engage in no missionary activity as in Mark 5:20 and Luke 8:39. In all three Gospels Jesus is asked to leave the area by the people. Matthew in particular provides no rationale for this response in 8:34. Jesus is either bad for business because he destroyed the pig herds or he causes too much commotion with such acts of power. Better in these colonial contexts to keep your head low, or, as the Mishnaic tractate *Pirke Abot* says, "Love work, hate authority, and do not let yourself be known by the government" (1.10).

This severely truncated story in Matthew when compared to Mark 5:1–20 or Luke 8:26–39 serves as another brief episode that illustrates Jesus' healing power and authority. The healing of the paralytic child in 9:1–8 expands on the same theme of Jesus' personal authority. The healing of the child puts the question of authority, and specifically by whose authority Jesus acts, squarely on the table. Matthew, following Mark, has put this question out in the open. Until now this question has been a subtext (save 7:29) in the story. Jesus heals the child by saying, "Your sins are forgiven" (9:2). This provokes the first open conflict with the local leaders who, in this instance, are scribes. Does

Jesus, and through him the Matthean community, as the author has several times claimed, have the authority to forgive (or not forgive) sins? The scribes call this blasphemy. This is the precise charge that resurfaces at the trial scene in 26:57ff. when Jesus is asked if he is "the Christ, the son of God" (26:63).

What possible "sin" has the boy committed? We are not told. It is offensive to our sensibilities to think of a young child (*teknon*) as a sinner. Yet it is widely acknowledged that diseases in the ancient world were associated with some sort of miscue with the gods, or sin. This assumption is evident in John 9:2. Jesus actually admits that he did not need to say, "Your sins are forgiven" (9:5). But to make it clear to those who are around that he can do it — that is, to push the issue — Jesus says, "Your sins are forgiven." The issue of authority — who is in charge, who lays down the rules and interprets them, and above all who speaks for the God of Israel — emerges as the central contention. This is the fundamental issue coming to the fore at the start of chapter 9. It has been brewing throughout the story. It was made explicit for a moment in 7:29, and has been the issue surrounding the healings in chapter 8. Here in 9:1–8 Matthew makes the issue prominent. Who has authority to act in this manner in Israel?

An important feature of this story is the corporate or collective faith honored by Jesus. In the three synoptic Gospels it is a group of people who bring the paralyzed child (he is a "man" in Luke 5:20) for healing. Upon seeing their (*autōn*, genitive plural) faith, that is, the faith expressed by those acting on behalf of the child, Jesus moves to heal him. Corporate or communal acts of faith, it is asserted here in this originally Marcan story, can effect change and healing even in particular or individual situations. Where the sin of another is concerned, one wonders if, in the antique mindset, that too could be inflicted as a result of corporate dereliction or omission? If collective expressions of faith can heal an individual, is it possible corporate sins can be reflected in the ills of one person?

"So that you may know that the Son of Man has the *authority on earth* to forgive sins." This is the point of the story and, really, the other healing stories leading up to this. The title "Son of man" goes back to Daniel 7 and dates to roughly 165 B.C.E. The

Son of man is a corporate, heavenly, redemptive figure known among apocalyptic groups in Israel in this period. The operative clause in Matthew 9:6 is probably "authority on earth" to forgive sins. The Son of man is a heavenly figure with heavenly authority. Here Jesus claims, as Son of man, he possesses the power and authority *on earth* to forgive sins. Matthew stresses this point in the conclusion of the story of the paralytic child when he writes, "When the crowds saw it [the healing] they were afraid and they glorified God, who had given such *authority to people* [*anthropois*]." Mark 2:12 and Luke 5:26 conclude with "We never saw anything like this," and "We have seen strange things today," respectively. Only Matthew punctuates again the issue of authority in 9:8 at the conclusion to the story. The miracles of Jesus for Matthew more than any other writer are meant to display the authority he has been given by God. This authority has been passed onto the Matthean community as heirs and guarantors of the message and authority of Jesus. The story ends with people (that is plural, *anthropois*) receiving authority. The community now carries that same authority to forgive, to bind, to loose, to decide who are members in the church of the kingdom of heaven and who are no longer "sons of the kingdom." They received this authority from Jesus, who received it from God. The miracles intend to reinforce this Matthean claim.

## Discipleship and Faith

Matthew uses the popularity that appears to come from Jesus' healing as an opportunity to teach about the cost of discipleship and membership in the Matthean community. The Matthean order here is to use the miracles in 8:1–17 to teach first about authority, and then discipleship. Matthew utilizes a famous Q logion to teach about discipleship, "Foxes have holes, and the birds of the air have nests, but the Son of Man has nowhere to lay his head" (Matt. 8:20 ‖ Luke 9:58). In Matthew 8:19 the one coming to Jesus saying, "I will follow [*akolouthaso*] you wherever you go," is actually a scribe (*grammateus*), and not Q's unidentified person (Luke 9:57). I suspect, along with others, that by this point in the development of traditions about Jesus the term "to follow" had become nearly a technical term, or code word, for members of the Jesus movement. This certainly seems to be the case in the Matthean community. The scribe addresses Jesus in terms familiar to the scribe. "Teacher" (*didaskole*) he says, and not "Lord" or "Sir" (*Kurie*) as the leper and centurion had done earlier. The term "scribe" is already associated with the Matthean opponents. Yet this is the most neutral of local leadership terms in Matthew's vocabulary. Matthew speaks about "their" scribes (cf. 7:29), suggesting that there are other scribes. And Matthew likens members of his community to well-trained or truly trained scribes, that is, "scribes trained for the kingdom of heaven" (13:52).

This scribe appears to mean well in his declaration. Jesus suggests, however, that he doesn't know what he is getting into. After the scribe a disciple (one would assume a follower, given the intimacy of this term in Matthew) speaks to Jesus and he too demonstrates a less-than-complete understanding of the cost of discipleship. The response he receives is one of the harshest and most often recited of Jesus' words on discipleship. " 'Lord [*Kurie*], let me first go bury my father.' But Jesus said to him, 'Follow me and let the dead bury their own dead' " (8:22).

This is a very harsh and unbending saying on what it means to be a follower. Jesus' teaching on discipleship, at just about every point, is hardly supportive of modern notions of the nuclear family. On the contrary, his demands strain traditional and family relationships. This is supported by the vocabulary Matthew uses to describe disciples and members. They are "brothers" and "mothers" (Matt. 12:49 ‖ Mark 3:34). The demands placed upon the followers supersede the traditional responsibilities associated with family and village life. "Home" takes on a new meaning, as Jesus' response to the scribe suggests, and family responsibilities are reappraised. As A. J. Saldarini has recently pointed out, Matthew employs kinship language to describe the social relations within the community. At points he affirms traditional roles to honor one's mother and father (15:4–5; 19:19), but these commands are put in a new perspective and relative priority. The hyperbolic but no less biting saying on discipleship from 8:22 denotes this change. A. Schlatter commented accurately some time ago, "That pietas could be denied at this point, and the duty of a son overridden, was completely unthinkable to Jewish sensitivities. It was a purely sacrilegious act of impiety" (237). I would only add to Schlatter's comment that this would constitute a supreme act of sacrilege in any culture in the Greco-Roman world: Jew, Roman, and Greek alike.

The nature of discipleship in this section of chapter 8 probably reflects the divisions in families within the Jewish community in Palestine in the first century. As we pointed out before, such intimate division is frequently part of a colonial or seemingly totalitarian setting. It is not uncommon in such colonial situations for brother to fight against brother, and for family loyalties to be severed. Are the members willing to turn their backs on the family for the sake of their new, fictive family? In such a context family support fails and traditional bonds dissolve as a result of one's allegiance to the (new) cause. In fact, in 10:21 and 10:35 Jesus is explicit about the division and enmity within families he, Jesus, will cause. Family relations now constitute an obstacle and potential threat. Also, the ideology of the group exacerbates the gap between a member and his or her family through heightened rhetoric and excessive demands for loyalty. The community becomes the family and attempts to fulfill the roles formerly associated with family and other traditional ties. The Q logion about leaving the dead to bury their own dead is suggestive of such a context.

The disciple who approached Jesus only asked "first" (*proton*) to bury his father. There is every indication that the person intends to follow. Jesus' response to him does break with traditions about the priority of a dead person in most any stream of Jewish thought. "He who is confronted by a dead relative is freed from reciting the *Shema*, from the Eighteen Benedictions, and from all the commandments stated in the Torah" (*Ber.* 3.1a; also *Sanh.* 47a). But this later rabbinic summation of the rights and priority of the dead reflects a period of more developed control and order. For many the period between the revolts in Palestine was a state of emergency. As is so often the case, the numerous popular movements, rebel and bandit groups, many of whom died in trying to effect their particular visions within early Roman Palestine, lived life outside traditional roles and sources of security. In this period of conflict and uncertainty such daily, familial, and traditional routines and responsibilities were held in abeyance by reforming or rebel groups. The Jesus movement(s) was one such group. Matthew employs this logion to underline that membership in the Matthean community will also strain relations at home and within the local setting of his church. Those who are true disciples must inevitably be prepared for these painful divisions and hard choices.

Matthew 8:23–27 can be thought of as both a miracle story and a parable about discipleship. Following on the heels of the instruction about discipleship, as only Matthew has it, the story emerges as a parable about following Jesus. This story is taken from Mark 4:35ff., but Matthew explicitly makes this a story about "following" (*akolouthasan*) in 8:23. The disciples follow Jesus into the boat and are overcome by the storm that catches them off guard. In all the synoptic accounts the faith of the disciples is called into question, though characteristically Matthew softens the critique of the disciples compared to Mark (8:26 ‖ Mark 4:40). In Matthew, however, the cry of the disciples is made into a unison prayer or exclamation, "Lord save!" (8:25). G. Bornkamm and others have noted the corporate and ecclesial character of this brief parable. The parable of "the little boat church" addresses the fears about following that confront the Matthean church. Matthew returns to this theme and develops it further in 14:22ff. Some traditional relationships and forms of security have been put in peril by the followers' allegiance to Jesus and certainly their membership in the Matthean community. It has been rough sailing for members of the church. This reworked parable aims at teaching them they are not alone in the fears they face as followers and disciples.

## Dissension and Doubts about Jesus and the Kingdom

Much of the rest of the chapter from 9:9 forward picks up on the conflict begun in 9:3 when the scribes brought the question about Jesus' authority and the charge of blasphemy out in the open. The call of the disciple who was a tax collector in 9:9ff. is the start of tension over the company Jesus keeps. In Mark 2:14 and Luke 5:29 the follower and tax collector is named Levi. In Matthew 9:9 he is "a man called Matthew." Here we have the passage that almost certainly accounts for the Gospel ultimately being called "Matthew." The Gospel was not written by this man, or anyone else who actually followed Jesus. Even the very oldest of the first followers of Jesus would have died by the time of the writing of Matthew's Gospel. The death of that generation, though, might be cause actually to write a book like Matthew's. Matthew's Gospel is a recollection of Jesus' life, ministry, and death aimed at the issues surrounding followers of Jesus in Palestine at the end of the first century. The original manuscripts of the Gospels have no superscripts. That is, no title or name is associated with them. Church tradition subsequently gave names to the Gospels, usually as a result of some piece of internal evidence or hint that could be taken as potential (though doubtful) autobiographical glosses on the part of the author. Such is the case with Matthew 9:9.

After his meeting and calling Matthew, Jesus is seen sitting at a table at "the house" in Capernaum with *many* tax collectors and sinners. These two infamous groups, "tax collectors and sinners," represent a formulaic pair in synoptic parlance. The two, it seems, naturally go together. It requires no elaboration or explanation that tax collectors would be counted with and among sinners. It is one of the surprising features of the synoptic Gospels that they so freely associate Jesus with a group of people that, given the colonial setting of Palestine, must have been among the most hated groups in the land.

Others in the empire seemed to share this view of tax collectors as well. Cicero (*De offic* 15–51), Diogenes Cynicus (*Ep.* 36.2), and Dio Chrysostom (*Orat.* 14.14) lump them together with beggars, thieves, and robbers. Similarly, later rabbinic literature groups them with murderers, sinners, and robbers (*m. Tohar.* 7.6; *m. Ned.* 3.4). Tax collectors also appear in lists of despised trades that Jews should not follow (*b. Sanh.* 25b). In colonial settings even the colonialists don't respect the indigenous population who do their bidding. These well-established writers and, in their own right, powerful and influential people from the broader Roman world include tax collectors among a very low level of imperial society.

Feelings about local people who officially served the Romans directly, or Roman client-lords like Antipas, must have run very high in Palestine. It is attention-getting that these people make their way into the Gospel tradition. The Pharisees in Matthew call attention to Jesus' association with these people. "Why does your teacher [*didaskalos umon*] eat with tax collectors and sinners?" (9:11). The Pharisees use some of the same "us/them" language we saw in Matthew: "your" teacher, as opposed to the teachers with whom they are familiar and friendly. Only in Matthew do the Pharisees describe Jesus as a teacher in this pericope. This is the first instance of open opposition to Jesus from the Pharisees.

What we know about the party of the Pharisees comes primarily from Josephus with a little help from the Gospels and later rabbinic literature. Josephus says there are three main parties or philosophies (*haireseis*) among the Jews. They are Sadducees, Pharisees, and Essenes (*J.W.* 2.119). In the parallel passage in *Antiquities* a fourth group is added, the Fourth Philosophy, who are just like the Pharisees, only much more revolutionary and zealous for the liberation of Israel (*Ant.* 18.11). Josephus first mentions the Pharisees in the context of a discussion about John Hyrcanus who ruled from c. 134 to 104 B.C.E. The Pharisees gained and then lost the political support of Hyrcanus, who switched from being a Pharisee to a Sadducee (*Ant.* 13.288). There is an indication later in *Antiquities* that Hyrcanus initiated a repression of Pharisaic beliefs and practices (*Ant.* 13.409).

The Pharisees are mentioned again in a story about Alexander Jannai (c. 76 B.C.E.). On his deathbed Jannai gives his wife and successor, Alexandra, advice about how to successfully rule the kingdom (*Ant.* 13.399–417). If she wishes to stay in power, Jannai tells her, she must put some of her power in the hands of the Pharisees. Because they are so popular with the people, they will reconcile the nation to her. Their popularity, Josephus says, was due to the Pharisees being "the most accurate interpreters of the law" (*J.W.* 1.108–12). Alexandra takes her husband's advice and enjoys a successful reign. But the Pharisees then work their way into the political framework of the government, and into Alexandra's favor. Josephus claims that under Alexandra the Pharisees become "the real administrators of public affairs, enjoying royal authority." *Antiquities* 13.405 describes the steps Alexandra takes to empower the Pharisees, and that she orders the multitude to obey them. In the parallel passage in *J.W.* 1.111–16 Josephus says that the Pharisees could set free whomever they wished, retain whomever they wished, and are granted the power "to bind and to loose" under Alexandra. The Pharisees emerge again in Josephus during the reign of Herod. In *Jewish Wars* 1.567 Herod becomes angry with the Pharisees. He suspects they are doing something behind his back. He believes his wife is supporting the Pharisees and encouraging them to oust Herod.

The picture we get of the Pharisees from these passages is a political interest group, or *retainer* class (as discussed by A. J. Saldarini), who are popular with the people, around or near those in power, and whose fortunes can rather quickly turn from enjoying power to having none. Such is the fate of the retainer class, or educated elite in an agrarian society, depending as they do on the favor of those in power. That they should be concerned about the law and turn up to debate legal issues makes sense in light of Josephus's description. Popularity with and respect of the people are important for the Pharisaic party. The Pharisees' influence and position with those in power depend on their popularity and influence with the people. The highly stylized and polemical debates with the Pharisees in Matthew's Gospel frequently have as their focus the popular support of the people or crowds.

The Pharisees were one of the few groups to have survived the destruction of Jerusalem and the first revolt in any number. We never hear again of Essenes or the Qumran community, or a number of rebel groups, and apocalyptic groups are in very short supply after 70. The Sadducees are mentioned only a few times in rabbinic literature and the Gospels. The Pharisees' position and influence seem to get stronger as we approach the end of the first century C.E. It is generally held by J. Neusner and others that a strong Pharisaic component to rabbinic Judaism took shape after 135 C.E. As Neusner has pointed out, the Pharisaic system, as best we can reconstruct it, did not require a literal temple, though it was based on the temple. The rites of ritual purity, tithing, and calendrical observance were all founded on and related to the temple. The Pharisees took this system, applied it to everyone (no longer only to temple priests), and encouraged their fulfillment in a domestic or local setting. The debates with Jesus over these matters later in Matthew are largely consistent with this picture. The rules pertaining to the temple could now be enacted in a home or village setting. The regulations about temple life pertained, but a temple as such was no longer required. If Neusner is correct, we can see at least one reason why the Pharisees might have fared so well after 70 C.E. and the destruction of the temple in Jerusalem. By the way, the allegorization of the temple and the replication of the temple in the domestic setting were also practiced by so-called early Christianity. Herein we can see yet another potential cause for conflict and competition between these two groups.

The question asked by the Pharisees in Matthew 9:11 is an attempt to discredit Jesus by drawing attention to something most or all people would have found revolting. A contest for who will have influence and constitute the local leadership and authority is clearly underway. Matthew has been making no secret of his polemic with these leaders and now we see the contention goes both ways. There has been considerable debate among scholars over whether Jesus would have really dined with such a questionable lot. The scenario of Jesus seeking out such outcasts has played a large role in certain Christian reconstructions of Jesus. The social application of the Gospel, which has meant so much in terms of work in the inner cities, starting and funding Christian aid organizations, and other similar expressions have often been predicated on this picture. The consensus among scholars today is that Jesus probably did make such associations, if even very occasionally. This conclusion cannot be without some qualifications.

The first point, made particularly by E. P. Sanders, is even if Jesus did dine with "tax gatherers and sinners," this is not necessarily a violation of Jewish law. This is the significance many Christian writers have given to this scene. Jesus, the "inclusive" master, is demonstrating the limitations of "exclusive" Judaism. These prejudices are Sanders's concern, and he does a good job of showing that such presuppositions about Judaism and Jesus' place within it are based on assumptions by interpreters and not an informed knowledge of second-temple Judaism. Judaism in all its diversity in the early Roman period was no less informed or compassionate about sinners and outsiders than what has come to be called their early Christian counterparts.

Second, the possibility exists that this charge against Jesus was a rumor that started with his opponents. If so, the earliest recorders of the tradition took the rumor as authentic and found ample warrant within the scriptures of Israel for this behavior. They clearly did not view this as a very damaging charge. Was this a false charge against Jesus which made its way into the Gospel tradition, or did the earliest writers have the knowledge or sense that this charge was in fact true, and could be made into a virtue, as Matthew does in 9:13? Most scholars incline toward the latter view. But even those scholars who incline toward the former, like R. Horsley, allow for the possibility of some limited instances of contact between this population and Jesus.

It is likely that Jesus had contact with a tax collector and other marginalized people. Remember, reforming, rebel, or other deviant groups usually do not draw from the mainstream of society, at least initially. It is quite plausible those around the edges of Galilean society would have had entrée to the movement or had cause to engage this popular leader. It is not necessarily the case that the tax collector is a Gentile. In fact, he probably was not. And it does not matter whether he was working directly for Rome, or Herod Antipas, or Agrippa. His reputation preceded him. He was part of a profession which, if not utterly despised, had at least very low stock in the colonial setting of Roman Palestine. I think it is significant that this story is embedded within the Gospel tradition. When coupled with several of Matthew's other stories about officials involved in the imperial system it helps indicate just where Matthew sees the crisis coming. He takes aim at (another) local political group that is lobbying for the ear and allegiance of the people.

In 9:11 we are not even informed about the issue associated with Jesus' behavior. The Pharisees do not accuse Jesus of breaking the law; they are only surprised that he is eating with the tax collectors. The offense here may only be that Jesus is not dining with the Pharisees. Therefore, they ask innocently, "Why is your teacher dining with tax gatherers and sinners?" That is, why has he chosen to dine with them and not us? It is a fair question. Jesus' choice here is an unusual one. Matthew's response and scriptural citation, however, signal that this is the beginning of hostilities between the two groups. The Pharisees' question about Jesus dining with tax collectors and sinners and, above all, Matthew's response make this impending crisis very clear.

Matthew's Jesus responds to the Pharisees' question to the disciples by quoting an ancient proverb about the role of a physician followed by Hosea 6:6: "I desire mercy and not sacrifice." Matthew alone among the Gospel writers cites Hosea 6:6 and does so twice. The other instance is found in Matthew 12:7. The only other occasion I am aware of when this passage is cited for support of certain behavior is in *Avot Rabbi Nathan* (*ARN*). This post-Mishnaic rabbinic tractate, which contains some early traditions, mentions this passage in the context of a lament over the destruction of the temple. "How will sacrifice be made?" Yohan ben Zakkai quotes this passage from Hosea to explain how sacrifice will continue in the post-70 period. Matthew concurs with the sentiment from *ARN*. He believes that the Pharisees, in light of their question, do not. This scriptural citation, then, is obviously aimed at Matthew's opponents in the law in the post-70 period in Palestine.

The dissension and doubts concerning Jesus do not only come from the Pharisees in this section of the Gospel. The Baptist, too, has developed some doubts about Jesus. In 9:14–17 John's disciples (also *mathatai*) come to Jesus with a question about fasting. "We and the Pharisees fast, but your disciples do not fast" (9:14). Here we see a break between the Baptist and the Pharisees on one hand, and Jesus and his disciples on the other. The particular behavioral issue is fasting. Jesus' followers do not fast but

several other groups of disciples do. Matthew makes clear that
it is John's disciples who come with the question. Luke 5:33
obscures this point.

Who fasts and when to do it remained in dispute for some
time within Jesus-centered and formative Judaism. The *Didache*
captures some of this debate in 8:1 where it states, "Hypocrites
fast on Monday and Thursday. Christians therefore should fast
on Wednesday and Friday." We know already from chapter 6 that
Matthew's community does fast. Like the *Didache*, he contrasts
his fasts with those of his opponents, "the hypocrites." Jesus'
answer, which is obviously a post-facto explanation on the part
of the Evangelist, explains that while Jesus (the bridegroom) is
here, there is no mourning (i.e., fasting; contrast though Matt.
6:16). The time will come when Jesus, the bridegroom, is gone.
Then they will fast.

The somewhat complicated response to this simple question
finds its significance in the way this begins to distinguish and
distance the Jesus movement from other related movements.
The issue of fasting was a concrete and visible way in which
groups began to lay out boundaries and assert the differences
that existed between their community and their contemporaries.
Matthew knew this and utilized this passage, like others, to ar-
ticulate divisions and distinctions between the Matthean church
and other local leaders. In this pericope the party of the Pharisees and the followers of John the Baptist are both distanced
from Matthew's community. People are noticing the external
marks of Matthean Judaism. Such boundary-setting invariably
raises questions from outsiders, and very often creates questions
and friction. This section of the Gospel gives expression to the
questions, and eventual friction, that arise from outsiders about
the behavior of Matthew's church.

## Further Acts of Power and Popular Support

Chapter 9 concludes with a series of miracle stories that demonstrate Jesus' growing popularity among the crowds. The first
miracle in 9:18–26 involves a ruler (*arkon*) who has come to

Jesus saying, "My daughter has just died, but if you lay your hand on her she will live" (9:18). In the parallel stories in Mark 5:21 and Luke 8:40 the official is a "ruler of the synagogue" (*arkisynagogon*). Matthew deletes this designation. There are no friendly exchanges in Matthew between Jesus and synagogue officials. The term is reserved for the leadership group with whom he is contending. The language of simply "ruler" (*arkon*) in Matthew tends to suggest a gentile official or prominent civic figure. This is not necessarily so, but I suspect this is part of Matthew's aim in the deletion of the Marcan term here. This would accord rather well with a theme in this section of the Gospel where people associated with the foreign system and powers are portrayed quite positively. This authority knows enough also to go to Jesus for help. Jesus' power and ability, and his desire to do good works, are somehow clear to him, but not others.

In all three synoptic versions this story is interrupted by the healing of the woman who has hemorrhaged for twelve years. Matthew uses the more precise term here, *aimorroousa,* instead of Mark and Luke's more general "flow of blood." Jesus' power being recognized by even those people whom he passes on the streets is depicted here. Matthew shortens the Marcan version considerably. The woman's frustration with physicians, her impoverished state, and her fear are all missing from Matthew's account. In fact, the woman is actually not healed from touching Jesus' cloak, as is the case in Mark and Luke. In Matthew Jesus feels her touch him, turns around, and says, "Take heart, daughter; your faith has made you well." And at that time (*apo tas opas*), the woman is made well (9:22). The healing is not emphasized—even downplayed—and the more magical elements of the healing have been deleted. In Matthew this is a short story about a person's ability to recognize the healing power of Jesus and her faith in that power.

Matthew returns quickly to the story of the ruler and his daughter. Following the healing of the hemorrhaging women Jesus arrives at the house of the ruler and announces, "The girl is not dead but sleeping" (Matt. 9:24 ‖ Mark 5:39 ‖ Luke 8:52). In all three Gospels the crowd laughs at this statement. He goes into the house by himself in Matthew (he is with Peter, James, and John in Mark 5:37), takes the girl by the hand, and she gets up (Matt. 9:25). This is the end of Matthew's story. He does not record Jesus speaking with the child. The familiar Aramaic saying, "Talitha cum" ("Little girl I say to you, arise"), in Mark 5:41 is not repeated by Matthew, nor is the amazement of the crowd, her parents, or the command to silence (Mark 5:43 ‖ Luke 8:56). Matthew does add this summation, "and the report of this went through all that district" (9:26).

Matthew 9:27–31 is a skeletal version of the healing of two blind men also found in Matthew 20:29–34. This is an instance of what has been called "Matthean doubling." For some reason Matthew will repeat a story, or a very similar version of it. We saw something like this in our discussion of the love command or Golden Rule above. This is the case with the issue of taxes, divorce, the disciples at sea in a boat, and more. This story is an example of this odd Matthean convention. Matthew 20:29–34 is closest to the Marcan original. In both Matthean versions of this healing there are two blind men. Matthew prefers even to double the actors in the drama when possible. This can be seen in Matthew's Gadarene demoniacs story (8:28ff.) where, unlike Mark and Luke, Matthew records the healing of two demoniacs by Jesus.

As was the case with the "little boat church" in Matthew 8:23, Matthew alone inserts the notion of "following" (*akolouthasan*, i.e., belief and membership) into the story of the blind men. They cry out to Jesus, "Have mercy on us Son of David" (9:27). Matthew identified Jesus as the Son of David in the first verse of his Gospel. This significant claim that Jesus is of the line of David and is a leader in Israel like David of old is literally given voice by the two blind men. Matthew's contemporaries knew what this claim meant. It is high praise, yet a provocative claim in the face of other leaders and rulers in Israel. Jesus does not rebuke the men or the title in Matthew. Jesus speaks with the blind men "in the house" (only in Matt. 9:28). In this truncated healing story Matthew leaves out or, in his rush to shorten the story, overlooks the request of the blind men (Matt. 20:32; Mark 10:51; Luke 18:41). In the other versions Jesus asks what the men want him to do for them and they answer, "Lord, let our eyes be open." The question and response are missing here. When inside the house Jesus simply asks the men, "Do you believe I am able to do this?" and they say, "Yes Lord" (9:28). D. Duling has helped demonstrate that, in fact, an association existed in this period between the notion of the Son of David and healing. These two Matthean and synoptic stories seem to reinforce Duling's findings.

After the healing, in a fashion more like Mark than Matthew, Jesus warns the men not to let others know about this. This is a rare instance of Matthew replicating the so-called Marcan Messianic Secret. This refers to the number of places in Mark's Gospel where people Jesus helps or heals are told to keep it to themselves. They almost never do, but instead spread the news far and wide. Matthew tends not to follow Mark on this point but here he does. After being so charged by Jesus in Matthew 9:30 they "went away and spread his fame through all the district" (9:31).

The final miracle in this Matthean cycle of stories is about a mute demoniac. Interestingly, this is also an example of Matthean doubling. Virtually the same story appears in 12:22–24 where the title "Son of David" is again invoked. This brief healing involves an exorcism, with no details or drama provided, which results in the man getting his voice back. There is no christological confession in this story, as is the case in 9:27 and 12:23. But the crowds (*oi oxloi*) marvel and say, "Never was anything like this seen before in Israel" (9:33). However, the Pharisees, seemingly in response, say, "He casts out demons by the prince of demons" (9:34). Their response is the same in the parallel story in Matthew 12:24.

Matthew has inserted the Pharisees as opponents into this story. The Marcan version has "scribes who came down from Jerusalem" (Mark 3:22), and Luke has only that some of the people said this. As has been widely acknowledged by commentators, Matthew inserts the Pharisees whenever possible as the opponents of Jesus and antagonists in his story. The Pharisees and their opposition to Jesus and his followers become more visible and vocal as the story progresses. We are now at a turning point in the story where the scene is being set and the wheels are put in motion for an inevitable clash or crisis between two different groups, two contrasting interpretations and competing sources of authority.

This miracle cycle pushes the Pharisees to the fore as the group most obviously opposed to Jesus and, by extension, the Matthean community. Matthew's characterization of the Pharisees is contentious, polemical, and affords no response by the accused. His tenor is emotional, and perhaps frightened. This strident tone increases as the Gospel goes forward. Were the historical Pharisees as bad as Matthew would have us believe? Most certainly not. There are other ancient sources to balance Matthew's caricature. This one-sided portrayal suggests two things. Matthew's shrill account betrays he is on the declining or losing side of this struggle between two, roughly analogous, groups. Second, this struggle is certainly not over. The struggle for popularity, obtaining an audience and platform from which these forms of Judaisms can lay out their interpretations and beliefs, goes on, though Matthew may be feeling the heat.

The miracle cycle from chapter 9 stresses two things. Jesus' fame and popularity are spreading. Matthew 9:26, 31, 33, and to a lesser extent 9:10 all claim this. This is one of the fundamental points of Matthew's miracles, which he significantly shortened from his earlier sources. He does not belabor or embellish on these stories. The people are healed and this contributes to Jesus' popularity throughout the region.

Most miracles in the Gospels intend to highlight the authority and power of Jesus and often contrast that with other putative powers. Matthew is no exception. The actors in his healing stories attest to the authority of Jesus by coming to him, and by being walking examples of that authority. But it is this theme of authority that provokes the tension and opposition. The Pharisees are mentioned in connection with either the healings or Jesus' public behavior in 9:11, 14, 34, and, in a related way, 9:3. The healings performed by Jesus and his public teaching in Matthew contributed substantially to his popularity among the crowds or Galilean masses. However, this notoriety and popular support with the people, and the public displays of authority in the form of the miracles and teaching, served to quicken the conflict with the Pharisees and other regional authorities.

## Further Reading

Bornkamm, G., G. Barth, and H. Held. *Tradition and Interpretation in Matthew.* Philadelphia: Westminster, 1963.

Danker, F. *Benefactor: Epigraphic Study of a Greco-Roman and New Testament Semantic Field.* St. Louis: Clayton, 1982.

Donahue, J. R. "Tax Collectors and Sinners." *CBQ* 33 (1971): 39–61.

Duling, D. "The Therapeutic Son of David: An Element in Matthew's Christological Apologetic." *NTS* 24 (1978): 392–410.

Goldin, J. *The Fathers According to Rabbi Nathan.* Trans. with introduction and commentary by J. Goldin. New Haven: Yale University Press, 1955.

Hengel, M. *The Charismatic Leader and His Followers.* Trans. J. Greig. New York: Crossroad, 1981.

Horsley, R. *Jesus and the Spiral of Violence.* San Francisco: Harper and Row, 1987.

Kingsbury, J. D. "Observations on the 'Miracle Chapters' of Matthew 8–9." *CBQ* 40 (1978): 559–73.

Kloppenborg, J. *The Formation of Q.* Philadelphia: Fortress, 1987.

Kraabel, A. T. "Immigrants, Exiles, Expatriates, and Missionaries." In *Religious Propaganda and Missionary Competition in the New Testament World: Essays Honoring Dieter Georgi,* ed. L. Bormann, K. Del Tredici, and A. Standhartinger, 71–88. Leiden: Brill, 1994.

Neusner, J. *From Politics to Piety: The Emergence of Pharisaic Judaism.* Englewood Cliffs: Prentice-Hall, 1973.

———. "Two Pictures of the Pharisees: Philosophical Circle and Eating Club." *ATR* 64 (1982): 525–38.

Overman, J. A., and R. S. MacLennan. *Diaspora Jews and Judaism: Essays in Honor of, and in Dialogue with, A. Thomas Kraabel.* University of South Florida Studies in the History of Judaism 41. Atlanta: Scholars Press, 1992.

Saldarini, A. J. *Matthew's Christian-Jewish Community.* Chicago Studies in the History of Judaism. Chicago: University of Chicago Press, 1994.

———. *Pharisees, Scribes, and Sadducees in Palestinian Society: A Sociological Approach.* Wilmington, Del.: Michael Glazier, 1988.

Sanders, E. P. *Jesus and Judaism.* Philadelphia: Fortress, 1985.

Schlatter, A. *Der Evangelist Matthäus.* Stuttgart: Calwer, 1948.

# Chapter Five

# Jesus and Mission in Matthew — 9:35-11:1

## The Waning of Missionary Zeal and the Twelve

Matthew's mission discourse begins at 9:35, with 9:35–38 serving as a preamble to the sending. It starts with another typical synoptic summary of Jesus' activity. "He went about all the cities and villages, teaching in *their* synagogues and preaching the gospel of the kingdom, healing every disease and every infirmity." Matthew, typically, has inserted the phrase "their synagogues" into this synoptic summary to draw attention again to the venue of Jesus' ministry and to highlight the failure of the present local leadership. It is in "their gathering places" where there is no leadership and compassion. The impression is Jesus was with the people, saw them, and had contact with them. In seeing the crowds, "he had compassion for them, because they were harassed and helpless, like sheep without a shepherd" (9:36).

Matthew depicts Jesus as having an understanding and resonance with the people the other leaders do not. In fact, Matthew records Jesus thought the people were "like sheep without a shepherd" (9:36). Israel as a flock is a common image in the Hebrew Bible (Num. 27:17; 1 Kgs. 22:17). The sheep as "scattered" is a usual image among postexilic writers. Above all, 9:36 recalls Matthew's citation from Micah 5:2 in the birth narrative. "And you, O Bethlehem, in the land of Judah, are by no means least among the rulers of Judah; for from you shall come a ruler [*hegoumenos,* not *arkon*] who will shepherd [*poimanei,* the same term as 9:36] my people Israel" (2:6). Matthew asserts here that the people are without adequate leadership. The promise and citation announced in chapter 2 are being fulfilled in this passage and, more, in the mission of the twelve to "the lost sheep of the house of Israel."

In these verses Matthew has combined material he inherited from Mark and from Q to make his point. Matthew 9:35 is from Q found in Luke 8:1. Matthew 9:36 is from Mark 6:34, and Matthew 9:37 is Q from Luke 10:2. Matthew has combined these sayings from his different sources to prepare the way for the call of the twelve disciples and their mission to the people of Israel. Matthew's arrangement of this material makes more vivid the portrayal of Israel as a people without leadership and direction (9:36). They are vulnerable and harassed (from *skullo,* meaning to be weary and troubled; cf. Herodian 7.3.4). This condition serves as the pretext and preparation for Matthew's sending out of the twelve disciples.

The saying from Matthew 9:37–38 (cf. Luke 10:2) is significant and telling. There is much work to be done. And it is the right time for the work Matthew has in mind. "The harvest is plentiful." But it appears there are few people to go out on such mission work: "The laborers are few." Verse 38 is a prayer that the community is encouraged to pray with Jesus for more missionaries. The request to pray for such volunteers would also at the same time serve as a prod for those who might be sitting on the fence where their own involvement in missionary activity is concerned.

In fact, there is some indication that Matthew himself is not particularly focused on "going out," or mission. This, perhaps unwittingly by the author, reflects the larger Matthean community's general view of this activity. For example, Matthew, unlike both Mark and Luke, has only one sending, not two. Both Mark in 6:31 and Luke in 9:10 record the disciples returning from their mission and providing a successful report. There is nothing comparable in Matthew. We noted above how the Gadarene demoniacs in Matthew, again unlike Mark and Luke, do not become missionaries after their healing (Mark 5:20 ‖ Luke 8:39). And Matthew has deleted the interesting story in Mark 9:38–41 and Luke 9:49–50 called the unknown or strange exorcist, about a person who casts out demons in Jesus' name but is not a member of the group. The disciples try to stop him for this very reason. Jesus, though, says, "Do not forbid him; . . . for he that is not against us is for us" (Mark 9:40; Luke 9:50). While Matthew deletes this story about people outside the community engaged in missionary work, he retains this synoptic logion about allegiance. However, significantly, he has reversed it. In Matthew 12:30 Jesus says, "He who is not with me is against me, and he who does not gather with me scatters."

Matthew's emphasis here is so clearly on the community, membership, and discipleship within the church that his focus beyond the bounds of the community has faded. He does not seem to envision people engaging in mission work except for those who are already a part of the Matthean church. Allegiance is much more strictly defined by the subtle but significant shift in the synoptic saying in Matthew 12:30 and the parallels in Mark 9:40 and Luke 9:50. If you are not obviously part of the Matthean community you are viewed as "against" the group, while Mark and Luke allow for people outside the community doing the work of the apostles or "sent ones." With the one notable exception of the end of the Gospel, which we will treat later, Matthew's own perspective is not focused very far beyond his community's immediate horizon. He concentrates much more on the internal life, conflicts and crises, and educational life within the group. This focus on the group is reflected in the lack of energy devoted in the book to mission. In 9:35ff. is an admission from Matthew that few people engaged in the work initiated by Jesus. "Few" went out, yet the need to help "out there," beyond the bounds of the Matthean community, remained great. "The harvest is plentiful, but the workers are few." The dangers were great for missionaries, and the issues in Matthew's setting were much more local. There were crises to contend with closer to home, and most people did not feel "called" to this work. "Pray," therefore, Matthew says, "to the Lord of the harvest to send out laborers into his harvest" (Matt. 9:38). While mission work was once a priority in Matthew's setting, it had passed to only a (specialized?) few who actually went out and engaged the wider world. Matthew's church was focused on issues and crises much closer or, as K. Stendahl once said, with the gathering place (synagogue) across the street from Matthew's community.

Mark and Luke both record this sending of the twelve (Mark 6:7-11; 3:13-19; Luke 9:1-5; 6:12-16; 10:3). Matthew, though, made some changes in this synoptic sending. Matthew makes clear in 10:1 that the twelve being sent are "disciples." These are the very members and followers who have received special instruction from Jesus, are persecuted "for righteousness sake," and who have sacrificed family ties and other relationships for membership in the community. Mark and Luke record only that "the twelve" were called to Jesus and given authority. Matthew expands the authority given to these twelve and the acts they are called to perform. In 10:7ff. Matthew adds "preaching that the kingdom is at hand, heal the sick, raise the dead, cleanse lepers, cast out demons" to the charge of the twelve.

Appropriately, the term "apostle" (*apostolon*) is introduced in 10:2. This Greek term means literally "to be sent." The twelve disciples are now also "sendees" in Matthew, and Jesus is the sender. There is no fundamental contradiction in the terms "disciples" and "apostle." They do not necessarily denote different offices within the ecclesia and they certainly are not mutually exclusive. As with Mark and Luke, Matthew provides a list of the names of those who were sent. Once again, as in 4:18, Simon, "who is called Peter," heads the list. Peter's priority is emphasized here by Matthew's use of the adjective "first" (*protos*). Peter is first among the disciples, usually spokesperson for the group, and the one granted unusual authority. As J. Kingsbury has said, Matthew's community may be a "brotherhood," and he may ideally promote equality in the kingdom, but nevertheless, Peter emerges in this Gospel as *primus inter pares,* or first among equals. Along with a number of other important passages, 10:2 captures this interesting role for Peter in Matthew.

Matthew prefers to provide the disciples' names in couplets. This is not unlike the literary convention of doubling actors in his pericopae, mentioned above. D. Harrington has pointed out the parallel between this list and the list in *Pirke Avot* where the great teachers of Israel are listed in pairs. There was also an early tradition that the apostles were sent out in "pairs" (Mark 6:7; 10:1) and Matthew may have been reflecting this older tradition in naming the apostles by twos. All three synoptic writers include "Matthew" in the list of names, as does a list in Acts of the Apostles 1:13, but only Matthew designates him "the tax collector" (Matt. 10:3 ‖ Mark 3:18 ‖ Luke 6:15). The name "Levi" does not appear in any of the lists. This was the name for the tax collector in Mark 2:14 and Luke 5:29 who was called Matthew in Matthew 9:9.

The significance of the number 12 in this sending section has been discussed at great length by many commentators. Even those with only a passing acquaintance with the Hebrew Bible can recognize the allusion to ancient Israel and its first political federation. The number 12 here belongs to an early strata of the Gospel tradition. There is little doubt here that it is intended to be a symbolic number representing Israel. There are other places in the Gospel tradition where symbolic numbers figure in the broader narrative and the mission of the church specifically. In chapter 10 Luke sends out "seventy others" on a mission. This second Lucan mission has been viewed as a symbolic mission to the world, or "ends of the earth," because it was believed that there were seventy nations in the world. The appointment of seven hellenists to serve within the church alongside the circumcised in Acts 6 has been interpreted similarly. The number 12 makes its way into all the synoptic accounts and Acts of the Apostles. Very early on, the number 12 was fixed as the number Jesus initially called to follow him and begin the mission to Israel. What might this tell us?

There were many people around Jesus during the course of his ministry. There are many in the Gospel narratives who are viewed as bona fide followers and disciples. The women who "follow" him from Galilee and who are the first to see the empty tomb are clearly followers and members of the band. A number of people, as we have already seen, both Jew and Gentile, are affirmed as full members of the movement. The earlier strata of the Gospel tradition depicts the boundaries of the Jesus movement as rather amorphous and vague. People perhaps moved in and out. But there were obviously more than twelve who were counted among the "followers."

The Gospel narratives that focus on Jesus calling twelve are an indication of how the early church understood itself and its ministry. This group focused on the renewal of historic Israel. I do not think this necessarily meant they would reconstitute the tribal confederacy as a form of government. But they would renew Israel's fidelity to the covenant and law, they would lead aright the people of the flock who had gone astray, and they would secure the future, politically and eschatologically, for God's Israel. The calling of the twelve, then, is a bold symbol. It claims a lot. Many of these followers' peers may have thought them guilty of hubris. But the selection and sending of twelve disciples reveals the church's self-understanding as a body called to renew and revitalize God's people Israel.

## Charlatans, Evangelists, and Philosophers: Obtaining Credibility in the Mission Field

Jesus sends the twelve out on their "journey" (*hodon;* Mark 6:8 ‖ Luke 9:3; Matt. 10:10) and charges them to take very little with them. Luke's Jesus says, "Take nothing for your journey" (Luke 9:3). Mark allows only for a staff and sandals (Mark 6:8–9). Matthew's instruction does not contain the general statement "take nothing" (*maden airete*), but provides a more expanded list of what not to take. "Take no gold, nor silver, nor copper in your belts, no bag for your journey, nor two tunics, nor sandals, nor a staff; for the laborer deserves his food" (Matt. 10:9–10).

A great deal has been made over the years about this description of the apostles on their mission. It has served as an ideal portrait of the one who serves the Lord. Such disciples should desire little in the way of pay, possessions, or worldly concerns. This has contributed in no small way to the assumption that the modern laborer also should have little care for pay or possession and, indeed, too many have had little opportunity to develop such an illicit concern. This portion of the sending has provoked analogies between the earliest Jesus movements' lifestyle and missionary methods. In 1968 M. Hengel wrote a book that explored certain parallels and differences between Jesus' teaching on "following" and popular Cynic-Stoic philosophy. While the Cynic-Stoic background to the life and thought of the Apostle Paul had been recognized for many years, there had been relatively few attempts at connecting this thought-world with Jesus and the Gospels. Hengel was followed by G. Theissen, who saw some connections with certain schools of ancient philosophy and the Jesus movement in the sending discourse. Theissen has used the phrase "wandering charismatics" to describe the people involved in this phase and part of the Jesus movements. The role and influence of Cynic-like beliefs and conventions in Palestine, and within the Jesus movement in particular, have developed into a current lively discussion.

The apparent itinerancy of the apostles, along with their lack of possessions, cause this group to appear to some scholars like the wandering Cynic philosophers of the Hellenistic and Roman periods. These Cynics were both famous and infamous in antiquity for their often harsh critique of society and its norms. A contemporary of Matthew's, Dio Chrysostom (c. 40–120 C.E.), provides a lengthy account of the different types of philosophers. Of particular interest to us are his discussions of "Wandering Charlatans" and "The Ideal Philosopher." The charlatans were found in great number in cities, on street corners, and temple gates. They told puns and jokes and "philosophical commonplaces," and passed the hat around and deceived the crowds (*Diss.* 77/78.34–35). Unlike the true philosopher, they did not speak with "boldness" (*parresia*), but rather they deceived through flattery. (Indeed, the early-second-century writer Plutarch devoted an entire work to "How to Tell a Flatterer from a Friend.") These charlatans were viewed as being out for their own glory, gratification, and money (*Diss.* 32.7; 35.8; 48.10; 66.26). This perception of the popular philosopher was not rare. There were many accounts of false philosophers out for their own gain who possessed no real wisdom or truth. Lucian (*Peregrinus*), Philostratus (*Lives of the Sophists*), and Plutarch, among others, all produced works where these traits of certain philosophers were exposed. Charlatans were not new, and they were apparently not in very short supply. The ancient world was no less on guard for these "bastards and ignoble race of men," as Dio Chrysostom describes them, than we moderns.

The Cynic philosophic tradition was known in particular for its renunciation of possessions and the daily comforts of life. A Roman contemporary of Matthew's, Stoic philosopher Epictetus (c. 50–135 C.E.), captured the essence of the Cynic philosophical teaching on possessions in his *Dissertationes* when he wrote, "I lie on the bare earth; I have no wife, no children, no palace from which to rule but only earth and heaven and one cloak. Yet what do I lack? Am I not without sorrow, am I not without fear, am I not free? . . . Who on seeing me will not consider that he is looking at his king and his lord?" (*Diss.* 3.22.45–49). Elsewhere in his *Enchiridon,* Epictetus continually warns against the trap of "externals." The freedom of the philosopher is the freedom from all ties, whether property, family, convention, or custom. Such ties will encumber the true philosopher and lead people astray, away from truth. This radical freedom from all ties was a hallowed tradition within Greek philosophical thought. Certain traditions about Socrates claimed he lived in utter poverty "for the sake of serving God" (cf. Plato *Apol.* 23c; Xenephon *Memor.* 1.2.1; 1.6.1–10). But it is said that it was Socrates' pupil Antisthenes who was able to be content with the few possessions of a staff, a bag, and one cloak. Closer to the time of Jesus, Matthew, Dio Chrysostom, and Epictetus, these few items became the symbols of the spartan but "free" life of the Cynic philosopher.

The honesty and genuine nature of the followers of Jesus would have received no less scrutiny than any other popular movement that had disciples, teachers, and promoters of a school or philosophy. At first glance this is how the apostles would have appeared to many of their contemporaries. Built into the mission discourse are tangible signs that hopefully signal the virtue and trustworthiness of the twelve. They take no money on their journey, receive no pay, and carry no bag. This spartan journey necessitated the twelve living off the hospitality of those in the towns they visited, which evolved into another problem. How long before such hospitality wears out and the missionaries appear to be simply living off the goodwill of others? This concern may be reflected in the Matthean passages on hospitality (10:11–13), and emerges obviously in the *Didache* in the saying, "An apostle who remains more than two days is a false prophet" (11.5). Earlier, and in a related way, the Apostle Paul boasted that he did not receive anything from his churches and did not burden them with having to provide for him. This became a bone of contention in some of his churches, if not an offense (2 Cor. 11:7–15).

These passages alone show that people like Matthew had to walk a fine line in their teaching about discipleship and missionary zeal. If one were to travel with nothing (in Matthew not even sandals or a staff), they would be dependent on the gifts of others. However, one must not let that dependence give the appearance of seeking or desiring such gifts and rewards as an apostle. Paul and the *Didache* demonstrate two slightly different approaches to the same issue. The dramatically scaled-down luggage of the twelve in the sending discourse is a reflection of a concern that circulated more widely within the Roman world and the early church. I do not mean to suggest here that the Gospels were trying to depict Jesus and his movement as Cynic-like. There were some widespread conventions in the ancient world about "schools," their teachers and disciples, and I think it not unusual that Matthew and others would have been familiar with these traditions. But even more people had a widespread, and perhaps even commonsense set of expectations about philosophers, disciples, missionaries, or self-proclaimed righteous people of God. A finite set or list of expectations about their motives and behavior would occur to most people. Like the Greco-Roman writers above, the Babylonian Talmud (*b. Ber.* 29a) warns Torah teachers, "Just as Moses received Torah without payment, so teach it without payment." And *Pirke Avot* (1:13) says, "The one who makes worldly use of the crown [Torah] will waste away."

That there was a fairly universal description about the behavior and ideals of true and false philosophers and teachers in Matthew's day reinforces the point that quite naturally a reasonable and rather obvious list of expectations would develop around the empire for people pursuing these calls or careers.

One need not have been a philosopher, have encountered Diogenes Laertius or any other Cynic writer or speaker to expect teachers and philosophers to believe in what they were saying, not lie, and act — more or less — from pure motives. This, I think, could be described as a commonsense list of moral conduct for teachers, preachers, and *sophoi* in the ancient world. All this concern about purity and honesty, on the one hand, and charlatans, greed, and liars on the other demonstrates a fairly significant credibility gap for the average person. The numerous charlatan philosophers, preachers, and disciples in the Roman world had put the motives of most teachers and preachers in doubt. It seems clear to me that the Jesus movement, and specifically Matthean Judaism, were not spared this suspicion. The demand to leave all possessions behind, neither take nor accept any money, and receive only food and a bed from a village when on the road was Matthew's way of anticipating and overcoming the bad press and suspicions associated with traveling teachers, preachers, and "wise men."

Still, the saying about "only one coat" (Matt. 10:10 ‖ Mark 3:9 ‖ Luke 9:3) is reminiscent of Epictetus's description of only one cloak in *Dissertationes* 3.22 for the true philosopher. The command to take no bag, sandals, or staff in Matthew 10:9 is extreme, even when compared with the other Gospels. One cannot help but wonder if here Matthew is one-upping the traditional, or usual portrait of the philosopher-teacher pursuing the life of radical freedom from the ties of possessions? The inference here is the life expected of the Matthean disciple is even harder and more austere than those of the philosophers, teachers, and pupils of the broader Roman world and Greek East in particular.

## Gentiles, Samaritans, and the Lost Sheep of the House of Israel

Matthew alone among the synoptic writers has the charge by Jesus to the twelve disciples to "not go the way of the gentiles or into the city of the Samaritans, but rather go to the lost sheep of the house of Israel" (10:5–6). The geographical dimensions of the disciples' work is limited in this Gospel. It has already been noted that Jesus' own ministry was confined mostly to Galilee in Matthew. People from other regions (e.g., Tyre, Sidon, the Decapolis), came to see him in Galilee. While it was nothing to have contact with people outside of Israel when living in Galilee, this was not the focus of Matthew's ministry. Matthean Judaism was dedicated to the renewal of Israel through what the author thought was a true interpretation of the law, a new appreciation of Israel's faithful past, and the elevation of new leaders drawn, primarily, from the Matthean community.

The literal rendering of Matthew 10:5a is "Do not journey in the direction of the gentiles/nations/foreigners [*ethnon*]." That is, stay within the narrow borders of what was then defined as historic Israel. And 10:5b reads, "Do not go into the city of the Samaritans." As has been noted, the term *ethnos* has a range of meanings, and Matthew seems to employ the term with this breadth in mind. Among most classical writers the term can mean a company or body of people — like colleagues, a group of soldiers, trade organizations or guilds. Plato uses *ethne* for the various groups who have different functions and positions in his ideal city as if they comprise social or cultural classes (*Rep.* 421c). The term can also mean simply the rural or common folk. Somewhat like the term *barbaroi, ethne* can denote simply "them," or all those who are not us.

It is related to this final sense that the term is used to refer to a larger group of people, like a tribe, ethnic group, or a defined people. As Saldarini points out, after Homer *ethnos* acquires the meaning of "people" or "nation," referring to a group with cultural, linguistic, geographical, and political unity. One of the most celebrated examples of this use of the term in the ancient world comes from the so-called *ethne* reliefs from the Sebasteion in the city of Aphrodisias in Asia Minor. Dating from the period of the emperor Augustus this magnificent structure has statues and reliefs around the perimeter of the building. Each relief represents an ethnic entity or people who comprise the expanding empire under Augustus. R. Smith has written several articles on this fascinating building, its design and significance. Among those identifiable *ethne* portrayed in the Sebasteion are

the *ethnous Ioudaion:* "the people of the Jews." The reliefs from
Aphrodisias provide for us a picture of how cultural and ethnic
entities were understood and identified in this part of the Roman world. These "people" did not necessarily denote a nation
or proscribed political entity in our modern sense. The notion of
the nation-state is relatively recent, and these political construc-
tions were far more fragile and short-lived than the ethnic and
cultural identities the reliefs from Aphrodisias signify.

Josephus uses the term *ethnos* often in this regard. In *Antiquities* 12.135, quoting Polybius, he says Antiochus "subdued
the Jewish people" (*Ioudaion ethnos*). Here Josephus describes
his people, the Jews, with this term. Acts of the Apostles does
the same in 10:22. The Samaritans are described as an "ethnos" in *Antiquities* 18:85, as is the case in Acts 8:9. Josephus also
describes Galileans and Judeans as different *ethnos* (*B.J.* 2.510,
4.105). And he uses the plural form of the term to describe the
"foreign people" that make war on the Jews (*Ant.* 13.196).

*Ethnos/ethne,* then, is a common Greek term that very broadly
designates a group of people. This can be a smaller association
within a certain cultural or political region, or it can be a larger
ethnic group. By "ethnic group" I mean a body that defines itself, as well as being defined by others, as a category distinct
from others of the same order. That is, they more or less know
who "they" are, and they know they are not "them." The con-
verse is also the case. The group constitutes a semi-independent
"interaction sphere," and they share a set of values and symbols
(including language) that serve to define the nature and boundaries of the group. The repeated use of this broad but important
notion of *ethnos* in many Greco-Roman writers, and Jewish and
Christian writers in particular, should tell us that these issues of
definition, or "us/them," loomed large in this period.

While such questions of definitions and boundaries are always important, the period in which Matthew was living and
writing was particularly concerned with these questions. The
hellenization or "Greeking" of the world through the spread of
Greek language and culture had foisted the issue of cultural
and ethnic identity versus assimilation upon many people in
the East. Indigenous languages were taking a back seat to Greek.

Greek symbols, beliefs, and philosophies were everywhere and were quite influential. The advent of Roman rule added to these cultural tensions the reality of imperial power and the loss of political autonomy. In such an environment issues of identity and ethnic definition emerge with regularity and tenacity, as they did repeatedly *within* Jewish society and culture in Israel in Matthew's day. Issues of identity surface and resurface within a given *ethnos* as well as between *ethne*. Matthew was working in an environment where two questions loomed large: How do we relate to, or how are we different from the other Jews we live with? And how do we relate to other members of our *ethnos?* But, like most people in the Greek East at the close of the first century, Matthew also had to ask how we relate to the world. How does what has happened to us, the Matthean community, affect our relationship to other *ethne,* people, groups, and nations throughout the *oikoumene,* or inhabited world? Matthew's varied use of the term *ethnos/ethne* signals his community's involvement in these important and widespread issues.

When a specific group or people are not identified, this term tends to mean something like "foreigners," or those who are "not us" (Polybius 1324b; Cassius Dio 36.41; Acts 14:27; Matt. 5:47; *Ant.* 13.196). The use of this term to designate a people or groups of people suggests that those employing the word also see themselves as an *ethnos,* that is, a distinct group of people different from some other group. Matthew's community is an *ethnos,* as are the Jews as a whole, as are other nondescript foreigners whom Matthew references in only a passing manner. One crucial question in this Gospel and in the community it represents is, how do Matthew's people or *ethnos* relate to the larger people or *ethnos* of which they are historically a part, that is, Israel?

In the mission discourse in chapter 10 we get a glimpse of Matthew's response to this important question. Matthew's Jesus wants the mission to begin with his definition of the land of Israel (10:6). Here the dual terms "Gentiles" and "Samaritans" in 10:5 help us to see that Matthew is contrasting three *ethne,* groups, or ethnicities: Israel, Samaritans, and those people/lands that are not Jewish and not considered, geographically speaking, Israel. Matthew believes his missionaries should begin with the group or people Israel. He advised them not to travel in the direction of those areas that were not Israel (the Decapolis, Syria, and the ancient Phoenician plain), and not to go to the city of the Samaritans.

Matthew defined Israel in terms similar to the Maccabees, that is, he considered Galilee part of Israel. The expansion of the Hasmonean kingdom into the Galilee is recorded in 1 Maccabees 5:9ff. Prior to this expansion the region was described as gentile or a land of foreigners (*ethnon*), but was claimed or redeemed for Israel. Galilee, the traditional land of the tribe of Naphtali and Zebulun, was no longer viewed as part of *ta ethne,* but rather part of the land of Israel. Matthew shared this view. His citation from Isaiah 9:1–2 about "Galilee of the gentiles" is a passage about the redemption of Galilee. It is the region of Galilee, together with Judea, which will serve as the starting point for the disciples' mission.

Jesus' mission begins with Israel. There is no reason to assume that this means some nation, group, or ethnic group is therefore excluded. Our discussion of the term *ethnos/ethne* above demonstrates that the term does not imply exclusion. And Matthew's passage in 10:6 does not say that because Jesus sends the twelve first to the lost sheep of the house of Israel that others are consequently out of the kingdom of heaven. On the contrary, we have already seen where Jesus praises so-called Gentiles or foreigners and tells them they will come from east and west and sit at table with Abraham, Isaac, and Jacob in the kingdom of heaven (8:11). In 10:6 no one group or ethnicity is left out or denied. Here the mission begins appropriately with Israel and the people Jesus, according to Matthew, has been sent to save.

Conversely, it is just as important to understand that the term *ethnos/ethne* does not automatically mean "no Jews." There has been a strong tradition within largely German biblical scholarship which saw in Jesus' ministry a movement from Jews to Gentiles and the wider world. There was a plan and progression in this beginning with the Jews but ending with the Gentiles. This scheme was called *Heilsgeschichte* or salvation-history. This scheme basically saw in Jesus' ministry a periodization of his work. Jesus began among the Jews, but as a result of their rejection of his message and God's plan he moved on to the Gentiles. Where the Jews would reject Jesus the Gentiles would receive him and the Gospel.

Nothing could have been further from Matthew's mind. The thought that God would reject God's people and God's promises, I suspect, was unthinkable to Matthew. Such a hypothetical scheme emerges only when one juxtaposes Matthew 10:6 with the close of the Gospel, Matthew 28:19, "Go into all nations [*ta ethne*], baptizing them." When compared with one another and read through the lens of the salvation-history scheme some scholars see in the combination of these passages the rejection of Jews and Israel and the embrace of Gentiles by Matthew. This scheme owes much to latent anti-Semitic tendencies in New Testament scholarship that have not gone away altogether, but which controlled much of New Testament scholarship during the middle decades of the twentieth century. To arrive at this reconstruction one must first not understand the breadth of the term *ethnos/ethne,* which we discussed above. One must lift 10:6 and 28:19 out of their immediate context of Matthew's Gospel and read them without reference to a host of other passages in the Gospel. Also, one must presume a gentile author, writing to Gentiles who believe a monolithic Judaism exists which has rejected Jesus and his subsequent followers. Such assumptions are not the least bit informed about the historical and cultural context of the Greek East, second-temple Judaism, and certainly not Matthew's Gospel. This author is a Jew describing his community as the people who fulfill and carry on the traditions, responsibilities, and promises of historic Israel. Matthew 10:6 does not suggest that people are excluded from Matthew's community, and in no way does 28:19 suggest that henceforth Jews are no longer members of the kingdom of heaven.

The mention of the city of the Samaritans in 10:5b is an interesting Matthean addition to the sending. Samaritans had been a despised people or *ethnos* in the eyes of most Jews for a long time by the writing of Matthew's Gospel. Tension existed between Samaritans and "Jews" because Samaritans had their own temple and cultic center at Shechem (modern-day Nablus in Palestine). Samaritans claimed Mount Gerizim, their temple, was the true and original cultic center. Those loyal to the Jerusalem temple charged the Samaritans with syncretism; they were half Yahwistic, half pagan. This claim goes as far back as 1 Kings 17 and is still expressed in Josephus (*Ant.* 9.288). They had their own version of the Pentateuch and they were thought by some to have been supporters of Antiochus Epiphanies, the Seleucid ruler who conquered Israel and finally desecrated the Jerusalem temple in 165 B.C.E. This event paved the way for the Maccabean revolt and a brief stint of political autonomy for Israel, which ended in 63 B.C.E. under Pompey. The Samaritan temple was destroyed by John Hyrcanus around 125 B.C.E. The movement continued and even developed a diaspora. There is epigraphical evidence of Samaritan communities in Thessalonia and on the Island of Delos. Interestingly, a Samaritan popular movement developed during the first century B.C.E.–first century C.E., led by a figure named Dositheus. He was viewed by some as a messiah, argued about scripture and law, and some believed he would finally be resurrected.

Tension among Samaria, Galilee, and Judea continued well into the first century. Passages like John 4:9, the irony of Luke 10:33 and his parable of the Good Samaritan, and at some level Matthew 10:5b in the New Testament capture some of the charges and tensions relative to Samaritans which circulated in Matthew's time. Josephus tells a story about a first-century riot between Galileans and Samaritans (*J.W.* 2.232). A group of Galileans were traveling to Jerusalem for a festival. In the village called Gema (modern-day Jenin), a Galilean was murdered by a Samaritan. A considerable crowd gathered quickly from Galilee with the intention of "waging war on the Samaritans." News of the murder reached Jerusalem and an angry mob rushed off to Samaria. As they approached Acrabatene (near Shechem), they massacred the inhabitants and burned down the village. Rome ultimately had to get involved in settling this dispute. Eighteen of the Jews from Jerusalem were punished and beheaded. Three pairs of the most prominent Samaritans were executed in Rome and the procurator Camunus was banished.

The hostilities, prejudices, and enmity that existed between Galilean movements and Samaritans were real. The occasional slam against Samaritans in the Gospels is grounded in the real political and religious tensions of this period. The city (*polis*) of the Samaritans in Matthew 10:5b is unclear. It may be Shechem, the traditional holy place of Mount Gerizim and the place of the riot mentioned by Josephus, or it may be a reference to Samaria Sebaste. This was one of the cities built by Herod the Great toward the end of the first century B.C.E. This city honors the emperor Augustus. "Sebaste" was Augustus's Greek nickname and is found in many Greek inscriptions in the East honoring Augustus. The term means "holy," "pious," or "revered." Parts of this city in modern-day Palestine are still visible today. It was a large city and would have served as an administrative and political center in Palestine during the first century. Much like the absence of the mention of the large cities of Galilee in the Gospel tradition, Matthew's strategy may be to steer clear of those centers where the political and military authorities are concentrated. Therefore, do not go into that city. In either case, Matthew may have some concrete reasons for counseling the disciples to stay away from this Samaritan city.

## Persecution: Civil and Political Animosity for the Movement

The opposition and animosity some members of the Matthean group may have been experiencing is given expression in 10:17–20. There is a core of this tradition in Q (Luke 12:11–12) and more fully in Mark 13:9ff. But this is expanded considerably in Matthew. The disciples will be delivered up (*paradosousiv*) to councils (*sunedria*) and flogged in *their* gathering places (10:17). This passage is full of Matthew's language and particular concerns. "Delivered up" is the same term used in describing Jesus' betrayal to the authorities and his crucifixion (27:2, 18, 26), "councils" is his term for the courts that his community must avoid at all costs (5:22), and, of course, Matthew's distinctive "their gathering places" betrays his hand.

There is additional indication that Matthew is speaking about opposition to his community in chapter 10 because of the slight but telling change he made in Matthew 10:42. In this verse Matthew calls those who are on mission "little ones" (*mikron*). This is a favorite Matthean term for certain members of his community (cf. 18:6). Also, Matthew has altered the Marcan saying from Mark 9:41 in a significant way. In Matthew 10:42 the cup of cold water is to be given to the missionary in need "because he is a disciple." In Mark the cup of cold water is given "in the name of Christ" (Mark 9:41). This is a small but significant change on Matthew's part. He has made it clear he is speaking about followers and members of the Matthean community who are on mission and who are enduring the hardships of rejection and betrayal.

The Matthean community feels persecuted. People are turning them in or over to local authorities (10:17). As Jesus was "delivered up," so the Matthean church is being arrested by or turned over to the councils or local courts (*synedria*). These are the very places the community was warned to stay out of because "they will never get out of there until they have paid their last cent." This is the institution about which Jesus taught the disciples to strike a deal on the way: "Make friends with your accuser while on the way to court." Matthew asserts that some form of public punishment or humiliation takes place in the opponents' gathering places. And here emerges a possible connection between these local venues, which we have encountered before, and other, more substantial political officials. "You will be dragged before governors and kings [*basileis*] for my sake to bear testimony [*marturion*] before them and the foreigners [*ethnesin*]." Here the courts, venues, and personnel of the foreign forces are introduced and there is an apparent connection between the local persecution the Matthean community feels and the trouble they may experience before the ruling foreign authorities. The stakes have been raised. A possible coalition hinted at here would have grave consequences for the Matthean community. The local opposition to the group may be gaining entrée to the larger and ruling political authorities in the region, the Roman authorities and their appointees. Even the term "testimony" may imply that some people do not come back from appearing before the governors, kings, and foreigners.

The disciples will be brought into court. They need not be anxious about remembering the right words and they need not worry about what to say. This is a Q saying (Luke 12:12), together with material from Mark's "little apocalypse," chapter 13. A similar saying appears in the so-called Last Discourse in John's Gospel, 14:26. The court is the one specific setting in the Gospel tradition where followers of Jesus are promised the presence of the Holy Spirit, the *Paraklete,* or as Matthew says, "the Spirit of your father" (10:20). The Jesus movements were apparently suspect, deviant, or perceived as dangerous enough to have themselves in court on a fairly regular basis. These court and persecution sayings developed as a response to the fear members felt and the abuse they thought they suffered when forced to appear in the dock.

Matthew, however, developed and rearranged this material. He devoted more energy to the explanation and instruction to members about the courts and the possibility of punishment. Matthew says members are brought into court "for my [Jesus'] sake" (10:18). The reader, though, is given no indication of the charge. Why were the members dragged into court in the first place? Were they violating an actual, if not reasonable, law but, as can so often be the case, the accused was claiming oppression and persecution? We are not given sufficient information to know how and why the members ended up in court. We have too little indication from the outsiders of what the church's crime may have really been. The reader will remember, however, that the community felt John the Baptist was the first martyr in their collective history. Josephus's account of John's death stresses that he was killed, much like Jesus, for "sedition" (*Ant.* 18.118). Herod feared John's eloquence might lead the crowds that followed him to sedition, for they appeared as though "they might be guided by John in everything that they did."

The account of the Baptist's death in Matthew 14:1ff. gives little hint of the issue of sedition and the anxiety John's popular movement provoked in Herod Antipas. Matthew's group, seeing itself in some respect as the religious heirs to some of John's ministry, might have emulated some behavior that also would appear seditious. Of course, all the Jesus movements were aware the hero, Jesus, was himself killed by the Romans, ostensibly for sedition. The Matthean community understood itself in this train of prophets and righteous people in Israel who were unjustly persecuted and even killed. What happened to John and Jesus may well happen to the Matthean community. Matthew interprets the trouble and conflict the church was feeling with local leaders in the form of the so-called scribes and Pharisees as the same trouble that ultimately got John and Jesus. As Jesus says in Matthew, "A disciple is not above his teacher, nor a servant above his master" (10:24).

Exactly what is that trouble? The only thing we are told is that there is an issue in Matthew's setting about how to interpret the law. The Matthean community's perceived lawless behavior ("Do not say I have come to destroy the law") may have landed some of the followers in court. This did not necessarily mean death at the hands of the Roman client-lords, as with John and Jesus. But it felt like that to the community. They were harassed, punished or humiliated, hated (10:22), and on the run from town to town (10:23). This may perhaps be hyperbolic but Matthew and his community believed this captured, or might soon accurately capture, their reality. Indeed, if the local leaders and Matthean opposition were able to work effectively with the foreign occupying forces and personnel, as 10:18 suggests, then the Matthean community really did have something to worry about.

Even allowing for hyperbole on Matthew's part, these few passages from the sending discourse, 10:17–20, reflect a heightened concern for the animosity the group, or some in the group, were feeling. Some in the towns were turning against the group. They should "beware" (10:17), some will turn them in. This again is a feature of a colonial context, where the indigenous population turns on each other. Some Matthean Jews were delivered to the gathering places of their opposition and, most likely, the local leaders. These local civic issues, however, seem to be turning into larger political issues involving some major officials ("governors and kings"). This is exactly what happened to Jesus and John and their respective popular movements. The Matthean Jews understood themselves as standing in the same tradition as John, Jesus, and the many righteous prophets before them in Israel who were persecuted and condemned, they believed, falsely. Something was telling Matthew that the tide was beginning to turn in his setting against the group and its message.

For Matthew, these political and social changes were signs of the end. Betrayal and falling away from the group as a result of this political and civil pressure were seen as an indication that the end was near (10:33). Despite the opposition the community encountered, the work and mission of the disciples had to continue. "You will not have gone through all the towns [or cities; *poleis*] of Israel before the Son of Man comes" (10:23). The mission of the community — or more accurately some in the community — was tied to Matthew's understanding of the end and Israel's political rehabilitation. The apocalypticism, or dramatic descriptions of the end of history by Gospel writers like Matthew, though morose and violent, are actually expressions of the hope the authors had. For them, the troubles they experienced or suspected confirm for them the beginning of the end. This then means their version of how Israel will be set right by God is starting to unfold. The mission of the disciples and the opposition they encounter signaled for Matthew the beginning of the restoration of Israel which was, after all, why Jesus came in the first place (Matt. 2:21).

## Israel as a Divided Home: Ruptures within the Family and Community

This shift in the political winds is a painful and poignant moment in the Gospel. The division and conflict the sending discourse highlights in 10:17–20, as might be expected, is manifest also within families. I have said before that Matthew's Gospel has all the emotion, pain, and, perhaps from time to time, the same lack of objectivity as a family falling apart. In 10:21ff. Matthew makes this painful reality of his setting explicit. "Brother will deliver up brother to death, and the father his child, and the children will rise against parents and have them put to death."

The divisions are manifest socially across Israel. Matthew's Jesus teaches the disciples to condemn those who will not listen to or receive the words of the missionaries (10:14). "It will be more tolerable for Sodom and Gomorrah than for that town" (10:15). Great enmity, division, and emotional, strident words and actions now characterize the Matthean setting. "Do not think I have come to bring peace on earth," Jesus says here (cf. 5:9); "I have not come to bring peace, but a sword" (10:34). Nation, village, and now families are being divided over the behavior and beliefs of the Matthean community. Chapter 10 makes clear what has been implicit and felt up to this point. These words of judgment from Matthew's Jesus seem to fly in the face of his teaching on the Golden Rule, loving your enemies, and turning the other cheek. Remember, in many ways Matthew and his community resembled the scribes and Pharisees. They both fasted and prayed, they both provided a central place for the law (otherwise one could not have such spirited debates about it), they both had scribes, gathering places, and laid claim to the same heroes of their national past. Concerning this Matthean contradiction between damning those who will not listen and the command to love those who are one's enemies, I would only quote Matthew: "Do what they say, but do not do what they do" (23:3). Here again Matthew's instruction parallels that of his opponents. He is not able to act out the law he teaches. In this instance, too, he seems to be guilty of the same charge he levels against the scribes and Pharisees.

The similarity between Matthean Judaism and their opponents is an important point. It helps us understand the emotion and deep division that is captured in these verses from the sending. As many sociologists of social conflict have observed, competition and animosity require some proximity. That is, one must care, live close to another, or have similar enough belief systems to clash — complete alienation and difference will not provoke a good fight. There must be some contact, competition, and, often, claims and desires for the very same thing. This, I believe, we can see happening in Matthew's setting. There is much Matthew and his contemporaries, particularly his opponents, had in common. There was proximity, closeness, even at points, intimacy. This sociological truism helps us understand the highly charged and hyperbolic rhetoric, the very personal attacks, and the deep emotion that characterizes this story of crisis and conflict.

Matthew and his debate partners unwittingly played into the colonial reality of their setting. With so much in common, with their great shared past of historic Israel, with the law and the covenant and much more in common, they were divided against one another. Writ large, when one examines the history of Palestine in the first century B.C.E. through the second century C.E., the division between Matthean Judaism and their rivals is hardly a meaningful statistic. This division and rupture between communities was played out many, many times in Palestine leading up to the first revolt against Rome and beyond. So viewed, this is just two more Judaisms competing and having it out with one another in early Roman Israel. The colonial reality of Israel in this period succeeded in dividing many in the land against one another.

When we come closer and look carefully at the words of this document the pain and impact of this rupture take on greater definition: clearer contours, deeper face lines, a grimace, shouts and panicked glances, teeth that are set on edge, a torn garment, backs irreconcilably turned. These Matthean words put a human face on two particular communities or groups that have come to a crossroad in their life and struggle together. "Brother will deliver brother up to death, and the father his child, and the children will rise against their parents and have them killed, and you will be hated by all." With these words the Matthean community reached a point of no return in their struggle with neighbors, friends, and even family.

## Further Reading

Hengel, M. *The Charismatic Leader and His Followers.* Trans. J. Greig. New York: Crossroad, 1981.

Isler, S. *The Dositheans: A Samaritan Sect in Late Antiquity.* Leiden: Brill, 1976.

Kingsbury, J. D. "The Figure of Peter in Matthew's Gospel as a Theological Problem." *JBL* 98 (1979): 67–87.

Kriesburg, L. *The Sociology of Social Conflict.* Englewood Cliffs, N.J.: Prentice-Hall, 1973.

Levine, A. J. *The Social and Ethnic Dimensions of Matthean Social History. "Go nowhere among the Gentiles..." (Matt. 10.5b).* Lewiston, N.Y.: Mellen, 1988.

Malherbe, A. J. *Paul and the Popular Philosophers.* Minneapolis: Fortress, 1989.

Overman, J. A. *Matthew's Gospel and Formative Judaism: The Social World of the Matthean Community.* Minneapolis: Fortress, 1990.

Saldarini, A. J. *Matthew's Christian-Jewish Community.* Studies in the History of Judaism. Chicago: University of Chicago Press, 1994.

Smith, R. R. *"Simulacra Gentium: The Ethne* from the Sebasteion at Aphrodisias." *JRS* 78 (1988): 50–77.

Stendahl, K. *The School of St. Matthew and Its Use of the Old Testament.* 2nd ed. Philadelphia: Fortress, 1968.

Theissen, G. *Sociology of Early Palestinian Christianity.* Philadelphia: Fortress, 1978.

# Chapter Six

# Jesus Falls Out with Local Leaders — 11:2–12:36

## John's Question

Following the sending discourse in 11:1 Jesus continues his own preaching and teaching in "their cities" (*polesin auton*). Once again Matthew's insertion of the pronominal adjective "their" suggests a hostile environment and a setting where the teaching and authority of Matthew's opponents, in one way or another, hold sway. Matthew 11:2-6 is material adapted from Q. These passages contain the question from John the Baptist to Jesus. The Baptist is in prison so the question is carried by disciples of John. "Are you the coming one [*ho erxomenos*], or should we look for another?" (11:3).

This question suggests that even those who are close to Jesus and in some manner support him are now having some doubts. In Matthew's version, John "hears about the deeds of *Christ*" (11:2). In Luke's version Jesus is referred to as "Lord" or *Kurion* (Luke 7:18). This is the first mention of the term "Christ" in Matthew's story since the birth narrative. Nevertheless John has his doubts. "Should we look for another?" Jesus' response to John's disciples is a recitation of the works Jesus has initiated in Israel, which sounds like a paraphrase of Isaiah 61:1-2. "The blind receive their sight, the lame walk, lepers are cleansed, the deaf hear, the dead are raised up, and the poor have the good news preached to them" (11:4-5). The answer to John's question is found in the deeds that are transpiring as a result of Jesus' ministry.

It is important to realize that there was no single uniform expectation about a messiah (meaning "anointed agent of God"), salvific figure, or "coming one" within second-temple Judaism. Jewish communities and the texts they produced offer various pictures of messianic figures and the deeds they would accomplish. The Qumran community was "messianic" but in a very different sense from most of the New Testament texts. First, Qumran seems to have hoped for two messiahs. The Qumran messiahs are probably less actual persons and more representatives of two traditional authorities within Judaism (cf. 1QSb 3:2–4). These messiahs appear at and preside over the heavenly banquet at Qumran (1QSa 2:11–22). These messiahs do not play a personal role in the redemption of community members or Israel. The community also has an authority figure called the Teacher of Righteousness who controls the interpretation of scripture for the community (1QpHab 2:2–10; 7:4–14). The mid-first-century B.C.E. Psalms of Solomon also reflect a messianic hope in the closing chapter of these psalms. Recently, R. Horsley has drawn our attention to the fact several popular leaders were called or thought of as "messiahs" around the time of Jesus. And it should be stressed that Paul and the Gospels do not speak monolithically about messiahs. As a recent volume edited by W. S. Green reminds us, there were many Judaisms in Matthew's day and many messiahs to go along with those Judaisms.

Jesus' response to John's question reflects some of the Matthean community's expectations associated with "the coming one." I am not sure John had someone specific in mind when he asked if Jesus was the one. What is meant here is, is Jesus the one who will set things right in Israel? Jesus' work, in Matthew's mind, is the sort of activity Israel needs. These are also the actions that announce that he indeed is the one to provoke the necessary changes. John asks this question from prison. Can he hope to get out of prison? Is there going to be a change soon in Israel? And John may believe that part of the change will be an open challenge to Roman rule. According to Josephus, John was in prison for sedition (*Ant.* 18.118).

Even Roman writers and officials, from time to time, expressed an awareness of a need for political change in Judea.

It was only Tacitus who wrote the oft-repeated, but odd sentence (when one has read Josephus, the Gospels, and a few other sources), "Under Tiberius all was quiet" (*Hist.* 5.9.7). In fact, to the contrary, Tacitus himself implies that the people of Judea had much to put up with under the procuratorship of Felix (52–60 C.E.) because "he exercised the authority of a king with the mentality of a slave" (*Hist.* 5.9.8). Similarly, one may recall Pontius Pilate's reputation in Judea, which was not lost on some Roman officials. Pilate was finally recalled through the legate of Syria, Vitellius, back to Rome because of ineffectiveness as procurator of Judea (*Ant.* 18.88–89). If certain prominent Roman officials and politicians were aware of a need for change in Judea, how much more the Judeans? And wouldn't some Judeans interpret this need for change in language and terms familiar to them and associated with their religiopolitical expectations? This generally perceived need for political change would reinforce, for certain politically active Judeans, their interpretation of history and events, and more specifically their hope for a figure who would redeem them from their Roman yoke.

Sitting in prison John may well have wondered when this change would be initiated. Based on his exchange with Jesus at the baptism (3:13ff.), it seems John believed Jesus was the one to provoke this much-needed change. John probably shared the belief echoed by Tacitus and Suetonius that men from Judea would gain world power (Suetonius, *Vesp.* 4.5). Tacitus says this very oracle encouraged the outbreak of the first revolt (*Hist.* 5.13.4ff.) against Rome. Josephus points out that his popular oracle was actually about Vespasian (and Titus), and it was misinterpreted by many upstart Judeans (*B.J.* 6.312ff.). Is "the coming one," whom John asked about in prison, really the divine agent he believed would inaugurate the obvious and necessary changes he had been speaking about in his apocalyptic-type preaching? John may well have been hoping that the "coming one" would also, along with healing and preaching, do away with the foreign presence and rule in Israel. This would be the beginning of the judgment John had predicted and pronounced.

While in prison John hears things about Jesus which lead him to suspect that he will not finally do away with the occupying forces and their local puppets. Jesus is beginning *not* to fit John's expectations of the coming one. We are given no indication of how Jesus' answer was received by John or his disciples. Was this what he was hoping to hear? We do not know. Jesus, in summarizing Isaiah 61:1–2, suggests this is enough of an answer. These are the works he has been called by God to enact. But it is also possible that this passage made its way into the Gospel to further distance John from Jesus. The question John asks reflects some doubt or misunderstanding about Jesus. If any competition or comparison between John and Jesus persisted in the early years of the movement this would put John in quite a different light than Jesus. Interestingly, in Acts 18:24 an Alexandrian Jew named Apollos was in Ephesus when Priscilla and Aquila were there. He was eloquent, quoted the law, and was viewed as a believer in Jesus, yet "only knew the baptism of John" (Acts 18:25). Paul encountered "some disciples" of John's in Ephesus and persuaded them to be "baptized in the name of the Lord Jesus" (19:5). If support and devotion to the Baptist continued at all during the second and third generation of the movements, these passages, while paying honor to John, do so while putting him in his place in relation to Jesus.

After the disciples leave, Jesus begins to praise the Baptist in 11:7–19. Jesus emphasizes that John is a prophet and more (11:9). Malachi 3:1 is quoted in Q and taken over by Matthew to explain John's person and role. John's ministry is linked to Jesus'. John's austere lifestyle is highlighted by the description of his dress, his life in the desert, and the suggestion that this was no "reed shaken in the wind" (11:7). The sturdy, honest and true, and unequivocating nature of the Baptist is emphasized by the image of the reed that does not shake or bend. It has been suggested by Theissen and followed by Harrington that this may also be an allusion, or bit of "local color," pointing to Herod Antipas. A reed was the prominent symbol on Herod Antipas's coins minted at his newly constructed city in Galilee, Tiberias. Construction on Tiberias was probably completed around the year 18–20 C.E. Having built a city out of nothing on the western shore of the Sea of Galilee in honor of and named after the emperor would not have endeared Antipas to people like John. The

city of Tiberias would have been the largest building project going during the life and times of both Jesus and John and would
have created a lot of discussion and certainly some consternation. It was also a new center for the political, military, and
administrative elite of which certain popular leaders like John
and Jesus would have to be cautious. In this saying, Q may be
contrasting John with Antipas, the reed that bends and shakes in
response to the winds of Rome.

John, Jesus says, is the greatest born among women yet even
the least in the kingdom is greater than he. While John is a great
prophetic figure, and the ministry of Jesus is directly related to
his, one is not a member of the kingdom of heaven by virtue of
being a believer or supporter of the Baptist. "Even the least in
the kingdom of heaven is greater than he" (11:11). While there
is continuity and a relationship between these two movements,
in Matthew's mind (and Luke's in 7:28), they are not the same.
These two leaders, and the movements they spawned, though
kindred, are different. To follow the Baptist or have embraced
his message is not the same as membership in Matthean Judaism. Great though John may have been, Matthew and other
earlier traditions within the Gospels and Acts feel it necessary to
emphasize this point about the Baptist and his movement.

## The Kingdom of Heaven and Violence

In chapter 11, verses 12ff. attempt to capture the pivotal role
John played in the history of Israel and the chronology of
the kingdom of heaven. John's persecution and execution were
viewed by Matthew's community as the beginning of hostilities against them. This violence and persecution continued to
Matthew's day (*eos arti*). Luke has a similar view of John's watershed role in the history of the kingdom of God, but he does not
add the saying about violence against the kingdom (Luke 7:16).
In Matthew's cosmic timeline the violence against John was the
start of violence against and rejection of the community and its
message. As we saw in chapter 10, this is how Matthew knew it
was the beginning of the end, or at least this is how he inter-

preted the harm being done to some members of the church. Therefore, John is like Elijah. He paved the way for Jesus and the age when the expectations of the community will be fulfilled.

As we have already seen in a number of ways, for Matthew to say "the kingdom of heaven has suffered violence" is to say members of the Matthean community, past and present, have suffered and are suffering violence. This reality must have created considerable dissonance for some members of the church. Certainly the violence and perceived persecution made some members wonder if they had made the right choices. The division and brokenness within families and traditional villages, and the rejection that created, must surely have given some Matthean Jews pause. "Brother will deliver up brother to death, and the father his child, and children will rise against parents and have them put to death." (10:21). Surely this was not the way things were supposed to be.

It fell to Matthew and other leaders within Jesus-centered Judaism to offer a defense of what was happening to them and their people. Matthew explained and justified this Matthean reality by tying it to the violence done to two of the most prominent people in their church's story, namely Jesus and John the Baptist. If the group revered John and Jesus, and if Matthew linked the biographies of these two with what was happening to Matthean Jews, then the pain and confusion associated with this violence might be more tolerable. This helped to justify the violence. What happened to John (and to Jesus) was also happening to the community members ("a disciple is not above his teacher"). The persecution and violence against them were part of the process that started with John, continued with Jesus, and now finally would be consummated with the Matthean community. The suffering of the members and their heroes was tied to the coming of the end and the fulfillment of theirs hopes for Israel. The violence against the members and the kingdom was associated apocalyptically. That is, in Matthew's reasoning the persecution would be short-lived, and it represented the dawn of the fulfillment of the group's plans.

Matthew's apocalypticism, however, is tempered in my view. There are still undeniably apocalyptic strains in his thought and message. Chapters 10–11, 24–26, and some of the Matthean parables have apocalyptic elements. By "apocalyptic," I mean an emphasis on the imminent end of the world or prevailing order, the judgment of one's enemies and those who reject one's message, the vindication of one's group, and the restoration of Israel and the way things are supposed to be. Apocalypticists have a negative, even hostile view of the world. It is a place that will "get you." This pejorative view of the world colors most of their views and attitudes.

Matthew's apocalypticism is selective and sporadic. This was not his dominant worldview, but a piece of his world, part of many second-temple Judaisms, and occasionally is the point of view to which he turned to explain troubling or perplexing events, particularly the persecution of his fellow members. Apocalypticism is not the perspective and attitude that fundamentally shaped Matthew's thinking. This is confirmed above all in the institutionalization in which Matthew and his community were involved. The Sermon on the Mount is almost antiapocalyptic. That is, the Sermon constitutes community instruction for the long haul. How will relationships be structured long-term? How is life within the community going to be guided and shaped over time? Legal instruction, and ways of getting along with those in power (certainly not their celebrated demise, as for most apocalypticists), are the themes of the Sermon. These themes concern the "everyday" and the present order, not the imminent end of that order. Chapter 18, as we will see, as well as a number of the Matthean parables and Matthew's instruction about the law and debates with other local leaders address issues of the *ongoing* life of the community. He may be wrong but Matthew sees a place for his community in the present order and in the future. There must be some shifting and changing of roles, but this will not ultimately require a conflagration. Matthew sometimes takes recourse in the anger, frustration, even disgust of an apocalyptic perspective. He does this usually in conjunction with the theme of the community's persecution. This topic brings his anger and desire for revenge to the fore. But this is not finally his point of view. He hoped his community would reason and argue their way into a leadership role locally within Israel where they could "save," guide, and teach the people.

Violence was a feature of fragmented Israel in the period leading up to and between the two revolts against Rome. Matthew's community lived through much of this violence and, apparently, some measure of violence had been directed against them. Matthew seeks to assuage the concerns of the members by explaining that this violence goes back to the beginning of the movement. John and Jesus suffered in this manner and so then would the Matthean community. The violence they suffered was not a mistake, it did not reflect poorly on the community, its leaders, or its message. The sayings about John and violence against the kingdom then serve, among other things, to legitimate the current troubling plight of Matthew's own church. The community is also told that this will not last too long. These very struggles serve as signals of the end, *telos,* or fulfillment of their aspirations. Matthew connects, then, violence against the kingdom and his apocalyptic hopes.

## Jesus Pronounces Judgment

Matthew's apocalypticism continues in this portion of chapter 11 in the pronouncement of judgment against the cities of Chorazin, Bethsaida, and Capernaum. A standard element in most any apocalyptic scenario is the judgment and rejection of those who reject you and your message. Matthew's apocalypticism is certainly not without this feature. Matthew 11:20–27 contains such a judgment against those who refused to believe in Jesus.

The judgment pronounced against these three cities situated along the western shore of the Sea of Galilee is found in Q (Luke 10:12–15). Matthew has taken over this Q material and expanded it. The rejection of Jesus' message by some or many of his contemporaries is met with anger by Matthew as well as earlier writers within the Gospel tradition. This blast against those seemingly closest to Jesus comes out of nowhere. This does not accord well with the earlier indications of Jesus' popularity and following among the people or "crowds." The notion that wholesale cities had failed to repent in light of what had been happening in their midst has not been suggested until now.

This denunciation is tied to the earlier passages (11:16–19) where Jesus excoriates "this generation" (11:16). The notion of "this generation" among apocalyptic thinkers is a slogan for the resistant and errant among them. "This [evil] generation," so much responsible for the current state of affairs, will be judged at the end that is coming soon. Matthew himself employs this term on a number of occasions (12:39–42; 16:4; 23:36; 24:34). Matthew, following Q, likens "this generation" to spoiled children. They cannot be pleased or entertained, and they choose not to participate in the events and acts that transpire around them.

"But to what shall I compare this generation? It is like children sitting in the marketplaces and calling to their playmates, 'We piped to you and you did not dance; we wailed, and you did not mourn'" (11:17). This logion is reminiscent of children at play. One of the partners is obdurate and selfish. So it is, Matthew's Jesus claims, with "this generation." As the spoiled children did not take advantage of the opportunities before them, however chided, so this generation failed to take advantage of the opportunities — in the form of John and Jesus — which were availed to them. "For John the Baptist came neither eating nor drinking and they say, 'He has a demon'; the Son of man came eating and drinking and they say, 'Behold, a glutton and a drunkard, a friend of tax collectors and sinners!'" (11:18–19). This generation is compared with the negative, even cynical attitude of the children who refuse to play. Like them, this generation is unmoved by what has been happening around them. So they are looking at judgment worse, Jesus says, than that of Sodom.

But why the villages along the Sea of Galilee that were home to the movement? Shouldn't the large cities, home to the foreign powers and those most inclined toward Rome, be the places that receive the woes? Why not woes against Sepphoris, Scythopolis/Bet Shean, and Tiberias? That might make a little more sense.

But, as we said about the necessity for proximity where any social conflict is concerned, the same abides for apocalyptic judgment. After all, judgment of this nature is itself a powerful expression of social conflict and division. Tyre and Sidon are cut a fair amount of slack in this pronouncement of judgment by Jesus. It is his contemporaries, those in his backyard — we would insist typically — who receive the harshest words and judgment. Israel is being spilt over the message of Jesus (and Matthew's) group and other such groups; villages, families, and finally, in 66–70, the nation was split. Israel is still more or less in that state during the time of the writing of Matthew's Gospel and up through the Bar Kochba revolt. Jesus and his movement, and perhaps even Matthew's community, were centered in and around the densely populated western shore of the Sea of Galilee.

The mixed reception of the message of the Gospel of the kingdom of heaven and the division it provoked hurt the most, and created the most dissonance, close to home. In a recent book on the earliest Gospel strata Q, L. Vaage has highlighted the local division and conflict present in this earliest recitation of the teaching and nature of the Jesus movement(s). This conflict and division did not go away, and may have in fact increased over time. Those people close to home, however few or many, who ultimately did not see things the same way as Jesus, Q, or Matthew, were among those most vigorously denounced. They really were in the marketplaces and streets of these cities and villages of eastern Galilee and heard the message, and were unmoved. The woes against these home cities of the movement in Matthew 11:20–24 capture the hostility and pain associated with the rejection experienced by the group close to (or in) home. They, predictably, come in for the harshest treatment and judgment from their peers in the early Jesus movements and within Matthean Judaism.

Matthew ends this section not on a note of judgment, but rather with a promise to those who do decide to respond to the message of Jesus and the movement. Matthew 11:28–30 reads like an invitation to those who are still on the fence. Although there are some or many who have turned a deaf ear to the community, and therefore are denounced in the woes against the cities of Galilee, some may still be willing to become disciples in Matthew's community or "school." The words "yoke," "labor," and "rest" carry both pastoral and educational weight. The audience hears in these words a promise about their own safety, their own belongingness, and a promise about what membership in this movement will mean for them. For the beleaguered, for those who are emotionally or intellectually troubled about Matthew's church, and for those caught in the turmoil of Galilee in the period between the revolts, this passage is an invitation for comfort, rest, and a home.

"Come to me all who labor and are heavy laden, and I will give you rest. Take my yoke upon you and learn from me; for I am gentle and lowly in heart, and you will find rest for your souls. For my yoke is easy and my burden is light" (11:28–30). These passages are unique to Matthew. He inserted them as a description of life in the Matthean community for those who were troubled or perplexed about allegiance to or membership in the group. Clearly some people were weighing the choices in their setting. The choice between Matthean Judaism and the so-called scribes and Pharisees loomed large, at least in Matthew's view, as a crucial choice for the people. Indeed, the phrase about those who are heavily laden conjures up images of the Pharisees in chapter 23 who "tie up heavy burdens, hard to bear, and lay them on men's shoulders" (23:4). Another point of contrast with the Pharisees may well be 11:28. Matthew claims they place heavy burdens on the people, but the Matthean burden is light.

In a dramatic change of tone from the woes on Chorazin, Bethsaida, and Capernaum, Matthew describes his community as a place of rest, gentleness, and ease. The apparent anomaly between judging the Galilean cities one moment and inviting them to find rest with the Matthean Jesus the next highlights the ambivalence with which Matthew's group was viewed locally. On the one hand people are judged for their lack of response, on the other they are encouraged to come to the community and find in it a place that may represent a haven from the crises they are experiencing locally, whatever they may have been. This ambivalence toward outsiders reflects at best a mixed response toward Matthew's church.

It is important to remember also that "yoke" denotes sovereignty. It was often used as a political image in reference to the king or sovereign whom the people served. In 2 Chronicles 10 are some interesting passages about King Rehoboam who "placed a heavy yoke upon the people." Although his father placed a heavy yoke on the people and they complained to Rehoboam, he nonetheless announced to the people that his yoke would be even heavier than his father's (2 Chron. 10:4ff.). "Yoke," then, is also an image about rule, whether harsh or fair, and Matthew was not unaware of this. Jesus' rule or sovereignty is righteous, just, and an easy burden.

In the LXX "yoke" frequently takes on the sense of justice. The Greek term for yoke, *zugos,* can also be the balance on a scale. There are many references to justice and fairness involving this term. There could be false *zugoi* or weights, which allowed people to deceive and steal in the market or in commerce. The Book of Proverbs speaks about a just weight (*zugos*), which is pleasing to God (Prov. 11:1, 16). To Yahweh only belongs the scales and the balance (*zugos*). The scales or yoke (*zugoi*) must be fair, and false weights are unpleasing to Yahweh (Mic. 6:11; Ezek. 45:10). There is then a play on words in Greek concerning the word "yoke," or, at least, this word had multiple meanings and implications. All these nuances are carried in Matthew's use of this term in 11:28ff.

While retaining these nuances over time "yoke" began to develop some new meanings as well. The notion of the yoke began to be associated with wisdom, learning, and the law or Torah. Certain apocryphal second-temple texts and wisdom literature capture this meaning. Sirach 51 is the classic location for this sense of *zugos.* In the famous poem about wisdom Sirach reads, "Buy her without money, put your necks under her yoke; let your souls receive instruction; she is not far to seek. See for yourselves, how slight my efforts have been to win peace." In this passage we see the confluence of several of the Matthean concerns and notions present in 11:28–30. Wisdom is personified as the woman to whom people should submit. She is a teacher. She supplies peace. Matthew seems to be likening his teaching to personified Wisdom so prominent among certain learned circles in the second-temple period. His yoke, like that of Wisdom's, will teach and impart. "Take my yoke upon you and learn from me" (11:29). Jesus' instruction, like Wisdom's, is good for the soul and grants peace (11:29), a sentiment echoed later by 1 Clement who spoke about "the yoke of grace" (1 Clem. 16:17). Only a few verses earlier (11:19), Matthew introduces the idea of wisdom. "Wisdom," he says, "is justified by her deeds." That is, the justice and accuracy of what one says is confirmed, or not, in one's actions. This is a constant theme of Matthew's and relates directly to his interpretation of the law.

Through the use of the image of a yoke, Matthew ties into a current notion of wisdom and peace being obtained through careful study, a certain disciplined submission to the law and Torah, and through taking on the burden of your master's teaching. The *Didache* picks this up and understands "the Lord's full yoke" (*Did.* 6:2) as referring to Jesus' teaching. In doing these things the student will find fulfillment and peace. Study, learning, and knowledge are constant themes for Matthew. This passage — a homily on Sirach 51, if you will, fashioned for Matthean Jews — is in this way most appropriate for Matthew. He does not spend much time or devote much space to developing what some have called a "wisdom christology." But these verses do contain much of what Matthew wished to communicate to his audience. As W. D. Davies and D. Allison have said, in many respects this passage is a summary of Matthew's entire message. Jesus is the revealer of God's will and truth. He is the personal fulfillment of Israel's personified divine agent for the sophistic; he is Wisdom, and he is the one who correctly interprets and teaches the law. It is this last crucial theme — Jesus as the true interpreter and teacher of the law — which Matthew moves on to in chapter 12.

# The Conflict Stories:
## Sabbath; Jesus, the Devil, and the Spirit of God; Scribes, Pharisees, and the Sign of Jonah; Discipleship, Alienation, and the Matthean Family

Matthew 12:1–8 is a well-known controversy story between Jesus and the Pharisees. The story begins with the comical scene of Jesus and his disciples walking through a cornfield (for some reason) and out of nowhere the Pharisees pop up to catch them in a violation of the law. This artificial setting for this debate serves as a reminder of the constructed nature of these debates with the Matthean opponents. That is, these stories were developed and embellished over a long period of time by congregations of Jesus followers to help them recall the differences between them and other Judaisms of the day. Matthew, for example, inherited this story from Mark. Matthew has added some material to suit the issues and questions that loom large in his context.

Matthew has added, for example, that the disciples were hungry and therefore began to pluck the grain on a sabbath (Matt. 12:1 ‖ Mark 2:23 ‖ Luke 6:1). It is this action by the disciples which provokes the debate between Jesus and the Pharisees. In Matthew the Pharisees make the direct declaration that "your disciples" are doing what is not lawful on the sabbath (12:2). In Mark and Luke this is in the form of a question from the Pharisees. The synoptic writers offer a defense of the disciples by referring to the actions of David in the temple when he was hungry. This comes from 1 Samuel 21:1–6 where David and his men ate the bread of presence in the sanctuary at Nob (1 Sam. 21:6). There is no mention of the sabbath, however, in the Samuel text.

The mention of the David story, of course, is intended to demonstrate the basic lawfulness of the disciples and the misguided notions of the law and legal interpretation that inform the Pharisees. I do not think these are simply fictional stories to make the Pharisees look bad and Jesus and the twelve like legal *virtuosi*, though the stories also mean to do that. *M. Šabb.* 7:2, for example, provides a list of thirty-nine acts that cannot be performed on the sabbath. Further, while the scene for the narrative is obviously manufactured, Matthew, more than Luke or Mark, takes the question with utter seriousness. These were actual issues confronting and dividing second-temple communities.

Matthew adds another legal argument not present in the parallel texts. In Matthew Jesus responds further to the Pharisees by asking them about work done by the priests in the temple on the sabbath, like setting out the bread of presence or doubling the daily burnt offering (Lev. 24:8; Num. 28:9–10). He begins in good rhetorical fashion by asking, "Have you not read in the law...?" These priests, according to scripture, work on the sabbath, yet they are "guiltless." Matthew sets the actions of the disciples, as one would expect him to do, within the confines of the law. The disciples, too, then emerge from this explication as "guiltless" (12:5). Matthew further makes clear in this conflict story that the Pharisees, though posing as legal experts, really do not know, much less live the law. "If you had known what this means," Jesus continues, 'I desire mercy not sacrifice,' you would not have condemned the guiltless." Here Matthew has strengthened Mark's legal arguments considerably.

This scripture citation in 12:7 is the second instance of Matthew using Hosea 6:6. The first instance was in Matthew 9:13. Jesus was also debating with the Pharisees in that passage when he initially quoted Hosea 6:6. In 9:13 he said to the Pharisees, "Go and learn what this means, 'I desire mercy not sacrifice.'" In chapter 12 Jesus says to the Pharisees, "If you had known what this means, 'I desire mercy not sacrifice.'" In chapter 9 the Pharisees were encouraged to "go and learn." By chapter 12 their failure to learn the lesson results in Jesus determining they do not know what this means. The tone in chapter 12 is they will never grasp the importance of this Hosea passage, which is a central hermeneutical passage for Matthew and, perhaps, for Yohan ben Zakkai as well (*ARN* 3).

This conflict story highlights the lawful behavior of the disciples. It also provides an occasion, or a case study, for Matthew to demonstrate how his community interprets the law. Jesus emerges as more informed and skilled in understanding how the law relates to important issues like sabbath observance. Matthew contains the same concluding saying that Mark and Luke have. "The Son of Man is lord of the sabbath" (12:8 || Mark 2:28 || Luke 6:5). Matthew, however, has deleted a pivotal verse in the Marcan story. Mark's Jesus says, "The Sabbath was made for man, not man for the sabbath." In other words, the sabbath serves people, not the other way around.

This is far too radical, too reductionist a view of the sabbath laws for Matthew. The Sabbath laws absolutely abide. As E. Schweizer commented quite accurately, Matthew's congregation was still sabbath observant. Of course they were; that is what Jesus taught them to do. But Mark's Jesus makes sabbath observance too questionable. If the sabbath was made for man (Mark 2:27), then I am free to do as I wish on sabbath. This is far too extreme and dangerous a view for Matthew. Some of Matthew's opponents might think he and his community were loose interpreters of the law, but Matthew thinks they completely fulfill it and would never set it aside. In another Jesus movement, which held to Mark 2:27, sabbath laws might be broken because they believe they are free to do that, being "lords of the sabbath." This was not Matthew's community. Their actions, though viewed sometimes as anomic by their rivals, are always explained and defended by Matthew as correctly fulfilling and interpreting the law. So Mark 2:27 had to go because it did not accord with Matthew's understanding of his community's relationship to the law. There are sabbath laws that must be followed and submitted to. Matthew understands this and explains that in fact, contrary to the Pharisees, his community understands and fulfills these laws.

Matthew 12:9–14 introduces another conflict story. This is also a healing story involving the sabbath and the Pharisees. The venue is one of "their gathering places" (12:9). There was a man with a withered hand in the synagogue and "they" (the Pharisees; see v. 14) ask Jesus if it is lawful to heal on the sabbath. The synoptic writers add that the Pharisees ask this "so that they might accuse him" (Matt. 12:10 || Mark 3:2 || Luke 6:7).

Matthew responds by asking the Pharisees a question. "Which one of you, if you had one sheep and it falls into a pit on the sabbath, will not lay hold of it and lift it out? Of how much more value is a man than a sheep?" Jesus' response in Matthew is reminiscent of Qumran's concern over saving an animal, or not, on the sabbath. "If a beast falls into a cistern or into a pit, let it not be lifted out on the sabbath" (CD 11:13–14). This injunction is part of a long list of prohibitions for the sabbath at Qumran. One may not assist a beast giving birth, carry a child, clean house, or spend the sabbath near Gentiles.

The versions found in Mark and Luke ask more directly about an issue that is well attested within early Rabbinism. Mark and Luke ask specifically about doing good or saving a life on the sabbath. *M. Yoma* 8:6 states, "A case of risk of loss of life supersedes the sabbath." This is Jesus' question in Mark (3:4) and Luke (6:9). Matthew's Jesus is getting at the same point but does so with a question about sheep and their owners. Matthew's question about the fallen sheep once again expands the legal argument when compared to Mark or Luke. The case of the beast in the pit is additional legal weight on the side of Matthew's particular interpretation of the law. One might say here that Matthew's Jesus sides more with Mishna's answer to the sabbath question than with Qumran. The man's hand, therefore, is healed by Jesus.

But the Pharisees do not accept this interpretation and Jesus' actions. This is the first time the reader sees the opposition deciding to put Jesus to death. "The Pharisees went out and took counsel against him, how they might destroy him" (12:14). This verse, like certain verses in the birth narrative, prefigures the trial and death scene at the end of the Gospel. The Pharisees "counsel together" (*sumboulion;* 28:11) as to how "to destroy" him (*apolesosen;* 27:20), language that also reappears at the trial and death of Jesus. Luke tones this down a bit. He records that the Pharisees "discussed with one another what they might do to Jesus" (Luke 6:11). He is missing the definitive term *apolesosen,* that is, the decision to destroy Jesus.

Mark has the Pharisees form a coalition with "the Herodians" in 3:6. This is a curious and, at first glance, not altogether logical pairing. While Matthew does not mention this group in chapter 12 he does associate them with the Pharisees in 22:16 in the context of a question about taxes. Josephus uses the term in *Jewish Wars* 1.319 to refer to those who fought on the side of Herod the Great while regaining control of Judea in 37 B.C.E. For the most part, however, "the Herodians" have been viewed as a political group of aristocrats or locally powerful people aligned with Herod Antipas. This view was expressed long ago by H. H. Rowley and has been followed by a number of others in this regard, including more recently R. Pesch and R. Guelich.

But A. Hultgren has sought to revive B. W. Bacon's thesis concerning the Herodians. Bacon, based on Tertullian (*Against All Heresies* 1.3.649) and Epiphanius in his "Against the Herodians" (*Epiphanii Opera* 1.330), says that this was a group who considered Herod the messiah. They applied to him the prophecy in Genesis 49:10 that "the scepter shall not depart from Judah." Tertullian and Epiphanius have Herod Agrippa I in mind to whom Claudius granted sovereignty in Galilee in 40 C.E. and Judea in 41. Palestine was then united under the rule of Agrippa I. Herod Agrippa I is said to have gained favor with the people of Galilean and Judean society. Josephus says, "He scrupulously observed the traditions of his people. He neglected no rite of purification, and no day passed for him without the prescribed sacrifice" (*Ant.* 19.331). *M. Sotah* 7:8 has a tradition about Agrippa I reading Torah in the temple at the feast of Tabernacles. He read a portion from Deuteronomy 17:15 which says, "Thou may not put a foreigner over thee to rule which is not thy brother." Agrippa's eyes filled with tears, but the people called out, "Our brother art thou, our brother art thou, our brother art thou!"

Bacon suggests that the description of Agrippa I accords well with some of the popular traditions about the Pharisees. Along broad lines the description of the beliefs and practice of the Pharisees from J. Neusner and A. Baumgarten would support Bacon's suggestion. Agrippa I's reputation for attention to purity laws, the traditions of the people, and all the laws and sacrifices while in Jerusalem, not to mention his positive reputation in early rabbinic tradition, all point to a possible Pharisaic-Herodian connection. This connection would have started after the death of Jesus and during the reign of Agrippa I. Such a relationship also accords with the picture of the Pharisees in Josephus as a political interest group who become aligned with political leaders and lobby for their platform and the "traditions of the elders." This relationship would have continued after Agrippa I's death.

The picture of the Herodians as a group of politically powerful local elite and as a religious group that fixed some sort of messianic hope on Agrippa's reign are not mutually exclusive. On the contrary, they almost necessarily converge. These two parties could have formed an alliance that continued throughout most of the first century. The religiopolitical hopes of the Herodians as expressed by Epiphanius and Tertullian point to another source of potential conflict with Jesus-centered Judaism. If Epiphanius is right about the identity of the Herodians, then the titles "king of the Jews" and "messiah" appear even more provocative in the Matthean setting. These groups are trying to garner and maintain popular support, advocate for their particular messiah, and claim to speak for God about the future of Israel. These two movements are heading toward a confrontation with one another. In this regard, then, the Pharisees and Herodians do make a sensible, and for Matthew a potentially dangerous, coalition out to stop Jesus and his following.

For Matthew the Pharisees are the fundamental opponents of the Matthean community. Therefore, the Herodians are quite minor figures in his Gospel. They do perhaps represent a vestige of some political alliance set against the early Jesus movement. This alliance, though altered, may have continued in the form of the local leader's coalition with larger political authorities. The Pharisees joining with the Herodians represent such a relationship. But it is the Pharisees' opposition and hostility that preoccupies Matthew. The conflict story in Matthew 12:9–14 is significant because it contrasts yet again the Matthean church's interpretation and application of the law with that of the local leaders. And these passages make clear that the violence and conflict brewing throughout the story have broken out into open conflict. There is no secret now of the opposition's desire to do in Jesus and, by extension, his followers in the form of Matthew's community.

In 12:18–21 Matthew inserts a fulfillment citation from Isaiah 42:1–4. This is one of the famous so-called Suffering Servant poems from 2 Isaiah (chapters 40–58 and dating to the Babylonian exile c. 535 B.C.E.). These poems were understood in Matthew's setting as ancient songs of Israel's redemption fulfilled in the person of Jesus. He is that person of whom Isaiah spoke. The citation reiterates Jesus' fulfillment of the expectations of God's people Israel. But in this section of conflict stories the citation from Isaiah also reminds people that Jesus could not possibly be the one who misunderstands the law or leads his people astray. According to Isaiah, he is the one who came to fulfill the law and the prophets, and the political and religious aspirations of God's people.

This citation from Isaiah stresses the view that this messianic figure will be also a redemptive figure for the nations, that is, for all people. Matthew carefully follows the LXX text, as over against the Hebrew, which has inserted "the nations/gentiles/people will hope" into Isaiah 42:4b. Matthew's crisis with the local leaders has quickened the realization, as well as Matthew's interpretation of scripture, which stresses that the nations will also be included in this kingdom of heaven. This message will be announced to the nations (12:18), and in his name the nations will hope (12:21). Again, rendering this term *ethne* "people" is understandable and acceptable. The point here is Matthew sees this as something the world can be a part of and benefit from. There is no indication that those who join play by different rules. Those who are a part of the community or people must follow Matthew's interpretation of the law, the Matthean rendition of Israel's history, and Jesus the wise teacher of Israel. This passage more than any other prepares the reader for the close of the Gospel and the so-called final commission.

Like all Matthean fulfillment citations this quotation from Isaiah stresses Jesus as the fulfiller. His actions and attitudes seem strange to many of the crowd and the local leaders. But Matthew keeps stressing the fulfillment of Israel's laws through the actions of Jesus. He is gentle and meek (Isa. 42:20), he will establish justice (42:20), and all the people will hope in Jesus (42:21). The Pharisees fail to see this and, of course, beg to differ with Matthew.

Matthew 12:22–30 is the second story about a blind and mute demoniac. Jesus casts out the demon and he is healed. A very similar story appeared in 9:32–34. This story follows Mark and Q more closely than 9:32ff. and is another occasion to debate the Pharisees. The charge of Jesus having a demon is repeated, and is responded to more fully by Matthew. "It is only by Beelzebul, the prince of demons, that this man casts out demons," the Pharisees say (12:24). In response to this charge Matthew follows Mark's analogy of a house divided. "If Satan casts out Satan, he is against himself; how then will his kingdom stand?" (12:26).

And Jesus says he casts out demons because he has rendered Satan powerless. Or, as the synoptic writers have it, "he has bound the strong man so that he can plunder his house" (Matt. 12:29). That demons are being cast out by Jesus is proof that he has put Satan to flight, or "bound the strong man."

The charge that Jesus was beside himself or had a demon was apparently a fairly widespread charge. All the synoptic writers and John contain this charge and the debate with the Pharisees which was associated with it. This charge was taken with certain seriousness by the writers. Matthew includes the outline of this controversy twice in his Gospel. By taking the time to respond to the charge of the Pharisees against Jesus, he hoped to put to rest the accusation that must have occasionally surfaced in his day — that Jesus was really a crazed man or a magician gifted by Satan.

The saying about blasphemy against the holy spirit follows the discussion of Jesus having a demon and the Matthean (and Q: Luke 11:23) saying about absolute allegiance to the group (cf. Mark 9:40). This is a rather obscure verse and historically has provoked considerable debate. Mark helps explain the meaning of this passage (3:30) when he says Jesus referred to the blasphemy against the Holy Spirit because "they had said, 'He has an unclean spirit.'" That is, ascribing the power to the wrong spirit is, in this case, the blasphemy. Matthew, as is often the case, deletes or mistakenly omits a Marcan explanation. For example, in the passion scene Matthew omits the Marcan blindfolding of Jesus and, therefore, the slap of Jesus' face, and the taunt, "Prophesy to us Christ, who slapped you" (Matt. 26:67 || Mark 14:65), makes no sense. Similarly, there is not adequate explanation here by Matthew for this particular verse.

Luke has put this passage about blasphemy in the context of

persecution and legal action against the followers (12:8ff.). The inference here has to do with denial or speaking falsely in the court setting. Interestingly, Matthew and Luke record that "whoever says a word against the Son of Man will be forgiven; but he who blasphemes against the holy spirit will not be forgiven" (Matt. 12:32 ‖ Luke 12:10). In this context the title "Son of man" as used by Jesus appears to be a circumlocution for "I," or self-referential. For both writers blasphemy against Jesus can, strictly speaking, be forgiven. Taking a hint from Mark here, it is the false attribution of Jesus' power, or the whence of his power, that is blasphemy. If you recall the centurion from Capernaum who came to Jesus because his servant was sick (8:5ff.), he was praised by Jesus because he understood — through analogy — where Jesus' power came from, or from whom he was taking his orders. "I too am a man under authority, with soldiers under me, and I say to one 'Go,' and he goes, and to another 'Come,' and he comes." Jesus marveled when he heard this and said, "Not even in all of Israel have I found such faith" (Matt. 8:10). The failure to correctly attribute the source of Jesus' authority, not necessarily devotion to the Son of man, is the definition here of a "sin against the holy spirit." It is this charge of blasphemy against Jesus which resurfaces in the trial (Matt. 26:65).

Following the blasphemy saying, Matthew's Jesus inserts one of his favorite themes of those who bear good fruit. Trees bear either good fruit or bad. This is how judgments are to be made within the Matthean setting. There are many issues and concerns within Matthew's church that emerge throughout the course of the Gospel. There are some important decisions and judgments to be made by members. There are people who are in the community but are really false members. They will be rooted or sorted out in the end. There are many whose external behavior and actions are very much like those of the Matthean community, but they are not true disciples either. And there are many who will lead the members astray. They "make people twice the sons of hell than they are."

How will these judgments be made by the community? The pressure and cost associated with important choices and judgments are nearly palpable in Matthew's Gospel. Matthew mentions in a number of places that the litmus test for judgments by the Matthean members is the actions, or "fruits," of those in question. It is, as B. Gerhardsson has said, through one's particular acts that they are known and judged. This is as true for the Matthean members as it is for the Matthean opponents. The "fruit of their lives" is the decisive criteria in legal interpretation and personal judgments the members must make.

This, it seems, is the primary difference, and Matthew's primary rub with his debate partners. "Good things come out of good people, and evil things from evil people" (12:35). The Matthean opposition "speak," Matthew claims, but they do not act or "do." This is ample material for people to make a judgment about their wisdom, legal interpretations, and leadership abilities.

Chapter 12 includes another confrontation between some of the scribes and Pharisees (12:38). They come to Jesus wishing to see a sign from him. This passage also is repeated by Matthew in 16:1–4 with the Sadducees substituting for the scribes. Mark's version of this provides no sign (Mark 8:12). The apparent "sign of Jonah" comes from Q (Luke 11:29). The sign of Jonah in Q and Luke, as L. T. Johnson has pointed out, is the preaching of Jonah (cf. Jon. 3:1–10). The sign of Jonah is his preaching of repentance to the city of Nineveh. Also, in Luke the scribes and Pharisees are not the provocateurs, but rather "the crowds" receive the appellation of "an evil generation." In Matthew the scribes and Pharisees represent "an evil and adulterous generation [that] seeks for a sign." As Jonah's preaching was a sign and occasion for repentance in Jonah's day, so Jesus constitutes such a sign in his day. The Queen of South (Queen of Sheba; cf. 1 Kgs. 10:1–13) came to Solomon from Arabia "to hear the wisdom of Solomon, and behold, something greater than Solomon is here." The men of Nineveh repented at the preaching of Jonah; "something greater than Jonah is here" (Luke 11:32). Curiously, the Queen of Sheba and the men of Nineveh will arise and judge or condemn "this generation" because they sought wisdom and were able to repent. Matthew believes those living now, and during the days of Jesus, have been granted an even greater sign.

Matthew makes some considerable changes in the sign of

Jonah material from Q. In 12:40 Matthew inserts his interpretation of the sign of Jonah. "Jonah was in the belly of the whale three days and three nights, so will the Son of Man be three days and three nights in the heart of the earth." Matthew has taken Q's interpretation of the sign of Jonah being his preaching to the Ninevites, and interpreted the sign as representing Jesus' resurrection. This is obviously a development later in the church's life. The belief in the resurrection on the part of some Jesus movements has spawned a new interpretation of "the sign of Jonah." In a setting like Matthean Judaism the resurrection is used as proof that Jesus is who he said he was, as well as validation of the community's allegiance to him. At the end of the Gospel we are told of a rumor circulating among Matthew's people that the resurrection never happened but, rather, Jesus' body was stolen. "This rumor circulates among Jews to this day" (28:15).

Matthew's rendition of "the sign of Jonah" provides another opportunity to use the scribes and Pharisees as a foil. This generation, largely through the leadership and influence of the so-called scribes and Pharisees, is in worse shape than many "generations" before them. Even Jonah's "generation" repented as a result of his preaching (Matt. 12:41). This evil generation is like a demon-possessed man who has the spirit cast out, but the spirit subsequently returns with seven other spirits more evil than the first (Matt. 12:43–45). Such is the state of this generation, the audience and opponents in Matthew's setting. Even the resurrection, Matthew says in his redacted version of the sign of Jonah, has not helped this generation change.

These passages help explain to Matthew's church the lack of positive response to their message and mission, slight as it is, and may help assuage the doubt that could arise in the face of such disinterest from "this generation." No sign will help the scribes and Pharisees. They are portrayed as a lost group of leaders and scholars (they usually call Jesus "teacher"; cf. 12:38), from whom the Matthean community is being increasingly distanced.

Matthew concludes this chapter with a Marcan story about allegiance and commitment within the kingdom of heaven (Matt. 12:46–50 ǁ Mark 3:31–35 ǁ Luke 8:19–21). While Jesus is teaching, his mother and brothers stand outside waiting to speak with him. While there has been some debate in certain wings of Christianity about Jesus having any siblings, this is certainly not a concern of the Gospel tradition. The synoptic Gospels hold that Jesus had siblings. When Jesus is told that his mother and brothers are outside he responds, "Who is my mother and my brothers?" In 12:49 Matthew records, *"stretching out his hands toward his disciples,* he said, 'Here are my mother and my brothers! For whoever does the will of my father in heaven is my brother, my sister, and mother'"* (12:50). Matthew makes clear that membership and discipleship in the Matthean church is like a family. That is, it constitutes the primary set of relationships in one's life. Identity, protection and nurture, belongingness, and training (the traditional roles of the family) are now provided by the Matthean community. This passage captures the transformation of a term like "brother" (*adelphoi*) from a biological term to a sociological term that depicts fictive kinship in Matthew's setting. As the group experiences rejection and, at best, a lukewarm response from "this generation," support, solace, and protection can be found through allegiance to and membership in the family of the kingdom of heaven (12:50). Matthew asserts the community can provide what Matthean Jews can no longer find, or are unable to find, in their families, villages, and city. Matthew's church appears to be increasingly isolated and set in opposition to the traditional relational and kinship structures, and against the local leaders in their setting.

## Further Reading

Bacon, B. W. "Pharisees and Herodians in Mark." *JBL* 39 (1920): 102–11.

Baumgarten, A. "The Pharisaic *Paradosis.*" *HTR* 80 (1987): 63–78.

Davies, W. D., and D. Allison. *A Critical and Exegetical Commentary on Matthew,* vol. 2, *Chapters 8–17.* Edinburgh: T. & T. Clark, 1991.

Deutsch, C. *Hidden Wisdom and the Easy Yoke: Wisdom, Torah and Discipleship in Matthew 11:25–30.* Sheffield: JSOT, 1987.

Edwards, R. A. *The Sign of Jonah in the Theology of the Evangelists and Q.* Naperville, Ill.: Allenson, 1971.

Gerhardsson, B. "'An ihren Früchten sollt ihr sie erkennen': Die Legitimitätsfrage in der matthäischen Christologie." *EvTh* 42 (1982): 113–26.

Green, W. S., J. Neusner, and E. Frerichs, eds. *Judaisms and Their Messiahs at the Turn of the Christian Era.* Cambridge: Cambridge University Press, 1987.

Guelich, R. *Mark 1–8:26.* Word Biblical Commentary 34a. Waco, Tex.: Word, 1989.

Harrington, D. *The Gospel of Matthew.* Sacra Pagina 1. Collegeville, Minn.: Michael Glazier/Liturgical Press, 1991.

Hultgren, A. *Jesus and His Adversaries: The Form and Function of the Conflict Stories in the Synoptic Gospels.* Minneapolis: Augsburg, 1979.

Johnson, L. T. *The Gospel of Luke.* Sacra Pagina 3. Collegeville, Minn.: Michael Glazier/Liturgical Press, 1991.

Neusner, J. "The Idea of Purity in Ancient Judaism." *JAAR* 43 (1975): 15–26.

Pesch, R. *Das Markusevangelium.* HTKNT. Freiburg: Herder, 1977.

Rowley, H. H. "The Herodians in the Gospels." *JTS* 41 (1940): 14–27.

Schweizer, E. "Matthew's Church." In *The Interpretation of Matthew,* ed. G. Stanton, 129–55. Philadelphia: Fortress, 1983.

Smith, M. *Jesus the Magician.* San Francisco: Harper and Row, 1978.

Theissen, G. "Das 'schwankende Rohr' im Mt. 11, 7 und die Gründungsmünzen von Tiberias. Ein Beitrag zur Lokalkoloritforschung in den synoptischen Evangelien." *ZDPV* 101 (1985): 43–55.

Vaage, L. *Galilean Upstarts: Jesus' First Followers According to Q.* Valley Forge, Pa.: Trinity Press International, 1994.

# The Parables of the Kingdom —
# 13:1–13:51

## The Sower

Chapter 13 is Matthew's parable chapter. This chapter contains seven parables, with a brief conclusion about scribes trained for the kingdom and a postscript about Jesus' rejection in his own country. Matthew's parables are primarily "parables of the kingdom of heaven." Jesus is still by the Sea of Galilee and is followed by a large crowd. Matthew has Jesus come out of "the house" and sit by the sea as the crowd begins to gather. Due to the size of the crowd, Jesus is forced into a boat, where he begins to teach them "many things in parables" (13:3). Matthew follows Mark closely in his version of the first parable, the so-called parable of the sower (Matt. 13:4 ‖ Mark 4:3).

This parable is accurately described as an allegory because of the interpretation the Gospel writers assign to it. The two powerful images in this story are the sower and the seeds. The ground is not as prominent as some interpreters have asserted. The point is quite clear; some seeds grow and some simply do not. Their environment and, above all, their own internal disposition — something to which Matthew pays considerable attention — is not always suitable for growth. This parable is considered the first of the so-called Matthean growth parables.

This parable appears in Matthew, Mark, Luke, and the *Gospel of Thomas* (*Gos. Thom.* 9), though there is no accompanying interpretation in Thomas. As M. Meyer has observed, the image of the field, or soil, as the place where wisdom, knowledge, or truth flourishes is not unknown in either Jewish or Roman literature (cf. Sir. 6:19; Quintillian, *Or. Instr.* 5.11.24). The early-second-century Roman rhetor Quintillian wrote, "If you would say that the mind needs to be cultivated, you would use a comparison to the soil, which if neglected produces thorns and brambles, but if cultivated produces a crop." We can see just from the Quintillian example that the images of soil and field were not limited to Palestine, and their use does not necessarily suggest a thoroughly agrarian environment. These images were widespread and, rather obviously, lend themselves to morals and fables about human growth and frustration.

The Gospel writers, including Matthew, found the soil and the field apt images for communicating what they needed to about faith and following, and in Matthew's case the kingdom of heaven. As the reader will no doubt recall, some seeds were sown on a path, birds came and ate them. Other seeds fell on rocky soil, they sprang up quickly, and the sun scorched them because they lacked depth. And some seeds fell on thorns that grew up and choked them. But some seeds fell on good soil and brought forth grain — some a hundredfold, some sixty, some thirty.

Matthew uses the neuter plural *alla* (meaning "others," or "other seeds") as opposed to Mark's singular subject *allo* or "another" seed. However, even in English we speak of "seed" in both the singular and the plural and the Evangelists seemed to have some of the same confusion. Mark switches to the plural from the singular (from *allo* to *alla*) in 4:8 so that the crop can yield a hundredfold. Even Mark's use of the singular carries the sense that he is talking about *seeds* that are sown. When one is talking about sowing, whether to use the singular or plural for "seed" can be as awkward in Greek as it is in English. Matthew remains grammatically consistent and uses the plural throughout.

The sower is actually only mentioned in the opening of the parable. The focus of the story, after the first verse, is the seeds, though the presence of the sower is implied with the verb *epesev*, that is, "sown" or "fallen." The parable would be most accurately termed "the parable of the seeds." But the title "sower" has been part of popular Christian discourse for a long time and will probably not be changing soon. Commentators on the parables from earlier in this century consistently referred to the parable as that of "the sower" and this contributed to the title remaining. The focal point of the story, however, are the *seeds*, and their fate after being sown.

The parable describes three types of seed that do not "bear fruit." The term used here is Matthew's usual term for "bearing fruit" (*karpon;* Matt. 13:8 ‖ Mark 4:8 ‖ Luke 8:8). This is not a story describing the contrast between "the Word that remains unfruitful among *the Jews* [my emphasis] and the Word that becomes productive in the disciples, or church," as J. Kingsbury has said. We can see even within Matthew's Gospel that there are good and bad crops within the community. And certainly nothing in the parable suggests it is talking about Jews who reject Jesus and his message. This is a story about why the seed, which Matthew identifies as "the word of the kingdom" (13:19), does not catch on with more listeners. The parable is an apology, hoping to explain the meager results of Jesus' teaching and/or the Matthean mission, and also serves as a hortatory warning to followers. The presence of this parable demonstrates the author's awareness that there are those in the community who will not remain, and may ultimately refute the Matthean message.

As mentioned above, Matthew, Mark, and Luke, but not Thomas, add an interpretation to the parable. Matthew explains that the first seed represents "any one who hears the word of the kingdom and *does not understand it,* the evil one comes and snatches away what is sown in his heart." Matthew alone connects the lack of understanding (*sunientos,* 13:11; cf. 13:15, 19, 23) with the work of the evil one snatching away the word of the kingdom. Neither Luke nor Mark add this interpretation of the first batch of seed. The second seed represents "he who hears the word and immediately [*euthus*] receives it with joy" (13:20). However, "he has no root in himself, but endures for a while, and when tribulation or persecution arises on account of the word, immediately he falls away" (*ethus skandalizetai;* 13:21).

The notions of "root" and "falling away" or, literally, "stumbling," are noteworthy. Appropriately for a parable, the term "root" lends itself to several levels of meaning. The second seeds have no "root," and therefore do not last when the times get tough "due to the word." "Root" (*riza*) can refer loosely to a family or nation (cf. Aelius Aristides 30.16). John the Baptist uses the term in a related way in Matthew's lone use of the term outside of this parable. You may recall John says to the Pharisees and Sadducees, "Do not presume to say to yourselves, 'We have Abraham for our father'; for I tell you, God is able to raise up children to Abraham. Even now the axe is laid to the root of the trees; every tree that does not *bear fruit* is cut down and thrown in the fire" (3:9–10). Lineage, family tree, and collective or corporate identity are captured in the image of the "root."

Jesus portrayed as "the son of David" in Matthew also suggests "the root of Jesse" from Isaiah 11:10; "The root of Jesse shall stand as a signal to the people. It will be sought out by the nations." This passage is echoed in Sirach 47:25: "It shall be granted to Jacob a remnant, and to David a root springing from him." Isaiah 53:2, in one of the so-called suffering servant poems, uses the term in relation to the servant: "For he grew up before him like a young plant, and like a root out of dry ground." First Clement seems to be following this Isaiah passage when he writes, "He [Jesus], was like a child, like a root in thirsty ground" (1 Clem. 16:3). So the term "root," along with the notion of family or, loosely defined, nation, would also be suggestive of Jesus, the son of David and root of Jesse, to some of Matthew's members. Within the parlance of Jesus-centered Judaism this image, when used within the context of a story about Jesus, would take on added significance. One would not want to be "without root," though it can be the root itself which causes the trouble and hindrance.

All of these connotations are carried by the term "root" and could easily come to mind for the Matthean Jew reflecting on this parable. These meanings are not mutually exclusive. However, Job 5:3, Sirach 40:15, probably followed by 1 Clement 39:8, seem to relate most explicitly to Matthew 13:21. These passages are about the "foolish [or "unclean" in Sirach], taking root." They only find *rock* as a foundation, and soon their homes are swept away. These are the foolish who lack wisdom or understanding — they have no depth and cannot endure the hardships of *following*. This portion of the parable helps to explain, among other things, those within Jesus-centered Judaism, and in this case Matthean Judaism, who have left the community and abandoned the precepts spelled out in the Gospel. The author maintains these people never really understood the true nature of following Jesus and the word of the kingdom of heaven, and they did not finally understand the Matthean interpretation of the law and Israel's past and future.

The seeds that are choked by the "cares of the world" are those people warned about in the Sermon on the Mount. They have, unfortunately, laid up treasures on earth and have been caught up in those earthly concerns. They are among those people whom Matthew criticizes constantly, those who do not bear fruit. Those who are caught up in "the cares of the world and delight in riches" are *akarpos*—unfruitful. The Matthean followers are well aware of what, according to Matthew, happens to those who do not bear fruit (cf. 7:17ff.). These "cares of the world" are among the leading "stumbling blocks" to fulfilling the Matthean mandate to "bear fruit" as a follower and member of the kingdom of heaven.

In Matthew 13:21 the one who has no root endures for a while, but falls away, or stumbles, "when tribulation or persecution arises on account of the word." The term "fall away, stumble, or take offense," *skandalizetai,* was already in the tradition when Matthew took over the parable of the sower. But this is an interesting word and one that Matthew uses with great regularity (5:29, 30; 11:6; 13:41, 57; 15:13ff.; 16:23; 17:27; 18:6–9; 24:10; 26:31, 33). This term has several related meanings and is a very important term for Matthew. It stresses the theme of enduring hardships and avoiding the traps that will take people away from the community and into *anomia,* or lawlessness, and eventually judgment. This term represents the elements in the followers' lives which obstruct their life as a disciple and disrupt communal relations and affairs. These obstructions can be Jesus himself, as in 11:6 where Jesus responds to John the Baptist by saying, "Blessed is he who does not stumble over me," or the Pharisees in 15:13ff., who "take offense" at his language and teaching about the law. The obstructions, or point of stumbling, can be having your mind on the things of this world, or people, and not God, as in the case of Peter in 16:23. Playing off certain Hebrew Bible texts like Isaiah 28:16 and Psalm 118:22, other Jesus movements, notably Pauline groups, understood Jesus and his crucifixion as *the skandalon,* or stumbling block (Rom. 9:32–33; 1 Cor. 1:23; 1 Pet. 2:8).

According to Matthew, one of the most grievous acts one can commit is causing someone (a little one, or *mikroi*) to stumble or *skandalisae* (18:6ff.). This word, then, while appearing casual if not insignificant in the immediate context of the parable of the sower, is actually a crucial concept for Matthew. The stumbling — whether it is over Jesus himself, the "word of the kingdom," worldly concerns, or the teaching of the Pharisees — is happening in some significant ways in Matthew's community. He must confront this problem and reality, both to support those who feel besieged and to try to put a stop to the "falling off" within the church. In an interesting Matthean verse in 13:41, toward the end of the interpretation of the parable of the tares, we read, "The Son of Man will send his angels, and they will gather out of his kingdom all causes of sin [*skandala*] and all evildoers." The falling away or stumbling is because of evil influences and forces. In the end the Matthean Son of man will take those things away from the community. And, not surprisingly, they will be judged and thrown into the fire, and "the righteous [true Matthean Jews] will shine like the sun in the kingdom of their father" (13:43).

## Why Parables?

In between the parable of the sower (13:1–9) and its interpretation (13:18–23), Jesus is asked to provide an explanation of why he teaches in parables (13:10–17). In Matthew it is explicitly the disciples who ask Jesus about his parabolic teaching. Matthew's answer includes both Marcan and Q material. This question was raised earlier in the Gospel tradition, at least by Mark's time. Matthew takes Mark's lead, but alters the answer to suit his understanding of the disciples.

Jesus is quoted as saying his parabolic speech is "for those out-side" (Mark 4:11), or Matthew's "them" (*ekeinois*) in verse 11. Matthew's disciples make clear in 13:10 that they are not taught in the obtuse language of parables. "Why," they ask, "do you speak to them [*autois*] in parables?" Luke (8:10) and Matthew have Jesus respond, "To you it has been given to know the *mys-teries* [plural in Matthew and Luke, singular in Mark 4:11], of the kingdom of heaven, but to them it has not been given." The explanation, though seeming inherently unfair, is clear. Disciples receive a more prosaic and easily understood message, while outsiders must hear in the confounding language and imagery of the parable. Matthew has no trouble with the special tutoring the disciples receive. This happens throughout his Gospel, and he has inserted here, in contrast to Mark, the explicit importance of the disciples "knowing" (13:11). This is an important theme, as we have noted already, for Matthew's community. Disciples, members, or *followers* do understand Jesus' message, are well taught, and are in effect "scribes trained for the kingdom of heaven" (13:52).

This is quite a change from the Marcan portrayal of discipleship. One may almost say Mark celebrates the mystery and shrouded nature of faith and following. It has often been noted that the disciples in Mark are among the slowest learners in his story. As several scholars have observed, Matthew consistently cleans up Mark's picture of the disciples. There is much they are unsure of, and much that they (most notably, Peter) get wrong. And, as is widely recognized, even — or particularly — at the resurrection, ambiguity, fear, and uncertainty persist. Fear is a prominent feature in Mark's Gospel. It may be taken as a sign that one is getting close to the meaning of the story when one is afraid. But knowledge, quite unlike Matthew, is not something to be prized in the earliest Gospel.

But the answer of the Gospel writers to the question about the obfuscating nature of parabolic language is that those who hear the parables are outsiders. Their instruction is purposefully obtuse. All Gospel writers try to buttress this argument through recourse to Isaiah 6:9–10. Even John offers a truncated citation of Isaiah 6:9–10 in John 9:39 and 12:40. Matthew provides a full citation of the passage in 13:13–15. Mark, however, does not follow his own argument from Isaiah too rigidly because in Mark 4:13 Jesus complains about the disciples' failure to understand the parable. This exchange is not present in Matthew and Luke. It should be remembered, however, that the disciples not understanding it is as important to Mark as the disciples understanding it is to Matthew. Matthew would be clearly uncomfortable with Mark 4:13 and this, indeed, is not present in Matthew's version in 13:18. Matthew may think the confusion in Mark's version comes from Mark 4:10. Matthew makes it clearer than Mark that parables are taught to "them" (*autois*), and not to the disciples. And if the disciples hear a parable they either understand it, or are given private instruction to insure their comprehension. Matthew and Luke conclude their explanations about parables — and in Matthew's case his biblical citation — with a *makarioi:* "Blessed are your eyes for they see, and your ears, for they hear. Truly, I say to you, many prophets and righteous people have longed to see what you see, and did not see it, and to hear what you hear, and did not hear it." The Matthean understanding of Jesus is not incorrect or aberrant; it is, rather, revealed. Many have tried or waited to hear and see what their community now sees and hears. Because of this special position, Matthew insists, they are blessed. Not so with the outsiders and those who do not see, hear, or, in particular, understand.

Matthew, however, does not have a refined and consistent theory of Jesus' parables. For example, in contrast to this explanation in chapter 13, people other than the disciples do understand parables elsewhere in the Gospel, as in the case of the chief priests and Pharisees in 21:45. The parable of the house built on a rock in 7:24ff. may perhaps serve as another example, though "the crowds" seem more like an afterthought in the Sermon, which is really about the internal life of the community. But we do have conflicting views of how parables function in Matthew. Is it language only insiders are allowed to hear and receive and at the same time intended to confound the outsider (13:11)? Or are the parables of Jesus understood, though perhaps interpreted differently, by friend and foe alike within the

Gospel and Matthew's setting? On this point the author is not consistent.

The question and explanation(s) about parables probably do not belong to the words of Jesus, though many of the parables may. This question is a result of communities of Jesus followers trying to make sense out of polyvalent and ambiguous stories that had been part of their traditions about Jesus from very early on. The first place most authors and scribes from these communities looked for answers to such questions was scripture. The citation from Isaiah 6, quoted in some form in all four Gospels, represents one answer to this question. This scriptural citation and the recitation of it up until the time of Matthew, Luke, and John chooses to make parables "insider language." It is our language, our meanings and interpretation, and our images that we control, so this answer to the parable question maintains.

The communities of Jesus followers took parables as defining elements in their social and intellectual life. This is one identifying characteristic of Jesus-centered communities. The shadowy and figurative language and stories of Jesus told within the communities became mythopoetic badges of identity for the group. Each story reinforced their status as insiders and comprehenders — no matter how arbitrary the interpretation — and at the same time punctuated the boundary between their group and those who did not give assent or "understand." When a parable of Jesus was told within one such group it would have been met with a chorus of silent nods, much like a twentieth-century audience hearing a Latin Mass, affirming its content and meaning, knowing it is about *them,* but not really knowing what on earth it means.

Once again the parables are not about Gentiles emphasizing the rejection and subsequent judgment of Jesus by the Jews, as Kingsbury has said, following (it appears) Lohmeyer and others. There is no way a neutral reader can take Matthew's *autois* ("them") in 13:10 as "a *terminus technicus* designating the Jews." Therefore, one cannot read the Matthean parables as portraying "the Jews as a people who stand outside the circle of those who participate in the joy and salvation of the Messianic age." Such readings are not supported, and should not be imported into the text. These interpretations lead to destructive and lethal beliefs and attitudes about Jews and Judaism within Christianity.

When we, as did they, read the parables we are confronted with imaginative untethered speech. That is, the nature of the parables, even more than the imprecise nature of usual discourse, is loosed from the confines of usual meanings. There is then, as A. Wilder has said, a "freshness" to parables because of their openness and polyvalence. The potential for new meaning is always there. The church tried, as evidenced in the question of the parables, to corral this unconventional manner of speech and make sense out of it. One of the first questions to emerge among Jesus followers was "Why parables?" The citation from Isaiah and the language of insider/outsider attributed to parables is an attempt to answer this immediate and understandable question. But the communities also saw in these stories vestiges of Jesus' person and imagination, and what they held to be his revolutionary teaching, though concrete and earthy, about life, faith, and the future. For many of the first followers those lessons were in the shadows, at times obscure and uncertain. Wilder quoted Shakespeare when thinking about these early attempts at recalling and interpreting the parables: "What is thy substance, whereof art thou made, that thousands of strange shadows on thee tend." The shadows were characteristic of Jesus and his teaching very early on in the life of different Jesus movements. This figurative instruction, possessing multiple and elusive meanings, also became a hallmark of the community members. Although ambiguous and difficult to tame, in the hearing of the parables these followers could listen and nod, knowing that these were their stories and they, whatever they meant, understood them.

## Other Parables of Growth

Matthew continues his parable chapter with one of his own, the so-called parable of the tares or the parable of the good and bad wheat. Again, this is a Matthean parable of growth. He begins the parable by likening the kingdom of heaven to this story.

The language here is that of a simile. The parables are not to be taken as absolutes or as direct representations of the kingdom of heaven. The parable may be "like" (*homoiothae*) the kingdom of heaven. We are aware in this Gospel that the phrase "kingdom of heaven" carries both eschatological and contemporary ethical connotations. That is, the phrase "kingdom of heaven" refers to a future hope for the community following the fulfillment of their expectations, but it also stands for the community *now*. In this parable the emphasis falls on the now. There is an eschatological aspect to this parable but it is referred to as "the harvest."

In the kingdom of heaven there is both good and bad. We know, then, that this is before the putative judgment or end. The key feature of this parable is how the problem of the Matthean *corpus mixtum,* that is, the presence of both good and bad in the community of the kingdom of heaven, should be handled. An enemy (*exthros*) sowed weeds among the wheat in the field of the owner while he slept. Servants (*douloi*) of the householder came and notified him of the weeds. They also were unaware of the enemies' attack on their crop. An enemy person (*anthropos*) has done this. The "anthropos" in 13:28 should be rendered here in light of the subsequent interpretation and not skipped, as in some translations.

We have seen evil or enemy forces in the fields corrupting the crops before in 13:19, but there the more usual Matthean term for evil, *poneros,* is used. This is a rare term for Matthew and tends to denote a human enemy or opponent. This is stressed in 13:28 with the addition of *anthropos* to *exthros* or "enemy." The servants ask if they should go out and separate the wheat from weeds now. The householder says no. There is fear that some of the good wheat will be taken up with the bad weeds. Wait, therefore, for the harvest, when the weeds will be bound up and burned and the wheat will be gathered into the householder's barn (13:30). The interpretation of the parable says the enemy is the devil (13:39). But the language of 13:28 suggests a more human opposition to the householder and his servants. In this version of the story human enemies, not evil ones, have sown bad seeds in the fields of the household. Matthean opponents are to be blamed for the *corpus mixtum* that presently characterizes the Matthean church. Yes the evil one, the devil, is ultimately responsible, Matthew would believe, because his opposition is in actuality "children of Ghenna" (23:15). Yet the human agency involved in this Matthean internal struggle between good and bad influences and instruction cannot be avoided in 13:28.

Matthew's counsel should not be missed on this point. Not unlike chapter 18, in this parable Matthew urges restraint on the subject of judging the membership. One does judge in Matthew's church, but that takes a very long time and involves a protracted process of observing the actions or "fruits" of the member. Matthew encourages forgiveness within the group, to be exceedingly deliberate in judgment and, if at all possible, hold off until the eschaton or, big time, when all will be judged, gathered, or destroyed.

This parable is the only other parable to have an accompanying interpretation besides the parable of the sower. Like the sower, roles are assigned to each part of the story. It is the disciples again, like the start of the sower interpretation, who come to Jesus while he is in "the house" at Capernaum, and ask about the meaning of the parable in 13:36–43. Jesus says the sower is the Son of man, the field is the world, the good seeds are the sons of the kingdom, and the weeds are the sons of the evil one, the enemy is the devil, the harvest is the close of the age, and the reapers are the angels.

Not all the dramatic personae in the original parable are accounted for in the later interpretation. The men, the servants, and the householder from the original story are not provided a place in the interpretation. "The Son of Man will send his angels, and they will gather out of his kingdom all causes of offense, or stumbling, and doers of lawlessness." Some translations render this phrase from 13:41 "sin and evil doers." Both terms here, *skandala* and *poiountas tan anomian,* are part of Matthew's particular vocabulary. These are elements that cause members to stumble or fall away (*skandala*) and "people who commit lawlessness." Both of these terms signal concrete actions with which, we can see through the course of the Gospel, the Matthean church is struggling. *Anomia,* or lawlessness, is something

over which Matthew expresses great concern. His community
is not *anomia;* far from it. There are those who have accused
the community of lawlessness (5:17ff.), but that is only because
they do not really understand the law and the prophets. Matthew 7:23 is an example of Matthew's concern over "lawlessness"
within the community and is nearly synonymous with 13:41.
The notion of *anomia* does not suggest the presence of a particular party who hold to a certain, more liberal interpretation
of the law within Matthew's church. Groups as different from
one another as the so-called charismatics in Matthew 7:23ff. and
the scribes and Pharisees are *anomia.* "Woe to you scribes and
Pharisees . . . you also outwardly appear righteous to others, but
within you are full of hypocrisy and lawlessness" (*hupocriseos kai
anomias;* 23:28).

Lawlessness is any type of action, behavior, or attitude that
runs counter to the Matthean interpretation of the law and the
nature of following as taught by Jesus. Some of the lawless have
made their way into the Matthean community and are influenc-
ing the good seeds. Here Matthew encourages others to hold off
on deciding just who are the true Matthean members and who
are the false ones who "look righteous on the outside but inside
are hypocrites and lawless." The parable and interpretation of
the good and bad wheat hardly conceal the issues within Matthew's setting. The influences in his context, largely those of the
Matthean opponents or "sons of the evil one," are having an impact within Matthew's own community. His church is made up,
he believes, of those who actually and honestly embrace the precepts of the group, and those who are not true members of the
community. This is not an unusual situation for any human organization, much less a church. Matthew decides to let the great
harvest deal with these issues and people and, for the sake of
the overall safety of the other members, forego any attempt at
rooting out those who are becoming partial to the Matthean
opponents.

Prior to the interpretation of the parable of the good and bad
wheat Matthew inserts two other growth parables in 13:31–33.
One, the parable of the mustard seed, is taken from Mark, and
the other, the parable of the leaven, comes from Q. Both para-

bles assert the subtle and modest presence of the kingdom of heaven. In time, the presence, impact, and ministry of the kingdom ("the birds of the air come and make nests in its branches") can be demonstrated. Right now, the kingdom of heaven is present but quietly, subtly, and in surprising ways.

Although the Matthean community constitutes a minority in their setting—theologically and politically, and almost certainly numerically—they are having a small and gradual impact. This is the claim of these two short parables. In time the community of the kingdom of heaven will grow and fulfill its hopes and the claims it makes about Israel's future. To Matthean detractors or those with doubts, this would sound like wishful thinking. But this helps supporters gauge their expectations. These parables encourage them to look for signs of the kingdom in subtle and inconspicuous events. Small gains and very minor victories, in light of these parables, can now be interpreted as a little more growth on the part of the kingdom of heaven. This is how all movements who view their struggle as one of good against evil have had to interpret their impact on the world.

Before moving on to three other parables, Matthew includes another brief apology for Jesus teaching in parables. Matthew found another passage from Psalm 77:2 in the LXX. The Psalm begins, "Draw near my people to my law [*nomon*], incline your ears to the words of my mouth. I will open my mouth in parables; I will utter what has been pronounced from the beginning; that which we have heard and known and our fathers have told us" (LXX Psalm 77:1–3). Matthew copies 77:2a exactly as the LXX has it. Matthew's version of 77:2b, however, bears little relation to LXX 77:2b, certainly in vocabulary. Matthew continues, "I will utter [*ereugomai,* lit. "roar," or "pour forth"], what has been hidden [*krupto*] from the foundation of the world." The LXX has more simply, "I will utter what has been pronounced from the beginning."

I do not know where Matthew came up with his version of Psalm 77:2b found in 13:35b. It is, however, mistaken to think that at Matthew's time the LXX was in any final form. The myth of the translation of the Hebrew Bible into Greek found in the mid-second- to mid-first-century B.C.E. document *The Letter of*

*Aristeas* portrays the translation and reception of the LXX as happening in one specific moment in history. It required a long process for the LXX text to be settled and generally received. It is, in fact, misleading to speak of *the* LXX. There were many versions of the LXX in Matthew's day. Josephus is an interesting case in point. Which texts and languages Josephus referred to when citing scripture is still contested among scholars. L. Feldman maintains that at points Josephus used a Greek translation of the Hebrew, some form of the so-called LXX, but one we cannot always place. Matthew's situation, in this instance, is similar to Josephus. Matthew is copying a version of the LXX which at Psalm 77:2b is quite different from the LXX text we know today.

In any case, in Matthew's view LXX Psalm 77:2 is one more scriptural citation that supports Jesus' unusual mode of instruction as it is portrayed in the Gospel. Matthew treats this as a fulfillment citation and uses his usual catchword, *pleroma,* to emphasize this. Matthew claims in 13:35a that Jesus' teaching in parables is the fulfillment of his version of LXX Psalm 77:2. It is the crowds (*oxlois*) who receive everything in parables, while the disciples receive a clearer and more personal form of instruction. Indeed, "He said nothing to them [the crowds] without a parable" (13:34).

## A Treasure, a Pearl, and a Net Full of Fish

The three concluding parables of chapter 13 are the parables of the hidden treasure, the pearl, and the net (Matt. 13:44–50). The hidden treasure and the single pearl emphasize the unequaled value of the kingdom of heaven. Upon finding the treasure or the pearl, the subjects sell all they have to possess that one thing: a field and a pearl respectively. The kingdom of heaven is worth sacrificing or giving up everything for it. It is not unlikely that many Matthean Jews felt as though they had done just that. Matthean Judaism caused divisions within their homes and villages, it put them on the outs with local leaders and authorities, and created considerable conflict in their setting and in their lives.

These parables attempt to reinforce that, yes, in fact, it was worth it for these followers to have done just that.

The hidden treasure of the kingdom of heaven (13:44) does not suggest esoteric or hidden knowledge. This would be more compatible with Mark's Gospel than Matthew. The hidden treasure suggests more the surprise of the kingdom of heaven when one becomes a follower and disciple in Matthew's church. In participating in the life of the community of the kingdom of heaven, much to his surprise and joy, the man has found something of greater value than anything else he has. The hidden treasure and leaven (13:33) underscore the great surprise of the value and joy found in the kingdom.

The parable of the net is a parable about the "end of the age" and is related to the interpretation of the parable of the tares. The net, like the field in the parable of the tares, is full with both good and bad fish. "So it is," Matthew says in this story, which is unique to his Gospel, "at the close of the age" (13:48). As in 13:41, "The angels will come and separate the evil from the righteous, and throw them into the furnace of fire; there men will weep and gnash their teeth" (13:49–50). Matthew does anticipate some sort of end to this present order and age. He expects judgment for the evil and lawless. But this is not the Matthean community's concern. Twice in parables only found in Matthew he has said at the end angels will come and separate out the evil from the righteous (i.e., Matthean disciples), and throw out causes of sin and all people who commit lawless deeds.

The kingdom of heaven is like this full net. The kingdom of heaven now is full of all kinds (*pantos genous*): good, bad, the lawless, and the righteous. No community, once it decides to include people, can claim to be without problems, struggles, and even corrupting and destructive elements. Such is the case with the kingdom of heaven even now; that is Matthew's community. It is significant that Matthew reminds his audience that there are some good and righteous people mixed in with the offensive and lawless. One must be careful not to throw the proverbial baby out with the bath water. Matthew is here encouraging discretion and caution in the judgments the community will make. The community is a mixed bag. Matthew does not believe it is ultimately the task of the community to purge the *anomia*. Matthew's people should wait for the judgment he believes will come at the end of the age, when this present order passes and the order he has been advocating and arguing for prevails.

Matthew is not, as we shall see, perfectly consistent on this point. There are judgments the community makes. The disciples in Matthew are invested with unusual authority to make such judgments. Life and order within communities are never as neat as one would like. There are principles and guidelines, but there are also extenuating circumstances. At some point in time Matthean Judaism had to come to grips with the reality that some decisions, judgments, and "throwing out" had to be done. Matthew confronts that reality in chapter 18. Also, the disciples, and whomever they represent in the contemporary Matthean setting, are given authority from Jesus for the expressed purpose of making some very tough and weighty judgments. The parables of the tares and the net offer a principle Matthew is advocating but one that cannot, in every instance within the long life of a community, be followed.

## The Educated Scribe and the Kingdom of Heaven

Matthew 13:51–52 has been taken by some scholars as self-referential verses added by the Evangelist to summarize this teaching section. In many ways these verses serve as apt summaries of the author's philosophy of Matthean Judaism and not just a summary of the parable chapter. "Have you understood all this? They said to him 'Yes.' And he said to them, 'Therefore every scribe trained for the kingdom of heaven is like a householder who brings out of his treasure what is new and what is old.' " Matthew begins the verse by asking rhetorically if the disciples have understood all of this. They say, of course, "yes." Again, the well-trained scribe is one who does indeed understand what is being taught, and can act on it. The disciples' understanding (*sunakate*) determines that they truly are "scribes trained for the kingdom of heaven."

A scribe (*grammateus*) was originally understood within the

Greek world as a clerk or secretary. The scribe was a learned or lettered individual who performed official tasks for a person or institution like, as Liddell and Scott tell us, Thucydides' *grammateus tou sunedriou,* or "secretary of the council." The second/third-century C.E. Apollonius of Tyana (*Philostratus* 1.352, 7) contains a similar use of the term referring to an official in Ephesus. Acts 19:35 uses "scribe" to describe the "town clerk" who quieted the crowd in Ephesus in connection with a riot caused by the Apostle Paul. These are people concerned with administrative duties, finance, and taxation; frequently, they were legal experts. The term in Greek above all draws attention to the fact that these people are literate; they can read, count, add, subtract, keep records, and help interpret when that is necessary.

The Hebrew Bible contains many references to scribes (*soper*). Judges 5:14 contains a reference to a *soper,* and the chief scribe in the Jerusalem court was one concerned with finance and administration (1 Kings 22; Jer. 36:10). And Baruch, who served as Jeremiah's amanuensis, was an influential scribe (Jer. 36:32).

In the second-temple period "scribes" obtained a prominent role and status within society. This was frequently due to the fact that they could read, write, interpret, and were knowledgeable about the law. The importance of the scribe parallels the importance of the law, as in the case of Ezra 7:6, 1 Enoch 72–82, Ben Sirach 38:24–39:11, and so on. In the post-70 period scribes continued to grow in importance, and within Jewish groups and society their role was further associated with the law, though not necessarily at the expense of other administrative functions.

Josephus refers to scribes of various social status (*J.W.* 1.479, 529; 5.532). The importance of the scribe is seen in post-destruction literature like 4 Ezra and 2 Baruch and the renaissance of these two scribal figures, Ezra and Baruch, in other apocryphal and pseudepigraphical literature from this period. The Mishna refers to scribes often and in association with legal disputes, but their authority is not always viewed as equal to the sayings and rulings of rabbis (*m. 'Or.* 3:9; *m. Sanh.* 11:3; *m. Yad* 3:2; *m. Kelim* 13:7; *m. Tohar.* 4.7).

In his fixing on the term and image of the scribe as an ideal figure for the community Matthew immediately posits education, training, and learning as goals — if not requirements — for the community members. These, of course, are the distinguishing features of the scribe. The members of Matthew's church, however, are "scribes trained for the kingdom of heaven." This is what distinguishes them from scribes for other communities (cf. Matt. 7:29).

The term for "trained" (*mathateutheis*) is a form of the word for "disciple," and closely related to the name of the book. A disciple, a follower and member of this group, is one who is also in "training." The disciple in Matthew is one who has much to learn. Again, there is little mystery in Matthew, but a lot to be mastered. This is the student's Gospel. Knowledge, study, understanding, and correct interpretation of the law are vital elements in the members' training. Members are debaters with others, whose views they encounter in their setting and city, and they are prepared to assume administrative and judicial functions that, most likely, "their scribes" now control and execute. At the closing of this age, Matthew's scribes will assume those roles and positions of teaching and authority. In their preparation they take out of their "house" things that are "new and old" (13:52), representing the traditions, laws, and promises of ancient Israel going back to Abraham, Moses, and David, as well as the new interpretation and fulfillment of these things the community has found in Jesus.

Matthew concludes this chapter with the story of Jesus' rejection at his own country or town (Matt. 13:53–58). The Greek term here is *patris,* which means "region," "home country," or "town." In German works until the 1950s this term was rendered *vaterland,* or "fatherland," but is now usually rendered *heimat,* or "region," as in the case of J. Gnilka's commentary on Mark and the parallel passage there.

Only Luke makes it explicit that the rejection takes place in Nazareth (Luke 4:16 ‖ Mark 6:1–6). Matthew has inserted his characteristic "their" (*auton*) into Mark's verse "he taught them in the synagogue." Matthew has deleted the sabbath controversy present in Mark. Matthew had his requisite sabbath conflicts earlier, as we have already seen. His insertion of the pronoun "their" into his Marcan source highlights the rejection that is about to occur. "Their" places are those places where his teaching does not prevail. It is the assumption of the writer, often made explicit, that this is because the current leaders and opposition have influenced the crowds.

The crowds are "astonished at this wisdom and mighty works" (*sophia auta kai ai dunameis*) and ask, "Where did he get this?" (13:54). Jesus is recognized as "the carpenter's son" (Mark says Jesus is a carpenter; Mark 6:3), and the crowd recalls the names of those in his family, including mother, four brothers, and his sisters (13:55–56). Their familiarity with Jesus' family suggests Nazareth as the site of the rejection. In Matthew the crowd asks again, "Where did this man get this?" The question from Matthew's crowd underscores the claim that Jesus must get "all this" from God, since they know his family, his background, and "they [the family] are all with them." They are aware of Jesus' ordinary upbringing and beginning. Where, then, did he get the wisdom and the power? Matthew is offering yet another argument for the authority of Jesus' actions and teaching. Even those who know Jesus best assume he got this from somewhere, and it surely wasn't Nazareth, the village crowds, or his family. But they ultimately "take offense at him" (*skandalizonto*). The claim to wisdom and power cannot be accepted by these people because of the familiar face put on it. Because of this "unbelief [*apistian;* 13:58], he did not do many works of power there." Jesus explains this by quoting an apparently well-known aphorism, "A prophet is not without honor, except in his own house" (13:57). A variant of this is found in Mark 6:4, Luke 4:24, John 4:44, *Gospel of Thomas* 31, and P. *Oxy.* 1:5. Again, the rejection of the message of Jesus and, by extension, the Matthean community continues to be an issue. Even those who knew Jesus best did not embrace what he had to say. This is a problem within the early life of the Jesus movements. Matthew and a number of writers from other Jesus movements enlist a familiar wise saying to support and defend what happened to Jesus on an apparently well-known visit home. Although his wisdom and power are visible, the crowd is uncertain of its origin. This may have scared them. Jesus once again, as in his saying to John in 11:6, has become the stumbling block or cause of offense. Jesus then returns,

based on 14:13, to his center along the eastern edge of Lower
Galilee and never returns to his *patria*.

## Further Reading

Bultmann, R. *The History of the Synoptic Tradition*. Rev. ed. Trans.
    J. Marsh. San Francisco: Harper and Row, 1963.
Cope, L. *Matthew: A Scribe Trained for the Kingdom of Heaven*. Washing-
    ton, D.C.: Catholic Biblical Association, 1976.
Crossan, D. *Finding Is the First Act: Trove Folktales and Jesus' Treasure
    Parable*. Semeia Supplements 9. Missoula, Mont.: Scholars Press,
    1979.
———. *In Parables: The Challenge of the Historical Jesus*. New York:
    Harper and Row, 1973.
Dodd, C. H. *The Parables of the Kingdom*. London: Fontana, 1961.
Feldman, L. *Josephus and Modern Scholarship*. New York: de Gruyter,
    1984.
Gnilka, J. *Das Evangelium Nach Markus (Mk.1–8, 26)*. EKKNT 2.1. Zürich:
    Benziger, 1978.
Jellicoe, S. *The Septuagint and Modern Study*. Oxford: Clarendon Press,
    1968.
Jeremias, J. *The Parables of Jesus*. 2nd rev. ed. Trans. S. H. Hooke. New
    York: Scribner's, 1972.
Kingsbury, J. D. *The Parables of Jesus in Matthew 13*. Richmond, Va.:
    John Knox, 1969.
Meyer, M. *The Gospel of Thomas: The Hidden Sayings of Jesus*. San
    Francisco: HarperCollins, 1992.
Overman, J. A. "The Diaspora in the Modern Study of Ancient Ju-
    daism." In *Diaspora Jews and Judaism: Essays in Honor of, and in
    Dialogue with, A. Thomas Kraabel,* ed. J. A. Overman and R. S.
    MacLennan, 63–78. Atlanta: Scholars Press, 1992.
Schweizer, E. "Observance of the Law and Charismatic Activity in
    Matthew." *NTS* 16 (1970): 213–30.
Van Segbroeck, F. "Jésus rejeté par sa patrie (Mt 13, 54–58)." *Biblica*
    49 (1968): 167–98.
Wilder, A. N. *Early Christian Rhetoric: The Language of the Gospel*.
    Cambridge: Harvard University Press, 1971.
———. *Jesus' Parables and the War of Myths*. Philadelphia: Fortress,
    1982.

## Chapter Eight

# Open Conflict and Political Alignments — 14:1–16:12

---

### Herod Antipas and the Death of John

Matthew 14:1–12 takes up the relationship between Herod Antipas, John the Baptist, and Jesus once again. In 14:1 Matthew correctly refers to Antipas as tetrarch or, literally, "Ruler of a Fourth." After the death of Herod the Great in 4 B.C.E. his kingdom was divided between his four sons. Herod Antipas was given control of Galilee and Perea until his death in 39 C.E. In the Marcan version Antipas is called a *basileus,* or king, but this is not technically correct (Mark 6:14). However, Matthew also calls Antipas king in 14:9. It may well have been that these ancient writers were less aware or interested in the precise administrative and political hierarchy (tetrarch, ethnarch, king), and viewed these terms, especially *basileus,* as meaning the man, or new or next man, in charge. One must not forget the colonial political reality that cast such a dramatic shadow over Roman Palestine. This reality colors virtually every document and movement we can recover from this period. This is also, if not particularly, the case with Gospels like Matthew's.

The story of John vividly recalls for us the political realities of speaking up or out, of leading a movement, or asserting objection or opinion in first-century Palestine. Jesus' popularity reached the tetrarch Antipas. Matthew placed the belief that Jesus is John the Baptist raised from the dead in Antipas's mouth. Mark's version shows people gathered around Antipas offering theories on the identity of Jesus. In Matthew it is Herod who says to his servants, "This is John the Baptist raised from the dead; that is why these powers are at work in him" (14:2). This phrase is also reminiscent of the questions from the crowds in Nazareth only a few verses earlier: "Where did he get all this [power and wisdom]?"

At this point Matthew seems to have a sort of narrative lapse. When this segment of the Gospel begins John is dead. Matthew 14:3ff. begins telling the story of John's imprisonment and death. But in 14:13 Jesus' ministry picks up again: "When Jesus heard [about John's death] he withdrew from there in a boat to a lonely place apart." In 14:3 John's death is an event that has already taken place. In 14:13 the story continues with the death as a present and pivotal part of the narrative. Mark does not make this synchronic slip in the narrative.

Matthew 14:3–12 tells the version of John's imprisonment and death current among Jesus movements in the first century. In the account found in the synoptic Gospels (Mark 6:17–29; Luke 3:19–20), followers of Jesus believed John was imprisoned for confronting Herod for marrying his brother's wife, Herodias. Consequently, Herodias held a grudge against John and once he was in prison schemed to have him beheaded. Herod wanted to kill John but "he feared the people because they held him to be a prophet" (14:5). Mark records, somewhat differently, that *Herod* feared John, knowing that he was a righteous and holy man, and kept him safe. In Mark it sounds as though Herod regularly entertained conversations with John and enjoyed them (Mark 6:20). This more positive portrait of Herod Antipas is missing in Matthew.

In a story familiar to many, Herodias's daughter danced for Herod on his birthday. He was greatly pleased and in a moment of excessive royal largess promised to "give her whatever she might ask" (14:7). The girl's mother prompted her to ask for the head of John the Baptist on a platter. Herod followed through on his pledge and ordered John beheaded. John's disciples took the body and buried it; and they went and told Jesus (14:12).

There is only a hint of this version of John's imprisonment

and death in the Gospels in Josephus, *Antiquities* 18.109–19. However, Josephus provides some other information about him which does impact our reading of Matthew. Josephus mentions Herod falling for his brother's wife, Herodias. They agreed to marry. What is significant in this section of *Antiquities* is the strife it caused among Arabia, Judea, and Rome, because Herod was already married to the daughter of King Aretas of Arabia. (Herod's grandfather Antipater had very good relations with the Arabian royal family while he was in power during the days of the late Roman Republic. Herod the Great and his sons bene-fited from this political foundation formed by Antipater.) While Herod was in Rome, Aretas's daughter made a run for the bor-der, having learned that Herod intended to marry Herodias and get rid of her. She made her way to Machaerus on the border of Aretas's and Herod's territory on the Dead Sea. *Antiquities* 18.112 states, "Machaerus was at that time subject to her father." In other words, having learned of Herod's plans his then-wife headed for home and for safety. This, along with a border dis-pute, Josephus says, was the beginning of discord between Herod and Aretas. This is the most significant part of this story for Jose-phus, given his constant concern for stability and concord to prevail in the region.

In the context of this story Josephus mentions John, his im-prisonment and death. The troops of Herod and Aretas clashed somewhere near the present Golan Heights, perhaps ancient Gamala (*Ant.* 18.113). In the battle "the whole of Herod's army was destroyed" through the work of some informants. Josephus adds here that many Jews believed Herod's army was wiped out by divine vengeance because of his treatment of John, surnamed the Baptist. This is where Josephus provides his description of John and his program.

Josephus describes John as a *agathon andra* (a good man), that he exhorted other Jews (*Ioudaiois*) to live virtuously, to ex-hibit justice (*dikaiosyne*) toward others and practice piety toward God, and "to come together in baptism." These are all posi-tive attributes from Josephus and describe John in terms any good Roman would support or embrace. "In his view," writes Josephus, this was a necessary preliminary if baptism was to be acceptable to God. They must not employ it [baptism] to gain pardon for whatever sins [*hamartadon*] they committed, but as a consecration of the body implying that the soul was already thoroughly cleansed by right behavior [*dikaiosyne*]. When others too joined the crowds about him, because they were aroused to the highest degree by his sermons, Herod became alarmed. Eloquence that had so great an effect on people might lead some to sedition. (*Ant.* 118.116–18)

This fear in Herod caused him, according to Josephus, "to strike first," and get rid of John before his work led to an uprising. Herod brought John in chains to Machaerus and had him put to death there. "The Jews held the belief [*doxa*] that the destruction of Herod's army [at the hands of Aretas's] was visited upon him by God as a verdict against Herod and a vindication of John" (*Ant.* 18.119).

There are several important features of Josephus's report about the Baptist when held alongside of Matthew's Gospel. Josephus makes no explicit mention of John upbraiding Herod for his marriage to Philip's wife. However, Josephus does mention the event as a source of discord in the kingdom. It is striking that Josephus should go out of his way to claim that John's baptism was *not* a baptism for the forgiveness of sins, but rather one that implied that the body was already clean by right behavior (*dikaiosyne*). Where would Josephus get the idea that some would think John's baptism related to forgiveness and a change of direction? This comes almost out of nowhere in *Antiquities* 18. Josephus had some awareness of or had some contact with those who held this view of the Baptist's program; and this view of his program is not unlike that which we see in the Gospels (cf. Matt. 3:6, 8; Mark 1:5; Luke 3:8).

The end of *Antiquities* 18.117 reads like a polemic against those who viewed, or view, John's baptism as a call for change. Of course the Gospels make this aspect of John's message quite clear. He is calling for change in people's behavior (Luke 3:10–14), he calls for the forgiveness of sins (in direct contrast to

Josephus) and, in the words of Q, for repentance or *metanoia* (Matt. 3:8 || Luke 3:8). The citations from Isaiah in the Gospels (Mark 1:2; Matt. 3:3; Luke 3:4) denote significant change. John is preparing the way for this change and, indeed, is part of it. The fuller citation from Isaiah 40 recorded in Luke 3 suggests even a change in the natural order, as well as repentance, a change of behavior, and forgiveness of sins.

These actions associated with John in the Gospels are or would have been viewed as revolutionary in Josephus. His description of John, however accurate or tendentious, portrays him as more stable, encouraging of general and positive qualities within the people, and he does not have John confronting the political leader Herod. I think Josephus's description of John suggests he was aware of this other interpretation of John, which is closer to the Gospel picture. Josephus's account, in certain respects, counters this picture.

The notion that forgiveness of sins could be interpreted as politically threatening or revolutionary is noteworthy. It is important to Josephus that John's baptism is "not to gain pardon for sins, but as a consecration of the body implying that the soul was already cleansed through right behavior." Right behavior here is being good (*agathon*), virtuous (*arete*), practicing justice or righteousness (*dikaiosyne*), and pursuing *pietas* toward God. These are standard hellenistic virtues encouraged by John, according to Josephus, which are apparently already in place and operative in the people. Why is it important that these traits are already in place and that people need not "gain pardon for whatever sins they committed"?

The notions of repentance and forgiveness denote change. They imply there is something wrong with the present order. Remember, Josephus, the Gospel writers, or other Roman authors hardly mean personal salvation and forgiveness when they speak about "repentance" or "forgiveness of sins." In late antiquity, and in the Greco-Roman social world especially, as B. Malina has reminded us, people "measured themselves in relation to one another, not as autonomous individuals as in the modern West." Calls for repentance and forgiveness of sins then would have been viewed as calls for some demonstrable social change.

Terms like "forgiveness" and "repentance," so ensconced within the Christian tradition and so often repeated, are really disturbing calls for significant communal and civil transformation. The Gospels realize this in the use of these terms, and so does Josephus. It is for this reason he rather curiously emphasizes the absence of forgiveness and repentance in the message of the Baptist. The presence of these elements in the Baptist's, or anyone's, message is necessarily a call for change. It is change that Roman rulers and their employees fear and resist. Their job is to maintain stability and order. Both forgiveness and repentance run counter to those goals and objectives.

In an awkward verse at the start of *Antiquities* 18.119, Josephus mentions a form of the word for repentance, or literally, "a change of mind" (*metanoeiv*). In this passage Josephus says Herod decided to get rid of John before his speaking out led to an uprising (and) which would have involved (Herod) in a difficult situation which would "force upon him the realization of his mistake [*metanoeiv*]." In this context the "mistake" must involve something about dumping Aretas's daughter and marrying Philip's wife. This would be the only "repentance" Josephus could mean when speaking of Herod in association with John. He got rid of John to avoid an upheaval, and found himself in a difficult situation where he would (the phrase is awkward here) "have repentance forced upon him." Even Josephus implies that Herod should have repented for his actions. The repentance, mistake, or change of mind must have something to do with his new disruptive marriage and John's "word" or preaching. Josephus, too, most likely believed God judged Herod in the defeat of his troops. However, he could never be accused of this by the way he constructed the story: "The verdict of the Jews was that the destruction of Herod's army was a vindication of John, since God saw fit to inflict such a blow on Herod." If pressed by someone, Josephus could say he was only reporting the view "of the Jews." But why has he included it in the first place? This note of repentance from Herod in *Antiquities* 18.119 suggests that part of John's preaching, and what he was stirring up, had to do with the difficulty Herod's relationship with Herodias had made for the people. This is what

John would be fomenting. We cannot be certain, but it appears Josephus thought Herod Antipas was aware of his "sins." Antipas, therefore, acted to try to avoid "metanoia." Here is a rather indirect suggestion of what the Gospels were proclaiming explicitly.

Herod had John killed finally because he feared his words would lead to some form of sedition. The term here, *stasis,* is used in a number of places to denote a disturbance or lively argument in an assembly (Acts 15:2; 23:7; 24:5; 1 Clem. 1:1; 46:9; 57:1; *Ant.* 18.374), or an outright revolt (Mark 15:7; Luke 23:19; Acts 19:40; *Ant.* 20.117). It is in this second sense that *stasis* seems to be used in *Antiquities* 18.118. It was John's preaching and popularity, and perhaps his broaching the subject of Herod's dubious marriage, that did him in. Herod, according to Josephus, performed a preemptive strike on the Baptist and his growing movement in an attempt to head off a possible revolt. John's popularity with the people is stressed by Gospel writers in Jesus' question about the nature of John's baptism to the chief priests and elders (of the people) while in the temple in Jerusalem (Matt. 21:23 ‖ Mark 11:27 ‖ Luke 20:1).

According to Josephus, there was no indication that Herod feared the crowds in his decision to kill John. In fact, quite the contrary. He killed John because of his popularity. Herod wanted to keep the peace and, therefore, nipped the Baptist movement in the bud. It was the fear of sedition prompted by John's authority and popularity with the people that led to his demise. In the passion narrative Barabbas, whom Pilate putatively is willing to release instead of Jesus, is charged with *stasis,* or sedition, in Mark 15:7 and Luke 23:19. John's Gospel refers to Barabbas as a *lestes,* or bandit, which is the same term applied to Jesus in the arrest scene (Matt. 26:55 ‖ Mark 14:48 ‖ Luke 22:52). Matthew does not describe Barabbas, though he is mentioned in the scene with Pilate.

This discussion of John the Baptist, his description in Josephus and in the Gospels, is important because in John we probably have our closest parallel to what might have happened to Jesus and why. John's movement would have seemed similar to Jesus' to the Romans and other officials who were removed from the followers and communities associated with these popular leaders. Indeed, Matthew treats John's death as prefiguring Jesus' own death. John's death signals the open hostility that will be forthcoming from the political leaders aligned against the movement. What happened to John is going to happen to Jesus, and may in turn happen to the Matthean community.

Josephus implies it was a mistake for Herod to kill John. Josephus also makes John sound like a rather civil teacher of central Greco-Roman values. Both Josephus and the Gospels mention, or stress, that justice (*dikaiosyne*) is central to John's message, though what these authors meant by this term may have varied considerably. Josephus stresses John's was not a baptism for repentance and forgiveness of sins. This is perhaps the most notable difference between the Gospels and Josephus. Josephus makes a somewhat fine but crucial distinction between his version of John's baptism and one associated with sin and repentance. According to Josephus, John's baptism signifies qualities already present in people; they are qualities the Roman world, broadly speaking, embraced and celebrated. So viewed, John's baptism reinforces actions and an order already in place. The Gospels' version of John's message looks forward to change — eschatologically and ethically. A baptism of repentance and "forgiveness of sins" suggests change in one's behavior. Further, that change would have been on a social, collective, and political — as well as individual — level. Josephus hints at an example of "change" or repentance in describing Herod's thinking. His motivation for arresting John involved avoiding *metanoein*, whatever that meant for Herod in the tension involving Aretas, Herodias, and the popular opposition to his actions. It is the tension between change of behavior and structures on the one hand, and the desire to maintain the present order and mores on the other, that finally gets John, and plays a significant role in the death of Jesus. The forgiveness of sins declared by Jesus in Matthew's Gospel (cf. Matt. 1:21; 6:12–14; 9:2–6; 12:31–32; 18:21–35), which sounds so liberating to insiders, was taken by officials outside the movement as a dangerous and destabilizing political statement.

## Bread and Faith: The Feedings in Matthew

Matthew continues his narrative about John's death and its effect on Jesus in 14:13. When Jesus heard about John's death he withdrew by boat to a deserted place on his own. Luke records that Jesus withdrew to Bethsaida, whereas Matthew and Mark say simply that Jesus went to "a lonely place" (*eramon topon*). Matthew stresses Jesus being by himself, while Luke and Mark suggest the disciples were still with Jesus (Mark 6:32 || Luke 9:10). The impact of John's death on Jesus is highlighted by Matthew in placing Jesus both alone and in a lonely place after hearing the news. But crowds "followed him" on foot from the villages bordering the Sea of Galilee. Jesus then went ashore (Matt. 14:14ff.), saw the great crowd, and "had compassion on them." Matthew and Luke record Jesus healed their sick (Matt. 14:14 || Luke 9:11), while Mark records he "began to teach them many things" (Mark 6:34), something we might expect to hear from Matthew. In the verses that follow, Matthew supplies one of his feeding miracles.

Matthew provides two feeding stories in this section of his Gospel, 14:13–21 and 15:32–39. Both feedings begin with Matthew emphasizing Jesus' "compassion" for the crowd (*splagxnizomai*). In the first feeding this is because they need healing and in the second because they had been following "for three days" and have had nothing to eat. The second feeding provides a reason for the miracle. "I am unwilling," Jesus says, "to send them away lest they faint on the way" (15:32). In the first feeding the disciples encourage Jesus to send the crowd into the villages to buy food for themselves. In response Jesus says, "They need not go away; you give them something to eat" (14:16). In each instance the disciples have only a small amount of food. In the first feeding it is "five loaves and two fish," while in the second it is seven loaves and "a few small fish" (15:34).

The liturgical and ecclesial setting of these two feeding narratives can hardly be missed. Jesus commands the crowds to sit down on the ground or grass (14:19; 15:35), gives thanks (or blesses them in 14:19), breaks the loaves, and gives them to the disciples. The communal setting of the feedings is emphasized by three liturgical actions or verbs in quick succession: "he blessed," "he broke," "he gave" (Matt. 14:19; 15:36 ‖ Mark 6:41 ‖ Luke 9:16; John 6:11). This language reappears in the Last Supper in 26:26. In each feeding the food is given to the disciples, who in turn distribute it to the people. When the people finish they are able to collect twelve baskets full of leftover pieces. In Matthew's second feeding they collect seven baskets full of leftover broken pieces (15:37). All the authors agree that the number fed was about 5,000 (Matt. 14:21 ‖ Mark 6:44 ‖ Luke 9:14; John 6:10), noting the number was 5,000 "men" (*andres*); although Matthew clarifies this further with the phrase "besides women and children" (*xhoris gunaikon kai paidion*) in 14:21. In 15:38 Matthew changes this number to 4,000 men "besides women and children." Matthew provides a formal link between the two feeding stories with this uniform conclusion.

That early Jesus movements like Matthew's, and others that predate his Gospel, should have met together for meals, some form of worship, and teaching is not surprising, although in a different part of the world a communal meal and worship were part of the Corinthian church's life perhaps fifty years or more before the writing of Matthew's Gospel. Part of 1 Corinthians is devoted to disputes about the communal meal, as one can see in 11:23ff., where the liturgy for the meal is reiterated by Paul for the Corinthians.

As is widely recognized, a special eschatological meal was a central feature of the life of the Qumran community. These "messianic" or heavenly banquets in the Dead Sea Scrolls (1QS 6:4–5; 1QSa 2:11–22) were expressions of the community's hope in an imminent heavenly banquet. Matthew and Mark also add an eschatological element to their versions of the Last Supper (Matt. 26:29 ‖ Mark 14:25). In his version of the Last Supper Matthew once again adds the notion of the "forgiveness of sins" to his Marcan source. Matthew's belief in the notion of a heavenly banquet is given expression in Matthew 8:11–12 and 22:1–10. D. Harrington suggests that the background for the heavenly banquet and meal within second-temple Judaism is found in 1 Kings 4:42–44 and the story of the prophet Elisha feeding 100 men. In this Hebrew Bible miraculous feeding there is also some left after feeding 100 men. The heavenly banquet captures the hopes of these different communities that God will indeed provide for them, and that a day is coming when they can celebrate at ease and peace in their kingdom (Matt. 26:29 ‖ Mark 14:25).

The liturgical setting of the feedings reminds us also of the prayer the Matthean congregation said in their communal gatherings. In the Lord's Prayer the community connects bread and forgiveness (6:11–12). The material needs of the church are directly related to their spiritual and political needs in the connection Matthew provides between bread and forgiveness. In their gatherings, at some point after praying for both bread and forgiveness (from God and "their brothers"), the community "blessed, broke, and gave" each other bread. The disciples — that is, community members — gave the bread to one another as the feeding miracles indicated. The Matthean community believed Jesus started this ritual, based on Hebrew Bible stories and images, and the church continued to enact this ritual in their communal setting.

Many people have tied symbolic significance to the number of baskets in these two Matthean feeding stories, twelve and seven respectively. It has usually been held that 12 represents the twelve tribes of historic Israel and that, therefore, the feeding signifies an eschatologically renewed Israel. Similarly, the number 7 has represented the gentile world to some interpreters. It seems possible that 7 or 70 represents the Gentiles for the author Luke in both his Gospel (the sending of the seventy in Luke 10:1) and in Acts 6:1 (where seven "hellenists," in contrast to the "Hebrews," were selected to take care of their widows). Such an interpretation of the number of baskets in Matthew is, admittedly, possible. But there is not a great deal of evidence to support such a reading. A more plausible interpretation is that both 7 and 12 were symbolic, even hallowed, numbers within Matthew's biblical and cultural tradition. The selection of the numbers 12 and 7, rather than suggesting something about Israel and the nations specifically, denotes the involvement and hand of God. When one encounters these two numbers within the biblical tradition, including the Gospels, one is aware that God is at work.

## The Parable of the Fearful Church

Following the first feeding miracle Jesus "made the disciples get into the boat and go before him to the other side" (14:22). The Matthean disciples' boat was beaten by waves and the wind was against them (14:24).

> And in the fourth watch of the night he [Jesus] came walking to them on the sea. But when the disciples saw him walking on the sea, they were terrified, saying, "It is a ghost!" And they cried out for fear. But immediately he spoke to them saying, "Take heart, it is I; have no fear." (14:25–27)

Following these verses, which Matthew took from his Marcan source he adds some distinctive passages of his own involving his favorite dramatic persona, Peter.

In Matthew 14:27ff. Peter responded to Jesus by saying, "Lord, if it is you, call to me to come to you on the water." The familiar and popular scene of Peter coming to Jesus across the water follows in 14:29–33. When Peter saw the wind he "became afraid [*ephobatha*], and began to sink and cried out, saying, 'Lord save me.' Jesus reached out his hand and caught him, saying to him, 'O one of little faith why did you doubt?' When *they* [genitive plural of *autos*], got into the boat the wind ceased. And those in the boat worshiped him saying, 'Truly you are the Son of God.' "

This is the second incident in "the boat" for the disciples. As we noted briefly when discussing the first boat scene (8:23–27), Matthew's hand is evident in his shaping of these stories. In the first story Matthew alone describes the disciples getting into the boat as an act of *akolouthasan,* or following Jesus (8:23). The disciples' call in Luke (8:24) and question in Mark (4:38) become a prayer in the mouths of the disciples in Matthew: "Lord, save."

Also, Matthew makes this boat scene an example of little faith (*oligopistoi*), and through the story encourages the congregation to view threats and fear in the life of following differently. As Bornkamm asserted some time ago, Matthew has taken what was ostensibly a nature miracle and transformed it into a story about discipleship and the cycle of trial, fear, and rescue.

In this second boat story Peter emerges as a type for the follower in Matthew's community. Some of the same elements present in this story were present in the first. The little boat is beaten by the waves and has the wind against it. The disciples see "a phantom" or ghost, who turns out to be Jesus, walking toward them. This feature makes transparent the nature of this story as parable about the church's life following Jesus' death. As in the earlier boat story, they are terrified. In this story Jesus addresses the disciples, saying, "Take heart, it is I; have no fear" (14:27).

Peter, as if to symbolize the followers' attempt at trust, responds to Jesus' call to "come," and sets out on the water after him. He is soon overcome by fear (*ephobatha*) from the wind and starts to sink. Matthew puts the same exclamatory prayer in 8:25 in Peter's mouth in 14:30, "Lord, save me." Jesus reaches out his hand and catches him. While perhaps a noble attempt, the hydrawalk is a miserable failure. Again, the disciples, in this case Peter, model "little faith [*oligopiste*]" and doubt (14:31). This is as negative as Matthew gets about the behavior of the disciples in his Gospel. He frequently uses this term to describe inadequate responses to crises and fear (6:30; 8:26; 14:31; 16:8; 17:20).

That Peter serves as a type for discipleship *in this story* is demonstrated by Matthew in his use of "they" in verse 32. "And when *they* got into the boat, the wind ceased. And those in the boat worshiped him." Jesus' saving act brought not just Peter but "them" into the boat. After this saving act and calming of the wind those in the boat worshiped Jesus, saying, "Truly you are the Son of God" (cf. 27:54). H. Frankemölle and E. Schweizer have pointed out Peter's role as model for community leadership and a type for discipleship generally in Matthew's Gospel. Several verses in the Gospel — 19:27, 26:35, 26:40, and this verse, 14:32 — capture this second aspect of the function of Peter in Matthew. Although it is Peter who has come out of the boat responding to Jesus' call to come, it is the disciples ("they") who get hauled into the boat by Jesus. After this, "those in the boat" worship Jesus and call him "Son of God."

The communal and even liturgical features of the boat stories are quite transparent. There are prayers and liturgical formulas, christological titles are attributed to Jesus, he saves them from fear and trial, and, in the second story, they worship him. Matthew inherited the original boat story from Mark. But Matthew is the first interpreter of this tradition. He understands the story in a deeper, figurative sense as a fable about discipleship. He transforms the Marcan story, and building from that constructs a second narrative focusing on Peter which contains confessions, prayers, instruction about faith, and figuratively captures the perils and the thrill of following. When members' faith is paralyzed by danger or doubt the church of the kingdom of heaven is encouraged to find refuge in the protection they believe they receive from the "Lord who saves them."

These creative stories, and Matthew's allegorical interpretation of Mark's earlier stilling of the storm, have led commentators to think of these stories as Matthean narratives about "the little ship of the church." K. Goldammer drew attention to this interpretation of Matthew's boat stories in an article entitled "Navis ecclesiae." But apparently this interpretation goes back as far as Tertullian (*de Baptismo* 12). The fears and trials of Matthew's community emerge again with force in his construction of the stories of the boat church. His interpretive and narrative handiwork contains a number of lessons about discipleship and the nature of faith, but it signals also the crises the community at times feels surrounded by.

## Issues of Local Leadership: Who Is Breaking with Tradition?

Matthew 15:1–20 contains an extended debate with the Pharisees and scribes, and an exposition of Matthew's interpretation of certain crucial laws within his society. This story involves a legal dispute between Jesus and the Pharisees and scribes over unwashed hands and what constitutes pure and impure. This conflict story is really a dispute over local tradition and authority. Who will control behavior, possess legal authority, and determine what is proper or improper interpretation? To some modern readers this dispute may seem somewhat arcane and academic. This is hardly the case. The question about which set of traditions will be used to guide relationships and interaction — especially the most central of social activities until very recently, eating — and who will decide who is in conformity or not are fundamental questions of political and social life. These are the questions the Matthean dispute from 15:1ff. seeks to address.

Matthew has taken this story over from Mark 7. Mark uses this story to set aside the series of laws about which the Pharisees and scribes inquire. The Pharisees come to Jesus and ask, "Why do your disciples transgress the tradition of the elders [*paradosis ton presbuteron*]?" This is an appropriate and understandable question coming from the Pharisees. Josephus tells us that the Pharisees observe traditions (*paradosis*) not recorded in the law of Moses (*Ant.* 13.297). Some of these traditions were apparently banned for a time under John Hyrcanus (c. 120 B.C.E.) when he left the Pharisaic party and became a Sadducee. Josephus describes the Pharisaic adherence to a popular set of traditions.

> The Pharisees have delivered to the people a great many observances by the tradition from their Fathers, which are not written in the law of Moses; and for this reason the Sadducees reject them, and say that we are to honor those observances which are written word, not observing those which are derived from the tradition of our forefathers. Concerning these things great disputes and differences have risen among them.

It is precisely this sort of dispute that appears in Matthew 15:1ff. and Mark 7:1ff. Certain Jesus movements were clearly involved in this same rather central dispute. A. Baumgarten has pointed out how this Pharisaic-Sadducean contention continued well into the rabbinic period as the passage from *Abot Rabbi Nathan* (*ARN*) 5 demonstrates: "The Sadducees say: it is a tradition of the house of the Pharisees that they deny themselves [the pleasures] of this world, but in the world to come they will have nothing." The controversy between these two groups was strong enough earlier in the second-temple period to provoke a persecution of those who held to the Pharisaic traditions (*Ant.* 13.296). It may be recalled that these Pharisaic traditions were reinstated under Alexandra, the wife and widow of Alexander Jannai, when she assumed power in 76 B.C.E. This was a result of the political and administrative influence the Pharisees gained through her.

New evidence from Qumran points to these disputes being more widespread than we previously thought. J. Baumgarten, L. Schiffman, and others have pointed to several Qumran texts that may indeed reflect the Pharisaic-Sadducean controversy over purity and other halakhic points. The more recently discovered document 4QMMT, for example, catalogues at least twenty specific halakhic (pertaining to legal interpretation) disputes over the law. A. Baumgarten claims 1QH 4:14–15 contains a direct charge against the Pharisees using the code name "doresh halakot," claiming they follow the desires of their heart as opposed to the law of God. The arguments over law and tradition evident in the Gospels and Josephus appear also in these early documents from the Dead Sea Scroll community.

In *Antiquities* 17.41 Josephus implies the Pharisees follow "ancestral customs and claim to observe laws which the Deity approves." One of Josephus's chief rivals in first-century Palestine was Nicolaus of Damascus, who accused the Pharisees of "pretending to observe the laws of which God approves." Herein lies the conflict between these various groups and voices in late-first-century Palestinian society. The traditions, interpretations, and the authority they invoke form the basis for conflict and dispute within Jewish society for much of the Roman period. The Jesus movements, along with Josephus, Qumran, the Pharisees and Sadducees, were squarely placed in the middle of this tension. It should be emphasized for the modern reader how close the connection between seemingly religious observance and political power was in antiquity. The traditions and interpretations that prevailed were those groups and leaders who would finally have voice and influence with the people. Also, the claim to represent the traditions and interpretations that are most in consonance with historic Israel and its hallowed leaders gives added weight to the arguments of a group. In this regard, I see the Pharisaic claim to hold the ancient traditions and Matthew's claim to truly fulfill the law and the prophets, and Qumran's assertion that it does the same, analogous in at least one respect. This way of interpreting the past — whether textual or oral — is an attempt to traditionalize and venerate their movements. Each attempts to demonstrate — mostly to its own members — that its own interpretation is older, most consistent with the past, and is that interpretation inspired and sanctioned by God. I have said elsewhere that this might be described as each group's attempt at "filling out the background" of their collective and mythic past. They are old, true, and that body within Israel that correctly interprets God's law and will. Each group, in related ways, sought to make this claim. There were serious political consequences to the outcome of this debate, and the issue, as we have already seen, provoked strong feelings and emotions, like those evident between Sadducees, Pharisees, and some of the Jesus movements.

There is, then, an important context and background to the question of the Pharisees in Matthew 15:1. "Why do your disciples transgress the tradition of the elders?" is a loaded, though familiar, question in Matthew's setting. The question, of course, also aims at getting at the Matthean position on the disputed issue of "the tradition of the elders" mentioned in Josephus and the Saducean charges about the Pharisees. The original question has to do with eating with clean or unclean hands (Mark 7:5 ‖ Matt. 15:2). In Matthew Jesus responds with a question: "Why do you transgress the commandment of God for the sake of your tradition?" (15:3). Like Nicolaus of Damascus and the Sadducees, Jesus juxtaposes the Pharisees' traditions with the laws of God. The Pharisaic position about their oral traditions expressed by Josephus is rejected here by Jesus. In fact, in 15:6 the commands of God and the traditions of the Pharisees are explicitly contrasted. The putative Pharisaic tradition about Corban, giving to God, is contrasted with one of the Ten Commandments to honor one's father and mother. The point of the Corban example is that these Pharisees apparently used the tradition of money given to or reserved for God as an excuse not to provide for their parents. In doing this, they violate the commandment to honor father and mother. Mark and Matthew cite Isaiah 29:13 as further support for Jesus' response. The Pharisees' hearts are "far from God." In a charge we have encountered before, the Evangelists quote Isaiah claiming the Pharisees and scribes "teach as doctrines the commands of men" (Mark 7:7; Matt. 15:9). As Matthew says, "For the sake of your tradition you have made empty the word of God." The Pharisees and scribes recede into the background while Jesus calls the people to him so that he can explain his interpretation of this particular aspect of ritual purity.

Matthew has made some significant changes in his Marcan source. Matthew deletes the explanatory verses from Mark 7:3 about Pharisaic and Jewish traditions and laws about vessels. This is needless information for Matthew's audience. Matthew's Jesus handles the Pharisees' question quite differently. Both Matthew and Mark agree that the Pharisees "set aside the commands of God" primarily because they focus on external matters, failing to realize that it is really internal matters of the heart, desires, and attitudes that are the source of uncleanliness (Matt. 15:18; Mark 7:21). But Mark takes this insight from the Jesus tradition and thus "declares all foods clean." Like the Marcan statement about the sabbath ("the sabbath was made for man, not man for the sabbath"; Mark 2:27), this statement declaring "all foods clean" is too radical for Matthew. His community observed certain laws and traditions about ritual purity, as they also observed certain laws pertaining to the sabbath. Matthew, therefore, deletes Mark 7:19.

Matthew actually engages the Pharisees' question. He takes the question about clean and unclean hands seriously. Mark's response assumes he thought the question was really about food and finally dismissed it as no longer pertaining to his community. The question is about defiled hands and eating. Matthew recognizes this and offers an interpretation as to why the disciples' behavior does *not* violate certain laws of ritual purity. Impure and corrupt thoughts and motives that come from the heart defile. Defilement is an internal issue, according to the teaching of Jesus in Mark and Matthew. "But to eat with unwashed hands," Matthew says, "does not defile a person" (Matt. 15:20). The debate over washed or unwashed hands continued into the rabbinic period, as J. Neusner has shown. *M. Yad* 1:1 and *Ḥag.* 2:5 capture the ongoing discussion of this issue. There is no indication, despite Mark 7:3 ("the Pharisees and all the Jews"), that all Pharisees followed this particular interpretation of defilement. There were divisions within Pharisaism as well, and Matthew may have been taking aim at a certain Pharisaic group and interpretation.

This conflict story and legal debate are another opportunity for Matthew to offer an apology for his community's view of the law. This is also another attempt to assert the superiority of his community's interpretation over that of the Pharisees. The Matthean church upholds the law. They believe they fulfill it perfectly. Therefore, Matthew, in contrast to Mark, offers a reasoned defense and rationale, according to the law and based on scripture, of his community's interpretation and behavior. The Pharisees and scribes from Jerusalem are the ones who break God's laws, not the Matthean community.

In 15:12–14 Matthew attacks the Pharisees' role as teachers and leaders. Only Matthew records that the Pharisees were "offended" (once again *eskandalisthasan*) by what Jesus had said. They will be "rooted up," Matthew's Jesus responds. They are "blind guides" (cf. 23:16). Here and in chapter 23 the Pharisees are depicted as leaders. This also accords with Josephus, who maintains the Pharisees were more popular with the people because of their legal interpretations (*J.W.* 1.108ff.; *Ant.* 13.399ff.). That the Pharisees' interpretation seemed to be prevailing among the people (they were their guides and leaders) was a source of consternation for Matthew. His community possessed an interpretation of the law and enacted it in a way that was far more constructive and consistent with Israel's past than did the Pharisees, so the author believed. This conflict story about unwashed hands in 15:1–20 is a chance for Matthew to try to make his case and assert once again his community's role as the authentic local leaders and teachers. It is really the Pharisees, not Matthean Jews, who break with tradition and with God.

## The Canaanite Woman and the God of Israel

The story of the Canaanite woman is both an interesting and disturbing one which Matthew develops from his Marcan source. In this story Jesus draws near to the region of Tyre and Sidon, outside of Galilee on the Mediterranean coast. This was the traditional region of the Canaanites and was considered gentile territory in Jesus' day. In Matthew the woman comes out from that region crying out for help for her daughter who is possessed by a demon. The coming out from that region gives the impression she has come out to meet Jesus while he is still in Galilee. Matthew, therefore, is able to maintain his Galilean-centric story of Jesus. He prefers to keep Jesus in Galilee until he travels to Jerusalem to die.

Her plea to Jesus is a rather exalted one: "O Lord [*Kurie*], Son of David" (15:22). But according to Matthew, Jesus does not answer her. Mark does not contain this feature of Jesus ignoring the woman's cry. Her continued cries annoy the disciples in Matthew and they ask Jesus to send her away. The apparent lack of concern for the woman and her sick child on the part of Jesus and the disciples is a disturbing feature of this story.

Only in Matthew does Jesus respond, quoting himself (10:6) and saying, "I was sent only to the lost sheep of the house of Israel" (15:24). But the woman persists and kneels before him, saying, "Lord, help me." Mark's version contains little of this material. Mark's "Syrophoenician woman" does not praise Jesus in the christological and liturgical tones that Matthew's Canaanite woman does (Matt. 15:22). Mark's Jesus does not seem to have turned a deaf ear to the woman's cry. There is no explicit response from Mark which would obviously leave the woman out, as in Matthew 15:24, and there is no *"Kurie, Boathei moi"* or "Lord, help me!" This reads less like a cry in Matthew and more like a prayer.

Matthew rejoins the Marcan material at 15:26 and follows him, more or less, for two verses. Jesus finally responds to her plea by saying, "It is not fair to take the children's bread and throw it to the dogs." Even here, the slight modifications by Matthew in this verse make it even harsher than the Marcan source.

The woman answers, "Yes Lord, yet even dogs eat the crumbs off their master's table." This is a harsh and demeaning image in just about any culture, but most certainly in the Middle East. Matthew has employed this image before together with another unflattering image from the Middle East — a pig — in 7:6: "Do not give what is holy to dogs and do not throw your pearls before pigs lest they trample them under foot and turn and attack you." The woman ultimately is praised by Jesus — more so in Matthew than in Mark — where he says, "O woman, great is your faith! Be it done for you as you desire" (15:28). Her faith is not mentioned in Mark (7:29).

The meaning of the story and images seem clear enough. The children represent Israel and the dogs are Gentiles. Yet I believe the words placed in the mouth of the woman — the titles for Jesus, her submission to Jesus, her "kneeling" (15:25; *prosekunei*), and her prayer for help — all place her as a believing community member. That is, this gentile woman has come to Jesus and has engaged in all the requisite behavior expected of members. Only in Matthew is it exclaimed, "O woman, great is your faith!" Although a Gentile, she is a Matthean Jew in good standing. She behaves and believes in accordance with the community rules.

This story, as Davies and Allison warn us, should not be read as a foretaste of Jesus' rejection of Jews and Israel and his joyful acceptance of Gentiles. This story reflects the real-life tension of gentile admission and participation in the Matthean community and other similar Jesus movements. I do not think that there were many non-Jews in Matthew's community. But there were, most likely, some. In fact, I would say Matthew would have been unusual not to have had to cross this bridge and deal with this potentially volatile situation. The exact relationship between Jews and Gentiles, and when, if, and how Gentiles could be members of a Jewish community, were constant questions in the second-temple period. These questions divided some communities, as in the case of some Pauline churches (Rom. 9:25–30) and other predominantly diaspora communities (Acts 15:1–20). The first-century Alexandrian writer Philo took this question up regularly (*Mos.* 2.43; *Spec.* 1.97; 2.165–67; *Praem.* 114). Matthew also looked for scriptural and *haggadic,* or traditional narrative, support for the question of non-Jewish involvement in the ministry of Jesus and, therefore also, Matthean Judaism. In 12:18–21 Matthew provides scriptural support for the possibility of gentile participation in this form of Judaism. As with the centurion from chapter 8, so also with the Canaanite woman chapter 15: their faith is portrayed as modeling faith in the authority of Jesus. It is her great faith that finally gets Jesus to consider the Canaanite woman's prayer and plea.

We have already noted the interaction between Jews and Gentiles in the Greco-Roman period. Many texts and writers from this period highlight the reality and sometimes urgency involved with gentile involvement in Jewish communities. The debate over the so-called God-Fearers featured in the Book of Acts reveals some of the issues surrounding gentile involvement in Jewish life and worship. The same is true of the *Theosebes* inscription from the city of Aphrodisias in western Asia Minor. Despite one's position on either God-Fearers or the related *Theosebes*, the reality of gentile involvement, and the tensions and issues surrounding this reality, emerge with force in the period in which Matthew wrote his Gospel.

But this reality is not isolated to the diaspora. Non-Jews had been a part of life in Galilee and Judea for some time. Hellenistic culture and conventions, including Greek language, had been part of Palestinian life for many years by the end of the first century C.E. M. Hengel helped demonstrate the cultural confluence of Judaism and Hellenism in this period in his monumental *Judaism and Hellenism.* But archaeology in the Galilee and surrounding region over the last twenty years has helped also to lay bare gentile influence and elements in the Galilee. Greek influence, followed by Roman domination, coupled with the lively trade and cross-cultural character of the Galilee all helped to put the gentile question on the table. In this regard the diaspora is not distinct from the homeland. Both regions within ancient Judaism had to contend with gentile influence and involvement.

I am not sure that one could call gentile involvement — or not — a prominent issue in Matthew. His rather veiled discussions about this matter (such as the centurion and the Canaanite woman) do not compare to Paul, the Acts of the Apostles, or

Philo in the degree and vigor with which the gentile question is pursued. In a recent book G. Porton has helped highlight the dimensions of the discussion about non-Jews or *Goyim* within rabbinic literature and thought. So, for several hundred years after Matthew, and roughly in the same geographical region as Matthew, rabbis continued to discuss the role of Gentiles in, and their relationship to, historic Israel.

The story of the Canaanite woman teaches about faith but also takes up the rather widespread question of gentile involvement in a Jewish community, in this case, Matthew's community. Jesus' response to the woman's plea is less than hospitable. When compared to Mark, his source for the story, Matthew appears less enthusiastic about gentile participation, if we may allow for the woman to represent non-Jews, which in this instance seems reasonable. The first priority of Jesus' ministry and mission was Israel. He was sent to fulfill the laws and the prophets of Israel. This is stressed more by Matthew than his earlier sources. Matthean Judaism believed that this was Jesus' role and purpose. Others, of course, might join in and find their hope in Jesus (Matt. 12:21; Isa. 42:1–4), but this message was first for Israel (Matt. 10:6; 15:24). As with many other Jewish communities in the Roman period, Gentiles could be involved and, to some degree, already were. But they had to participate by the rules and traditions of the community. That is, there was no indication that there was another set of rules or interpretations for Gentiles. That would seem quite unlikely coming from Matthew.

The Canaanite woman, like the centurion, indicates that great faith can be found among the Gentiles. This woman came to Israel, leaving her native region (15:22). She calls Jesus "Lord" and "Son of David." This later title has particular meaning for Matthew and demonstrates her willingness to participate in the hope, traditions, and legends of Israel. She persists in coming after Jesus and the disciples, she seems to understand her place within the kingdom of heaven (15:26–27), and she accepts and worships Jesus (15:25). This Gentile has become a follower and believer, if not a member, within the Matthean community. Gentile participation could happen within Matthean Judaism and such people could, in fact, serve as models for faith and play an important role in the church of the kingdom of heaven. However, this may have been a rather new phenomenon for Matthew's group, and such Gentiles were not present in the Matthean community in any significant number.

## Beware the Leaven of the Local Leadership

Matthew 16:1–12 is another instance where Matthew takes aim at local leaders. In these verses it is the Pharisees and Sadducees who come under attack by Jesus. In 16:1–4 Matthew includes another episode of Jewish leaders seeking a sign from Jesus. Matthew's first account of this appears in 12:38–39, where the scribes are named with the Pharisees. Matthew 16:2 appears to pick up on a Q logion about reading the signs in the sky. "When it is evening, you say, 'It will be fair weather; for the sky is red.' And in the morning, 'It will be stormy today, for the sky is red and threatening'" (16:2–3). Jesus chastises these leaders because "they know how to interpret the appearance of the sky, but they cannot interpret the signs of the times." Matthew then returns to the saying he reported in 12:39: "An evil and adulterous generation seeks for a sign, but no sign will be given to it except the sign of Jonah" (16:4).

Luke does not use the request for a sign from Jesus as a polemic against Pharisees and some other leadership group (Luke 11:16). Mark places the question in the mouth of Pharisees in 8:11, but in 8:15 adds "the leaven of Herod" to the Pharisees. Matthew does not follow Mark in mentioning Herod. In the first Matthean version, scribes and Pharisees ask the question and in the second Sadducees and Pharisees. In 16:1 it is clear the Sadducees and Pharisees ask not out of any authentic desire to find an answer but to "test him." Making their ill will in approaching Jesus explicit, Matthew takes this apparently misguided question and uses it as yet another negative example of the current leadership in his setting. In 16:1–4 Jesus asserts that these leaders are surrounded by signs but they are unable to read them. The only sign they will be given, once again, is the sign of Jonah.

One must consult Matthew 12:38ff. to discover how Matthew interprets the "sign of Jonah."

At one level the question about a sign is understandable in light of the sociopolitical context of first-century Palestine. As Horsley and others have shown, at the level of the average person, at least, many popular leaders and prophets were springing up and leading movements in response to their imperial predicament. Was Jesus such a figure? Many of his actions and teaching would have led some to think so. If Jesus was in the mold of one of the prophets of old, a sign would not be out of order. Was Jesus a true prophet and one whom the people should follow? Historically speaking, this is an understandable question of Jesus, and from the people's perspective it was a critical one.

By the time we get to Matthew's Gospel, however, this is not a question from the people seeking to know if this is the prophet — among many — whom they should follow and give their allegiance. By this time in the Gospel tradition the question emerges as a lack of faith and wisdom, and actually is in opposition to Jesus and his movement. Matthew places this question in the mouths of the Pharisees and Sadducees to highlight both their opposition and their lack of understanding as local leaders.

In 16:5–12 Jesus and the disciples "reach the other side, and had forgotten to bring any bread." Between the "toing and froing" across the lake and the perpetual shortage of bread, the reader is expecting a third Matthean feeding story. Instead, the image and problem of bread, treated already in 14:13–21 and 15:32–39, become the material for further attack on the Sadducees and Pharisees. "Beware," Jesus says, "of the leaven of the Pharisees and Sadducees" (16:6). The disciples discuss this saying among themselves. Although they are obviously confused, Jesus charges them with being "little trusters," and not with a failure to understand. This is the most common charge Matthew made against his own members and disciples. They did not lack, for the most part, wisdom or understanding; they did, however, from time to time lack trust or faith.

Jesus references his earlier feedings: "Do you not remember the five loaves of the five thousand and the seven loaves of the four thousand? How is it that you fail to perceive that I did not speak about bread? Beware of the leaven of the Pharisees and Sadducees" (16:9–11). Then the disciples understand that Jesus is not talking about the leaven of bread, but rather the teaching of the Pharisees and Sadducees.

In this brief polemic with local leaders Matthew has transformed the miracle stories about feeding the multitude into stories about the inadequacy of the teaching of these leaders. Much like the apocryphal saying sometimes attributed to Rev. William Spooner, who said, "In the sermon which I have just completed, wherever I said Aristotle, I meant Saint Paul," so Matthew teaches his audience, "In the stories I have just told you, when I said bread, I meant the teaching of the Pharisees." In retrospect, the feedings in Matthew become allegories for the fullness of the teaching in Matthean Judaism and a reminder of the inadequacies of the teaching of the local leaders. In this way 16:1–12 makes some of the same claims about these leaders as were made in the dispute about unwashed hands in 15:1–20. The teaching and leadership of this group or groups fail to provide the necessary and needed wisdom for the people. When you think of bread, henceforth, don't think of eating, but of teaching. And remember the fallacies in the teaching of the Pharisees and Sadducees and the truth and accuracy of my teaching, Jesus says. This is the result of the Matthean Jesus' response to the disciples wondering about bread and leaven.

## Further Reading

Baumgarten, A. I. "The Pharisaic *Paradosis.*" *HTR* 80 (1987): 63–78.

Baumgarten, J. M. "The Pharisaic-Sadducean Controversies about Purity and the Qumran Texts." *JJS* 31 (1980): 157–70.

Bornkamm, G. "The Stilling of the Storm." In *Tradition and Interpretation in Matthew,* ed. G. Bornkamm, G. Barth, and H. Held, 52–57. Philadelphia: Westminster, 1963.

Cope, L. "The Death of John the Baptist in the Gospel of Matthew." *CBQ* 38 (1976): 515–19.

Davies, W. D. and D. Allison. *Matthew 8–17: An Exegetical and Critical Commentary.* Edinburgh: T. & T. Clark, 1992.

Fowler, R. M. *Loaves and Fishes: The Function of the Feeding Stories in the Gospel of Mark.* SBLDS 54. Chico, Calif.: Scholars Press, 1981.

Frankemölle, H. *Jahwebund und Kirche Christi*. Münster: Aschendorff, 1974.

Goldammer, K. "Navis Ecclesiae." *ZNW* 40 (1941): 76–91.

Harrington, D. *The Gospel of Matthew*. Sacra Pagina Series 1. Collegeville, Minn.: Michael Glazier/Liturgical Press, 1991.

Hengel, M. *Judaism and Hellenism*. Philadelphia: Fortress, 1974.

Horsley, R. H., and J. S. Hanson. *Bandits, Prophets, and Messiahs: Popular Movements at the Time of Jesus*. Minneapolis: Winston, 1985.

Kraabel, A. T. "The Disappearance of the God-Fearers." *Numen* 28 (1981): 113–26.

Malina, B. "The Individual and the Community — Personality in the Social World of Early Christianity." *BTB* 9 (1979): 126–38.

Minear, P. "The Disciples and the Crowds in the Gospel of Matthew." In *Gospel Studies in Honor of S. E. Johnson*, ed. M. Shepherd and E. Hobbs, ATR Suppl. Series 3 (1974): 28–44.

Nau, A. J. *Peter in Matthew: Discipleship, Diplomacy, and Dispraise*. Collegeville, Minn.: Michael Glazier/Liturgical Press, 1992.

Neusner, J. "First Clean the Outside." *NTS* 22 (1975–76): 486–95.

Overman, J. A. "The God-Fearers: Some Neglected Features." *JSNT* 32 (1988): 17–26.

———. *Matthew's Gospel and Formative Judaism: The Social World of the Matthean Community*. Minneapolis: Fortress, 1990.

———. "Recent Advances in the Archaeology of the Galilee in the Roman Period." *Currents in Research: Biblical Studies* 1 (1993): 35–58.

Porton, G. *Goyim: Gentiles and Israelites in Mishna-Tosefta*. Atlanta: Scholars Press, 1988.

Reynolds, J., and R. Tannenbaum. *Jews and Godfearers at Aphrodisias*. Cambridge: Cambridge Philological Society, 1987.

Schiffman, L. "The New Halakhic Letter (4QMMT) and the Origins of the Dead Sea Sect." *BA* 53 (1990): 64–73.

Schweizer, E. "Matthew's Church." In *The Interpretation of Matthew*, ed. G. Stanton, 129–55. Philadelphia: Fortress, 1983.

Trilling, W. "Amt und Amtsverständnis bei Matthäus." In *Mélanges Bibliques: Festschrift for B. Rigaux*, ed. A. Descamps, 29–44. Gembloux: Duculot, 1969.

Vermes, G. *The Dead Sea Scrolls in English*. 3rd ed. London: Penguin, 1987.

# Leadership and Succession in Matthew's Church — 16:13–17:20

## The Confession at Caesarea Philippi

Matthew 16:13–20 is a memorable and pivotal point in the Gospel. This is the so-called Petrine Confession and may well represent the apex of the disciples' understanding and "following" in Matthew. This story comes from Mark (8:27–30) and appears in a modified form in Luke (Luke 9:18–21). Luke does not indicate where this discussion took place, but both Mark and Matthew say it was near Caesarea Philippi, or Banias, in Upper Galilee near Mount Hermon. The *Gospel of Thomas* contains a vaguely related version where the response to Jesus' question is, "Simon Peter said to him, 'You are like a messenger.' Matthew said to him, 'You are like a wise philosopher.' Thomas said to him, 'Teacher, my mouth is unable to say what you are like'" (*Gos. Thom.* 13). One can recognize a faint connection in this Thomas saying which bears little on the Matthean version.

The Petrine Confession is the only narrative in Matthew's Gospel which explicitly places Jesus outside of Lower Galilee. In Caesarea Philippi Jesus is still in Galilee, but Upper Galilee. As E. Meyers has pointed out, archaeological excavations in the Galilee over the last twenty years have helped illumine some of the cultural and political differences between Upper and Lower Galilee. Upper Galilee was less urbanized than Lower Galilee. The primary corridor of trade and cultural influence in Upper Galilee and the four villages, or tetracomia, ran between the Phoenician coastal towns of Tyre and Sidon on the Mediterranean coast and Damascus to the east.

This town was originally called Panias (Polybius 16.18.2; Pliny, *N.H.* 5.74). This name is derived from a natural spring at Banias which was dedicated to the god Pan. In 20 B.C.E. Augustus gave this region to Herod. Herod built a marble temple near the cave of Pan in honor of his emperor and patron. When Herod died, the region passed to his son Philip, who expanded the city and named it Caesarea to further honor Augustus (*Ant.* 18.28; *J.W.* 2.168). This expansion and rededication of the city would have occurred around the time of Jesus' ministry. Most notably, this city was known as a pagan city and center in antiquity. Recent excavations by Z. Ma'oz and others have confirmed this. In late antiquity the city reverted to its earlier name of Panias (Eusebius, *Onomast.* 215.82; 217.40; 275.36). The Arabic form of this name, Banias, persists today as the name of the site.

In Mark's version of this story Jesus asks the disciples the decisive question of the pericope, "Who do men say that I am?" while they are on the road. In fact, the question is preceded by a distinctive Marcan redactional phrase, "and on the way" (*en ta hodo*). Mark's story of Jesus, as pointed out by W. Kelber and others, frequently utilizes the metaphor of movement and walking while Jesus and the twelve are talking in order to highlight Mark's understanding of discipleship. This pivotal conversation happens in Mark "while they were on the way" (Mark 8:27). In Matthew's version he and the disciples have already arrived in Caesarea Philippi. Throughout his story Matthew depicts the disciples as far more settled than does Mark. It is also significant to note that Mark's version has Jesus ask this question in the first person: "Who do people [*anthropoi*] say that I am?" (Mark 8:27). In Matthew Jesus asks, "Who do people say the Son of Man is?" (Matt. 16:13). In 16:21 Matthew deletes this title and adds simply "he," where Mark includes the title "Son of man" in the parallel passage in 8:31. This seems to reflect that "Son of man" serves simply as a circumlocution for "I," which is what G. Vermes has maintained the Aramaic term (*Bar Nasa*) originally meant.

The disciples do attempt to answer Jesus' question. Some say

John the Baptist (e.g., as we have seen, Herod Antipas), some say Elijah, and others one of the prophets (Mark 8:28 ‖ Luke 9:19 ‖ Matt. 16:14). Matthew has added another possibility, namely, Jeremiah. Matthew alone among the Gospel writers mentions the name Jeremiah. He not only adds the name here in 16:14, but also in 2:17 and 27:9. In post-70 Judaism in Palestine Jeremiah was associated with a renewal of the temple cult. Long ago Jeremiah helped provoke a renewal, but also a harsh critique, of the temple cult and a lament over Jerusalem and its judgment. In the post-70 period, he was occasionally utilized to explain the recent catastrophe of the temple's destruction, and he represented hope for the future. His faithful secretary Baruch is also an important figure in the post-70 period in Palestine and several significant pseudepigraphical works bear his name.

"Your ways and your doings have brought this upon you. It is your doom and it is bitter" (Jer. 4:18). Such words carried great meaning in certain circles in the post-70 period. "I looked, and lo, the fruitful land was a desert and all her cities were laid in ruins" (Jer. 4:26). What laid in waste could be restored, so some felt, in the aftermath of the revolt and destruction of 70 C.E. Jeremiah predicted destruction but held out hope for renewal and reconstruction. "If you return, I will restore you, and you shall stand before me. If you utter what is precious, and not what is worthless, you shall be as my mouth" (Jer. 15:19). The Jeremian cycle of rejection, destruction, and renewal fits Matthew's context and theology very well. The person and message of Jeremiah provided a useful theodicy for Matthew and other faithful Jews in Palestine who were struggling with the meaning of recent events in their setting. I have pointed out elsewhere that the figure of Jeremiah is an important and logical figure within post-70 Jewish polemical literature and rhetoric. It makes sense, therefore, that Jeremiah should make his way into Matthew's thought-world and Gospel.

In all three synoptic Gospels Peter responds to Jesus' question about who people say he is. In Mark, Peter replies, "You are the Christ" (Mark 8:29). In Luke, Peter responds, "The Christ of God" (Luke 9:20). Matthew develops Peter's response considerably and turns this exchange between Jesus and Peter into a central passage in his Gospel about discipleship, authority, and community. Matthew's Peter responds, "You are the Christ, the son of the living God" (Matt. 16:16). In Mark and Luke, Jesus provides very little response to Peter's claim. In fact, in these two Gospels Jesus uses a word reserved for demons in Mark's Gospel (*epitiman*) to quiet Peter and the twelve. Jesus, in effect, rebukes the disciples in light of Peter's response in Mark. I would translate Mark 8:30, "And he [Jesus] rebuked them in order that [*hina*] no one would speak about him." Arguably, Peter's response is wrong in Mark. Not so much because of his choice of the word "Christ" to describe Jesus, but rather because of what Peter may have meant by this title. If, in Peter's view, Christ meant a king to rule in power in the here and now (cf. 15:32), he had another thing coming. In Mark, more so than any other Gospel, discipleship means sacrifice and suffering. Peter and the twelve are slow to comprehend this. This is also the message of Peter's famous denial at the end of the Gospel. For him to say "Christ" and mean an earthly king (though this is largely the freight of this term) is a great mistake in Mark. Therefore, Peter and the disciples are told in words reserved only for devils — a rebuke — to reevaluate the meaning of being a follower. "The Son of man," Jesus continues, "must suffer many things, be rejected by elders, chief priests, and scribes, and be killed" (Mark 8:31). Peter cannot accept this (8:32), but this is the nature of discipleship in Mark.

By contrast, Matthew celebrates Peter's answer to the question posed in Caesarea Philippi.

> Blessed are you Simon Bar-Jona. Flesh and blood did not reveal this to you but your father who is in heaven. I tell you, you are Peter, and on this rock I will build my church, and the powers of death shall not prevail against it. I will give you the keys of the kingdom of heaven, and whatever you bind on earth shall be bound in heaven, and whatever you loose in heaven will be loosed in heaven. (Matt. 16:17–19)

In Matthew 16:20 the technical Marcan term of rebuke (*epitiman*) is deleted. This is a pregnant passage full of distinctive Matthean terms and concerns.

Once again, Matthew, being one of the first great interpreters of the Jesus tradition, has interpreted Simon Peter's name in terms of the faith and life of the community. Mark does not attach any significance to Simon's name change to Peter (Mark 3:16 ‖ Luke 6:14). It is Matthew who finds in this name a message for his church and interprets the name accordingly. "You are Peter, and upon this *rock* I will build my church." The play on words Matthew finds in the twin terms "Peter" (*Petros*) and "rock" (*petra*) form the substance of the message. Peter is the foundation (cf. 7:24) of the church of the kingdom of heaven.

Peter has consistently functioned as leader and spokesperson for the disciples, as we have already noted. In many respects this is not a great surprise for the informed Matthean follower. But the *makarios* or blessing Jesus bestows on Peter in 16:17 deserves further attention. First, Peter's confession and insight, Matthew claims, did not come from another person but from God. Peter's confession was a revelation. "Flesh and blood did not reveal this to you but my father who is in heaven." This adds tremendous weight and authority to Peter's position and claims about Jesus.

In Matthew's Gospel the figure of Peter oscillates between representing the quintessential disciple and being a type or model of a community leader. Peter is not only an example of a disciple, as Strecker and others have maintained, but he is also a model for leadership in the Matthean community. This oscillation and dual role for Peter must be kept in mind as one reads Matthew's story. In this instance, Peter emerges more as a transparent type for a community leader. He is the foundation. His interpretation of who Jesus really is comes directly from God, and he possesses extraordinary authority within the community.

The terms Matthew employs in this exchange between Peter and Jesus suggest authority and office. Peter is a rock, a foundation, illustrative of constancy and truth. The term "rock" is elsewhere used by Matthew to describe the person who depends on the teachings of Jesus (7:24ff.). But this term was used more widely than simply Matthew's community. As O. Betz has pointed out, the term "rock" was important in the Qumran community. 1QS 11:4ff., 1QH 6:25ff., and 1QH 7:8ff. all use this term to describe the truth of God. In 1QS 8:5–10 the Qumran community is depicted as the "rock," the true Israel. The *Odes of Solomon* 22:12 records that the "foundation of everything is your [God's] rock. And upon it you have built your kingdom, and it has become a dwelling place for your holy ones." In these contexts and communities the term "rock" emerges as a rather exclusive term. It denotes the teachings and principles of the community — or the community itself — which is a rock: true, constant, and placed by God. Matthew, too, uses the term *petra* to assert the same claims about his community, Jesus' teaching, and the church's interpretation of the law. The connection between Peter's name and the loaded legitimating term "rock" is more than cute or convenient for Matthew. The leadership of the community and their exalted claims about Jesus rest on sure ground. God alone has revealed these things to the community through its leaders prefigured, in this instance, by Peter. The Matthean church, as a result of its true teaching, interpretation, and leadership, rests on a rock and nothing, not even the powers of death or hades, shall prevail against it.

Jesus grants Peter the "keys of the kingdom of heaven, and whatever you bind on earth shall be bound in heaven, and whatever you lose on earth shall be loosed in heaven" (Matt. 16:19). The term "keys," like "rock," was also common in post-70 literature from Palestine and carries with it some important connotations. This passage appears to be based on Isaiah 22:22: "And I will place on his shoulder the key of the house of David; he shall open, and none shall shut; and he shall shut and none shall open." The keys of the temple in Jerusalem become an important image and the subject of some debate in post-70 Palestinian literature. In 4 Baruch 4:4 Jeremiah himself takes the keys of the temple and casts them up toward the sun, saying, "Take the keys of the temple of God and keep them until the day in which the Lord will question you about them. Because we were not found worthy of keeping them, for we were false stewards." In 2 Baruch 10:18 the priests are ordered to take the keys of the sanctuary and cast them up to heaven "because, behold, we have been found to be false stewards." The priests ask God to "guard your house yourself." Chapter 64 of 2 Baruch claims it was the wickedness of the priests and their profaning of the sanctuary which led to the destruction and God withdrawing from the temple. In a very similar passage in *ARN* 4, the keys of the temple are thrown into the heavens and a hand comes out of the clouds and catches them. "O Master of the Universe, here are the keys which you did hand over to us, for we have not been found trustworthy custodians to do the king's work and to eat at the king's table." The keys are to be kept until such time as "they" are found to be worthy. In 3 Baruch 11:2 the angel Michael retains the keys due to the falsehood of the priests. And in Revelation 3:7 it is Christ who holds "the key of David."

"Keys" in this period is a polemical term that provoked questions about true and faithful leadership. In these pseudepigraphical texts the priests and leaders are depicted as unworthy and faithless and, therefore, relinquish the keys (of the temple in Jerusalem), giving them back to God. At once the image of the keys provides an explanation for the destruction of the temple and offers a critique of the leaders during that painful period in Israel's history. By bestowing the keys on Peter Matthew makes the opposite claim about the leadership in his community. His leaders are faithful and worthy to possess these important and authoritative symbols, the keys. God has given them to his group. This is "the time" 4 Baruch spoke of. Matthew's community are those people, they claim, worthy "to do the king's work and sit at the king's table," as *ARN* says. Matthew claims that where the recent and current leadership has failed, his group, and their leaders as exemplified by Peter, will succeed.

These documents, which date to around the time of the writing of Matthew and probably come from the same or related provenance, fill out the background of this important term in Matthew 16:19. In Matthew's context the use of the term "keys" conjures up images of the temple, its destruction, and a loss of authority, and reminds people of the wickedness of the priests in Jerusalem during the time of the destruction. These priests are consistently the object of attack in polemical literature such as Matthew, from the post 70–period. I think there is little chance that the power and import of this term would be lost on Matthew's audience. The lost or temporarily hidden keys of authority are now in the possession of the Matthean leaders. God has granted to them the authority, the insight, and the office associated with this symbol.

Peter is also given the authority "to bind and to loose" in Matthew's Petrine Confession. These Greek terms, *deo* and *luo* respectively, have provoked extensive debate for many years. Matthew uses this couplet of authoritative terms twice in the Gospel, here and in 18:18. In 16:19 this authority is granted to Peter and in 18:18 it is granted to the community. This very fact highlights the Matthean ideal that leadership and community coalesce. There were leaders and authoritative roles operative in Matthew's church, but he tried to view the community as the primary focus of attention and the locus of authority and wisdom. This helps account for the oscillation in the portrayal of Peter serving both as a type for leadership and the archetypical disciple.

Matthew does not really unpack these two important terms for us. There are numerous rabbinic parallels to these terms but, for the most part, these traditions are too late to be of use in trying to ascertain what Matthew might have had in mind. But we do have a very important parallel in Josephus — Matthew's first-century contemporary also from Palestine — who uses these terms to describe Matthew's narrative opponents, the Pharisees. In a document written toward the end of the 70s, *The Jewish Wars,* Josephus describes the authority of the Pharisees during the reign of Alexandra (c. 70 B.C.E.). During her reign the Pharisees "became the real administrators of the state, at liberty to banish and recall, to loose and to bind whomever they would. In short, the enjoyment of royal authority were theirs" (*J.W.* 1.111).

Is Josephus describing the authority of the Pharisees — and thus the meaning of these two terms — around 70 B.C.E., or is he anachronistically describing the authority of the Pharisees in his own day with reference to this event almost 150 years before the writing of *Jewish Wars?* The answer is almost certainly a combination of each. S. Cohen has painstakingly tried to tease out the historical accuracies and personal biases of Josephus, and while this is an important question, it goes beyond the bounds of this commentary. There is a parallel passage to this in Josephus's *Antiquities of the Jews,* 13.407–11. In this passage Josephus writes, Alexandra may have held the title of sovereign (*basileias*), but the Pharisees held the power. "For example, they recalled exiles, and freed prisoners, and, in a word, in no way differed from absolute rulers [*despoton*]."

Alexandra liked the Pharisees and she permitted them to do as they pleased. She commanded the people to obey the Pharisees and to follow whatever regulations they instituted in accordance with "the traditions of the fathers" (*Ant.* 13.408–9; cf. Mark 7:5 ‖ Matt. 15:2). The Pharisees enjoyed free reign. This passage in *Antiquities* goes on to describe an uprising against the influence of the Pharisees and a subsequent persecution of those who resisted.

It is important to recognize the differences here between the account in the earlier *Jewish Wars* and the later *Antiquities. Antiquities* was written in the 90s of the first century, almost twenty years after *Jewish Wars.* Things had changed back in Palestine. There were new clients and local leaders dealing with the Roman imperial reality and personnel working in Israel. I think this passage in *Antiquities* reflects Matthew's current setting more so than the section in *Jewish Wars.* Josephus's treatment of the Pharisees here, like Matthew, probably makes the Pharisees seem more important than historically they really were. Pharisees were important to Josephus and to Matthew, but we do not know if they were important to many people beyond the small circles these two represented. But what Josephus describes in *Antiquities* is like what was happening in the Matthean context. Matthew's opponents were growing in power and influence. They had obtained authority somehow, much to Matthew's chagrin, and this made the life of his community more difficult and has called into question his interpretation of the law and history of Israel, which is now refracted through the life and teaching of Jesus.

The phrase "to bind and to loose" is also a description of the quite local authority of the Pharisees in the Matthean setting. Josephus's description of this authority helps us understand the civic, judicial, and political freight these terms carried. The authority to bind and to loose had concrete political and judicial consequences. Those possessing this power could commute a sentence or retain it. They could mete out punishment or forego it. According to Josephus a number of people were apparently uncomfortable with this measure of authority and resisted the Pharisees. This resulted in a short-lived persecution of those who would not embrace the traditions and rules of the Pharisees. Josephus also uses the story about Alexandra figuratively in *Antiquities* to describe the role of the Pharisees in the later part of the first century in Palestine.

Matthew makes the claim in 16:19 that the leaders of his community now possess the political, civil, and judicial authority to "bind and to loose." The community exercises the same authority in chapter 18. Matthew's hope that his group would exercise this authority more broadly within Palestinian society at the close of the first century never came to pass. His group was probably shrinking even while he was writing. What he does assert here, however, is that his community can fulfill these tasks internally and can try not to depend on the external offices and authorities outside of his church. Do not depend on the courts, local officials, or the accepted means of ordering life in the city or town, Matthew counsels here. He offers the same advice in the Sermon on the Mount. If the community does, they will find themselves in difficult situations and be submitted to destructive influences, interpretations, and teaching. Therefore, the community leaders now execute these tasks and possess the authority contained in the idea of "binding and loosing." In case this should cause any doubt on the part of the community members, the narrative reminds the church that Jesus himself bestowed this authority on the leadership (16:19) and community (18:18).

This is a rather blatant attempt to rival, if not replace, the authority of the Pharisees in the Matthean setting. Again, Matthew does not opt out of the parochial contention and struggle that characterize his setting. He does not dismiss such earthly authority. He does not advise the community to withdraw to an isolated place where they can live out their version of Jewish life and religion at the close of the first century. Matthew's story takes aim at the authorities and leaders in his setting. He directly engages in the competition and struggle for influence and authority in his context. Whatever the dominant authorities in his city — or part thereof — possess or enact, so also do the Matthean leaders. This, again, sets the stage for a confrontation between the Matthean community and the authorities in his neighborhood.

## Death and the Problem of Succession

The Petrine Confession in Matthew plays a fundamental role in the author's handling of internal issues of church life and structure. Sociologically Peter plays a key role in Matthew's narrative. The Gospels, especially Matthew's, can be described as "second-generation" literature. P. L. Berger in particular has used this phrase to describe the sociological and communal needs of a movement after the initial thrust and impetus of the movement — and above all the founder — have passed. Berger and others take their lead from the famous German sociologist Max Weber. Weber talked about this process in terms of "the routinization of charisma." Weber claimed "charisma" was a profound and powerful force in the world. This force was found in gifted and inspired, if not asocial, people. These leaders are *virtuosi*. They possess a passion and vision, and gift (therefore the term "charismatic") which drives them to break with tradition. Their message and example compel others to do the same. Weber took the Matthean Jesus' words from the Sermon on the Mount, "You have heard of old, but I say to you," to be an example of the charismatic's innovative, inspiring, but anomic message. Weber was wrong in his interpretation of the Sermon on the Mount, but he was absolutely right about the reality of this charismatic impulse and people, and the inevitable sociological necessity to try to tame or regularize this powerful force.

The Gospels then are "second generation" — or with W. Meeks, "community forming literature" — because they are literature that dates to a period in the history of the Jesus movement(s) when Jesus followers were trying to organize or routinize their beliefs, practices, and self-understanding. These stories called Gospels attempt to respond to issues, questions, and crises typical of the "second generation" of followers and devotees in a movement. They intend to help the communities formed around the message and person of Jesus survive and flourish long after the charismatic figure has passed from their midst. These questions and issues arise after the group has a history, a track record, and time enough to develop problems within the group and beyond the group in their relationship with the wider world. Speaking metaphorically, Berger says children always have questions and parents must provide answers. "The second generation always posits a problem of compliance." The Gospels attempt to provide answers to questions that emerged through the day-to-day and real-life questions of certain Jesus movements. What could Jesus have meant? Should we pay taxes? What are the responsibilities of a "disciple"? What is our relationship to local leaders and authorities? Where do non-Jews fit in? Why are we persecuted? These and many other related questions and crises are typical of the "second generation." Matthean Jews had to try to interpret and enact the insight and instruction of Jesus several generations removed from those who first encountered him.

The passion and inspired ecstasy of the charismatic no longer typified life in the Matthean church. As Weber himself pointed out, the pressures and problems of the everyday prevail on the spirit of charisma and those whom it has enthralled. The German word Weber used to describe "routinization" (*Veralltäglichung*) draws attention to the issues and questions of the everyday. Although it may seem otherwise for a time, life does go on after the death of the impassioned and inspired charismatic leader. Inevitably the community must turn its attention to the problems and questions of the everyday which break in upon the group with regularity. The charismatic person lives outside such concrete questions and obligations and persuades others to do the same. The structures, rules, and questions of the everyday tend to be treated as obstructions on the way to fulfilling the charismatic's vision. But no community can live perpetually outside the structures and norms of the everyday. Some agreement must be struck with the outside dominant culture. Also, subsequent members will not find the apparently glib discounting of the immediate and worldly sufficient. Answers must be supplied, modifications must take place, and a social development must occur if the movement or community is going to survive. This is the routinization of charisma and it is the task of second-generation literature to facilitate this transition for the group that remains devoted, though perplexed. Matthew's Gospel is, given such a definition, most certainly "second-generation" literature.

Perhaps the biggest problem where the routinization of charisma is concerned is what Weber called the problem of succession. That is, after the leader is gone, who will run the group? Not many schools specialize in graduating charismatics. How does the group find another suitable leader? In most instances, the first choice is a relative of the leader. In fact, there is some evidence the early church made just such a choice. James, "the brother of the Lord," is depicted as the authority in the church in Jerusalem in the days following the death of Jesus and was instrumental in resolving a potentially very divisive issue between Jews and non-Jews in the church (Acts 15:13ff.). But typically, this mode of determining leadership and authority through kinship does not last indefinitely. Weber pointed out that another way authority is passed on, after the cessation of charisma, is through "designation." This is the significance of the Matthean version of the Petrine Confession.

In the conversation between Peter and Jesus at Caesarea Philippi in Matthew, we have an example of "designation" in this sociological sense. Matthew has shaped a narrative based on his earlier Marcan source which anticipates and responds to questions about leadership and authority. Who is in charge now? Who will be the carrier of the distinctive Matthean interpretation of the Jesus tradition? Who will help shape the community as it tries to face the challenges and competition of the everyday? Matthew supplies answers to this question with his version of the Petrine Confession. In many respects, this conversation between Peter and Jesus constitutes a response to the inevitable second-generation question, "Says who?" How do we know we are right? What voice should we listen to? What interpretation should prevail? Matthew has posited answers to these crucial questions in his depiction of community leadership in 16:16ff.

This passage has been of particular interest over the centuries where ecclesial and papal authority are concerned. This question remains vital in some parts of the world, as evidenced by the recent book by U. Luz. Was Peter the first pope? In a sense, based on Matthew, one could say yes. Peter was also the first bishop, the first moderator, the first authoritative voice in a Quaker meeting, leader of a house church, base Christian community, or any other local, ecclesial version of authority. That is, Peter is the first developed portrait of an authoritative role within a local congregation. The frequent distinction between the person of Peter on the one hand and his confession on the other being the foundation of the church is an erroneous one. The person and the confession cannot be distinguished here. The astute reader will have noticed Peter's development, his knowledge, repeated questions and function as spokesman for the disciples. There is a reason in the Matthean narrative that Peter should receive the revelation in 16:17. The confession made by Peter goes hand in hand with the knowledge and experience he has obtained up to this point. It is Peter who emerges as the leader and rock of the community.

Matthew, being an early and sophisticated interpreter of the Jesus tradition, provides one of the first explicit examples of how leadership and authority could function within the structure of the followers' communities. It should be stressed that Peter represents a very local leader in the Matthean setting. As is the case with Matthew's characterization of the local Jewish leadership, one should not universalize this portrait. Matthew's response to the second-generation question about leadership and authority was shaped by his context and setting. His answer to the inevitable question, "Says who?" is different from Paul, Luke, or the Pastoral Epistles. Matthew's answer may have worked for Matthew, but less so for Luke, and certainly not for the Pastoral Epistles. Matthew's treatment of local authority and communal hierarchy was shaped by and for his community in their particular setting. This should be remembered and emphasized when trying to interpret his message. The New Testament does not speak in one voice about virtually anything, and certainly not on the question of authority. Matthew's portrait of local authority and leadership, exemplified in Peter, is a response to the competition and pressure his community was feeling toward the end of the first century in Palestine when another similar group was emerging as the dominant voice and power. Matthew's portrayal of Peter provides a response to this emerging Matthean reality and crisis.

In all three synoptic Gospels Jesus follows the Petrine Confession with an announcement of his suffering and death. Matthew 16:24–28, Mark 8:34–9:1, and Luke 9:23–27 contain the claim present in all the Gospels that being a follower requires sacrifice, suffering, and perhaps death. Jesus' death at the hands of the Romans left an indelible mark on those who shaped and wrote down the Gospel traditions. Because his death became so central in the subsequent recital of the Gospel, suffering and possibly death were treated as conditions of discipleship. What happened to Jesus may very well happen to his followers. Also, any suffering or injustice that occurred in the life of the followers was interpreted in light of this theme. Whether or not the injustice and suffering the church experienced was directly a result of belief in Jesus, it was interpreted that way. Suffering and injustice as a result of an arbitrary imperial system are interpreted as persecution "for the sake of righteousness."

This passage on sacrifice also contains aspects of judgment. Mark (8:38) and Luke (9:26) mention those who are ashamed of Jesus and his words, "the Son of Man will be ashamed of them when he comes in glory." Matthew has deleted this passage. However, in 16:27b Matthew has added, "He will repay every person for their actions [*praxis*]." Again, Matthew believed actions, behavior — "bearing fruit" — were marks of being a follower. The failure to produce fruit or exhibit the appropriate praxis was cause for judgment in Matthew's view.

Matthew is not alone on this score. Mark and Luke join him in this section on suffering. There is a cost for failing to remain true to Jesus. The reality of those leaving the group or denying allegiance to Jesus is probably what originally provoked these judgment sayings. In a colonial setting, such as Roman Palestine, where the group in question understands itself as aligned against the dominant voices or those in power, desertion, collaboration, or abandoning the cause is always treated with the greatest seriousness. This pressure and reality were part of the life of a Matthean Jew. Adoption of the community's precepts meant living at odds with those wielding influence, if not de jure authority, locally. To entertain second thoughts about the veracity of such an existence was viewed as tantamount to rejecting God. Very early on in their development the Jesus movements represented by the synoptic writers codified the priority of suffering and sacrifice over saving one's skin. Matthew, however, goes further, to say that the issue here is not only one of failure to profess Jesus as the Son of man, but also has to do with the behavior and *praxis* (16:27) of the followers. One's deeds had to be consistent with the Matthean version of the law, and one's relationships had to exhibit the contours called for by the community. Failure to do this, no matter how great the external, political and civic pressures, might garner an eschatological payback (*apodosei;* 16:27) at the end. There is no mistaking this conviction in the Gospel.

Matthew had clear bounds for the community. One could not participate in his group and at the same time live a life in the broader community that appeared at odds with Matthean Judaism. This kind of double standard would ultimately require an explanation. The establishment of this principle reflects that some indeed reconsidered their commitment to the church. It also served to warn those members who lived one way within the context of the Matthean community, yet practiced another way beyond the bounds of the group. Matthew's Jesus teaches one should expect and accept the struggles associated with membership rather than try to live in both worlds.

## The Transfiguration

The Petrine Confession and the teaching about sacrifice are followed by the familiar pericope of the Transfiguration. Matthew follows Mark quite closely in this story. The Transfiguration is depicted as a divine disclosure about Jesus and his intimate connection with two pivotal heroes in Israel's history. Taking his three closest disciples with him, Jesus ascends a mountain — a traditional venue for revelation within Hebrew lore — and there he is changed or transfigured (*metamorphothe*). At this point Moses and Elijah appear and all three begin to speak with one another (17:3). In his transformation Jesus' face shines like the sun and his garments become like light (17:2). These are traditional signs of the presence of God, a divine messenger, or revelation. Here Peter, James, and John see that Moses and Elijah (about whom there have been several questions) are met in the person of Jesus. Here, this story maintains, is the fulfillment of Israel's hopes.

Peter, once again serving as spokesperson for the group, suggests that they build three booths or tents (*skanas*) in honor of these three heroes of Israel. At this point in the narrative a voice from heaven announces, "This is my beloved son, with whom I am well pleased; listen to him" (17:5). In Matthew this passage parallels exactly the baptismal voice declaring Jesus' special relationship with God found in 3:17. The voice in 3:17 and again in 17:5, and the centurion's acclamation in 27:54 serve as cyclical refrains in Matthew's story reminding the audience of the nature and authority of Jesus, his actions and instructions.

The purpose and meaning of the Transfiguration scene has long been debated. The famous German biblical scholar from earlier in the twentieth century, R. Bultmann, believed, following J. Wellhausen and A. Loisy, that the Transfiguration was originally a resurrection story that somewhere in the development of the Gospel tradition was misplaced in the center of the story instead of the end. This interpretation is made more plausible when one notices the odd opening verse to the story, "and after six days...." This introduction does suggest a period of waiting, whether anticipation or mourning, followed by a revelation. Some contend that 2 Peter 1:17 is in fact a reference to the Transfiguration with language reminiscent of Matthew's version of the voice from heaven. The 2 Peter version treats the Transfiguration as an indication of the resurrection, for Jesus, but more immediately for the believers who struggle in the present hour, as 2 Peter 1:10–11 makes clear. As far as 2 Peter is concerned, the Matthean version of the Transfiguration carries a message about the hope of a resurrection at the end of time. This is a very early and suggestive interpretation of this unusual story.

Matthew seems to have anticipated some of the confusion that the Marcan version may have provoked by inserting the term "vision" (*horama*) into his story in 17:9. Matthew tries to suggest that the three were party to a vision when Jesus, Moses, and Elijah were presented to them, with Jesus clearly the greatest among the three. Matthew 17:6, which has no Marcan parallel, presents the disciples' response in terms of adoration and worship. They "fall on their faces and are filled with awe." This action is in direct response to the voice affirming Jesus as God's son. Only Jesus is left when the bright lights and radiant garments subside. He approaches the three followers with this admonition found only in Matthew, "Rise, and have no fear" (17:7). The language both of rising and fear is employed later by the angel in the resurrection narrative in Matthew 28:5–6. This is the messiah or anointed leader of Israel. The three disciples are asked to keep the vision on the mountain to themselves until the Son of man is raised from the dead (17:9).

The Transfiguration prompts another discussion about Elijah and John the Baptist (17:10–13). "Why do the scribes say that first Elijah must come?" It is clear that for some within early communities of Jesus' followers the question of Elijah was a troublesome conundrum. The scriptural background for this conundrum is found in Malachi 3:23–23 (=4:5–6). The Malachi passage speaks about Elijah as a precursor, but of the coming Day of the Lord, not the messiah as such. This seems to have provoked some confusion and question. Further, within certain early, particularly apocalyptic Jesus movements these two events — the arrival of God's anointed agent and the arrival of God's great day, and therefore judgment — seem to coalesce. John the Baptist, therefore, is portrayed as both a preacher of judgment and a messenger of the one who is to come. Following Mark 9:11–13, Matthew records that in John the Baptist Elijah has come. Matthew found Mark's response to the disciples' question too ambiguous. Mark failed to make John explicit in his version of the story and so in 17:13 Matthew makes it clear that when Jesus says, "Elijah has come," he means John the Baptist.

The phrase "listen to him" in 17:5 is a reiteration of Jesus' authority as teacher and guide. Following as it does on the heels of the Petrine Confession in Matthew, this short phrase carries even more weight. Matthew was very much concerned with the perception of and problems surrounding Jesus' authority. Why should Jesus' teachings and assertions, as they were being presented in the context of the Matthean community, be adhered to? Why were they in any way binding or superior to the other teaching and injunctions the community heard beyond the bounds of the ecclesia or assembly? Whether displaced resurrection narrative, Petrine vision, or some other original source, the Transfiguration, like so many other passages in Matthew's Gospel, underscored the authority of Jesus, Matthean Judaism's interpretation of him, and the risk one took in dismissing that authority.

## The Kings of the Earth and the Freedom of the Children: The First Question about Taxes

Matthew follows the Transfiguration pericope with an exorcism story involving an epileptic boy who could not be helped by the disciples. The point of this story is the "little faith" (*oligopistoi*) of the disciples. This Mattheanism captures an element of Matthew's understanding of discipleship. As Luz and others have shown, Matthew's disciples grow in their faith as they grow in their understanding and knowledge of Jesus and his designs for them. Matthew's purpose in this story is instructional for the purposes of discipleship. Mark's earlier version in 9:14–29 has little to do with discipleship and more to do with the nature of evil and the ensuing struggle with demonic power. In Matthew faith is not merely caught or granted. It is also learned, tried, and developed through the course of travels and trials with Jesus. The disciples are pushed toward greater faith and authority through the instruction they receive from Jesus.

Matthew 17:22–27 begins a new narrative unit, signaled by Jesus and the disciples regrouping in Galilee. Between the Petrine Confession and 17:22 the group has moved from the northern extent of Upper Galilee back again into Lower Galilee. The intervening Transfiguration story may be understood as having occurred on or around Mount Hermon or one of the many high points of the upper Galilean, lower Lebanese hills. Jesus and the disciples gather once again at their base in Capernaum in Lower Galilee along the shores of the Sea of Galilee. Prior to the discussion about taxes in Capernaum, Jesus issues another warning about the imminent suffering, death, and resurrection of the Son of man (17:23).

Back in Capernaum Peter, again perceived in some sense as the leader of the group, is approached by "those who receive the double drachma" (17:24). The double drachma was roughly equal to half a shekel. This is usually taken to be referring to the tax Jews placed on themselves in support of the Jerusalem temple (Neh. 10:32; Exod. 30:11–16), though in this passage the tax is clearly conflated with the explosive issue of Roman imperial rule. The practice of collecting the temple tax continued after the fall of the temple in 70 C.E., as evidenced by the extended discussion in the Mishna in the tractate *Shekalim*. The collectors ask Peter, "Does your teacher not wish to pay the double drachma?" Peter, without consultation, answers, "Yes." Later in "the house" at Capernaum Jesus asks Simon (Peter), "What do you think? From whom do the kings of the earth take toll or tribute? From their sons or from others?" Peter correctly answers, "From others." Jesus responds to him, saying, "The sons are free" (17:26).

The importance and relevance of this question for Jesus and his followers can hardly be overstated. Matthew, somewhat characteristically, has two stories about taxes: one in 22:17ff., which he inherited from Mark, and this story, which is found only in Matthew's Gospel. The question of taxation strikes at the heart of the political and religious situation in Roman Palestine. While the tax to the temple in Jerusalem had been in place for a long time, Roman rule, and the Roman client-lord system in particular had added several layers of new taxes and an inordinate burden on the people of Palestine. The Herodian dynasty had been particularly brutal where taxation and tribute were concerned. The famous Herodian building projects, and the military exploits of Rome, the protection of the eastern frontier of the empire, and the exploitation of the Galilean and Judean land all were exacted in large measure from the people and peasantry of Palestine. M. Goodman has ably demonstrated the debt cycle that characterized Palestine during the early Roman period. This question is actually a broad question about the movement's views on taxes generally.

For many in Palestine, taxes, and therefore debt, had become symbols of their imperial context and the oppression they were being forced to live and labor under. At the outbreak of the first revolt against Rome Josephus records that the popular forces destroyed the debt records at the house of the high priest Ananias and the palaces of Agrippa and Berenice (*J.W.* 2.426). The pressure from taxes, together with the related larger reality of imperial rule, provoked a number of bandit and popular movements devoted to some form of resistance to the client-lord and colonial system, if not outright rebellion against Rome. Scholars now widely recognize, through the work of R. Horsley and others, the widespread phenomenon of social banditry around the time of Jesus. The noted rebel and contemporary of Jesus, Simon bar Giora, amid his own bandit activity was known to proclaim to the peasants of the Judean hill country "liberty for slaves and rewards for the free" (*J.W.* 4.508). Many popular movements at the time of Jesus proclaimed messages to the people of Palestine which combined the hopes and demands of the God of Israel with the realities of Roman imperial rule.

Perhaps most notably in this regard in the first century was the so-called Fourth Philosophy headed by a Galilean named Judas. A wise man (*sophistes*), he headed a group very much like the Pharisees except they possessed a tremendous "zeal for liberty" (*Ant.* 18.23). Judas was known to urge his countrymen to resist paying taxes to Rome. To pay tribute to Rome was to deny the God of Israel. Judas inspired his followers to resist Rome, believing they would succeed in obtaining freedom with God on their side. Should they fail, at least they would obtain glory and honor for their high ideals (*Ant.* 18.3). An extremist resistance group called the Sicarii, from the Latin word for "dagger," developed around the 50s of the first century in and around Jerusalem and were perhaps originally related to the Fourth Philosophy (*J.W.* 7.253).

According to Josephus, the Sicarii were urban terrorists who took up an extreme form of resistance against Rome and its local supporters as the first century of the common era progressed.

> This group murdered people in broad daylight right in the middle of the city. Mixing with crowds, especially during the festivals, they would conceal small daggers beneath their garments and stab their opponents. Then, when their victims fell, the murderers simply melted into the outraged crowds.... The first to have his throat cut was Jonathan the High Priest, and after him many were murdered daily. (*J.W.* 2.254–56)

Notice that the Sicarii, like many other popular resistance movements, attacked leaders among the indigenous population, not the Romans directly. Eventually, resistance movements in Palestine did coalesce to resist Rome directly in 66 C.E. This, however, was short-lived. (Even during the siege of Jerusalem under the Roman general Titus, civil war and struggle broke out among the rebels within the walls of Jerusalem.) Jonathan the High Priest, like many other local elite and leaders, was viewed as a collaborator with Rome and therefore an obvious target for this urban terrorist group. A stark reality of the colonial setting that characterized much of the Roman Empire, especially Palestine, was the division colonial rule provoked among the local population. Where a leader or group lined up vis-à-vis Rome was a defining element in Palestinian life and relations.

The question posed to Peter about taxes, therefore, was also at the same time a question about the movement's allegiance to Rome. Few questions loomed larger in first-century Palestinian life. It is no surprise that this question makes its way into the Gospels and twice into Matthew. To an outsider, the Jesus movement would have looked very much like a popular resistance movement. Was this movement ultimately out to get rid of Rome and establish political sovereignty for Israel? Jesus looked like some of these other popular leaders. And his message bordered on revolution at numerous points. It is then no surprise that

Jesus was finally tried and killed for sedition and in crucifixion suffered a decidedly Roman form of death.

The colonial context and the problem of taxes did not improve greatly following the first revolt either, as one might expect. Emperor Vespasian imposed a tax of two denarii on Jews to go toward the rebuilding of the temple of Jupiter Capitolinus in Rome which was burned in 69 C.E. (*B.J.* 7.218). Later in the 90s, Suetonius writes, Emperor Domitian's agents imposed the tax on Jews "with a peculiar lack of mercy" (*acerbissime;* Suetonius, *Dom.* 12.2). These are just two incidents from the post-70 period which highlight the ongoing struggle and tension that surrounded the issues of taxation for Jews in Palestine and beyond.

In Matthew's day the question of payment of taxes to Rome or its hirelings in Galilee-Judea remained a crucial issue. This was not simply a historical question reflecting the situation in Palestine leading up to the first revolt. As in the pre-70 period, one's position on taxes revealed one's position on a wide range of religiopolitical issues. Peter, seen as the leader of the disciples and in some traditional sense the spiritual leader of the Matthean community, was confronted with this vital issue. The answer to this question would, of course, define Jesus among and in relation to many other popular charismatic leaders in his day. Also, and most important, Peter's answer would serve as a guide for Matthean Jews in their setting in the post-70 period. Peter's answer, as noted above, was an unequivocal yes (17:25).

But later on in this distinctly Matthean passage Jesus follows up with Peter "in the house." In a colonial context, too swift an answer to the loaded question about taxes can be highly problematic. An outright denial of tribute will result in retribution from those in power. An unbridled yes, like Peter's, can easily result in punishment from the local population for collaboration with the enemy. In questioning Simon, Jesus instructs the group in a more nuanced approach to the huge symbolic issue of payment of tribute. "From whom do the kings of the earth take toll or tribute? From their sons or from others [*allotrion* = foreigners or those different or alien to you]?" "From others," responds Simon. "Then the sons are free," says Jesus.

But Jesus goes on in the Matthean passage to chart a more delicate course. Obviously, outright denial of tribute would mean certain retribution for the followers of Jesus or the later Matthean community. There is ample proof of that in the Roman world. "But in order [*hina*] not to give offense [*skandalisomen*] to them, go to the sea and cast a hook, and take the first fish that comes up, and when you open its mouth you will find a shekel [*stater*]; take that and give it to them for me and yourself." In this passage Jesus sides with those who say the people do not have to pay the tax Rome and its local allies are collecting. But in order not to be killed (*skandalisomen;* literally, so that they do not stumble over you or are offended by you), give them the money. The *stater* (17:27) equals four drachmas, enough to pay the temple tax for both Jesus and Peter. D. Harrington has noted that in later rabbinic literature is a similar story about obtaining a pearl from a fish (*b. Šabb.* 119a).

Jesus' instruction to Peter, and therefore the Matthean community, is a middle ground between the Sicarii, or even the Fourth Philosophy, and those cooperating with Rome. This Matthean passage about taxes attempts to emphasize the integrity of "the sons," that is, the Jews of Israel who are free, but counsels a payment for the short term to avoid destruction and punishment. No doubt some in Matthew's setting and day would have found this counsel prudent, while others would have viewed this as a sellout. In the post-70 period this Matthean advice might well have sounded better and wiser than it might have prior to the first revolt and the destruction of the temple in Jerusalem by Rome. As we will see in chapter 13, Matthew believed that his community could be true to and fulfill the demands of the God of Israel better than others, while at the same time work effectively with Rome and its lords. Matthew believed a *modus vivendi* could be sketched out in this volatile context, and he believed his community were the people to do it. Both Judaism and Christianity ultimately did develop ways of getting along with those in power.

Matthew's position is a difficult one to maintain and balance. Here Jesus is affirming the inalienable freedom of the sons from tax, but appears to be counseling payment anyway. It is jumping to conclusion, though, to assume that this is simply the "counsel of compliance." Matthew remains rather more ambiguous. Note the manner in which the tax was paid. The form of payment was quite accidental or coincidental. The payment did not come out of the resources of the group but, quite miraculously, from the mouth of a fish. Even here a tension remained and one senses the issue was still alive in Matthew's congregation. Matthew's Jesus asserts the obligation to pay is not present, but it is best to find a way to pay, whether by crook or by hook.

## Further Reading

Berger, P. L. *The Sacred Canopy: Elements of a Sociological Theory of Religion.* Garden City, N.Y.: Doubleday, 1969.

Betz, O. "Felsenmann und Felsengemeinde." *ZNW* 48 (1957): 49–77.

Bornkamm, G. "The Authority to Bind and to Loose in the Church in Matthew's Gospel." In *Jesus and Man's Hope,* ed. D. G. Miller, 1:37–50. Pittsburgh: Pittsburgh Theological Seminary, 1970.

Bultmann, R. *The History of the Synoptic Tradition.* Rev. ed. Trans. J. Marsh. San Francisco: Harper and Row, 1963.

Cohen, S. *Josephus in Galilee and Rome: His Vita and Development as a Historian.* Leiden: Brill, 1979.

Goodman, M. "The First Jewish Revolt: Social Conflict and the Problem of Debt." *JJS* 33 (1982): 417–27.

———. "Nerva, the *Fiscus Judaicus* and Jewish Identity." *JRS* 79 (1989): 40–44.

Harrington, D. *The Gospel of Matthew.* Sacra Pagina 1. Collegeville, Minn.: Michael Glazier/Liturgical Press, 1991.

Horbury, W. "The Temple Tax." In *Jesus and the Politics of His Day,* ed. E. Bammel and C. F. D. Moule, 266–73. Cambridge: Cambridge University Press, 1986.

Kee, H. C. "The Terminology of Mark's Exorcism Stories." *NTS* 14 (1967–68): 232–46.

Kelber, W. *Mark's Story of Jesus.* Philadelphia: Fortress, 1979.

Luz, U. "The Disciples in the Gospel According to Matthew." In *The Interpretation of Matthew,* ed. G. Stanton, 98–128. Philadelphia: Fortress, 1983.

———. *Matthew in History: Interpretation, Influence, and Effects.* Minneapolis: Fortress, 1994.

Ma'oz, Z. "Banias Excavation Project—1988." *Exploration and Surveys in Israel* 7.8 (1989): 10–11.

Meyers, E. "The Cultural Setting of Galilee: The Case of Regionalism in Early Judaism." *ANRW* II.19.1 (1979): 686–702.

Murphy, F. *The Structure and Meaning of Second Baruch.* SBLDS 78. Atlanta: Scholars Press, 1985.

Nau, A. J. *Peter in Matthew: Discipleship, Diplomacy, and Dispraise.* Collegeville, Minn.: Michael Glazier/Liturgical Press, 1992.

Overman, J. A. "Heroes and Villains in Palestinian Lore: Matthew's Use of Traditional Jewish Polemic." SBLSP 29 (1990): 390–98.

———. *Matthew's Gospel and Formative Judaism: The Social World of the Matthean Community.* Minneapolis: Fortress, 1990.

Strecker, G. *Der Weg der Gerechtigkeit: Untersuchung zur Theologie des Matthäus.* Göttingen: Vandenhoeck and Ruprecht, 1966.

Trilling, W. "Amt und Amtsverständnis bei Matthäus." In *Mélanges Bibliques: Festschrift for B. Rigaux,* ed. A. Descamps, 29–44. Gembloux: Duculot, 1969.

Vermes, G. *Jesus and the World of Judaism.* London: SCM, 1983.

Weber, M. *Economy and Society.* Ed. G. Roth and C. Wittich. Berkeley: University of California Press, 1978.

# Chapter Ten

# Discipline and Order in the Church — 18:1–18:35

## True Greatness and Care for the Little Ones

In chapter 18 Matthew has concentrated a large measure of his instruction on community order and discipline. Here he lays out his views on the principles and priorities that should govern the collective life of Matthean Jews. The main theme of the chapter is dissension and erring members, but Matthew's message is rather carefully couched in terms of deference and forgiveness, which should typify ecclesial relations. W. Thompson and W. Pesch have both shown that the emphasis in this chapter is on forgiveness and reconciliation, though quite clearly there is an extent to which Matthew simply will not bend.

That these issues are set out so clearly signals certain important social and institutional developments in the history of the Matthean community. Discipline, excommunication, an explicit internal judicial process, and priorities by which the assembly should guide its life all denote significant developments in the life of a church. Matthew's Gospel reflects that the community behind the Gospel has moved away from whatever charismatic beginnings Jesus-centered Judaism may have once possessed. Sociologically, Matthew's community is far beyond its infancy. Structure, authority, guidelines, and modes of discipline exist and are being exercised. These developments and structures are necessary if the community is going to fashion its own identity, stave off the threats of its foes — real or imagined — and survive over the long haul. Chapter 18 is where Matthew attempts to lay out his community's social and institutional expectations for members.

The chapter begins with the synoptic question about greatness. In Matthew Jesus simply poses the question to the disciples: "Who is the greatest in the kingdom of heaven?" (18:1). Mark's version of the question suggests that Jesus had overheard the disciples arguing about who was the greatest (Mark 9:34). This somewhat unflattering glimpse of the disciples is absent in Matthew. In response to his own question in Matthew Jesus calls a child to him and utters the familiar logion, "Truly I say to you, unless you turn and become like children, you will never enter the kingdom of heaven. Whoever humbles oneself like this child, he is the greatest in the kingdom of heaven. Whoever receives one such child in my name receives me" (18:3–5).

Aside from the obvious evidence that Jesus was not a parent, what else can be said of this familiar passage? Matthew tends to employ kinship categories metaphorically and uses terms of endearment to describe community members. "Child," "brother," and "little ones" all serve as common titles for fellow members. "Child" here is being used metaphorically to capture the traits of deference, dependence, and openness that traditionally and romantically have been assigned to children and are encouraged within the Matthean community. Matthean members must not claim priority, position, or acumen. These do not constitute true greatness and Matthean Jews should eschew such usual marks of accomplishment. As we shall see in chapter 23, Matthew explicitly rejects titles for the community and advocates the abandoning of hierarchy.

In 18:6 the shift is made from "child" to "little ones" (*mikron*). Here Matthew ties together two pieces of Mark's Gospel. He was trying to make his redaction appear seamless and, indeed, one can almost read this first section of chapter 18 without stumble or pause. Matthew intended the child and the little ones to be synonymous. They both represent the community members, some of whom were exposed or vulnerable to teachings and perspectives that might take them away from the group. The idealization of Matthean members as childlike, or in character diminutive "little ones," of course, raises questions about how the members, if they embraced these traits, would survive in the "real world." Matthew anticipated this question with his apocalyptic caution to those who might prey on the children of the flock. Those who caused the little ones to stumble would suffer a dreadful fate.

This apocalyptic warning provides the occasion for Matthew to encourage members to examine their own lives and behavior. This is how he utilizes the Marcan material about cutting off one's hand, foot, or plucking out one's eye if any cause one to stumble or give offense (not "sin"; the word here is *skandalon* in 18:6-9). Once again this metaphorical language is intended to instruct the members to avoid the errors or dissension that divide the community or, in some extreme instances, result in the expulsion of members. Such divisive and destructive behavior had to be avoided at all cost because it would imperil the vulnerable members of the group. The cause or threat of offense had to be cut out for the good of the church and the protection of certain members.

Matthew's counsel in this regard was based on his deep and emotional concern for the members of the community. To him they were like children, family members, "little ones" who had the forces and authorities in the Matthean context set against them. The unity and preservation of the group was a paramount concern. Matthew's position was that it was not acceptable to lose even one of these "little ones' (18:14). Every single member counted and could not be lost. His attention to "the little ones" — those members put at risk — has provoked this arrangement of the Marcan material in Matthew 18:6-14.

The careful reader who compares Matthew and Mark will discover that Matthew deleted the Marcan story of the strange exorcist — the exorcist who cast out demons in Jesus' name but refused to follow with the disciples (Mark 9:38-41). Mark's Jesus finds this acceptable, though it bothers the disciples. Matthew did not include this Marcan story because that was not the way discipleship and membership worked in Matthean Judaism. To be a disciple was also to be a member of the Matthean community. Each member counted, and each one would be counted. The unity, preservation, and presence of the members was a fundamental concern and worry for the author. It is quite clear, then, that at the very least Matthew believed there were those in his setting who were out to get the members. Allegiance to the group was perceived as increasingly difficult and threatening, but absolutely crucial. The community itself had to provide the security and the support necessary to remain a faithful member of Matthew's church.

## Jesus Teaches about Forgiveness

Matthew begins to highlight the prominence forgiveness must take in Matthean social relations in 18:12ff. He adds greater weight to this principle by placing a question about forgiveness in the mouth of Peter (18:21–22), and he draws a connection between God's forgiveness and human forgiveness in the distinctly Matthean parable usually titled "The Unforgiving Servant" (18:23–35). "What do you think," Jesus begins (v. 12). This opening rhetorical question (*ti humin dokei*) is characteristic of Matthew's own hand. "If a person has a hundred sheep and one has gone astray, does he not leave the ninety-nine and go in search of the one that went astray?... It is not the will of my father in heaven that one of these little ones should perish." Matthew's advice here is clear. Great effort should be expended to save or retrieve the lost, imperiled, or potentially erring member.

When Matthew wishes to punctuate a point he places a question or comment in the mouth of Peter. This can be seen in the second incident in the boat and the storm in chapter 14 involving Peter, the greatly expanded version of the Petrine Confession in chapter 16, the first question about taxes in chapter 17, and here again in 18:21. Peter asks Jesus, called *kurie* or "Lord" here, how often should he forgive his brother (*adelphos*, another common Matthean term for community members)? A core of this material originally comes from Q (Luke 17:4). But Matthew has reworked it considerably. Only in Matthew is the teaching provoked by a Petrine question about the limit of forgiveness. Jesus' answer about the limit of one's forgiveness is "seven times seventy" or, of course, limitless. The number seems to be derived from Genesis 4:24 where the avenging of Cain and Lamech are referenced.

The point and rationale for forgiveness within the Matthean context is developed at length in 18:23–35 in the Matthean parable of the forgiving king and the unforgiving servant. This is a so-called Matthean parable of the kingdom. In the parables of the kingdom, which begin as though they are similes or analogies about the kingdom, the priorities and objectives of Matthean corporate life are laid out. Matthew's church is ideally a mirror or reiteration of the principles and conviction operative in God's kingdom. His community is, in his view, the community of the kingdom of heaven. The relationships and priorities in the Matthean kingdom on earth are to be "as they are in heaven."

The parable of the forgiving king is Matthew's story about what he believes God has done for Matthean Jews. Once again Matthew uses the subject of debts (*opheiletas;* 18:24, 28, 30, 32, 34) to characterize right relationships and attitudes within the church. The forgiving king, God, has forgiven his servants, the Matthean Jesus-centered Jews, a debt they could not pay (v. 24). Yet there are at least some instances where the forgiven members continue to enforce the debt they are owed by other members or "their brothers" (*adelpho;* v. 35). In this parable Matthew is teaching about forgiveness *within the community*, and not primarily beyond the bounds of the church. This is a story about those who fail to forgive other servants or their brothers, that is, other Matthean Jews.

Those members who do not enact forgiveness in this manner and fail to see the core value forgiveness constitutes for the community are "wicked servants" (*doule ponere*), and God will ultimately enforce their own debt rather than forgive it. If members who have received mercy fail to show mercy to other members (18:33; 5:7), their forgiveness will be called into question. Decisions about members, their behavior, and above all the preservation of the community are grounded in the group's commitment to forgiveness. Matthew's arrangement of this material in chapter 18 highlights unmistakably the fundamental place of forgiveness in Matthean communal ethics and actions. The tough decisions and disciplinary action that eventually come to all communities, including Matthew's, must be informed by this principle of forgiveness.

## Discipline and the Erring Member

In the middle of chapter 18, couched within the instructions about forgiveness, Matthew inserts the method by which the community has to deal with those members who fail to conform to the Matthean definition of true membership. Matthew 18:15–20 is largely material unique to Matthew. No other Gospel contains such explicit instruction about how to deal with erring members.

> If your brother sins [*hamartia*] against you, go and tell him his fault alone—between you and him. If he listens to you, you have gained your brother. But if he does not listen, take one or two others along with you, that every word may be confirmed by the evidence of two or three witnesses. If he refuses to listen to them, tell it to the church [*ecclesia*]; and if he refuses to listen even to the church, let him be to you as a gentile and a tax-collector. Truly, I say to you, whatever you bind on earth shall be bound in heaven, and whatever you loose on earth shall be loosed in heaven.

Matthew's advice here is aimed at drawing back members who are perilously close to being lost to the community. The notion of "gaining a brother back" is distinctly Matthean. He uses this term elsewhere (*ekerdasas* from *kerdaino*, meaning "gain," "profit," or "win") in 16:26 and 25:20, 22. Indeed, there may even be something of a missionary overtone to this term, as D. Daube has indicated. That is, within early Jesus movements there was the reality of members losing faith or interest in the new group. Also, relatively new groups must struggle not just to reiterate, but to shape and develop the behavior and beliefs that will mark off the group from others. What were Matthean Judaism's identity and communal traits? Discipline is an albeit unpopular, but vital step in community formation and identity. What would they *not* allow? What behavior and beliefs were incongruous with Matthean membership? These questions, too, are crucial in shaping a strong sense of corporate identity. In attempting to come to grips with this social and theological necessity, there will inevitably be those who cannot agree or conform to the emerging community consensus. In extreme cases, excommunication and a decision to view the subject henceforth as a nonmember will be necessary. However, the goal of this disciplinary process is to win brothers back, not to drive them away.

The initial action that Matthew proscribes is the offended member seeking out the brother "alone" (*monou;* 18:15). Much of the dissension and strife between church members can and should be dealt with quietly and quickly between two people. The destructive role of gossip and innuendo was no less a reality in Matthew's day than in ours. When wronged, when there is something "between you and a brother, go alone and tell him his fault. If he listens to you, you have gained a brother."

Too frequently though, within the highly charged and emotional milieu of religious communities, this does not suffice and may in fact exacerbate the issue. Then, Matthew counsels, bring one or two others with you to impress the issue upon the member. Should this procedure fail as well, bring the brother before the church. Should he refuse to listen to the church, let him be to you as a nonmember and one who has virtually nothing in common with the community, that is, "as a gentile and tax-collector"; this is the meaning of this odd Matthean stereotype that he also employed elsewhere (5:46–47; 6:7). Those who refuse to acknowledge the advice and assessment of the community effectively become outsiders. It is important to note that here the entire *ecclesia* enacts the punishment on the erring member and not the small group who confronted the member or a clique of leaders or authorities.

While Matthew's hand and vocabulary are in evidence throughout this section, Matthew himself cannot be credited with fashioning this disciplinary action. The so-called testimony of two witnesses has its roots in Deuteronomy 19:15 and Leviticus 19:7. This procedure of having two witnesses when confronting an erring member can also be seen at Qumran (CD 9; also 1QS 5-6) and in Josephus (*Life* 49; *Ant.* 4.219). This principle of two witnesses, apparently rather common within and among second-temple Judaisms, adds a dimension of justice and balance where community tensions and issues are concerned. Apparently, private disputes between members really do effect the whole community. Where they cannot be resolved quickly and cleanly, the community should get involved. The wisdom and putative objectivity of other well-intentioned members can find a solution where the dispute between two people, when left to their own devices, can easily escalate out of proportion and control. Matthew took the wisdom of this advice from his forbearers in the Hebrew Bible and applied it to his own community. He was not alone in seeing the wisdom in this measure and the communal harmony it could very often preserve.

Matthew does include instructions about excluding members from the assembly. While other Gospel writers do not offer such instruction, the Apostle Paul does in the case of the man who is living with his father's wife (1 Cor. 5:1ff.). "Let him who has done this be removed from among you" (1 Cor. 5:2). Paul advocates excommunication here "so that [the man's] spirit may be saved in the day of the Lord Jesus" (1 Cor. 5:5). Paul reasons that excommunication will result in the salvation of the member in some eschatological sense.

Unlike Paul, Matthew does not reflect any reason for excommunication other than the preservation of the community. The failure to bring one's behavior into conformity with the values of the church will result in nonmembership and alienation from the community. They shall become like foreigners. Paul, driven by an immediacy and apocalyptic fervor not really evident in Matthew any longer, sees some ultimate virtue in excommunication that is not explicit in Matthew. The Matthean version of excommunication and community discipline, tempered as it is by the Matthean core value of forgiveness, is a mark of the organization and structure Matthean Judaism developed to rival other existing structures, and to try to insure the perpetuation of their corporate life and order. Unlike the Pauline excommunication in 1 Corinthians, there is no suggestion that this finally is the best thing for the erring brother. The focus of this action is the community and its health, not the pastoral care of the deviant member.

This passage on discipline ends with a verse that highlights the authority the community believed it possesses, and the degree to which their authority rivaled that of other civic structures within their setting. "Truly, I say to you, whatever you bind [*deo*] on earth, shall be bound in heaven, and whatever you loose [*luo*] on earth, shall be loosed in heaven" (18:18). On the surface this passage seems to be a reiteration of 16:19; 16:19, however, appears to have been spoken to and about Peter. Matthew 18:18, quite clearly, is spoken to and about the *ecclesia;* here it is the church that possesses the authority to bind and to loose.

In the context of chapter 18 the judicial and punitive measures of the congregation carry the weight and sanction of the courts of heaven. This is an exalted claim and one that Matthew makes on numerous occasions. The decisions of the assembly carry the weight and authority of heaven. This is at best a thinly veiled assertion of the authority of the church in the face of those who question it, or who embrace another authority in the broader Matthean setting. Such authority is claimed and enshrined in 16:19 and 18:18 precisely because the community and its leaders recently had their authority, beliefs, and decisions questioned and, perhaps, rejected. These two verses seek to invest the members and the positions the church has assumed with the utmost authority. The decisions and judgments of the community parallel judgments made in heaven. Clearly, the message is that one flaunts the decisions and judgments of the Matthean community at considerable risk.

What is the relationship between 16:19 and 18:18? These are the two places where the author is talking explicitly about the church (*ecclesia*) and its authority. The years surrounding the writing of this Gospel were fluid if not fragmented years. Matthew's community felt this fragmentation profoundly. The events of 70 C.E. and immediately thereafter left a political and religious vacuum locally. In the larger sense, and in the larger political scene, there was no vacuum and little confusion. Rome knew just what it was doing from 66 C.E. forward. Vespasian and the new Flavian line were in charge and Judea and Galilee were important pieces of Flavian political propaganda. D. Edwards has helped sketch the important role of Judea after 70 in bolstering the power and position of the Flavian rulers Vespasian and his sons Titus and Domitian. The Roman system was working for the time being. And, welcomed or not, Galilee and Judea were receiving the attention and designs of their Roman overlords.

The vacuum and confusion existed on a local and parochial level. The Roman imperial system was in place and functioned in its noted efficient but often unforgiving manner. The question that loomed large and, while unanswered, left the religiopolitical situation up for grabs was, who at the local level would help implement Rome's policies in Palestine? In the villages and cities of post-70 Palestine, who would speak for the people, extend Rome's reach, and carry the traditions and authority of historic Israel during these precarious in-between years? What body or person would emerge with an answer to this tension? And might a group emerge capable of standing in the pregnant breach between Roman imperial rule on the one hand and Israel's traditions and desire for autonomy on the other? Between the destruction of the temple in Jerusalem in 70 and the cessation of the Bar Kochba revolt in 135 C.E., who possessed authority in the traditional and civic political entities throughout Palestine? There was a struggle for power and voice in these formative and fragmented years. Matthew's Gospel is a document that essays this vacuum, tension, and struggle for power on a local level. And Matthew's Gospel claims to stand in the breach, understanding Roman realities but possessing the authority and insight to speak for historic Israel. However, Matthew's is not the only voice laying claim to this position.

The power to bind and to loose granted to the *ecclesia* represents Matthean Judaism's claim to supplant the judicial and legal powers in his immediate setting. He felt his community should levy the decisions and penalties of God in heaven. Usual avenues and local political leaders were not those to whom the community should turn. Indeed, they were rejected. The Matthean community possessed the highest possible authority. Even the broader community, those beyond the bounds of the Matthean church, should look to the *ecclesia* for insight, teaching, and judgment, and recognize this authority. The claim to possess this authority and to bind the judgments of heaven reflects this religiopolitical vacuum. Who was in charge in Matthew's context was, at least for some, an open question. Matthew's attempt to move into the breach was met with significant opposition. By chapter 23 Matthew is quite explicit about those other local authorities who rivaled and rejected Matthean Judaism as a viable response to this period of political and religious turmoil.

This conflict and struggle were happening in numerous settings in post-70 Galilee-Judea. Matthew's was but one voice. Bar Kochba and the dedication to resistance were another. Numerous apocalyptic documents reveal yet others. Matthew's particular response to the crisis did not endure for a long period. There is evidence of Matthean influence elsewhere, but very little evidence of the endurance of his brand of Jesus-centered Judaism. However, for a time, in the years in between, Matthew's response to the crisis and leadership vacuum of the post-70 period was significant enough to warrant the attention of other potential local leaders. Matthean Judaism was viewed as a threat by some, though it did not finally succeed in eclipsing its rivals.

In chapter 9 we noted the connection Josephus makes between the Pharisees and "the power to bind and to loose." Josephus uses these words to describe the judicial power of the Pharisees under Alexandra (*J.W.* 1.111 ‖ *Ant.* 13.407). Of course, the Pharisees, or some post-70 form of them, were Matthew's concern and competition. It is not surprising that he would claim for his community the kind of judicial and administrative authority another post-70 writer should ascribe to the Pharisees. Matthew's church has been granted that same power. Only Matthew's community was not given that power by a local lord or by a Roman official. The authority to bind and loose held by the Matthean church (18:18), and by Matthean leaders (16:19), has been given to them by God. This claim would have doubtless provoked much debate and perhaps enmity within the local setting of Matthew's Gospel.

If Matthean Judaism were to move into the breach and vacuum of the post-70 period, it would have to supply leaders and officials to govern and adjudicate on a local level. Indeed, Matthew's disciples and Peter in particular represent such a development. His portrait of the followers of Jesus is at the same time a portrait of a group of leaders trained and charged to lead, teach, and judge the people. Matthew 16:19 then claims not just that there are Matthean leaders to pick up where pre-70 leaders left off, but they are in a position to have learned from the mistakes of the past. These leaders will be faithful, law-abiding, and just teacher/leaders of the people. The leaders, through the teachings the community received from Jesus, and from the divine disclosure captured in the Petrine Confession, possess the authority to bind and loose, and to enact the decisions and dictates of heaven. The scribes and Pharisees falsely claim such authority.

In a related way 18:18 makes the same claim for the entire community when they are called upon to make decisions and establish order. Just when the local Matthean leaders exercised their authority and when the entire community was required to pass judgment is not entirely clear. Each possessed judicial authority and the absolute nature of that authority would have placed them in conflict with any other local judicial or legal authorities. Chapters 16 and 18 underscore what we saw in the Sermon on the Mount. Matthew rejects the role and authority of the court in his setting and posits his own leaders and assembly as the only viable and legitimate court. His community and its leaders will fulfill this role, which is presently being executed by other local figures whom the author asserts are illegitimate. There are leadership roles, ministries, or functions established within the Matthean church. There are teachers, judges, scribes, and role models. Peter symbolizes the presence of such types within the community. Yet, when one reads chapter 18, and after that chapter 23, it is clear that particular functions and authoritative roles that have developed in Matthew's group are not over and above the church but are embedded within the collective life of the community. That is, authority in Matthew's community, whether exercised individually or collectively, is based on the authority of the church, and not a person. It is the community that grants authority — even to individual *virtuosi* within the church — and it is the community that will decide who speaks for Matthean Judaism and who or what constitutes a threat.

## The Authority of the Church

The authority of the *ecclesia*, assembly, or church is stressed in 18:18 in the power the group possesses to bind and to loose, but also, quite clearly, in the unique Matthean saying, "I say to you, if two of you agree on earth about anything they ask, it will be done for them by my father in heaven. For where two or three are gathered in my name, there I am in the midst of them" (18:19–20).

Matthew claims, of course, that God has granted insight and authority to the Matthean community. Others in his setting who claim a similar authority are actually false guides, teachers and scribes whose authority is manmade and bankrupt. The Matthean church claims their authority is from God and was delivered to them in the form of instruction and revelation by Jesus. But the locus of that authority is now the gathered body, the community of Matthean Jews. While on a theological level Matthew would agree that all authority is from God, the locus and exercise of that authority takes place within the Matthean church. The assembly, no matter how large or small, constitutes the arena and setting of God's presence and power according to Matthew. "Where two or three are gathered in my name, there I am in the midst of them [*en meso auton*]." The community's belief in the ongoing presence of Jesus is confirmed and reinforced in the gathering together of even a few Matthean faithful. The reassurance of that presence fosters a certain power and enables the church to enact the authority it claims it has. "If two of you agree on earth about anything they ask, it will be done for them by my father in heaven" (18:19).

Some in the Matthean community misunderstood authority, position, and the exercise of power in the church. There were some who had come to see power as hierarchical and dependent on one's position. In 23:6–12 Matthew explicitly reacts against those in his community who view authority as tied to position and office. To Matthew this is a fatal flaw in the actions and attitudes of the Matthean opponents. To view authority in this erroneous manner renders one's God-given authority null and void.

Authority in Matthew's church is grounded in the local assembly itself. The people, that is, the community and collectivity, possess the authority. They make the tough decisions, exercise God's power through prayer, and through their gathering together provide for the ongoing presence of Jesus. While there are almost certainly leaders and teachers in Matthew's church, they do not possess authority. At best, they are granted what authority they have from the assembly. Authority still resides in the hands and body of the community. Time and again in Matthew's Gospel his high view of the group, its preservation and sanctity come across. Misunderstandings about authority, its whence and its locus, lead to division within and a corruption of the assembly. In chapter 18 Matthew instructs the *ecclesia* about authority and power. When the people come together, when they agree, this is where authority resides and power is manifest.

Like the Sermon on the Mount, the liturgical context of this instruction is clear. Coincidentally, in the *Mishna* (*'Abot* 3.2) there is a related phrase about the presence of God when studying Torah: "If two sit together and words of the Law pass between them, the divine presence abides between them." Assembling, prayer, the mystical presence of Jesus claimed by those gathered, and the invocation of Jesus' name are all aspects of these two short but loaded verses (18:19–20). With the division and tension so evident in this Gospel, and with the perceived threat from outsiders, why would this community persist and survive? In these verses Matthew asserts the benefits from remaining among the group and not forsaking its gatherings. In these gatherings some of the promises the church believes Jesus gave them are fulfilled. The presence of Jesus promised to the disciples at the close of the Gospel is, apparently, fulfilled in this Matthean saying about gathering together. The people gathered together fulfill promises made to the group about prayer and its power, and in their gathered church members feel the authority to resist threats and impose order that individually seems out of reach. In the group power and possibilities that alone seem implausible appear realistic. When even two of them agree on something, it can be done. In that action, the community senses the power and the presence of Jesus which was promised but, of course, is understandably so elusive.

## Further Reading

Daube, D. *"Kerdano* as a Missionary Term." *HTR* 40 (1947): 109–20.

Edwards, D. "Religion, Power and Politics: Jewish Defeats by the Romans in Iconography and Josephus." In *Diaspora Jews and Judaism: Essays in Honor of, and in Dialogue with A. Thomas Kraabel*, ed. J. A. Overman and R. S. MacLennan, 293–309. Atlanta: Scholars Press, 1992.

Forkman, G. *The Limits of Religious Community: Expulsion from the Religious Community within the Qumran Sect, within Rabbinic Judaism, and within Primitive Christianity.* Lund: Gleerup, 1972.

Lona, H. "In meinem Namen versammelt. Mt.18, 20 und liturgisches Handeln." *Archiv für Liturgiewissenschaft* 27 (1985): 373–404.

Pesch, W. *Matthäus als Seelsorger.* Stuttgart: Katholisches Bibelwerk, 1966.

Scott, B. "The King's Accounting. Matthew 18:23–34." *JBL* 104 (1985): 429–42.

Thompson, W. *Matthew's Advice to a Divided Community: Mt. 17:22–18:35.* Rome: Biblical Institute, 1970.

*Chapter Eleven*

# The Journey South to Judea and Jerusalem — 19:1–22:14

## Questions about the Law

In 19:1 Matthew signals a significant shift in his story through the departure of Jesus from Galilee. Galilee had been the movement's home, and the Matthean community understood Jesus and the disciples as having been centered in Capernaum. Matthew goes to considerable pains to have Jesus and his followers remain in the Galilee throughout the course of his ministry. The crowds come from other regions to Galilee to see, hear, and be healed by Jesus.

There is a dramatic shift in scene and the tension is heightened as Jesus heads south at the start of chapter 19. What has been ministry, teaching, and ongoing tension with local authorities seems to have escalated to a point of no return. Jesus is now starting to head south, into Judea, to Jerusalem, and to his death. In Jerusalem Matthew's story of Jesus will reach its culmination. Luke's Gospel captures this poignant turn in the story with the dramatic phrase, "He set his face to go to Jerusalem" (Luke 9:51). Matthew 19:1 is the beginning of the end of Matthew's story of Jesus. Jesus' decision to go to Jerusalem is itself a perplexing one. What could have motivated this? What was to be gained from traveling to Jerusalem? We will take this up when discussing Jesus and his relationship to the temple.

Matthew 19:3–12 and 19:16–22 comprise two more sections on the law. The correct understanding and interpretation, the right application and fulfillment of the law are crucial themes

277

for Matthew. This is one very important feature that distinguishes Matthean Judaism from other second-temple options in Matthew's view. His community is the form of Judaism that fully understands and enacts the law. The Matthean community "fulfills" the law (cf. 5:17). Matthew intends for his church to be in debate with those in his setting who see and interpret the law differently. So he places a great deal of emphasis on teaching and arguing about the true nature and interpretation of the law. He takes up this theme once again at the start of chapter 19.

Matthew 19:3–12 is a conflict story or dispute about the law (what German-speaking scholars have referred to as *Streitgespräche*) between Jesus and the Pharisees. The legal debate in this instance involves the question of divorce. Once again the Pharisees are portrayed as those who misunderstand the law and who constitute Matthew's legal and political nemesis. Matthean conflict stories always perform the dual purposes of further explicating the distinctive Matthean *halacha*, or legal interpretation, while at the same time attempting to discredit the views of his opponents, the so-called Pharisees. This story comes originally from Mark 10:2–12, but Matthew has made some notable changes in his version.

First, in Mark the Pharisees' question is whether Jesus believes divorce is permissible or not. "Is it lawful for a man to divorce his wife?" Matthew has changed the question slightly but significantly. In 19:3 the Pharisees ask, "Can a man divorce his wife *for any cause?*" Matthew has changed the question simply from "is divorce lawful?" to "on what basis is divorce lawful?"

Matthew's version more closely resembles the debates about divorce which come to us from the Mishna. Tractate *m. Gittin* devotes great attention to the procedures for divorce. It is clear from the discussion in *m. Gittin* that divorce was accepted, though the causes for divorce are not expounded upon at any great length. There is considerable debate early on in *m. Gittin* about writs of divorce; when is a divorce contract legal, under what conditions must it be signed, delivered, and who must be the witnesses of the writ? The parallels and distinctions between slaves and wives are also discussed in this context. In *m. Gittin* 9:9 the views of the House of Shammai and Hillel are compared concerning the question of *when* divorce is acceptable. The House of Shammai says, "A man should divorce his wife only because he has found grounds for it in unchastity." And those in the House of Hillel say, "Even if she spoiled his dish." And R. Aqiba says, "Even if he found someone else prettier than she." As J. Kampen and others have recently pointed out, this was also a crucial issue among Qumran sectarians and the Dead Sea Scrolls.

Clearly, the question of the grounds for divorce was a lively and important one in Matthew's setting and day. Mark seems less connected with this particular context and question. In Mark Jesus seems to deny the option of divorce, much less the debate over how to divorce and when it is lawful. Matthew, in contrast, places Jesus in the midst of this proto-rabbinic debate. Here Matthew's Jesus sides more with the School of Shammai, and in fact quotes the same "exception clause" that we read in *m. Gittin* 9:9 from Shammai. Matthew is consistent on this point. This is the second treatment of divorce in the Gospel. In the Sermon on the Mount, Jesus had also discussed divorce. There again, in 5:31–32, Jesus allows for the exception of *porneia*, though here the qualifying term *logou*, or "word of *porneia*," is included. Matthew 5:32 suggests merely the "charge" of *porneia* is sufficient for divorce. Nevertheless, in both instances, 5:32 and 19:9, Matthew allows for the "exception clause" of *porneia*.

The meaning of this crucial term, *porneia*, is important but rather elusive. In most versions of the Bible the translation leads us to believe the term means sexual promiscuity or cheating on one's husband. There is, of course, no mention of the man cheating on the wife. And it is clear in these divorce texts that it is the man's prerogative to divorce. But I think this crucial Greek term has a broader meaning than simply sexual promiscuity. *Porneia* was a very common term for prostitution, itself a common institution within the ancient world. But within Hebrew and second-temple Greek literature this term takes on a broader meaning. First, harlotry or sexual promiscuity becomes a metaphor for idolatry or faithlessness on the part of Israel. This is seen in Jeremiah 2:20 and 3:9, and in particular in the famous story of Israel's faithlessness in Hosea. But there are occasions when the Septuagint will translate unfaithfulness or immorality as *porneia*, as in the case of Numbers 14:33, and Isaiah 47:10 and 57:9.

In this regard, in the other instance when Matthew uses this term in 15:19, *porneia* seems to carry more of an overtone of immorality and corruption. *Porneia* in 15:19 appears in a list of vices that come out of the heart. Interestingly, it is obviously distinguished in this context from adultery (*moicheiai*), for Matthew lists both of them. *Porneia*, here, is like "evil thoughts, murder, adultery, *porneia*, theft, false witness, and slander" (15:19). This could be referring specifically to sexual promiscuity, but a married woman engaging in sexual promiscuity is committing adultery. If Matthew understands *porneia* in 5:32 and 19:9 to mean sex outside of marriage he is being redundant in 15:19. I believe the term is best understood as a broad term that stands for immorality and unfaithfulness of, potentially, many kinds. As Kampen has pointed out, incest, polygamy, and other kinds of idolatry could well be included here. An important possible instance often overlooked by modern interpreters might be intermarriage or marriage within the degrees of kinship as discussed in Leviticus 18:6–18.

The debate about divorce was so lively in the second-temple period and, in many circles, is still so today precisely because the meaning of this important clause is not clear. The meaning of the term *porneia* and Matthew's threefold application of it is broad and open to interpretation. D. Harrington points out that even in the early rabbinic debate, as evidenced in *m. Gittin* 9:9ff., the meaning of the Hebrew equivalent is similarly debated. The origin of the exception clause is Deuteronomy 24:1–4. The crucial Hebrew terms (*'erwat dabar* = because of some indecency), like the Greek *porneia*, were unclear and debated. The House of Shammai seems to have reversed the word order in Hebrew (*debar 'erwah*), meaning "something shameful." The House of Shammai thought this cleared up the ambiguity of Deuteronomy 24:1–4 and took it to refer to unchastity. So some of Matthew's contemporaries were not only arguing about divorce and its grounds, they were also arguing over the meaning of the terms of the discussion. Matthew's use of the exception clause and term *porneia* is no less vague. The force of the term seems to refer to immorality in a general sense. Here Matthew again articulates what he believes was Jesus' view, and by extension his own community's view, on this important and timely question. Corruption and unfaithfulness, in a rather broad sense, constitute grounds for divorce in Matthew's view.

This interpretation leads the disciples to wonder if it pays at all to marry. That is, immorality in the context of marriage is quite common, particularly if one accepts Matthew's definition of adultery in the Sermon on the Mount (cf. 5:28), as we assume many Matthean Jews did. In light of this, the disciples in Matthew respond to Jesus' teaching on divorce saying, "If this is the case of a man with his wife, it is better not to marry" (19:10). Jesus responds with one of the more elliptical sayings in Matthew's Gospel: "Not all can accept this teaching but those to whom it is given. For there are eunuchs who have been so from birth, and there are eunuchs who have been made eunuchs by men, and there are eunuchs who have made themselves such for the sake of the kingdom of heaven. Whoever can accept it, let him accept it."

It is extremely difficult to make sense of this verse in that it is the only mention of eunuchs in the Gospels. There is a well-known story from the Acts of the Apostles about the so-called Ethiopian eunuch in Acts 8:27ff. who met Philip somewhere along the Gaza strip on a desert road. The Acts story is rather more consistent with the meaning of the term "eunuch" as it came through the Hebrew Bible to Matthew's day. In Hebrew "eunuch" (*saris*) refers to a foreign official (cf. Genesis 37–38; 50:4; 1 Kgs. 22:9; Esther 1:10–11). It is an administrative official of some significant rank. This is the case with the Ethiopian eunuch in Acts 8:27. This man was "an official of the court of Queen Candace, the Queen of Ethiopia, in charge of all her treasure." The term then in both the Hebrew Bible and in Acts, as E. Haenchen and others have long noted, does not necessarily denote castration. Rather, it draws attention to the political and perhaps military rank of a foreign dignitary.

Matthew's verses about eunuchs in the context of a discussion about divorce do not seem to relate directly to the Acts passage.

Leadership and participation in the Matthean cause, and an embrace of Matthew's *halacha*, may result in the decision to forego marriage. An interesting and plausible interpretation of this odd passage has been that this phrase and charge had been leveled at the Matthean community. "Eunuchs for the kingdom of heaven" might be viewed as something of a slur against the community members. The devotion and sacrifice the members enacted has led some to avoid marriage and even practice celibacy, as the disciples' question in 19:10 suggests. Some doubtless viewed this extreme degree of devotion as a diminution of traditional family roles. Indeed, Jesus' challenge to the traditional family structure is well attested within the Gospel tradition, and Matthew is no exception. Peter captures the life of denial that many in the community were living in 19:27. Such ascetic-like behavior, which flaunts the usual and traditional social structures, often provokes question and criticism from those outside the group. Such may have been the case with this phrase. Matthew has taken this criticism and tried to put a positive spin on it. Some choose to be eunuchs, while men command it of others, but the Matthean community is "eunuchs" for the kingdom of heaven. The rejection of traditional social structures, lines of authority, and allegiance are not negative but positive symbols of Matthean devotion and commitment, so the author claims in this unique passage.

There is evidence that other groups practiced similar forms of denial or at least had the reputation of doing so. Some of the Essenes and another ascetic group, the Theraputae, practiced celibacy in advocacy of their cause and utter devotion to their call. The brief biographical information we are given about John the Baptist seems to suggest that he, too, had abandoned traditional familial and social relations to preach his baptism of repentance and the imminent arrival of the kingdom. Paul of Tarsus appears to have lived a life that inclined in this direction as well. I doubt that Matthew is implying that castration is a feature of Matthean discipleship. An argument in this direction could not be made from this lone use of the Greek term *eunouchoi*, or "eunuch," in 19:12. Rather, Matthew has taken this derisive slur from the outside and turned it into an expression, if not a metaphor, for the unusual devotion required of and reflected by the Matthean community. We have seen Matthew respond to charges from outsiders in the case of taxes in chapter 17 and the issue of the law in chapter 5. The saying about eunuchs for the kingdom of heaven is very likely another instance where he attempted to turn charges from outsiders into marks of veracity and honor within his church.

Matthew 19:16–22 is another section that pushes the issue of the law and Matthew's interpretation of the same. This is a story from Mark 10:17–22. Luke copies this story nearly verbatim, while Matthew makes some suggestive changes. In the earlier version the person who approached Jesus and asked about how he might obtain eternal life began by addressing Jesus as "Good Teacher" (Mark 10:17 ‖ Luke 18:18). In Matthew Jesus is addressed simply as "Teacher." Matthew has placed the term "good" (*agathon*) in a position to modify the deeds that must be done to inherit eternal life. Jesus' response is, "Why do you ask me about what is good? One there is who is good" (19:17). Matthew has lost the force and purpose of the Marcan saying about good and God. However, he has kept a rearranged version of the question. I suggest here Matthew was uncomfortable even reiterating the problem the Marcan text raises, that is, the suggestion that Jesus in some way may rival God. Even the term "god" is avoided by Matthew (Matt. 19:17 ‖ Mark 10:18 ‖ Luke 18:19). Matthew's theology is so high it prohibits him from even mentioning God's name or the Greek term *Theos*. It is for this reason that Matthew has consistently altered the Marcan formula "kingdom of God" and supplied instead the circumlocution "kingdom of heaven," which ostensibly suggests the same thing but avoids the use of the term/name "God." Matthew 19:16–17 evidences the same theological sensitivity on the author's part.

Matthew's Jesus responds to this reasonable question by saying, "If you would enter life, keep the commands." In Matthew the questioner asks, "Which?" The honest question implies that there are various views extant in Jesus' and Matthew's day where this question is concerned. The questioner seeks Jesus' interpretation of the law; that is, which laws are crucial and vital? What is the core of the law and, therefore, our life as faithful Jews?

Which laws must we keep? Jesus' answer begins with a recital of the decalogue. In 19:20 the person asks, "All these I have observed, what do I still lack?" Jesus tells the man, "If you wish to be perfect, go, sell what you possess and give to the poor, and you will have treasure in heaven, and come, follow me" (19:21). "When the young man heard this he went away sorrowful; for he had great possessions."

The authenticity of the questions and the apparent innocence and openness of the questioner provoke considerable pathos for the reader. One senses the genuine desire on the part of the man, particularly in Matthew's version of this story, to get to the bottom of this vital question. In Matthew the man is asking the questions. Jesus does not need to tell him he is still lacking something, as in Mark and Luke. The motivated, determined, and law-abiding man presses the point with Jesus. "What do I still lack?" This additional command from Jesus not found in the decalogue causes the man to leave heavy-hearted.

Matthew posits "perfection" as an obtainable Matthean goal in 19:21. This, too, is an addition to the earlier story supplied by Matthew. He used the same term to conclude a section of Jesus' teaching in the Sermon on the Mount (5:48). The term here, *teleios*, suggests something like "wholeness" or "fulfillment," as the English cognates to this term "telos" or "teleological" suggest. Matthew believed a certain attitude and a series of actions were required for his members. Actions and attitudes were indivisible for him. Following the Ten Commandments was required. "Not one jot or stroke will fall from the law" (cf. 5:20). But there was more. The relinquishment of earthly success and position was something Matthean Jews would have to learn to live with. This provides further opportunity for Matthew to explicate his interpretation of the whole law, but gives further expression to the sacrifice and difficulties the Matthean community faced in their setting.

This exchange between Jesus and the questioner provides the opportunity for Jesus to teach the disciples privately about riches and the kingdom. "It is hard for a rich man to enter the kingdom of heaven" (19:23). The disciples are astonished. "Who then can be saved?" they ask. "Only with God is it possible" is Jesus' answer. Peter rightly declares that they, the disciples, have left everything and followed Jesus (19:27). Peter's comment underscores the disciples as true followers of Jesus and accurate interpreters of God's demands upon God's people. As we have previously noted, those who *follow* in Matthew (*akolouthesamen*) are those who understand and apprehend the truth. This is a technical term or buzzword within the Matthean community for those who have taken the steps, embraced the principles, and suffered the rejection expected of Matthean Jews. These disciples, led by their spokesman Peter, will certainly obtain their reward.

Matthew borrows a saying from Q (Luke 18:30) and adds that in the new world (*palingenesia*) those "followers" will sit upon twelve thrones judging the twelve tribes of Israel. In this respect W. Trilling was correct in maintaining that Matthew, following Q, understood his community, or at least the faithful followers within it, to be the *true Israel*. In the end God will use them to judge the rest of Israel. Matthew's community was equipped to judge, the author would maintain, because they have been faithful, they have sacrificed and endured, and they have accurately understood *and acted out* the law. Here is where the well-intentioned wealthy questioner who simply could not bring himself to take that last step of denial and sacrifice can be distinguished from Matthean Jews. The faithful within the Matthean community have supposedly lived out the law fully and, therefore, would finally judge those others in Israel against this standard.

## Hierarchy in the Kingdom of Heaven

The disciples' question about who can be saved in 19:25 captures their surprise and amazement in hearing that the usual marks and categories of success and godliness no longer abide or suffice. Issues and tensions surrounding position, prerogatives, and hierarchy loom large in Matthew's Gospel. The discussion with the good questioner in 19:16ff. provokes a discussion in Matthew about priorities and hierarchy in the kingdom of heaven and

the Matthean community. Those who have not, who have sacrificed and left the usual marks of success and position within
the world, those will be rewarded (19:29). Matthew punctuates this with the thrice-repeated principle he inherited from
Mark: "Many that are first will be last, and the last first" (Matt.
19:30 ‖ Mark 10:31).

Matthew 20:1–16 contains a parable unique to Matthew which
is meant to illustrate Matthean Judaism's view on position and
place within the kingdom and community. This familiar parable of the laborers in the vineyard details a dispute between
workers and a vineyard owner. In the parable the householder
(*oikodespote*) hires workers for his vineyard at five different
points during the course of the day. In the end they all receive the same pay. This is a theologically significant point and
provokes consternation among those who were hired first. The
owner charges these early hires with begrudging others of his
generosity. One can see in this parable tension between older,
perhaps founding members of the Matthean community and
newer or younger members who see themselves as full partici-
pants in Matthean Judaism's life and discourse. As new members
come into an established community, or new ideas and principles come forth, tension and argument over who was here
first, whose voice should prevail, and who really constitutes the
proverbial backbone of the church will arise. Matthew's answer
here is all are equal and, like it or not, all have equal voice.

In 19:15b the owner says something interesting to the com-
plaining early workers. Literally translated, this passage says,
"Your eye is evil because I am good." The term "evil" (*poneros*)
is a common Matthean term for envy brought on by material things. This term represents money and position catching
one's eye. This is a common downfall of many within the kingdom of heaven. The grace or good God is willing to show
those who come late to the vineyard can easily cause dissension and envy within the community. This is a corrupting
influence, which is the essential meaning of the Matthean buzzword *poneros*. A degree of this tension and corruption seems
to have occurred within the Matthean church. Some members
perceived that there should be a rank or order of members

based on longevity in the group and, perhaps, other demonstrable accomplishments. Such a procedure and ranking were used in the Qumran community, as L. Schiffman and others have shown. This Matthean parable aims at responding to that understandable expectation. In this community the members are all theoretically equal. Not surprisingly, however, the number of times Matthew feels compelled to take up the issue of hierarchy suggests that this principle was not being enthusiastically embraced or endorsed by all. This parable is told for the benefit of the community. This instruction is intended to help guide, if not reform, the current state of relationships within the Matthean church. The parable concludes with the second recitation of the summarizing aphorism, "The last will be first and the first last" (20:16).

The next discussion about position and hierarchy occurs as Jesus and the twelve disciples are "going up to Jerusalem" (20:17–28). In 20:20 the mother of the sons of Zebedee, James and John, asks Jesus if her two sons may sit at his right hand and left "when he comes in his kingdom." This request from the mother is proceeded in Matthew by a prediction of Jesus' death and the suffering of the Son of man (20:17–19). The decision to go up to Jerusalem in Jesus' view means certain death and rejection. In the midst of this instruction about the struggles and rejection that lie ahead comes the question about position and power in the kingdom of heaven. It is worth noting that in the earlier Marcan version of this story the two disciples ask this question themselves. In Matthew their mother asks on their behalf. Once again Matthew has cleaned up an earlier Marcan portrait of the disciples which he views as unflattering. In Matthew it is the mother of James and John who is depicted as not fully understanding the principles that guide Matthean Judaism.

Jesus responds by saying essentially that this is not finally his call. It is God who makes such decisions. And, most important, this is not the way things will be done among "the followers." The rulers of the nations (*arkontes ton ethnon*) lord over others, and their great ones exercise authority. It is not so among the followers (20:26). Great ones among the followers are those who serve (*diakonos*). "Whoever would be first among you

must be your servant/slave" (*doulos*). The model for this philosophy about position and prerogative within the community
comes from Jesus' own biography. He did not claim position or
power, but chose to serve and sacrifice. "The Son of man came
not to be served but to serve, and give his life as a ransom
for many" (20:28). This is the principle that must inform Matthean relations and actions or the community will fragment and
fall apart.

Matthew's teaching does not utterly eschew position and
order, though he may well have meant to do so. To say the last
shall be first and the first shall be last does still posit a hierarchy, though in an ironic fashion he may have been trying to
do away with position altogether. Nevertheless, once priorities
are articulated and some notion of position or hierarchy is still
a possibility, competition and rivalry of some kind can easily
emerge. In the Matthean setting it may be nothing more or less
than who serves and suffers or sacrifices the most. This, too, is
a hierarchy. Also, Jesus' response to the mother of the Zebedee
boys does not completely reject hierarchy. He says, this is up to
God, though he is quick to add, we do not act as the rulers of
other nations act.

Leaders and authoritative figures are a sociological inevitabil-
ity within communities. There is ample evidence of teachers,
leaders, and judges, for example, within the Matthean community. The ever-present tension is, how can these inevitable and
necessary roles emerge within a community without corrupting
the communal relations and decision-making processes? This is
a local reality that Matthew must address. His answer is found,
he maintains, in the life and actions of Jesus as they came to him
in the Gospel tradition. Jesus was certainly a leader and authoritative figure. But he did not apply his leadership and authority
in a usual manner. Leadership and authority are demonstrated
through service and deference to others within the church.
Matthew is arguing for power, guidance, and leadership to be
present within the community that at the same time should
retain a collective and basically nonhierarchical form of communal life. This is a difficult balance to maintain. This view of
communal life would treat leadership as a gift exercised within

the church for the sake of the church. However, the leader would not possess any more de jure authority than any other member. All are servants to and for one another. Matthew will take up the theme and problem of hierarchy and office within the community once again in chapter 23.

## Jesus' Entry into Jerusalem

Chapter 21 begins with Jesus' entry into Jerusalem. This so-called triumphal entry is in each of the synoptic Gospels. Matthew follows Mark in 21:1–3. That Jesus should ride an ass into Jerusalem is supported by Matthew through a scriptural citation from Zechariah 9:9. Matthew's reading of Zechariah 9:9 may account for the confusion and emendation of Mark 11:2. Mark's earlier version has, naturally enough, Jesus riding into Jerusalem on a colt. Matthew 21:5 has Jesus mounted on a colt *and* an ass. Indeed, the two disciples in Matthew 21:2 were asked to bring both a colt and an ass to Jesus. This must come from Matthew's quite literal reading of Zechariah 9:9: "Lo, your king comes to you; triumphant and victorious is he, humble and riding on an ass, on a colt the foal of an ass." Matthew takes this passage to mean Jesus, in order to fulfill scripture, must ride both an ass and a colt at the same time into the city of the great king.

Jesus as king, of course, is punctuated with the imagery of the entry into Jerusalem, and by the citation from Zechariah utilized by Matthew. The crowds receive him as king in 21:8–9. This reception virtually assures that something will be done about this movement and its leader. In the view of Rome and their local lords it is the suggestion and possibility of Jesus' kingship which must finally lead to his death. The writers of the triumphal entry seem to be tying into a tradition of popular kingship that was very much alive during Jesus' day. The important mid-first-century B.C.E. text, the Psalms of Solomon, chapter 17, captures this vital tradition of popular kingship that was reinvigorated during the advent of Roman imperial rule:

> Raise up unto them their king, the son of David, at the time
> in which you see, O God, that he may reign over Israel your
> servant. Gird him with strength, that he may shatter the
> unrighteous rulers and purge Jerusalem from nations that
> trample her down.... He will be a righteous king taught by
> God.... He will rebuke rulers and remove sinners by the
> might of his word.

According to this psalm, probably written in response to General
Pompey's entry into Jerusalem in 63 B.C.E., the son of David will
rule as a true king and crush the current false kings and rulers.
This posits an inevitable conflict.

Josephus tells us also about numerous other popular royal pretenders during the reign of Herod and into the first century. In
chapter 17 of *Antiquities* Josephus mentions several popular leaders who asserted their claim to the title and position of king.
Judas, the son of the brigand chief Ezekias, possessed a "zealous
pursuit for the royal rank: and intended to secure it by the advantage of his superior strength" (*Ant.* 17.271). One Simon, a
servant of King Herod, "spurred on by the chaotic social conditions, dared to don the diadem. He organized some men and was
proclaimed king by them in their fanaticism, and he thought
himself more worthy of this than anyone else." In addition to
these two Josephus tells of Athronges, a shepherd who was remarkable for his stature and strength. "He dared to aspire to
kingship.... Putting on the diadem Athronges held council on
what was to be done, although everything ultimately depended
on his own judgement.... He and his brothers pressed hard in
the slaughter of both the Romans and the Herodian troops" (*Ant.*
17.278–85).

Josephus believed these popular movements and royal pretenders brought much harm to Galilee-Judea, and were finally
responsible for the destruction of the Jerusalem temple in 70 C.E.
He concludes this section of *Antiquities* 17 with these words:

> So Judea was filled with brigandage [*lesterion*]. Anyone
> might make himself king as head of a band of rebels whom
> he fell in with, and then would press on to the destruc-
> tion of the community, causing trouble to few Romans

but bringing the greatest slaughter upon their own people. (*Ant.* 17.285)

According to Josephus, who really worked for Rome after 70 C.E. and championed stability and cooperation with Rome at almost any cost, many popular leaders were claiming kingship during this period. These leaders were, obviously, viewed as hostile to the status quo and out to get Rome and its allies. One will note that all such pretenders came to a violent end in Judea during the first century.

Jesus' movement, and the triumphal procession as it comes to us in Matthew in particular, would have conjured up unmistakable associations with such popular royal movements. The triumphal entry as it is recorded in the Gospels aligns Jesus and his followers with popular groups out to set up their own political structure in Judea and intending, therefore, to dispense with Roman rule and the client-kings they were empowering. Such a posture on the part of popular groups led to inevitable confrontation with those in power, and death to the popular leader. Matthew's entry into Jerusalem, though treated as triumphant in Christian lyric and liturgy, when viewed in context is really a death knell for the leader. It is a bold claim flaunting the political realities and those in power. Death could not be far behind.

In 19:10–11 Matthew records the city "shook" as Jesus entered Jerusalem. In Matthew significant events are often accompanied by portents of phenomena from nature. At both the birth and the death, natural phenomena occur along with the events. The earth shakes and opens at Jesus' death in Matthew. As Jesus enters Jerusalem, the crowds (*oxloi*) recognize him as "the prophet from Nazareth of Galilee." The popular acclaim the narrative ascribes to Jesus at this point will melt away as the next five chapters move toward Jesus' crucifixion.

The Gospel of Luke makes clear the troublesome freight of the crowds' "hosanna" (a transliteration of the Hebrew meaning "save, please") by inserting Luke 19:39–40. "And some of the Pharisees in the multitude said to him, 'Teacher, rebuke your disciples.' He said, 'I tell you, if these were silent, the very stones would cry out.'" Here Luke makes clear that in his view Jesus is God's true appointed king, but also demonstrates he is fully aware of the political problems such acclaim provokes.

Early communities of followers of Jesus found Jesus' death a perplexing issue. If this was God's son and king, how did he come to this end? This theological issue, or theodicy, informs the shape and substance of the passion narrative as it unfolds. Also, if followers of Jesus in the post-70 C.E. period were going to discover a way to get along with Rome, how could they continue to celebrate a founder and hero who was best remembered for his death due to sedition and the threat he posed to Roman rule? The triumphal entry brings these questions to the fore, and Matthew means to address them in the remaining passion and resurrection narratives.

## Matthew, Jesus, and the Temple

The triumphal entry creates the opportunity for Jesus to take on the temple personnel, as well as what the temple has come to symbolize. Upon entering Jerusalem Jesus goes directly to the temple. In 21:12 Jesus enters the temple and drives out those who were selling pigeons for the purposes of sacrifice, and he overturns the tables of the moneychangers. Matthew, Mark, and Luke support this action by citing Isaiah 56:7: "My house shall be called a house of prayer, but you make it a den of bandits" (21:13 ‖ Mark 11:17 ‖ Luke 19:46). Matthew is missing the phrase "for all nations" originally contained in the Isaiah passage and included by Mark. Again, Matthew does not worry excessively about "the nations" or Gentiles, and understands Jesus' mission as directed primarily to Israel.

Jesus clears out the temple and begins to heal the blind and the lame who come to him in the temple. Matthew alone among the synoptic authors uses this scene as a *Streitgespräche*, or conflict story. He records that the scribes and chief priests, as a result of looking on and seeing "the wonderful things Jesus did" (21:15), and hearing the children crying "hosanna to the son of David," become indignant. This episode contributes substantially to Jesus' death, which grows ever nearer the longer he is in Jerusalem. That evening Jesus leaves Jerusalem for Bethany and lodges there (21:17).

From Matthew's viewpoint the temple, its corruption and subsequent destruction, is an issue and event that happened to all Jews and Judaisms in Matthew's recent past and context. The fate of the temple has changed the life and practice of many Jews forever. A new system and structure to govern the indigenous people of Roman Palestine and to shape their religious life must now develop in the wake of the temple's destruction. Matthean Judaism believed it offered a response to this malaise.

Even if Matthew was written as late as the turn of the first or early second century c.e., the destruction of the temple in Jerusalem still loomed large, and the socioreligious life of Jews in Israel had not recovered. Who was in charge? What sort of hierarchy and authority now prevailed in Palestine? And, perhaps most widespread was the question, who is to blame for this predicament and judgment upon God's people?

Issues and questions regarding leadership, responsibility, and culpability are a stock feature of second-temple literature, and post-70 c.e. literature in particular. Priests associated with the temple in Jerusalem consistently receive bad press in the post-70 period. Second Baruch 64 speaks allegorically about the wickedness of the priests in the wake of the temple's destruction. Fourth Baruch makes the same point and claims that Jerusalem itself has become a corrupt sinful place. It is because of this sin that the destruction occurred (1:2; 2:2; 4:4, 7). Frequently, the priests of the temple are portrayed as being behind the corruption and profanity. *The Testaments of the Twelve Patriarchs* (*T. 12 Patr.* 16:2–4; 10:3) claims the priests of the temple work, teach, and offer sacrifices out of greed. In *Testament of Levi* 10:4, in a passage reminiscent of Jesus' passion, the temple veil is torn in order to expose the shameful deeds of the priests in the temple behind it. An interesting but neglected first-century document, *The Lives of the Prophets* (3:15), says the people in the Jerusalem temple were faithless. Among the Dead Sea Scrolls the *Damascus Document* (CD) charges the priests and leadership in Jerusalem with corruption and falsehood. God has, therefore, deserted the sanctuary (CD 1). The priests had profaned the temple and had failed to observe the difference from clean and unclean (CD 5:2ff.). These false leaders misguided the people and were "teachers of lies" and "false prophets." They exchanged the law inscribed upon people's hearts for the "smooth things" which they speak (1QH 4). As column 2 of the *War Scroll* claims, the Qumran community will reconstitute the temple in Jerusalem once God's holy war against these false leaders and priests is fulfilled.

That Jesus should level an attack against the current state of affairs in the temple, then, as we see in Matthew 21:12–17, 23–27, is not at all surprising. The Gospel writers' portrayal of this series of events in the temple associates Jesus with a fairly common point of view concerning the temple and the leadership in Jerusalem. Jesus, too, was critical of the temple leadership and the role the temple had come to serve in Palestine under Roman rule in the first century. I do not think Jesus condemned the temple itself, which would have been a highly unusual claim in Jesus' day. But the temple personnel, like priests, the functions the temple had come to perform, and the corruption and faithlessness this institution had come to symbolize to many by the early Roman period, were what Jesus and many of his contemporaries attacked. Matthew has placed Jesus within a certain circle of popular leaders who rallied people to action through their criticism of the Jerusalem leadership and the temple and priests in particular.

It is clear that to some in Jesus' day the temple was viewed as an arm of Roman imperialism. In the eyes of many popular leaders the temple served to support and bolster Roman rule and Roman administration in the land of Israel. It had become an institution helping to facilitate the commerce and control of Rome. The leaders of the temple were complicit with Rome and sought, therefore, to extend Roman control, usury, and expansion. As Josephus said, somewhat hyperbolically, whoever was master of the temple in Jerusalem controlled the whole nation (*ethnos; Ant.* 15.248). It is in this context that Matthew's treatment of Jesus' attack on those in the temple must be viewed.

E. P. Sanders has recently detailed the important and central role of the temple in Jerusalem for the average person in Israel in this period. The great amount of space devoted to the temple, and criticism of the same, in the literature seems to support Sanders's position. I doubt very much that Jesus' position, or for that matter the position of numerous mid-first-century rebels, was that of wiping out the temple. Rather they sought to reform the temple. Their agenda claimed the temple was to function in a certain manner within their society. Roman imperial rule, together with the excesses of certain local lords like Herod, had corrupted this central and crucial religious, social, and economic institution. Jesus and his contemporaries were not hostile toward the temple but, rather, toward what the temple had become and the men who had made it that way. This is what Jesus sought to address when he entered the temple in Jerusalem.

That Matthew is writing about this story sixty or so years after the fact adds another interesting layer to the narrative. By the writing of Matthew's Gospel, of course, the temple was in ruin, destroyed by Titus in 70 C.E. Matthew and most of his literate contemporaries were concerned with who was to blame for this catastrophe. As mentioned above, many believed, in some manner, the local leadership in Jerusalem and their retainers were to blame. They acted in a corrupt and faithless manner. They perverted the laws, misled the people, and corrupted the temple. These leaders became the scapegoats for many in the post-70 years. What the temple had become, the decisions of local leaders, and the deals that were cut with Roman officials are complex issues indeed. There is no simple answer to the problems, much less the solutions, of colonial contexts. There are, however, easy and frequent scapegoats who symbolize the frustrations and crises of such a context.

Matthew attempts to connect these widespread, albeit stereotypical, assumptions about Israel's leaders with the leaders in his day. This is why the temple scene has been made into a conflict narrative involving the chief priests, scribes, and elders of the people (21:15, 23). In chapter 21 and the confrontation in the temple, Matthew attempts to connect the catastrophe of 70 C.E. and the events leading up to it with the struggle going on in his day with local leaders. The curious passage where Jesus destroys the fig tree that produces no fruit (21:18–19) foreshadows Jerusalem's destruction and the judgment upon the temple and its leaders. Matthew seeks to show that the leaders in an earlier day in Israel were like those leaders with whom his community is in conflict. The leaders who stand in the way of Matthean Judaism are like those earlier leaders in Israel who were faithless, corrupt, and brought widespread suffering upon Israel's people. Jesus in Matthew is portrayed as opposing those leaders who have turned the vital institutions of Israel against Israel's people. This is how Matthew treats the local leaders in his setting. These leaders are false. They teach the people poorly. They have led Israel astray. Matthew asserts they are like the storied poor leaders of Israel's past. Matthew therefore tars the leaders that seek to curtail the life of his community with the brush of these earlier, false and corrupt leaders. As the temple went, so will go Israel in the post-70 period if the leaders in Matthew's day prevail.

## Matthew Making Sense of the Death of Jesus: The Two Sons, Wicked Tenants, and the Angry King

The inevitable confrontation, which looms increasingly larger as Jesus is in Jerusalem, is further developed by Matthew in 21:28ff. Jesus is still in the temple and confronted by the chief priests and elders of the people. Jesus asks them a question about John the Baptist in response to their question about Jesus' authority. The chief priest and elders of the people dare not answer his question for they "fear the multitude" (21:26) around Jesus. The tension between the religious and political officials and Jesus is fast moving past the point of no return. A confrontation and Jesus' imminent death are palpable throughout the early stages of the Jerusalem visit. Matthew's material in this section is arranged to both delegitimate the current leadership and to try to make sense out of Jesus' death.

In 21:28–32 Matthew's Jesus tells a parable about two sons. Both sons are asked to work in the vineyard by their father. The first son refuses, but later repents (*metameletheis*) and works for his father. The second son, when asked, replies that he will work but never shows up in the vineyard. "Which of the two," asks Jesus, "did the will of his father?" (21:31). Of course, the answer is the first. "Truly I tell you, the tax collectors and harlots go into the kingdom of God before you" (21:31).

This parable is unique to Matthew. Here Matthew demonstrates the reversal that he believes is operative now and in the kingdom of heaven. Many of those whom people would assume would be first in the kingdom of heaven, in fact, are not. Many were given a chance to hear the message of the kingdom through John and Jesus, but they did not hear and act. On the other hand, many of those whom people would not expect to be in the kingdom are precisely those who heard and repented when John came preaching. Jesus attempts to support this claim through appeal to the popular leader John the Baptist. "John came to you in the path of justice [*dikaiosynes*] and you did not believe him. Tax-collectors and harlots did believe in him" (21:32). Such a critique of the current social structure and the local leaders by Jesus would have provoked a strong reaction and some animosity from his audience.

In 21:33–46 Matthew takes over a synoptic parable about corrupt and wicked land tenants (Mark 12:1–12 ‖ Luke 20:9–19). In this story a householder (*oikodespotes*) plants a vineyard, builds a fence (*phragmos*) around it, puts in a wine press, builds a tower, lets it out to tenants, and goes into another country. This parable, which Matthew has taken over from Mark and modified, captures accurately the economic and political realities of life in an imperial context like Roman Palestine.

The vineyard, of course, is Israel. There is now a foreign or absentee owner or occupier of the land who has hired clients to keep the land profitable. The owner has engaged in some building: a fence, a tower for protection and scouting the land and trade routes, and a wine press for additional produce. The client system requires the tenants to pay their fruits (*karpous*) to the one who has taken control of the land. This is very similar to the situation in the land of Israel in the days of Jesus and Matthew. In the Roman imperial system things tended to run smoothly if the local population and those working the land provided payment and the fruits of their labors on time to their Roman lords.

Matthew has changed the man (*anthropos*) of Mark 12:1 and Luke 20:9 to a householder (*oikodespotes*). This term denotes a wealthier, more powerful person who has servants, owns land, and is almost certainly engaged in trade. Matthew employs this term several times when the other Gospel writers do not (10:25; 13:27, 52; 20:1; 21:33). Matthew is familiar with the system, structure, and industry of the household and he tends to speak about them in positive terms. Matthew's congregation of both good and bad is described as a household in 13:27. The protagonist of chapter 13, the "scribe trained for the kingdom of heaven," is like an *oikodespotes* who brings out of his treasure what is old and what is new (13:52). Jesus himself is called a householder in 10:25.

In 21:34 the *oikodespotes* sends his servant to collect what is due the householder. This is, of course, how the economic system works in a colonial setting and, like it or not, this collection would have been no surprise to anyone, particularly the tenants working the land for the lord. What is unusual in this parable is the tenants' response. When the owner's servants arrive, the tenants seize the servants, beat one, kill another, and stone yet another (21:35). According to the parable the absentee landlord sends a second and larger delegation of servants (*doulous*), and the result is the same. Finally the lord sends his son, saying, "They will respect my son" (21:37). But the tenants kill the son and cast him out of the vineyard in the vain hope they might gain the son's inheritance (21:38).

Matthew addresses two important issues at once in this parable. First is the thinly veiled subject of the death of Jesus. God the householder has sent servants to those working the vineyard for God and they, like John the Baptist, have not been heard. Finally, when the householder sends his own son, he is treated in the same or even worse manner. The householder's son is killed by wicked people in Israel who are not able to respect and obey the just householder. It is actions and attitudes such as this that ultimately lead to the death of Jesus.

The second, related issue of theodicy that Matthew addresses here is the destruction that has happened to Israel in Matthew's day. How and why was Jerusalem destroyed, and who is responsible for this destruction? In this parable the two crucial issues of theodicy that shaped so much early Christian writing are in evidence. How and why was Jesus killed? And why were Jerusalem and the temple destroyed roughly forty years later? Responses to these two, not unrelated questions shaped a great deal of the writing and thinking of the early followers of Jesus.

Matthew combines these two issues in this parable of the wicked tenants. The wicked tenants have failed to deal responsibly with the householder, and have even killed his son (= Jesus). The tenants fail to provide what the owner has coming. They refuse to pay their tribute, or fruits. In 21:40ff. Matthew writes, "What will the owner do to these tenants? He will put those wretches to a miserable death and let out the vineyard to other tenants who will give him the fruits at the right time" (*tous kairos auton*). In 21:42 Matthew, like Mark and Luke, cites Psalms 118:22–23; "The stone which the builders rejected has become the head of the corner. This is the Lord's doing and it is marvelous in our eyes." Matthew, apart from Mark and Luke, concludes with this distinctive passage: "Therefore I tell you that the kingdom of God will be taken away from you and given to a people [*ethne*] producing fruit" (21:43). These tenants, because they have acted recklessly, have brought destruction upon themselves and have lost their chance to serve as tenants of the land for the owner. The land, and the role of tenant, will be given to those who "play by the rules," and pay their fruits on time.

Wicked leaders (=tenants) failed to see the significance of Jesus and his message. In Matthew's day, similar wicked leaders have brought destruction upon Israel and its people. This point is punctuated by the Matthean addition to this story, which says, "When the chief Priests and the Pharisees heard his parables, they perceived that he was speaking about them and they tried to arrest him but feared the crowd" (21:46). Matthew makes explicit that these parables are about the leadership in Israel. They killed Jesus, and they were poor tenants who brought the wrath of the landowner upon all of Jerusalem.

There is a clear political subtext to this polyvalent parable.

Indeed, with Matthew and many of his contemporaries, politics and theology coalesce. Those people who rejected Jesus and John the Baptist are also related to those people who tried to throw off the imperial system in Roman Palestine. The wicked tenants are people who think they can play fast and loose with the imperial client-lord system. That attitude is contrary to God's will according to the author, and will bring certain destruction upon Israel. Only poor and corrupt leadership could have cultivated such hubris and brought about the destruction that occurred in Israel as a result of the first revolt against Rome.

Consequently God will give the kingdom to those tenants who work the land and pay their fruits to the lords in a timely fashion. This theme is emphasized again in the next parable of the great supper (22:1–14). This appears to have been a parable from Q (Luke 14:15–24), but Matthew has made some significant additions. In Matthew's version a king gives a marriage feast for his son. In Luke 14:16 this is not a marriage feast, but a banquet, and there is no mention of the man's son. Again, Matthew uses this parable to work out the theological questions that surround Jesus, his ministry, and his death. In this parable many people are invited to the marriage feast but find reasons not to come. Again, only in Matthew, the king's servants who invite the people are seized, treated shamefully, and killed (22:6). Luke's version is missing this violence against the servants and the obvious resistance to this person of considerable means. Instead of the invited guests, other servants are told to invite all those they can find, "both good and bad to the wedding feast" (22:10).

Matthew makes the violence against the king's servants the provocation for the king's anger. In his anger the king orders his troops to destroy those murderers and burn their city (21:7). This important passage is only in Matthew. It is clearly a thinly veiled reference to the first revolt against Rome, the destruction of Jerusalem, and the anger of the foreign rulers. Matthew connects the revolt, the destruction of Jerusalem, and the wickedness of local leaders with the death of Jesus. For him these events are connected. The same reckless tenants who killed Jesus are related to those leaders who opposed the foreign king, brought about Jerusalem's destruction, and now oppose Matthean Judaism.

Matthew's theology and the political context of his day coalesce. The killing of Jesus and the rejection of his message and, no doubt, the continued rejection of Matthew's message are connected to the upheaval of 66–70 and its aftermath. For Matthew the first revolt and destruction of Jerusalem are directly related to the rejection and death of Jesus. In some manner the same group(s) are responsible for both. Various leadership groups in Israel did not recognize what was happening in their midst, ultimately became "wicked tenants," and provoked the wrath of the foreign king. This resulted in the destruction of their city. In Matthew's view his community represents those who are now the true leaders. They are responsible, they have heard the message of John and Jesus, they understand Israel's laws and traditions, and they now should have the kingdom passed to them. They can be the tenants who work with the king and can pay their fruits on time.

Somewhat like his contemporary Josephus, Matthew believed the foreign king and the client system were a given. He may even have believed that these foreign rulers had been chosen by God, as Josephus claims in many places (cf. *B.J.* 3.399ff.) What is now at stake is who is chosen to work within this imperial structure. Who are God's leaders in Israel who will lead the people and work with the king or absentee lord? M. Goodman has pointed out that a failure of the ruling class of Judea finally led to the first revolt against Rome. Goodman notes that the sole traditional institution that the Romans allowed to remain in Judea after 6 C.E. was the high priesthood. According to Josephus the high priest was the representative (*prostates*) of the nation (*Ant.* 20.251). They represented the nation to the Romans as well as to God. It would be Matthew's contention that representative leaders like these failed. First, they were largely responsible for Jesus' death. More, they did not hear or understand the God of Israel and did not work well with the king or foreign lord. This resulted in the pain, destruction, and chaos of the first revolt. It is noteworthy that the chief priests in Jerusalem are counted with the Pharisees as the leaders who perceive that Jesus told these parables "about them" and who try unsuccessfully to arrest Jesus (21:45–46).

Matthew believes his community constitutes a remedy to this malaise in Palestine. They are the true teachers and leaders in his setting. He believes his are the people to whom the kingdom will be given. In contrast to the current leadership, he maintains, his people can work with the post-70 realities, pay their fruits to the lords, and be true to Israel's heritage and identity. It must be remembered that Matthew's is not the only group laying claim to this role. This leadership vacuum in the post-70 period gave rise to the competition and contention between potential leadership groups, a competition and contention that informs so much of Matthew's church and shapes so much of his Gospel.

## The Kingdom Given to People Who Bear Fruit

Matthew 21:43 has garnered much debate. It has emerged recently as a *crux interpretum* for understanding Matthew's aims and the nature of the Matthean community. It is deserving of some particular attention. Those who want to see Matthew as a document that details the split between early Christianity and early Judaism, or those who see early Christianity as a gentile or non-Jewish movement from almost the start, seize upon this passage and employ a certain interpretation of it. Earlier in this century the renowned German scholar of the Gospels, J. Jeremias, claimed that the parable of tenants, for which 21:43 is the conclusion, explains the ruin of Israel and the transfer of the vineyard (=Israel) to the gentile church. This has been a popular rendering of this parable for a good portion of the twentieth century. J. D. Kingsbury offers what seems to be a similar interpretation in writing that in this verse we see that God will give Israel to the church, his eschatological people who will do God's will. G. Stanton offers a related interpretation and claims that this verse is the clearest indication in the Gospel that "the Matthean community saw itself as a separate entity over against Judaism." This is a basic but common flaw among interpreters grounded in the hard categories of the mid-twentieth century.

Despite the tremendous advances in the study of second-temple
Judaism over the last twenty years, many interpreters still assume, and here Stanton makes this assumption explicit, that
there is such a thing in the first century as *a Judaism.* That is,
that there is one monolithic Judaism with which the church can
be contrasted. Matthew could not imagine such a context, despite the inclination of contemporary interpreters to impose this
modern dichotomy. This anachronistic and destructive juxtaposition of "Judaism" and "Christianity" in the Gospel is hopefully
something those in biblical studies are learning to leave behind,
however slowly.

The key to understanding 21:43 is the Greek term *ethnos*, usually rendered "nation" in 21:43. Both D. Harrington and A. J.
Saldarini have stressed that the basic meaning of this term is
simply "a group of people," and there is no need to read into
this term the formation of a new people of God. Neither the
term "new" nor "other" is present in this passage, though both
are frequently imposed. Matthew does not have in mind a third
race. In no way does this passage or term denote the rejection
of Israel, or of Jews. And it does not denote that Matthew understands his community as somehow separate from other Jews and
from Israel. The people under scrutiny here, and those being
judged by Jesus' words, are the leaders with whom he is contending. Matthew makes this perfectly clear in the following
verse (21:45) when he records, "When the chief priests and the
Pharisees heard his parables, they perceived that he was speaking
about them." Matthew makes it clear for the reader that even the
leaders understood the parables as referring to them, not to all
Jews or to Israel.

The usual or traditional translation of the term *ethnos* in
21:43 is "nation." This translation implies the rejection of a
nation (Israel) and the embrace of another (Christians). This misleading translation of this important term has encouraged some
of the erroneous interpretations mentioned above. The term *ethnos* possessed a broad semantic field in antiquity, but the term
"nation" is probably inappropriate and implies a modern identity and political constitution that really did not exist in the
Roman world. *Ethnos* can refer to a guild or union, a group or

community, company, or body of people living together. The term can also refer to a social class, as in the case of Plato's *Republic* (421c).

As Saldarini points out, the Septuagint tends to refer to non-Jews in the plural form *ethne*. However, Greeks tended to use the same convention for referring to non-Greeks. Therefore, the term refers generally to a group of people who are "not us." In the context of this Matthean parable the "not us" stands for those who are "not the leaders of Israel." This term should be rendered "people" or "group" in 21:43. "The kingdom will be taken away from you [the chief priest and Pharisees] and given to a people producing fruit." These are the same people who will pay their fruits at the right time, who can work with the absentee lords, who do not do violence to their emissaries, and are dependable leaders. This group, this *ethnos*, is none other than the Matthean community and their followers of Jesus. This message is in no way lost upon the current leaders who try to arrest Jesus when he has finished the parable. They know their leadership is under attack by Jesus and some of his subsequent followers, such as Matthean Judaism.

## Further Reading

Goodman, M. *The Ruling Class of Judea: The Origins of the Jewish Revolt against Rome A.D. 66-70.* Cambridge: Cambridge University Press, 1987.

Haenchen, E. *The Acts of the Apostles: A Commentary.* Philadelphia: Westminster, 1971.

Harrington, D. *The Gospel of Matthew.* Sacra Pagina 1. Collegeville, Minn.: Michael Glazier/Liturgical Press, 1991.

Horsley, R. H., and J. S. Hanson. *Bandits, Prophets, and Messiahs: Popular Movements at the Time of Jesus.* Minneapolis: Winston, 1985.

Jeremias, J. *The Parables of Jesus.* 2nd rev. ed. Trans. S. H. Hooke. New York: Scribner's, 1972.

Kampen, J. "The Matthean Divorce Texts Reexamined." In *New Qumran Texts and Studies*, ed. G. Brooke, 149–67. Leiden: Brill, 1994.

Kingsbury, J. D. "The Parable of the Wicked Husbandmen and the Secret of Jesus' Divine Sonship in Matthew: Some Literary-Critical Observations." *JBL* 105 (1986): 643–55.

Malina, B. "Does *Porneia* Mean Fornication?" *NovT* 14 (1972): 10–17.

Neusner, J. *The Mishna: A New Translation.* New Haven, Conn.: Yale University Press, 1988.

Quesnell, Q. "Made Themselves Eunuchs for the Kingdom of Heaven." *CBQ* 30 (1968): 335–58.

Saldarini, A. J. *Matthew's Christian-Jewish Community.* Chicago Studies in the History of Judaism. Chicago: University of Chicago Press, 1994.

Sanders, E. P. *Judaism: Practice and Belief, 63 B.C.E.–66 C.E.* Philadelphia: Trinity Press International, 1992.

Schiffman, L. *The Eschatological Community of the Dead Sea Scrolls.* SBL Monograph Series 28. Atlanta: Scholars Press, 1989.

Stanton, G. *A Gospel for a New People: Studies in Matthew.* Edinburgh: T. & T. Clark, 1992.

Trilling, W. *Das Wahre Israel: Studien zur Theologie des Matthäus-Evangeliums.* Munich: Kösel, 1964.

Vawter, B. "Divorce and the New Testament." *CBQ* 39 (1977): 528–42.

Vermes, G. *The Dead Sea Scrolls in English.* 3rd ed. London: Penguin, 1987.

*Chapter Twelve* _____

# Questions of Authority and Leadership — 22:15–23:39

_____

## The Question of Taxes Once Again

The tension between Jesus and the leadership in and around Jerusalem continues to build and reaches its apex in 22:15–23:39. Here Jesus attacks the leader's authority and character, and the claim that Matthean Jews can replace these leaders is made explicit. First, a series of questions and debates between Jesus and the leaders takes place in 22:15ff. In chapter 23 Matthew's criticism of these leaders reaches its storied climax in the characterization of these leaders as hypocrites, false guides, and "whitewashed sepulchers full of dead men's bones." This language and highly charged rhetoric are characteristic of a divided and contentious social setting where elite and religious *virtuosi* vie for power and position.

The first of these contentious dialogues is about taxes (22:15–22). This is Matthew's second question pertaining to taxes. This version of the tax question originally comes from Mark (Mark 12:13–17 ‖ Luke 20:20–26). While Jesus is described as "true," and "teaching the way of God" (Matt. 22:16), the reader is made aware from the start of the narrative that the purpose of the feigned innocence and compliment is to "entangle" Jesus. The leaders are looking for a way to bring Jesus and his impact to an end. The leaders (here the Pharisees, "their disciples" [a Matthean addition], and the Herodians) believe that the question about taxes will make Jesus come down definitively in public on a highly charged and divisive issue. This will cause disturbance among Jesus' ranks and perhaps finally provoke the opposition of those who are directly responsible to Rome for keeping the peace in this province or region of the empire.

In the first discussion of taxes in Matthew (17:24–27), there is no mention of Caesar. In this distinctively Matthean pericope the questioners are simply "the collectors of the half-shekel tax." In chapter 22, however, it is explicitly the leaders who seek to trip Jesus up with the loaded issue of payment to Rome and its overlords. In the Marcan parallel passage Caesar is explicitly mentioned. In Matthew's earlier treatment of taxes in chapter 17 Caesar is implied by Matthew's use of the term "king" (17:25), but the emperor is not named. In Matthew 22:17 opposition to this tax, it is made patently clear, constitutes opposition to Rome and Caesar. Rejection of the tax collected in the name of the emperor would mean almost certain destruction for the movement and their popular leader.

Jesus recognizes their malice and calls them the name usually reserved for the false leaders in Matthew, "hypocrites" (*hypocrites;* 22:18). However, Jesus continues and finds a way to avoid the Gordian knot of payment of taxes in a colonial setting by providing an answer that cannot be understood as either "yes" or "no." Jesus' response to the not-so-innocent question is well known: "Show me the money for the tax. . . . Whose likeness and inscription is this?" Of course the answer is "Caesar's." Jesus' next sentence has become ensconced within Western vernacular and is often reiterated: "Render to Caesar that which is Caesar's and that which is God's to God" (22:21).

The key feature of this passage is the question about the image (*icon*) and inscription (*epigraphy*) on the coin. The role of coins in the Greek and Roman worlds in terms of political control and popular propaganda can hardly be overstated. Coins were ubiquitous in antiquity. Even the illiterate saw the coins, held them, and apprehended the messages, slogans, and images that were minted upon them. It was through coins and sporadic, often fantastic, building projects that leaders cultivated their image and reputation. Their intimate connection with the gods, accounts of their divinely guided military victories, and nicknames asserting some attribute of the ruler were common features of ancient coinage and their impressions.

As early as the Hasmonean leader John Hyrcanus (c. 134 B.C.E.) local leaders had imitated the hellenistic convention of personal coinage for the ruler. The coins of one of the last Hasmonean rulers, Alexander Jannai, are found everywhere in Israel including, if not especially, the Galilee. Herod the Great regularly referred to himself as king (*basileus*). Agrippa I referred to himself variously as "the Great king" and "friend of Caesar." His coins, as well as the coins of Agrippa II, celebrate an alliance with Rome. Around the time of the writing of Mark's Gospel, and probably still fresh in the mind of Matthean Jews, if not still held and read by many in that community, were the so-called Judea Capta coins, which celebrated the victory by Vespasian and his son Titus over the Jews in Israel. One coin, for example, has the image of Vespasian on it with the slogan, "Vespasian, Autocrator, and Revered" (the abbreviation SEB). The other side of the coin shows the goddess of victory, Nike, standing, resting her foot on a helmet, and writing upon a shield that is hanging from a palm tree the words "Judea Captive." Some coins show Nike standing over the female body of "Judea." The Judea Capta coins provide an example of the powerful political and propaganda role played by coins in the Roman period.

Some found the coins believable, and treated them as warnings. Others viewed the coins with disdain and as reminders of their existence in an imperial context. To others the coins were daily reminders of the power of the rulers and the favor the gods had shown to the king, tetrarch, or emperor. It is not at all surprising that Jesus should use a coin to make a point, that one should be readily available, and that average folk from the crowd should know the image, meaning, and message stamped on the coin.

The question about taxes in Matthew 22:17 is about imperial taxes. "Is it lawful to pay taxes to Caesar?" The coin that Jesus utilizes bears the image of the emperor. "Whose likeness and inscription is this?" They answer, "Caesar's." Imperial coinage was particularly potent in its message(s) and elaborate in its claims. The first emperor Octavian took the ancient sacral title Augustus, and was known from his coins as *Imperator Caesar divi filius Augustus*, that is, "Emperor Caesar, Son of God, Augustus."

The most widespread imperial coin in Jesus' day was a variation on this Augustan coin minted by Tiberius. The coin's slogan read, *"Tiberius Caesar Divi Augusti Filius Augustus Pontifex Maximus,"* or "Tiberius Caesar, august son of the divine Augustus, high priest." It may well have been a coin like this that the writers imagined Jesus held as he responded to the question about taxes.

How should we understand the answer Jesus provided to this question, and why did they marvel at his response? The inference is that the coin should be given to Caesar because the coin bears his likeness. Matthew more than the other Gospel writers has taken pains to try to neutralize the tax question. "Gentiles and tax-collectors" are part of Jesus' discourse and, in the case of Matthew from Capernaum, one becomes a disciple. In his treatment of the subject in chapter 17 Jesus instructs Peter that "the sons are free from tribute," but "in order not to give offense," one should pay the tax. Matthew, heretofore, has not supported the tax, but has tried to find a way the community can justifiably remain true to their beliefs, yet not provoke the wrath or offense of those in power in the Matthean setting.

But the ambiguous Marcan phrase utilized by Matthew, "Give back to Caesar that which is Caesar's and to God that which is God's" (22:21), does not wholeheartedly endorse the payment of the tax. Rather, a significant measure of interpretation on the part of the listeners and readers remains. If the predisposition of the audience or community is that paying taxes to Rome violates God's laws, then one would understand Jesus' answer as a "no." This, for example, would have been the understanding of the so-called Fourth Philosophy, should any of their adherents have heard this saying.

The Fourth Philosophy was led by a Galilean named Judas, who urged his countrymen to rebel and reproached them if they submitted to paying taxes to the Romans. This constituted tolerating human masters when they should be serving God alone (*J.W.* 2.118). Judas and his associate, a Pharisee named Saddok, pressed hard for resistance to the Roman tax. Resistance, they argued, would pave the way for Jewish good fortune and God would doubtless join them in promoting their good fight. Many listened to their scheme and their numbers grew. Josephus claims that these men filled the nation with unrest (*Ant.* 18.3–9). As far as the Fourth Philosophy was concerned, God was the only true master. To pay taxes was to deny God. Taxes, a priori, do not belong to Caesar, but to God.

However, this hypothetical rendering by followers of the Fourth Philosophy in no way exhausts the possible interpretations of this many-sided saying. At the same time Jesus has offered a justification for those who hold the position that the tax is tolerable, if not acceptable. God is not concerned with taxes, but with people. G. Bornkamm suggested many years ago that what was understood in this passage was who or what bears the image of God. That is, if the image of Caesar is on the coin, and the coin belongs to Caesar, then who or what bears God's image and, therefore, belongs to God? Of course, the allusion is to Genesis and the claim that humankind bears God's image. The coin may belong to Caesar, but the person, all people, belong to God.

Characteristically, this interpretation is not explicit. Rather, for those inclined to understand the tax as a reality, or necessary evil, this interpretation would seem plausible. We may be paying taxes to Caesar, but we are giving to God what God ultimately wants. Jesus, according to Matthew, has found a middle way through the minefield of payment of taxes in Roman Palestine. For this reason "they" are amazed by his answer and leave him alone (22:22).

There is a related and slightly expanded version of this logion in the *Gospel of Thomas* (*Gos. Thom.* 100). "They showed Jesus a gold coin and said to him, 'Caesar's people demand taxes from us.' He said to them, 'Give Caesar the things that are Caesar's, give God the things that are God's, and give me what is mine.'" This passage sheds little light on the central questions surrounding Jesus and taxes, but adds the additional task for the interpreter of deciding in addition to Caesar and God, what they, the adherents, must also give to Jesus.

We cannot finally answer the historical question about Jesus' position on paying taxes to Rome, as important as that question may be. There is not space in this commentary to analyze the many books and articles written on this subject. The question strikes at the heart of many crucial questions having to do with Christian support or opposition to governments and political structures and authorities. There is no overt hostility to taxes in Jesus' teaching. There are, as we have seen, several passages in Matthew which may be construed as a begrudging allowance for taxes. Yet this earliest passage about taxes in the Gospel tradition is obscure in its instruction for these early communities. It is not explicit in its endorsement of the Roman tax.

Many Jews struggling to be faithful to their God in the colonial setting of Roman Palestine wrestled with this important question. Could one be a faithful first-century Jew and still pay tribute to Caesar? This question provoked a range of responses; many communities were divided over this very issue. That Josephus should assert that the Fourth Philosophy's position concerning taxes ultimately led to the destruction of the nation bears witness to the magnitude and the explosive nature of this question in the first century. Communities and perhaps even families were divided over this very question. Early communities who gathered around the memory of Jesus were like any other form of Judaism in Galilee and Judea at this time. They, too, had to confront this issue and they, too, found a range of answers. The ambiguity surrounding the question of taxes in the Gospel tradition reflects that these early Jewish communities could not find one suitable single response. There was a variety of interpretations and, doubtless, a range of reactions and hostilities toward differing interpretations. These communities themselves were not sure, and probably did not all agree upon, whether or not Jesus taught them to pay the tax. Jesus died as a revolutionary, but his charge was not failure to pay the tax. He was killed for sedition, a royal pretender.

We cannot be sure Jesus himself had formulated a clear response to this loaded question, or that he intended to. His response in Matthew 22:21 is meant to highlight his shrewdness in the face of the opposition there to trip him up, and does not in the first place teach about taxes. But the question

still remains, where did he stand on this issue? His first followers must have wondered out loud and vigorously debated this
vital religious and political point. As his words come to the Gospel writers, Jesus' view is a clear "yes" or "no," depending on the
position of those who hear the passage.

Matthew is deeply concerned with this question for his community. When we take his two pericopes from chapters 17
and 22 together, we see that he ultimately believes that the
group is not compelled to pay the tax. It is, however, wiser to pay
as a way to avoid trouble. Unlike the Fourth Philosophy, Matthew
does not believe that paying the tax renders void one's devotion to God. It does not violate Torah. Technically, the Matthean
community is free from the tax, which is flirting with trouble.
In order to keep their noses clean, they are encouraged to pay.
Again, Matthew does not understand Jesus to have advocated
the tax. Rather, Jesus found a way for the community to live
with a measure of integrity in their imperial setting. Matthew
does not advocate overt resistance to Rome, which failure to pay
would signal. One should assiduously look to fulfilling all the
demands of the God of Israel without provoking a confrontation
with those in power. Unlike some of his contemporaries, Matthew did not believe that payment of the imperial tax was the
issue upon which Jesus would have the community fall or rise.
Unlike many local lords and leaders, Matthean Jews did not support the tax. Unlike some revolutionaries of an earlier period,
Matthean Jews did not believe resisting the tax was the way to
deal with the reality of Roman rule.

## The Sadducees and the Resurrection

In 22:23–33 another group of leaders come up to Jesus in order
to quiz him. Here the Sadducees, "who say there is no resurrection," ask Jesus about a woman who outlives six husbands.
According to the law, with each death the woman marries a
brother of the husband. This happens seven times. The question
is, with which husband will the woman live in the resurrection?

In his response Jesus points out to the Sadducees that the

premise of their question is incorrect. "In the resurrection they neither marry nor are given in marriage, but are like angels in heaven" (22:30). Concerning the resurrection Jesus quotes a suggestive passage from Exodus 3:6 saying that the God of Abraham, Isaac, and Jacob is "not the God of the dead but of the living." This response also, according to Matthew, "astonishes" them.

We know very little about the Sadducees in the second-temple period. In the New Testament and in later rabbinic literature, the Sadducees are most often mentioned in association with the Pharisees. In both canons the Pharisees emerge as more significant where the historical development of both early Christianity and rabbinic Judaism are concerned. In the New Testament the interest in the Sadducees by themselves usually has to do with their denial of the resurrection, as this passage from the synoptic Gospels suggests (Mark 12:18–27 ‖ Matt. 22:23–33 ‖ Luke 20:27–40). Acts of the Apostles 23:6 also picks up on this aspect of Sadducean theology and the tension it caused with the Pharisees.

In Josephus the Sadducees are depicted as part of the governing class. They are usually around the halls of power, and can wield considerable influence. The Sadducees are no friends of the Pharisees, according to Josephus. As early as the reign of the Hasmonean ruler John Hyrcanus (134–104 B.C.E.), tension between these two Jewish leadership groups erupted. At one point Hyrcanus was a disciple of the Pharisees. However, at a dinner where Hyrcanus was entertaining the Pharisees, one member of the Pharisees, Eleazar, suggested to the king that he relinquish the high priesthood because his mother was once a captive (*Ant.* 13.372). The question implied that Hyrcanus's mother had been sexually violated while captive. It was this belief about women in captivity that led to the injunction against priests ever marrying captives (Lev. 21:14). Hyrcanus was so angered by this offense that, with the encouragement of a friend and Sadducee, Jonathan, Hyrcanus switched allegiance from the Pharisees to the Sadducees.

The tension between these two groups, which may have had its start under Hyrcanus, seems to have continued into the first century of the common era. In Acts and the Gospels the Sadducees are portrayed as errant because they do not accept the Jewish notion of the resurrection. The Mishna continues to mention the Sadducees in the same context, as *m. Sanhedrin* 10:1 shows. In rabbinic literature Sadducees also appear as the opponents of the Pharisees.

In the Gospels, and particularly in Matthew, little attention is paid to the distinctions between various leadership groups. Matthew mentions the Sadducees a few times more than the other Gospel writers. They are present at Jesus' baptism (3:7). In the other five instances where Matthew mentions the Sadducees they are named with the Pharisees and are part of an attempt to test or trip up Jesus. In 16:1ff. they come with the Pharisees to "see a sign from heaven." Jesus lumps them together with the Pharisees when he says, "Beware of the leaven of the Pharisees and Sadducees" (16:6–12). In Matthew 22:23ff. the same is true. Matthew has the Pharisees and Sadducees come together to test Jesus. Both are simply depicted as leadership groups, all of whom, especially in and around Jerusalem, are threatened by and opposed to Jesus. In this passage from Matthew 22:23–33 some of the tension between the Pharisees and Sadducees may still be palpable just under the surface of this Matthean narrative.

Matthew, however, is not interested in detailing the differences between various leadership and political interest groups. In his post-70 C.E. period these differences may have waned or been obscured. He may not be able to explain fully the origin and nature of each group. His aim in this section of the Jerusalem narrative is to demonstrate the general and rather widespread opposition of the Jewish leadership to Jesus and his message.

The real meaning and the implications of the decidedly Jewish notion of resurrection are not often recognized by many modern interpreters. Resurrection relates to the notion of a definitive end to history. At that time, or on that day, the faithful or elect will be raised to life, and the wicked or corrupt will be judged. The idea of eternal life, and immediate ascension to heaven or the hereafter, is largely a Greek philosophical notion and one far more popular in the West than resurrection.

The Gospels, with only one exception, teach resurrection as the dominant eschatology. It is consistent with the apocalypticism that characterizes most of the Gospels that when people die they lie in the ground until the great day when all the elect, or saints, are raised. This is what is meant by resurrection. The discussion about resurrection, then, is a discussion about a particular eschatology and a particular view of God's intervention in history.

In the Gospel of Luke, at the crucifixion when Jesus is on the cross between two thieves, he declares to one of them, "Truly I say to you, today you will be with me in paradise" (23:43). This is a view of the afterlife at variance with the traditional notion of resurrection. This Lucan saying probably owes more to certain forms of Greek philosophical thought than to the eschatology that informed much of the Jesus movement, and Pharisaism for that matter. The Gospels hold that those who die wait for the day when God will act, end history as we know it, judge the wicked and vindicate the righteous, and, as Matthew 22:30 suggests, empower the believers to serve God.

The belief in an existence after death, as G. Nickelsburg and others have pointed out, is a rather late development in the religion of Israel. Third Isaiah (especially chaps. 65–66), and 1 Enoch 24–27 (c. third century B.C.E.) seem to reflect a belief in the judgment of the wicked and eschatological blessing for the righteous. This is expanded in the later "epistle" of Enoch (chapters 92–105). The righteous's plea for justice has been heard by God and their names are written in the heavenly book (104:1–6).

The Book of Daniel (c. 165 B.C.E.) is considered the classic location by many for belief in the resurrection in some postexilic Jewish communities. In 12:1–3 Daniel writes,

> At that time your people shall be delivered, every one whose name is found written in the book. And many of those who sleep in the land of dust will awake, some to everlasting life, and some to shame and everlasting contempt. And those who are wise shall shine like the brightness of the firmament; and those who turn many to righteousness, like the stars for ever and ever. Second Maccabees 7:9–11

and Jubilees 23:11–31, both written around the time of
Daniel, also suggest a belief in the resurrection at the end
of time, or at a time when God decides to judge the wicked
and redeem the righteous.

The belief in the resurrection, then, emerged with some clar-
ity between c. 300 and 165 B.C.E. By the time of Jesus and the
Gospel writers this was still a relatively new idea. Debate continued about this belief for sometime past the New Testament
period, as the Mishna shows. At the time of the Jesus movement and the writing of the Gospels Jewish groups were still
arguing with one another about the veracity of this somewhat
new notion. The Jesus movements, of course, believed in such a
resurrection, along, we presume, with most Pharisees, while the
Sadducees rejected this notion. In his answer to the Sadducees'
question Jesus tactfully avoids being trapped, but manages to
reiterate his support for the largely apocalyptic belief in a resurrection at the end of history. This is a belief that, to outsiders,
would have associated Jesus' movement with certain other Jewish groups, and would have distinguished the Jesus movement
from still others.

## The Great Commandment

The discussion with the Sadducees about the resurrection is
followed by the question about which is the greatest commandment. Matthew has made several significant changes in his
version of this story when compared to the Marcan and Lucan parallels (Mark 12:28–34 ‖ Luke 10:25–28). Unlike Mark or
Luke, Matthew has made this encounter into a conflict story.
In Mark the questioner is a scribe (*grammates*), and in Luke a
lawyer (*nomikos*). Only in Matthew is the person posing the
question a Pharisee. In both Mark and Luke the person asking
the question is praised by Jesus (Mark 12:34 ‖ Luke 10:28). Matthew has tellingly deleted these positive responses from Jesus
(Mark 12:34 ‖ Luke 10:28). In Matthew the Pharisees gather together and a representative, a lawyer, poses the question to Jesus

which is uniquely formulated in Matthew: "Teacher, which is the greatest commandment in the law?" (22:36). Significantly, only Matthew explicitly mentions "the law" (*nomos*). Luke's version asks only, "What shall I do to inherit eternal life?" (Luke 10:25). Mark's version reads simply, "Which commandment is the first of all?" (Mark 12:28).

This question is aimed at teasing out the core value of Matthean Judaism and the interpretive parameters, or hermeneutical principles, they employ in applying the Torah to their lives. Jesus responds by citing the so-called love command, which is a combination of Deuteronomy 6:5 and Leviticus 19:18. "You shall love the Lord your God with all your heart, and with all your soul, and with all your mind. This is the greatest commandment. And a second is like it. You shall love your neighbor as yourself. On these two commandments depend all the law and the prophets." Only in Matthew does the concluding phrase, "On these two commandments depend all the law and the prophets" appear (22:40). This concluding Matthean saying punctuates his community's belief that these two principles are comparable, and that they summarize and fulfill the law.

Jesus' answer in the synoptic Gospels, and perhaps in Matthew in particular, is not without parallel in the first two centuries. Indeed, several sages from this period would have most likely endorsed this synopsis of the whole law. A much later tradition associated with the famous first-century figure Hillel, said this: "What is hateful to you, do not do it to your neighbor. This is the whole Torah; all the rest is interpretation" (*b. Šabb.* 31a). Related summations of the whole law can be found in Mishna (*Abot* 2:9) and in the prolific first-century Jewish writer and philosopher Philo of Alexandria, Egypt (*Hypothetica* 7.6).

What is the sum and essence of the law was a fair, and not uncommon question among first-century Jewish groups. Several well-known Jewish leaders and writers offered their interpretation on this vital question, a question that would distinguish one Jewish group or leader from another. One's answer could place one on the map of first-century Judaisms. Jesus' answer would have found some resonance among several other first-century writers and groups both in and outside of Palestine.

It is, therefore, not surprising that the Gospel writers add their voices to this defining issue. Matthew, who stresses the law more than others, and makes the claim that his community both fully understands and fulfills the law, would surely want to make his view on this question known. To love God with all one has, and to love your neighbor as yourself — these two commands are equal and summarize the whole law. This answer helps place Matthean Judaism in relation to other forms of Judaism in the late first century. This is his hermeneutical principle. Failure to grasp this central or core value results, in Matthew's view, in the corruption and dissolution of the law.

What Matthew means by one's "neighbor" remains an important question for the modern interpreter. In the main, Matthew is concerned with actions and attitudes toward fellow members of his church. This is how and where his understanding of the "kingdom of heaven" is enacted. Proper relations among members within the group result in the reiteration of "the kingdom which is in heaven." Still, attitudes, actions, and consistency are high priorities for Matthean Jews. Not only actions toward other members count. To understand the law and to act it out is the highest command in Matthean Judaism. This is not with respect to other members only, but to members' lives and relationships generally. This consistency and correlation between beliefs and actions are a central value for Matthew and, in his view, ultimately reveal if one understands and fulfills the law. Therefore, the love command is the formulation that most captures the relationship between legal interpretation and human relations.

Matthew alludes to this principle when he quotes Hosea 6:6 in response to earlier questions by the local leadership (cf. 9:13; 12:7). In many more words, but in a similar respect, the Matthean antitheses of the Sermon on the Mount in 5:21ff., and the material on loving one's enemy in 5:44-48, seek to explicate this same Matthean core value of love of neighbor — or brother — as the summation and fulfillment of the law. Also, Matthew provides a succinct summary of the whole of the law in 7:12 with the so-called Golden Rule: "So, whatever you wish that others should do to you, do so also to them; for this is the law and the prophets." For Matthew this passage is the sum and freight of his

pet term *dikaiosyne* —justice. Justice, or righteousness, is summarized and fulfilled by the Golden Rule. That is, love others and,
above all, act or do (*poieite*) toward them as you would have
them act toward you. This is the law and the prophets. Hearing and understanding the law and the tradition and teaching of
the prophets are important to Matthew, but doing, or acting it
out toward others is crucial. This is precisely Matthew's charge
against those leaders in his setting whom he maintains are false
guides and bad teachers. They understand the law but they do
not act it out.

## Those with de Jure Authority:
## Matthean Political Realities

Chapter 23 is the culmination of Matthew's criticism of and attack upon the local Jewish leadership. His harshest words, which
unfortunately have found a way to echo across most of subsequent Western cultural history, are focused in this section.
Those living in such close historical and emotional proximity to the holocaust shudder when reading this chapter and
ecumenically minded Christians politely avoid these passages.

As A. J. Saldarini reminds us, however, to students and scholars of religion such rhetoric is not unusual. The claims that
religion and religious communities make are by nature emotional and exclusive. Matthew's contention with those in power
in his setting boils over in this chapter. If it has not been clear
before, chapter 23 now declares one cannot support the local
leaders and still be a faithful Matthean Jew. In this chapter
Matthew attempts to discredit and delegitimize the role and
character of the current leadership.

Yet this chapter also reveals most clearly the social and political station of the so-called scribes and Pharisees, and the social
location of the Matthean community in relation to them. Matthew 23:2–3 is a very significant passage in this regard. "The
scribes and Pharisees sit on Moses' seat; so do and observe what
they tell you, but do not act as they do; because they talk, but
they do not practice." In this passage we see clearly that the Mat-

thean opponents possess de jure authority; they are in control politically and judicially. Matthew's advice to his community is one of prudence, to keep one's nose clean in order to survive. The community should do what the leaders tell them to do because the leaders occupy the seat of authority. However, to retain good standing in the Matthean community, the community should not engage in the actions of these leaders. Their actions, according to Matthew, are not consistent with their words. This is Matthew's fundamental gripe with these leaders. Those Matthean Jews who exhibit the same inconsistency fail to truly fulfill the law.

It does not appear from this passage that Matthew has a problem with the leaders' interpretation and legislation. Rather, it is the inconsistency or hypocrisy he perceives in their failure to act on their own words. "They bind heavy burdens hard to carry on people, but they will not lighten them with even one finger" (23:5). "Moses' seat," mentioned in 23:2, was not yet a standard architectural feature of Jewish gathering places. This is a symbol or metaphor for the authority the Matthean opponents possess. Matthean Jews should publicly appear as though they are in accord with the rulings of these local leaders. This admission on the author's part clearly signals that his group has lost out or is losing out to these local leaders in their struggle for influence and authority. Matthew 23:2-3 reveals that the scribes and Pharisees are in charge and his community had better do as they say, but not emulate their behavior.

This social and political reality helps to put in focus the bitter and divisive tone of chapter 23. The Matthean community — though they feel as though they should lead, interpret the law for the people, and (based on the Matthean parables from chapters 21 and 22) be the people through whom the king exercises his rule — must instead take their lead and their instructions from the group they believe will lead the people astray. In the struggle to decide who would lead and guide the people in the post-70 C.E. vacuum, Matthean Jews lost out in their setting. The bitter reaction to that reality is palpable in this chapter. Although Matthew perceives the leaders as uninformed, corrupt, and hypocritical, his community must nevertheless take their interpretations and injunctions from them. No wonder the rhetoric of this Gospel is at points so highly charged and hostile. Much is at stake and much is being lost, so Matthew seems to believe.

Chapter 23 goes on to proclaim seven woes against the scribes and Pharisees, and makes charges of blindness, hypocrisy, and even murder against these leaders. The oracles against the scribes and Pharisees aim to discredit their teaching and their character as leaders. In 23:8-12 Matthew charges that the leaders cling to human hierarchies and positions of honor. Beyond loving the attention and deference of the public (23:5-7), they particularly like titles and being greeted with honorific appellations. Matthew claims instead that his community should eschew such titles. Titles proscribe a human hierarchy that should not exist in the kingdom of heaven. Only God should receive such appellations.

> You are not to be called rabbi, for you have one teacher, and you are all brethren. And call no one father, for you have one father in heaven. Do not be called masters, for you have one master, the Christ. He who is greatest among you shall be your servant; whoever exalts himself will be humbled, and whoever humbles himself will be exalted.

The local leaders have encouraged a hierarchy that stands in opposition to the Matthean ideal of equality. While there are functions and offices in Matthew's church, there are no titles, and all members are theoretically equal. This grows out of Jesus' admonitions to humble oneself. This, too, is a basic core value of the community and the local leaders in the Matthean setting apparently encourage quite the opposite.

The mention of avoiding the title "rabbi" is noteworthy. "Rabbi" was an honorific term meaning "teacher" or "wise one" until about 200 C.E. when it evolved into a technical term for teachers within rabbinic Judaism. By the writing of Matthew's Gospel, however, the process of this term being associated with a particular set of leaders and literati may have begun. In contrast to some of the other Gospels, Jesus is only called "Rabbi" twice in Matthew's Gospel, and that is by Judas, when he announces that it is he who will betray Jesus and when he comes with the chief priests and elders of the people to arrest Jesus (26:25, 49). It is quite striking that this term, so easily applied to Jesus in other Gospels, is avoided in Matthew. Only an informant, one who has gone over to the opposition, uses this title for Jesus. It may well be that in Matthew's setting this term was already associated with the local leadership and Matthean enemies. Matthean Jews, therefore, are to assiduously avoid using this term. In the mouth of Judas the term associates him with those who seek to do Jesus in. This title is now language taken over by the opposition and has been dropped from Matthean vocabulary.

Toward the close of chapter 23 Matthew attempts to associate the current leadership with all previous corrupt leaders in the history of Israel (23:29–31).

> Woe to you scribes and Pharisees, hypocrites! You build the tombs of the prophets and adorn the monuments of the righteous, saying, "If we had lived during the days of our fathers, we would not have taken part with them in the shedding of the blood of the prophets." Thus, you witness against yourself that you are sons of those who murdered the prophets.

The local leaders are handing out judgments and punishments in the local courts. This, after all, is their job as local retainers and officials. But Matthew believes these judgments are unfair and illegal. "I send you prophets and wise men and scribes, some of whom you will kill and crucify, and some you will scourge in *your* synagogues and prosecute [*dioxo*] from city to city" (23:34).

Like the storied villains of Israel's past, these leaders, Matthew contends, have killed wise and righteous people, agents of God, and, of course, Jesus. Therefore, as 23:35 asserts, these leaders are implicated in "all the righteous blood shed on earth, from Abel to the blood of Zechariah the son of Barachiah, whom you murdered between the sanctuary and the altar. Truly, I say to you, all this will come upon this generation." Here Matthew attempts to tar the present leadership with the brush of all former, notorious wicked leaders in Israel's history. The current leaders, the so-called scribes and Pharisees, are also guilty of shedding innocent and righteous blood.

The phrase, "all murders from Abel to Zachariah the son of Barachiah" is intended to encompass all the murders in Israel for all time. Zachariah the son of Barachiah is probably a reference to the Zechariah who was murdered in the temple area in 67 C.E., which Josephus reports in *Jewish Wars* 4.334–44. This is an important connection because these leaders are implicated by Matthew in all unjust murders in Israel, especially Jesus', but they are also being held responsible by him for the chaos and destruction associated with the first Jewish revolt against Rome in 66–70 C.E. This is made all but explicit in the famous lament over Jerusalem in 23:37–39. Jesus' lament over Jerusalem is originally from Q (Luke 13:34–35). Matthew has placed this poignant lament at the end of his protracted attack on the leadership in his setting. The destruction that came upon Jerusalem is clearly a result of the corrupt and misguided leaders in Israel. This is Matthew's view, in contrast to the parallel in Luke which has the lament follow on the heels of a positive portrayal of at least some Pharisees.

In Luke "some Pharisees" warn Jesus to "get away from here, for Herod wants to kill you" (13:31). One would not find such a sympathetic depiction of Pharisees in Matthew. Pharisees in Matthew do not have a concern to save Jesus' life; rather, they are implicated in his death and connected with the destruction of Jerusalem. In Matthew's view, the false oaths, impiety, hypocrisy, and murders leading up right to the eve of the first revolt (Zechariah the son of Barachiah in 23:35), all of which he attributes to the leaders in the form of "the scribes and Pharisees," have led to Jerusalem's destruction. Jerusalem, Matthew makes clear through this simple addendum to the Q material, has been made "desolate" (23:38). Through these illegitimate leaders judgment and ruin came upon the city of the great king.

These events are viewed by Matthew — some twenty years or so after the fact — as confirmation that those who are in charge are like, or related to, those wicked leaders of a prior generation. The events of the last few years show that these leaders should not be in charge. Rather, new and true leaders should emerge to lead God's Israel. Those leaders, the author believes, are the current members of the Matthean community.

## Matthew's Highly Charged Political Rhetoric

What are we to make of the highly charged rhetoric of chapter 23? How have such language and personal attacks made their way into the Christian canon and Western vernacular generally? While there is little reason to endorse such language, and it need not be excused, there is tremendous value in trying to understand where such language comes from. That is, what is the context of this language and how did it grow to such a strident and destructive level?

Indeed, Matthew's language, particularly in its hyperbolic form in chapter 23, does have a broader context within the late second-temple period. Matthew's Gospel needs always to be viewed as part of a body of literature written between the two Jewish revolts against Rome in Palestine. A vast amount of literature from this period and place both details, and seeks to make sense out of, the deep division and instability within Palestinian society. This body of literature reflects name-calling and finger-pointing, great hostility toward those in power — especially locally and, less so, the Romans directly — and these documents are very concerned with the future. What is God doing with Israel, who will lead God's people, and what went wrong over the last generation or two are all themes that pepper late second-temple literature. This is the broader literary and social context in which Matthew should be read and interpreted.

Out of this context comes the highly charged and profoundly alienating language of chapter 23, as well as other parts of Matthew's Gospel laced with invective. Heroic figures of Israel like Moses, the scriptures of Israel, and charismatic and prophetic characters were all employed by various writers to try to make sense out of the chaos of this period, indict the culprits, and vindicate the truly faithful. Matthew was by no means alone in this respect. Many of his contemporaries held a similar view of their reality. They utilized similar arguments and language that attacked their respective enemies and validated their own community. The only difference is each author seemed to view his own community as the rightful heir to authority and leadership in Israel. Communities behind documents like 4 Ezra, 2 Baruch, many of the Dead Sea Scrolls, and Matthew's Gospel all thought of themselves as the righteous or chosen ones who will inherit God's kingdom and effect God's rule. The wicked and false leaders will be judged or destroyed. Matthew's was not a solitary voice claiming the local leaders are corrupt and that his group should soon be granted the opportunity to lead Israel in faith and truth. Indeed, first-century Palestine seems to be full of rivals for this claim.

Such fragmentation and competing claims led, of course, to bitter charges and personal attacks on other groups and personnel. Matthew's community appears to have participated vigorously in this broader context and debate. Even a collection of stock language and terms emerges from the literature of this period. As I have tried to show elsewhere in *Matthew's Gospel and Formative Judaism*, Matthew's language is part and parcel of this larger fragmented emotional context. Terms like "righteous" and "justice," "lawless" and even "hypocrite," are part of the stock language of sectarian Roman Palestine. These potent terms reveal the divisions, enmity, and rivalry between competing groups. Also, these terms disclose an exclusivity on the part of those employing the terms which would have made reconciliation or negotiation nearly impossible. The sectarian and highly charged language of this period, of which Matthew 23 is so characteristic, must have made compromise very difficult. One's opponents were cast in stark and absolute terms, while the heroic but persecuted righteous ones were depicted as the only champions of God's truth and Israel's future. Such a cleavage and break makes any rapprochement highly unlikely. Matthew's language, like many of his contemporaries, set the stage for an all-or-nothing confrontation. The language of marginalized groups in Palestine between the revolts was exclusive, absolute, and showed no interest in resolving the local disputes and tensions. One had to choose between the so-called righteous and the groups they characterized as wicked. There was no middle way or compromise. This absolute stance surely was a contributing factor in the dissolution of many second-temple Judaisms — including Matthean Judaism — and helps account for their disappearance from the pages of history following the Bar Kochba revolt of 135 C.E.

As theorists of social conflict have long pointed out, those who use the highly charged and derogatory language such as is found in Matthew 23 invariably represent the minority. They feel powerless and may well realize they are losing out to the dominant culture or to those who wield real power. The language and the charges found in Matthew 23 and elsewhere signal something about the social location of the group. They have condemned those in power in the harshest words possible. They have promised the sanctions of heaven and exclusion from the world to come for the current leaders, and they hold out the pipe dream of a hope that one day, with God's help, the beleaguered and oppressed community will be in power. On that day they will make all things right.

To speak then of "whitewashed sepulchers full of dead men's bones," and accuse the leadership of corruption, lawlessness, and murder, reveals the frustration the marginalized group was feeling, and acknowledges once again, like Matthew 23:2–3, that these leaders were really the ones in power. The only power Matthew and his contemporaries possessed against the local lords in the colonial context of Roman Palestine was the power of their language. Their only recourse and hope was to wish the judgment of their God upon those who, in their view, had corrupted the law and the covenant, persecuted their people, and brought destruction upon Jerusalem. Matthew retained that apocalyptic dimension of his fragmented and sectarian setting. He believed the leaders who constituted the opposition to his community would soon be judged and his marginalized church would be vindicated. This view is put forth forcefully in chapters 26 and 27.

# Further Reading

Bammel, E., and C. F. D. Moule, eds. *Jesus and the Politics of His Day*. Cambridge: Cambridge University Press, 1984.

Bornkamm, G. *Jesus of Nazareth*. New York: Harper, 1960.

Donaldson, T. L. "Moses Typology and the Sectarian Nature of Early Christian Anti-Judaism." *JSNT* 12 (1981): 27–52.

Garland, D. *The Intention of Matthew 23*. NovTSup 52. Leiden: Brill, 1979.

Kriesburg, L. *The Sociology of Social Conflict*. Englewood Cliffs, N.J.: Prentice-Hall, 1973.

Meshorer, Y. *The Coins of Eretz Israel and the Decapolis in the Roman Period*. Jerusalem: Israel Museum, 1985.

Nickelsburg, G., Jr. *Resurrection, Immortality, and Eternal Life in Intertestamental Judaism*. Harvard Theological Studies 26. Cambridge: Harvard University Press, 1972.

Overman, J. A. "Heroes and Villains in Palestinian Lore: Matthew's Use of Traditional Jewish Polemic in the Passion Narrative." SBLSP 29 (1990): 585–96.

————. "Recent Advances in the Archaeology of the Galilee in the Roman Period." *Currents in Research: Biblical Studies* 1 (1993): 35–58.

Perkins, P. *Love Commands in the New Testament*. New York: Paulist, 1982.

Saldarini, A. J. "Delegitimation of Leaders in Matthew 23." *CBQ* 54 (1992): 659–80.

————. *Pharisees, Scribes, and Sadducees in Palestinian Society: A Sociological Approach*. Wilmington, Del.: Michael Glazier, 1988.

# Jesus and the End — 24:1–25:46

## MATTHEW'S APOCALYPTIC DISCOURSE

_____

### The Lament over Jerusalem and the Temple's Destruction

The lament over Jerusalem stirs memories and images associated with the destruction of the temple in 70 c.e. The desolation of this holy symbol, not to mention economic and cultural center for the region, must have surely been cataclysmic for many living in and around Judea-Galilee in the latter half of the first century. Matthew closes chapter 23 by bringing to mind for the reader those very images of Jerusalem's destruction and the poor leaders who either provoked or allowed such a thing to happen. In 24:1–3 Matthew's Jesus picks up on the theme of the temple and its destruction. His disciples point out the buildings of the temple to Jesus and he responds by saying, "Truly, I say to you there will not be left here one stone upon another, that will not be thrown down" (24:2). This brief sentence takes on added significance because this thinly veiled claim that the temple will be destroyed returns in the trial as part of the charge and case against him (26:61; 27; 40).

This passage is found also in Mark (13:1–2) and Luke (21:5–6). The earliest Gospel traditions seek to associate Jesus' death with the desolation of Jerusalem and the destruction of the temple. Jesus came to Jerusalem to push his point about the kingdom of heaven and his version of fidelity to Torah and the covenant and, perhaps, to force the hands of those in power. In certain respects, the temple stands at the center of Jesus' critique of the leadership and ruling elite. Power, influence, and wealth were gathered around the temple. The temple was both a crucial economic institution in Israel and the meeting place for local leaders and imperial forces. Banks, guards, judges, troops, priests, and provincial rulers are some of the personnel one finds in and around the temple area when reading Josephus. If Jesus offered a thoroughgoing critique of those in power locally, and Matthew certainly believed Jesus did, then the temple in Jerusalem was an obvious focal point for that critique.

But this does not mean that Jesus was hostile to the temple as such. His concern seems to have been those who were in power in and around the temple. Many writers from this period, characterized as it was by fragmentation and schism, attacked the local leaders. These groups and notables were held responsible for a wide range of social and cultural tensions. Second Baruch 64 attacks the wickedness of those priests. Fourth Baruch 4:4 (or, *The Things Omitted from Jeremiah the Prophet*) asserts the priests are no longer worthy of holding the temple keys and must relinquish them, as does the later rabbinic text *ARN* 4. The *Testament of Levi* (16:2–4) believes the priests in the temple are driven only by their own greed, and of course the Qumran community focused much of their literature on the corrupt priesthood in Jerusalem (cf. CD 5.2ff.). For many marginalized groups in this period the problem, in short, was the local leaders and politicians in Roman Palestine. If, many writers like Matthew believed, they could rid themselves of those religiopolitical leaders, then everything would be the way God wants it in Israel. Those local leaders, in a host of late second-temple literature, become the scapegoats for the struggles and hostilities within the colonial reality of Roman Palestine. A wide range of literature from this period maintains that they, the leaders, and not the temple per se, are the problem. The Gospels, and Matthew in particular, are not at all exceptional in this regard.

Jesus, then, defends and supports the temple as an institution; he is hostile toward what local leaders have turned the temple into, that is, "a den of thieves" (*leston;* 21:13). The temple is there for the people, a "house of prayer," a place where healing and transformation occur, and where the golden age of the rule of David is reiterated (21:14–15). The temple, though, Matthew's Jesus believes, has been seriously corrupted by bad leaders. Despite warnings, signs, and prophets, people's behavior did not change. The local leaders continued to serve other masters and to distort the traditions and laws of historic Israel. It was this corruption that eventuated the temple's downfall.

Mark, followed by Matthew and Luke, associated the destruction of the temple with the apocalyptic end of history that is so ingrained in the Gospel tradition. The earliest writers believed Jesus taught about the end of history. Part of Jesus' message to faithful Israel was the imminent end of this age. The destruction of the temple, and the suffering and terror that surrounded the period of the first revolt (so-called birth pangs), were interpreted by the first writers as signs that indeed the end Jesus predicted was near. The lament over Jerusalem and the saying about the temple's destruction are events out of time in the sense that the writers anachronistically understand the terrible events of 66–70 C.E. in light of the words of Jesus some forty years earlier. The cataclysm of the revolt and the temple's destruction made many late-first-century writers wonder out loud about how and why this had happened, and what the future now held for them. Jesus' words about the end were interpreted by the Gospel writers in a manner that attempted to make sense out this chaos. In the view of writers like Mark and Matthew, Jesus predicted the destruction of the temple long ago, and he explained why it was going to happen. This is God's judgment upon "this generation" (23:36) and the dawn of the vindication of the faithful within Israel. This destruction and desolation also served as a sign to believers that the current order of things was drawing to a close, and God's reign and order, articulated and directed by Jesus the Son of man, would soon begin. Following the saying about the temple and its buildings in Matthew (the temple in Jerusalem was not just one building but an area with a variety of structures and activities going on simultaneously), Jesus begins his apocalyptic discourse prompted by a question from the disciples: "Tell us, when will this be, and what will be the sign of your coming and the close of the age?" (24:3) The allusion to the temple's destruction, followed by this question from the disciples, constitute the beginning of Jesus' teaching about the end.

## The Coming Son of Man and the Persecution of the Community

Once again Jesus gathers with his disciples on a mountain to deliver a significant and extended time of teaching (Matt. 24:3–8 ‖ Mark 13:3–8). In 24:3–8 the mountain is the Mount of Olives. As D. Harrington points out, the Mount of Olives is an appropriate place for Jesus' eschatological discourse in light of the words of the late Hebrew Bible prophet Zechariah (14:4): "On that day [that is, the Day of the Lord], the Lord's feet shall stand on the Mount of Olives which lies before Jerusalem on the east; and the Mount of Olives shall be split in two." In Matthew all the disciples are privy to this crucial discourse, not just the four members of the inner circle, as is the case in Mark (13:3). With the disciples' question in Matthew Jesus begins his instruction about the future, coming events, and his understanding of where in the history of Israel he and his followers now stand.

In all three synoptic Gospels Jesus begins by saying, "Take heed that no one leads you astray. Many will come in my name saying, 'I am the Christ,' and they will lead many astray" (Matt. 24:4 ‖ Mark 13:5 ‖ Luke 21:8). Only Matthew supplies the term "Christ." Mark and Luke say simply, "I am he." The warning about being led astray only serves to confirm that this is precisely what was happening in the Matthean setting. Members were being lost due to the hardship of life within the Matthean community. This saying was intended to explain the attrition within the group, and to support those who remained but were nevertheless troubled by the doubts departing members had spawned.

Jesus goes on to set the context of terror and confusion that is symbolic of the end. "There will be wars and rumors of war." This was not a stretch and required little imagination for the Matthean community. They had quite recently lived through a war. Wars in any place and just about of any magnitude defy description. Even bizarre and highly symbolic imagery like this eschatological discourse fails to capture the brutal and utterly devastating reality of war. The Matthean community, unfortunately, was quite familiar with "wars and rumors of war." Josephus's description of the assault on Jerusalem and the destruction of the first revolt, though certainly hyperbolic, paints a picture of desolation and death, with the streets of the city running full with blood, that would put even the most gifted apocalypticist to shame (cf. *J.W.* 6.130–7.4). No wonder some believed this might be the end. Kingdoms will battle against kingdoms and people against people (or "tribes against tribes"; from the term *ethnos* in 24:7). There will be accompanying signs like famines, earthquakes, and suffering. These things are the beginning of the end (24:8).

A central piece of Jesus' teaching about the end is the persecution and struggles of the faithful community. Matthean Jews will be delivered up to "tribulation," and put to death. As a result the Matthean community believed they would be "hated by all people for my [Jesus'] name's sake" (24:9). And, as a result of this social and political alienation, many would "fall away," betray one another, and, in direct contrast to the paramount command and summation of the whole law within the Matthean church, "hate one another" (24:10). And Matthew adds this further descriptive saying, "Because lawlessness [*anomian*] is multiplied, the love of many will grow cold." As the distinguished Matthean scholar S. Légasse has pointed out, in Matthew's interpretation of the law and prophets the absence of love is the equivalent of apostasy. The dissolution of community and the fraying of relationships and commitments within the group are construed by Matthew as proof that the end is near. Matthew claims, "the one who endures to the end," this one will be saved (24:13).

The distinctively Matthean sentence about preaching the gospel of the kingdom to the whole inhabited earth (*oikoumene*) in 24:14 ends this section of the eschatological discourse. Matthew alone among the Gospel writers ties the end to preaching the Gospel of the kingdom to the whole earth. This message is intended to go to all people. When this has happened, "then the end will come" (24:14). What are we to make of this curious sentence? The most plausible interpretation of this verse inserted by Matthew is that it provides an explanation for the delay in the coming of "the end." The end Jesus spoke about began, Matthew believed, with the desolation of Jerusalem and the destruction of the temple. Yet Matthew's community was still struggling to live out their form of Judaism interpreted in light of Jesus a full generation or more after the events of 70. Where is the end? What accounts for the delay? Matthew maintains that Jesus inserted a proviso concerning the end. When the gospel of the kingdom has been delivered to the *oikoumene*, then, Matthew tries to explain, the end will finally come. This condition helps to explain the conclusion of the Gospel which mandates a mission for the community. There had been little talk of mission and, according to Matthew 9:37ff., little interest in mission on the part of the community up to this point. To the extent that there was any impetus for or interest in mission within the Matthean community, it was tied to the group's belief about the end. Mission is related to the eschatology of Matthean Judaism. When the inhabited world has the message of the kingdom preached to it, then the end will come. The message, of course, had not yet reached the entire world by the close of the first century and, therefore, the day of the Son of man had still not occurred. When all those on earth have had the Gospel preached to them, then the end will come, and come in a definitive and unmistakable fashion.

The persecution of the community also plays an important role in the teaching about the end. These struggles are interpreted as the prelude to the coming of the Son of man. The "desolating sacrilege" spoken of by the prophet signals the coming end. In the parallel passage to Matthew 24:15 (Mark 13:14 ‖ Luke 21:20) no particular prophet is named. In 24:15 Matthew specifically and characteristically names Daniel as the Hebrew Bible writer who wrote about the sacrilege. Matthew believed the words of Daniel's prophecy were being fulfilled in his day. When they write about the "desolating sacrilege," Matthew and Mark both have in mind something that has happened to or in the temple. This is indicated by the inclusion of the phrase about something or someone "standing in a holy place" in 24:15. This event, the destruction of the temple or its being overrun by foreigners, is the sacrilege that inaugurates the beginning of the end.

When this happens, "flee to the mountains." Matthew 24:17–18 stresses the urgency with which one must take flight. Do not return to your house or stop to get clothing. And one must recognize the severity of the situation. This period of tribulation will be very difficult for those with children, and for those fleeing in the frequently underestimated forbidding winter months in Israel. And finally, Matthew adds, pray that your flight from the desolation not be on the sabbath (24:20). Much has been written on this lone Matthean verse. G. Stanton has offered a recent review of interpretations of this curious passage. This verse probably suggests that in Matthew's overwhelmingly Jewish setting the flight on the sabbath would draw undue attention to the Matthean community. In addition, the possibility certainly exists that this would also have been viewed as a violation of sabbath laws by at least some Matthean Jews. Matthew 12:1–14 does not indicate, contrary to Stanton, that the community did not abide by sabbath laws, or that they held a more liberal view of those laws. Rather, the debate about sabbath interpretation in 12:1–14 is once again about the core value that should inform one's application of the law. The debate is not about the degree of activity allowed on the sabbath. The sabbath debate is about the attitude and hermeneutical principles that inform one's understanding of the law. The logion about flight on the sabbath pertains to Matthew's awareness of, and sensibilities to, certain Judaisms' sabbath observance.

Borrowing from Mark, Matthew describes in vivid terms the events surrounding the end. There will be many "false Christs," and false prophets will arise and show great signs and wonders so to lead people astray, "even the elect" (24:24). Do not believe these false voices who will lead many, even members of the Matthean community (*the eklektous*), away. The coming of the Son of man will be absolutely unmistakable: "As the lightning comes from the east and shines as far as the west, so will be the coming of the son of man" (24:27). After these struggles (*thlipsiv*), "the sun will be darkened, and the moon will not give its light, and the stars will fall from the heaven" (24:29). Typically with apocalypticists – and we have seen this already on several occasions in Matthew's Gospel – the coming of the end is declared through portents and signs in the heavens and in the earth. This was true in the birth narrative in Matthew, and is also the case in the death of Jesus. This trait is continued in his treatment of the end of the age. Sun, stars and moon, clouds, angels, and powers of heaven are all part of the "sign of the son of man" (24:30), and constitute the final act in the cosmic drama. The close of this apocalyptic play includes "a loud trumpet call, and the angels of the son of man gathering the elect from the four winds, from one end of heaven to the other" (24:31). Following the horrible events of the tribulation, and when the trumpet has sounded and the elect from all over have been gathered, then the day of the Son of man has come; the end is at hand.

The talk about the end in the Gospels periodically provokes speculation within particularly more conservative Christian communities about the end of the world. Conservative American Protestant Christianity, especially those inclined toward revivalism, have with some regularity studied this apocalyptic material from the Gospels with an eye toward figuring out again when the Son of man will return. For those who take this apocalyptic material seriously, if not literally, it is crucial to also take seriously Jesus' own admonition in Matthew 24:36: "But of that day and hour no one knows, not even the angels of heaven or the Son of man." This kind of speculation about the future is viewed as beyond the purview of human knowing in the Gospels. Matthew believed this ardently and was explicit in his caution against worrying about when these things will occur. No one knows when history will take its odd – if not final – turn. This is out of one's control. Matthew, as a review of the Sermon on the Mount, his legal material, and conflict the scribes and Pharisees shows, was far more concerned with living, and living in the manner he felt the God of Israel had called his people to live. That is, seek the kingdom of God and its justice, and love God and neighbor. This is the whole law and the prophets. If Matthean Jews remembered to do only this much, "everything else will be given to the community" (6:33).

For those who stand outside of Christian circles that still

take apocalyptic claims seriously, reading this Matthean material about the end is odd indeed. It is difficult for many modern
readers to understand the worldview that is behind this description of the end of history. The imagery associated with the end
in Matthew 24, and the assumption that God has planned such
a destructive end to God's creation, offend the sensibilities of
many modern believers and readers.

Much in Matthew is relevant for today. But Matthew and his
book are products of a context and environment quite different
from our own. This volume asserts that one must appreciate that
late-first-century context in order to make sense at all out of Matthew's Gospel. It will not help, and it does not do justice to this
text to pretend Matthew somehow anticipated or embraced the
values of modern postenlightenment believers at every point. In
certain instances Matthew's advice does correspond comfortably
to modern and so-called postmodern sensibilities. This is not the
case for many readers when we take up his view of history, the
future, and God's relationship to both.

For Matthew, despite the terrible events of the recent past,
the God of Israel is in charge. Unlike many people of our more
modern era, the crises and disappointments of life in the Matthean setting did not raise questions about God, God's existence
or fidelity. Rather, these events caused Matthean Jews to rein-
terpret and reevaluate the events that had recently transpired.
The problem was not with the God of Israel; this would not occur to Matthew. Rather, the problem was with certain people
in Israel. His story of Jesus seeks to highlight this point for his
readers. God will ultimately act and, Matthew 24 and 25 assert,
this action will occur soon. God will break into history, judge
the wicked, and vindicate the righteous, that is, the elect of
Matthew's church. This view of history and events strikes many
moderns as odd indeed. However, as we have seen, this is a view,
or eschatology (that is, view of the end), that was quite common
in Matthew's day. The apocalyptic discourse in Matthew, though
foreign to many of our inclinations and instincts, was usual and
comprehensible to Matthew's community and contemporaries.

Apocalyptic is not the only perspective offered concerning
the future in Matthew's Gospel. This may be one of several

distinguishing features between Matthew and Mark. The latter represents a group thoroughly focused on the end and the dawning of the new age. Matthew has conveniently and typically lumped his apocalyptic material together in the section leading up to the passion narrative. But elsewhere in his Gospel Matthew provides indications of other approaches to the problem of the future for believers in his community. Matthew reveals elsewhere in his Gospel that he and his community are preparing for the long haul. Matthew has imported and faithfully reported the apocalyptic discourse from Mark's Gospel — primarily Mark 13.

Matthew has made a few suggestive additions like the saying about love growing cold, preaching the Gospel of the kingdom to the whole world, and the warning about fleeing on the sabbath. His hand is in evidence in this apocalyptic section, but for the most part he has reiterated Mark's thoroughgoing apocalypticism in this chapter. But this in no way exhausts Matthew's view of how his community should face the future.

In the Sermon on the Mount, chapters 16, 18, and in his extended legal debates, Matthew has provided instructional material that is devoted to the ongoing life of the community. Relationships and guidelines for the internal life of the group are the foci of the Sermon on the Mount. Forgiveness and discipline within the membership are the foci of chapter 18. Issues of ongoing leadership and authority are the foci of chapter 16. The legal debates in chapters 12, 15, and 22, to name only a few, are really about the values and priorities the community will use in applying the law to their daily lives. Matthew's distinctive portrait of the disciples as understanding leaders and competent teachers for the church also corresponds to concerns about the future. These are trained and knowledgeable leaders who rival and could well replace the current leaders in the Matthean setting.

All of this does not sound like a community eagerly anticipating the imminent end of the world. In fact, I am quite confident, Matthew's focus was not trained on the end of history, despite chapter 24. We have already seen that Matthew has written a Gospel that responds to a set of real issues and tensions in his setting. His Gospel offers insight and instruction gleaned from traditions and memories about Jesus which will help Matthean Jews live in the world, not leave it abruptly. Matthew's savvy instruction about local political realities, his summation of the law and the prophets on several occasions in the Gospel, his highlighting of true leadership and authority, and his stress on communal relations and harmony all underscore that he expected his community to be around for awhile and was offering advice to make sure this was the case. Apocalyptic material is present in Matthew's Gospel, and was probably present to some extent among some Matthean members, but Matthew himself was a lukewarm apocalypticist.

Why, then, is this apocalyptic material in Matthew's Gospel at all? My view is that this has to do largely with how Matthew viewed Mark's Gospel. Matthew did not utterly distance himself from the apocalypticism he found in Mark. In some vague sense he believed the God of Israel would orchestrate a culmination to history and to God's plan. But this general eschatology on Matthew's part does not sufficiently explain the inclusion of the apocalyptic material in chapter 24. Along broad lines Matthew might endorse the scenario in chapter 24, but he did not focus on it, and his conviction in it was starting to wane in favor of developing a strategy and ethic for the future. Matthew did, though, follow Mark rather faithfully at many points. There is the sense when one reads Matthew closely in relation to Mark that Matthew felt compelled to faithfully report Mark's material unless he absolutely disagreed with it. Matthew, for example, broke with Mark on legal matters and with his portrayal of the disciples. Where Mark's story was found wanting Matthew added his own distinctive material. This is easy to spot because Matthew was inclined to concentrate his own distinctive material together. Outside of these Matthean sections, Matthew tried to follow Mark rather closely, making only subtle — though often significant — changes in the Marcan material as he went along.

I do not know why Matthew felt compelled to report Mark in this faithful, ordered, and at times pedestrian manner. But this tendency is clearly visible. He might have believed Mark's story carried some authority. All but 60 or so verses from Mark's roughly 660 verses are repeated in Matthew. This is a telling statistic. He was obviously deeply indebted to Mark's story. Matthew departed from Mark's narrative carefully and thoughtfully. His own creativity and themes were often inserted surreptitiously with the modest change of a word, the addition of a clause, or a verse. These subtle changes can be quite significant in terms of the overall meaning, but Matthew did this without making major editorial changes to Mark's story. Dropping a Marcan story was a last resort for Matthew. He was not opposed at all to adding his own material; in fact, there is no shortage of distinctly Matthean material. He was, however, slow to delete material from Mark. In this vein he has included and quietly modified the Marcan material on the end of the age. Matthew was not finally opposed to this eschatology, but he did not share Mark's zeal for it, and his commitment to this worldview appears faint when read in light of the broader context of Matthew's story.

## Apocalyptic Parables:
## Thoughts on the End of History

In Matthew Jesus tells several parables that are meant to instruct the community further about their beliefs and concerns about the end. Matthew 24:37–44 is material Matthew took over from Q (Luke 17:26–36; 12:39–40), not, in this instance, from Mark. The coming of the Son of man is likened in Q to the days of Noah. These days are like the days of Noah because then as now the people seem unaware that judgment is upon them. So sudden is this action or end that "two men will be walking in the field and one is taken and one is left. Two women will be grinding at the mill; one is taken and one is left. Watch therefore, for you do not know on what day your lord is coming" (Matt. 24:40–42).

In 24:37–44 Matthew picked up some material from Q (Luke 12:39–40) which is about a householder (*oikodespotes*) whose home is broken into by a thief. The transition from 24:42 and 24:43 is not a smooth one. Matthew has spliced together two disparate sections of Q, and done so rather unevenly. The reader may understandably wonder where the "householder" comes from in 24:43. J. Kloppenborg has a helpful discussion of the Q parallels to these Matthean passages in his book, *The Formation of Q*. It seems that both Q (Luke 12:39–40) and Matthew (24:37–44) have confused at least two themes within literature from early Jesus movements. The coming Day of the Lord is parabolically likened to a thief in 1 Thessalonians 5:2, 4, 2 Peter 3:10, and Revelation 3:3 and 16:15. But, as we have seen, Matthew and other Gospel writers contend that no one can know the day or hour, and dwelling upon the timing of this cosmic event is strongly discouraged.

Kloppenborg notes that this section of Q is "a secondary composition." Two themes, the unexpected and undetectable hour of the Son of man, and the failure to stay alert and keep watch over the proverbial house of the master, have been combined or conflated. The *Gospel of Thomas* (21b) retains a less conflated version that focuses solely on watchfulness and vigilance against the world. Matthew, through selectively combining Q material from at least two places (cf. Luke 17:26–36 and Luke 12:39–40), reflects some unevenness and conflating of two different themes related to the end.

From 24:45 through 24:51 Matthew can now take up the image of the householder and the stewards or servants who keep watch over the house. In Q (Luke 12:41) this discussion is prompted by a question from Peter, who asks if the story about the person given charge over the "house" is a parable "for us [i.e., the disciples], or for all." Matthew has made this a rhetorical question posed by Jesus himself (24:45). This is part of his longer instruction concerning the end and is still part of his lecture to the disciples. Matthew 24:45–51 (and its parallel in Luke 12:41–46) is a parable about the delay of the coming Son of man. The servant who is given charge over the house (presumably Israel) may say to himself, "My master is delayed" (Matt. 24:48 ∥ Luke 12:45), and begin to take liberties that he otherwise would not take. The servant may start to "beat fellow servants, and eat and drink with drunks" (24:49). Then the master of the house will come on a day when he does not expect him and at an hour he does not know, and he will punish him, and put him with the hypocrites; "there men will weep and gnash their teeth" (24:50–51). In 24:51 Matthew has added one of his favorite terms for the opponents in his setting, "hypocrites," who will be with the unfaithful stewards when the final day comes. They are like the wicked servants in the house who believed the master was long gone and they could get away with loose living and the oppression of other "fellow servants" (*sundoulous*).

In this brief parable Matthew shows that he believes the delay of the Day of the Lord has served to further identify the poor leaders who claim to be speaking on behalf of the God and traditions of Israel. This delay has provided more time to reveal the corruption and malice that Matthew believes motivate the present leadership and Matthean opponents. One clear expectation in Matthew's Gospel is that these poor leaders will one day, and perhaps soon, be judged and condemned. This is a prominent feature of Matthean eschatology as it comes to us in chapter 24.

Matthew 25:1–13 is the parable of the ten virgins, yet another story intended to instruct the community further about issues relating to the future and the close of the age. This Matthean parable possesses no clear parallel in the other Gospels. This, too, is a parable about the apparent delay of the end. The parable intends to encourage greater diligence and preparedness in the face of waning expectations that the end about which Jesus spoke is, in fact, near.

Like most parables this begins with a simile, "Then the kingdom of heaven is like ten maidens" (25:1). The ten maidens are waiting to meet the bridegroom. Five of the maidens are "foolish" (*morai*, as in the English cognate, "moronic,"), and five are wise (or "prudent," *phronimoi*). The foolish maidens do not take enough oil for their lamps, but the wise take flasks of oil with them. As the bridegroom is delayed, the maidens fall asleep. At midnight there is a cry, "Behold, the bridegroom! Come out to meet him" (25:6). By this hour the foolish maidens lack sufficient oil to "trim their lamps" (25:7), while the wise have enough for themselves, but not enough for both the wise and the foolish. The foolish go instead to barter for more oil (25:9), but while they are away the bridegroom comes, and those who are ready go into the marriage feast and the door is shut (25:10). Upon their return the foolish maidens are unable to gain entry into the feast. "Watch, therefore, for you know neither the day or the hour" (25:13).

This Matthean parable sounds like a warning to the community itself. That is, the maidens are all waiting and expecting the same thing: the coming of the bridegroom. They are like-minded and share the same hope. Some, however, have lost their hope and diligence prematurely. Members or faithful who do not maintain their watchfulness will be left out on the final day. Likewise, within the Matthean community are those who, while still members and believers in the message, have started to lose their belief in the Matthean version of the end of history. The delay of the Day of the Lord, the social and theological mechanisms the Matthean community has developed in order to successfully live life out in their setting, and the trials of their present circumstances, have all played a role in the waning of apocalyptic hope. The parable of the ten maidens is intended to counter this decline. The story asserts one never knows, one cannot be sure, and the community must try to stay ready and hold out hope that the end to history some believed Jesus preached might soon arrive. Despite ample evidence to the contrary, Matthew retains enough of an apocalyptic element that he still believes Matthean Judaism will ultimately prevail in its struggle with local opponents and internal members who have decided to abandon the precepts of Matthew's teaching and Torah interpretation, based as it is on the life and teaching of Jesus. These false voices within and without will be among those locked out from the age to come.

The so-called parable of the talents in 25:14–30 is yet another apocalyptic parable. While pieces of this parable seem to have originally derived from Q (Luke 19:11–27), there is much of Matthew's own hand in this story. In Matthew this is a story about a man who leaves on a journey and entrusts his property to his servants. To one servant he gives five talents, to another two, and to yet another one talent, "each according to his ability" (25:15). The servant with five talents takes what he has, trades with the talents, and makes five more. Also, the servant with two talents makes two more. But the servant with one talent hides his master's money in a hole.

"After a long time the master of those servants returned to settle accounts" (25:19). The first two servants are rewarded and called "good and faithful." Because they "had been faithful over a little," they will be set over much (25:21, 23). Both are told "to enter into the joy of your master." But the servant who only returns the one talent he had received to his master is finally "cast into the outer darkness; there people weep and gnash their teeth" (25:30).

The cruelty to this parable is hard to understand. Matthew's version of this parable is particularly confounding when compared with the parable in Luke 19:11–27. The parable in Luke is at least, according to Luke 19:14, 27, a pronouncement of judgment on those who "do not want [the Lord] to reign over them." The parable clearly lays out the punishment for those who stand in the way of Jesus and the kingdom of God. The Q parable concludes with the phrase, "Bring them here and slay them in front of me" (Luke 19:27). Matthew has altered this Q parable so that the judgment on the servant who failed to invest is even more confounding. While both parables advocate vengeance and judgment for those who do not embrace the values of the movement, the Matthean version stresses eschatological judgment on members — that is, fellow servants — not on people outside the group who are opposed to the reign of Jesus, as is the case in Luke's parallel.

The original intent of the earlier Lucan story is a political one. Luke's parable is a kingship parable. Matthew's version, on the other hand, is fundamentally about the servants' use of the talents they have been given. Luke tells a story, basically, about a king who, despite opposition from the citizenry, obtains a kingdom. He establishes his rule by getting rid of his opponents. It is important to recognize that the Lucan story is being told "because he [Jesus] was near to Jerusalem and because they supposed that the kingdom of God was to appear immediately."

The Lucan story lays bare the political and popular opposition to Jesus as a political power. Upon his return as king Jesus destroys those enemies who did not want this man to reign over them (19:14, 27). This is the outline and framework of the story. It details the fate of those who oppose Jesus — at least those who opposed Jesus while he was in Jerusalem. The aspect of the story that discusses the servants' use of the "ten pounds" (*minas*) is not incidental, but it is secondary. The servants who make the most out of what they were given by the king are honored and inherit cities to rule. The servant who merely holds the pounds, but does not trade for more pounds, is denounced, not given a city to rule, but is not judged beyond this. In Luke the servants are all given the same amount of money and told to trade with it. In Matthew the servants are given different amounts of money, "each according to his ability" (25:15).

Matthew's version, the parable of the talents, is fundamentally about the behavior of the servants. The political tensions and scenario in the Lucan version are no longer evident in Matthew's parable. In Luke the servants are explicitly told to trade their pounds and obtain more while the king is away. In Matthew no such explicit instruction is given. Nevertheless, when the man who gave the talents to his servants returns, he grants the reward of eschatological blessing ("enter the joy of your master"; 25:21, 23) to those who have doubled their talents. But the servant who only guards his one talent by burying it, out of fear of his master because he "knew him to be a hard man" (25:24), is severely chastised and judged. He is described as a "wicked and slothful servant." He should have at least invested the money to gain the interest. The one talent is taken from the wicked servant and given to the one who has turned his five talents into ten. "For to every one who has will more be given, and he will have abundance; but from him who has not, even what he has will be taken away" (25:29). This "worthless servant" is finally "cast into the outer darkness; there men will weep and gnash their teeth."

The difference between these two versions of this basic story is significant. Matthew has made this a story about the behavior and diligence of the servants while the master is away. In Matthew the concern about the delay of Jesus' return is emphasized through the verse that says, "Now after a long time the master of those servants came and settled accounts with them" (25:19). Matthew's parable is a story about the behavior of church members during the long delay of the parousia, or return of Jesus. The Matthean parable is a warning for community members who don't make the most out of what they have been given in this period prior to the return of the master. Some members of the Matthean community will be judged at the end of history.

Luke's story does intend to instruct believers in their actions and ethics while they are waiting, but Luke primarily aims at reassuring members that those who oppose them and reject Jesus, the king, will be judged and destroyed. The losers, or antagonists, in the Lucan story are outsiders who rejected the rule of the king. The losers, or antagonists, in the Matthean version are insiders who fail to live as they should in the period prior to the Day of the Lord. Matthew has stressed that members continue to make the most "out of their ability" (cf. 25:15) while the master is away. In this period church members should continue to live out Matthean ethics, conduct their work with a view toward profit, and expect a reward in the future for their life now. Those who do not embrace this feature of Matthean ethics at the end of time will be judged and left out of the "joy of the master."

Both versions of this story are harsh — Matthew's perhaps even more so because his story warns insiders of their final destruction if they do not live as they have been instructed. Once again, especially when compared to Luke's version of this story, Matthew's paramount concern for the health and life of the community comes to the fore. Matthew's parable has little instruction for or about the world. Matthew's parable does not concern itself with the issue of what will happen to nonmembers or those who fail to accept the message of the kingdom. These themes seem to be present at an earlier stage in the development of this odd story. The earlier Q substratum raises these broader concerns. Matthew, in contrast, has shaped this harsh story so that it addresses his community and the life and behavior of the membership. The Matthean parable of the talents is a foreboding message and warning for Matthean Jews. They are to remain active and vigilant in their tasks, continue to work hard for the master, though there seem to be many reasons presently to question that, and they should continue to look for the fulfillment of their version of history and the vindication of their message of the kingdom of heaven. Those who fail to do this will be judged on the last day.

This Matthean parable only thinly veils the fraying of the community around the edges and the doubts of some members as time in Judea-Galilee marches forward without Matthew's version of history and events coming to fulfillment. Things did not seem to be working out the way some believed they were supposed to. This created problems and dissonance for at least some Matthean Jews. Where are we headed? What has happened to our message? How do we explain the delay in the much vaunted fulfillment of history on the part of Jesus, putative king and Son of man? Matthew was well aware of these ecclesial problems and tensions. He knew, and the reader is made aware, of the dissolution of community and faith on the part of some as a result of these problems. Here Matthew fashioned a parable from an earlier Q story which attempts to respond to some of these crucial questions, and a parable that also serves as a warning to members contemplating abandoning certain fundamental precepts of Matthean Judaism.

This sort of view of the end, and the judgment and personal destruction it foretells, is troubling to most modern readers. But this view of history and accountability at the end of the age was quite typical of Matthew's day and context. Most of Matthew's readers would not have found this view of the end particularly unusual. Most of Matthew's contemporaries believed people would one day have to provide an account for their decisions and actions. Such apocalypticism did not persist too long into the histories of rabbinic Judaism and Christianity. But this worldview informed both religions at an early, formative stage. This perspective occasionally erupts in both religions even today, because this worldview, though foreign to most, has been codified and preserved in the canon of both the Hebrew Bible and the New Testament.

It is noteworthy that Matthew did not believe the community or its leaders engaged in the judgment of other members. Matthew's eschatology clearly includes a judgment of other Matthean Jews. He has stressed this at a number of points. But the community is called to forgive and not judge. The judgment is saved for the end, and God, or God's agent Jesus the Son of man, will do the judging, separating, and condemning. This is not the role or responsibility of the community. Such judgments, however harsh and disturbing, are saved to the end when God will judge. Matthew 18:35, the parables of the vineyard and the wedding feast in chapters 21 and 22, and the eschatological parables in chapters 24 and 25 bring out this feature of Matthean eschatology. Matthew seemed to be aware that his community was a mixed crowd. That is, there were good and bad, righteous and wicked mixed in together. Matthew dealt with this reality by stressing forgiveness, mutuality, and right relationships within the group. The judgment and the sorting out of good and bad, righteous and wicked will be done by God at the close of the age. This is not the task or charge of the *ecclesia*. Matthew warns his audience that this assessment will occur at some time in the (not too distant) future, and they should be watchful and vigilant in their behavior and actions in this interim time. But God will do the sorting out when the time comes, not Matthean members.

## "Unto the least of these": Ethics at the End of Time

Matthew ends this cycle of parables with his famous parable of the last judgment in 25:31–46. This story is distinctly Matthean. While only reported in one Gospel — Matthew — this parable has played a prominent and formative role in Christian history, and in the formation of Christian community and ethics. This, too, along with the previous Matthean eschatological parables is a story about ethics at the end of time.

This story is not so much about the delay of the parousia and how to live during this interim period, as is the case with the parables of the ten maidens and the talents, but is more about what will happen when the parousia finally does occur. The parable begins with the sentence, "When the Son of man comes in his glory, and all his angels with him, then he will sit on his glorious throne" (25:31). Gathered before the Son of man will be "all the nation's people [*panta to ethne*]." This is the same curious phrase we encounter at the close of the Gospel in 28:19. On this day he will separate the sheep from the goats. The subject or authority in the story quickly shifts from "the Son of man" to a king. From 25:33ff. this is a parable about a king judging those in his realm when he comes in his power.

The sheep are those who have lived in the manner the king expected. Specifically, they treated, served, and helped the king when he was in need. This is how the people were supposed to live. However, there are those in the fold who did not embrace these particular ethics at the end of time and they will be judged and condemned by the king. Those who have lived and behaved in the manner that meets the king's standards may "inherit the kingdom prepared [for them] from the foundation of the world" (25:34). The proverbial goats will be cast into the eternal fire "prepared for the devil and his angels" (25:41).

What sort of life are Matthean Jews supposed to be living now, prior to the return of the king? What are the ethical expectations these Matthean believers should be fulfilling now? Matthew's answer to this is well known and is frequently held up as an answer to questions about how Christians should live and act in the world. This parable has become a hallmark for guiding Christian ethics and ecclesial social responsibility.

"For I was hungry and you gave me food, I was thirsty and you gave me drink, I was a stranger and you welcomed me, I was naked and you clothed me, I was sick and you visited me, I was in prison and you came to me" (25:35–36). In 25:37 Matthew slips into his favorite terminology for the insiders, or members who in truth fulfill the Gospel, "the righteous" (*oi dikaioi*). These righteous seem quite unaware that they had been serving, helping, feeding, and visiting the king. In innocence they ask, "Lord, when did we see you hungry and feed you ... ?" The king's answer in 25:40 is a familiar and famous one: "Truly I say to you, as you did it to the least of these my brothers [*adelphon*], you did it to me."

The language of "least" (*elaxiston*) is reminiscent of the little ones, or *mikroi* of chapter 18 (cf. 18:6, 10). The language of "brother" (*adelphos*), as we have seen on numerous occasions, is also characteristic of Matthew's language to describe fellow community members. This is a story about those who lived in the Matthean community, and treated fellow servants, or Matthean Jews, in the manner Jesus taught and expected. When the righteous acted justly and empathetically toward "the least," the "little ones," or their *adelphoi*, that is, Matthean Jews, then they were really serving, helping, and consoling or pleasing the king. Right actions and behavior within the group and toward fellow community members are the mark of service to the king.

This passage has been used within the church to promote Christian care, mission, and service to the world. Matthew's personal parable in 25:31–46 has provoked much good: feeding, healing, hospitality, and charity. This story has served as a hallmark for the formation of the American Social Gospel Movement, Catholic Charities, the Catholic Worker Movement started by Dorothy Day, and many other international Christian service organizations. Matthew has unwittingly fostered an aspect of Christian history that has made a difference in the world. I say unwittingly because this is probably not the original meaning of this story. This is a story about care and service to others in the community, not beyond it, out in the world.

A recent dissertation by S. Gray provides a survey of the interpretation of this parable throughout church history. In his exhaustive review Gray has concluded that the phrase "least of these my brothers" was viewed throughout Christian history as referring to believers and, this author would add, specifically Matthean Jews. Gray consistently uses the anachronistic term "Christian" throughout his book to refer to Matthean members. This is confusing and historically misleading. The nomenclature "brother" and "least," as we have seen elsewhere in the Gospel, refer clearly to community members. Not all people who believed in Jesus (there was little uniformity in the earliest centuries of the church) were intended with these words, and certainly Matthew did not mean these people represented a new religion apart from Judaism. The people who are to be served and aided are fellow Matthean Jews. These people are fulfilling the will, law, and plan of the God of Israel. When they live and act out the ethics Jesus taught them, they are serving the king and will, therefore, "inherit the kingdom prepared for them." Most early church interpreters understood this Matthean parable in this manner.

Tertullian (160–225 C.E.), for example, understood this parable as proof that heretics, or erring members within the church, would be judged and condemned to the fire. In *De oratione* (26.1), Tertullian explains that in fellow Christian "brothers" one has seen their Lord. The first major Syriac figure in the church, Aphraates (280–345 C.E.), quotes Matthew 25:35–45 extensively in his *Demonstrations* 20. The function of the quotations is primarily to encourage believers to serve the Lord in the persons of the poor, sick, and needy. He collects a number of biblical passages to prove that the poor, small, and needy are really Christians. The "rich," he maintains, are the Jews. Already in this third- or early-fourth-century document we can see the words and injunctions of Matthean Judaism being used by later Christian writers to attack all Jews.

John Chrysostom (347–407 C.E.) was a Matthean scholar. Matthew's Gospel is the most quoted biblical book in his work. Gray counts over 170 quotes and 220 allusions to the last judgment scene in Chrysostom. This parable and the Sermon on the Mount are the two most quoted narrative units in Chrysostom's work. Chrysostom used this parable to sketch out his view and definition of Christian charity. Chrysostom seems to be among the first commentators to make a distinction between Christian poor and non-Christian poor, but he is not completely consistent on this point. He does seem to afford charity to all people, believers and nonbelievers. However, there are several instances (Gray can count at least eight unambiguous instances) when Chrysostom interprets the poor or needy of 25:31ff. as other Christians.

Most earlier interpreters of this passage understand Matthew's meaning as we do here. That is, Matthew intends with this parable to encourage charity among Matthean Jews. Service to the king is delivered by providing service to other members. The Matthean communal terms of endearment, "least," and "brother," signal to the reader that Matthew must have meant fellow members of his *ecclesia*. The king's command to be aided is fulfilled in providing help and service to those in need within the Matthean community.

By the late nineteenth and early twentieth centuries another interpretation to this parable started to emerge. This interpretation suggests that Matthew means to say that Christ has called his people to serve the world. The needy in the parable are not fellow church members, but rather are any needy in the world. It was primarily in this century and last that this so-called universalizing tendency in the parable was cultivated. That is to say, over the last 100 years or so more commentators have tried to assert that Matthew is advocating care, feeding, and charity toward all people — the world. This interpretive tendency corresponds with the rise of Christian missionary and social activity. Further, that Matthew might have all people in mind when he speaks of the "poor" or "needy" also corresponds to a setting where the dominant culture is Christian. It is easier to imagine a world where all people are the objects of Christian communal attention and affection — if not missionary activity — when Christian culture is dominant.

If we can imagine a context where a community of believers like Matthew's Jesus-centered Judaism was clearly a minority with great worries and threats, then the original thrust of Matthew's parable is easier to apprehend. Matthew was stressing care and concern for the members in light of the dangers and threats they felt they faced daily. This parable intends to warn people against the temptation to abandon members when they are in need, in trouble, or alienated. This parable charts a support system for the community that is beleaguered and in crisis.

This in no way is intended to diminish the tremendous work that has been done by Christians motivated by this verse. There is ample material in the Bible to support this kind of activity and these kinds of organizations. In honesty, however, when one reads this parable in the broader context of Matthew's entire Gospel, and when one recalls the broader context and setting of the Matthean community and the struggles that gave rise to the writing of the Gospel, the marvelous and positive interpretation of this parable which has moved to the fore in this century does not seem likely. While the recent Christian impulse to help, feed, and "take in" the world is crucial, its ground cannot reasonably be drawn from this parable. Matthew has in mind in this story the care and nurture of the community. In caring for fellow Matthean Jews one is caring for Christ. "As you did it unto the least of these my brothers, you did it unto me" (25:40).

## Further Reading

Burnett, F. W. *The Testimony of Jesus-Sophia: A Redactional-Critical Study of the Eschatological Discourse in Matthew.* Washington, D.C.: University Press of America, 1981.

Donahue, J. R. "The 'Parable' of the Sheep and the Goats: A Challenge to Christian Ethics." *TS* 47 (1986): 3–31.

Gray, S. W. *The Least of My Brothers: Matthew 25:31–46 — A History of Interpretation.* SBL Dissertation Series 114. Atlanta: Scholars Press, 1989.

Harrington, D. *The Gospel of Matthew.* Collegeville, Minn.: Michael Glazier/Liturgical Press, 1991.

Kee, H. C. *Community of the New Age: Studies in Mark's Gospel.* London: SCM Press, 1977.

Kloppenborg, J. *The Formation of Q: Trajectories in Ancient Wisdom Collections.* Philadelphia: Fortress, 1987.

Légasse, S. "Le refroidissement de l'amour avant la fin (Mt 24.12)." *SNTU* 8 (1983): 91–102.

Stanton, G. *A Gospel for a New People: Studies in Matthew.* Edinburgh: T. & T. Clark, 1992.

# Chapter Fourteen

# The Passion and Death —
# 26:1–27:54

## Preparation for Jesus' Death

The apocalyptic discourse and discussion about the end of history give way to the passion narrative in Matthew. Chapters 26 and 27 detail Jesus' arrest, trial, and death in Jerusalem. Matthew connects the coming of the end with Jesus' imminent death through his use of the predominantly eschatological title "Son of man" in 26:2.

In 26:2 (‖ Mark 14:1) Matthew notes that the Passover is two days away. The Son of man will be "delivered up" (*paradidotai*) to be crucified (*staurothanai*). "The chief priests and elders of the people [a distinctive and favorite Matthean term for local popular leaders] gathered in the palace of Caiaphas and took counsel together in order to arrest Jesus by stealth and kill him" (26:3–4). The reader has seen this association of local leaders and officials before. This political subtext and tension run throughout the story, and the convenient alliance of local leaders that Jesus' movement helped forge converges again in Jerusalem to help put an end to his influence. Virtually the same coalition of local and popular authorities emerged in Jerusalem during the birth of Jesus (2:4) when Herod had concerns about the child born "king of the Jews." This coalition is prominent throughout the trial and death in 26:5, 57, 59, and 27:1, 41, 62. The verb "to gather," or "assemble," is also present in the birth (2:4) as well as at the beginning of the passion narrative (26:3), along with themes of secrecy, deception or stealth, and the reasoning

353

together or "counsel" the leaders hold to figure out how to destroy Jesus. Matthew has placed a similar scene in the middle of his story at 12:14 involving just the Pharisees. This verbal and strategic link helps connect the Pharisees with the opposition and destruction of Jesus. The Pharisees also emerge in the passion narrative following Jesus' death.

Only Matthew adds the note about the leadership gathering in the courtyard or palace (*aulan*) of the high priest Caiaphas in 26:3. It is just outside of this courtyard that Peter denies that he knows Jesus or is even part of the movement in 26:69. The conflict and confrontation between local leaders and Jesus, which Matthew has been cultivating in his narrative from the birth of Jesus forward, culminates on the eve of the Jewish festival of Passover. It was not unusual in Jerusalem to have the festivals disrupted with public displays of dissatisfaction with those in power.

A celebrated instance of such trouble in Jerusalem during the time of a festival is recorded by Josephus in *Antiquities* 17.254ff. During the festival of Pentecost a huge crowd gathered in Jerusalem. Galileans, Idumaeans, and a multitude from Jericho, Transjordan, and Judea itself came for religious observance but also to express their resentment toward Sabinus, a procurator for Augustus around the time of the death of Herod. Sabinus was in charge of putting down some resistance that had developed while Varus was governor of Syria. The people's concern involved whether or not Herod's son Archelaus should become ruler of his father's kingdom. The people objected to Archelaus succeeding his father and resented the manner in which Sabinus had treated the Jews, even trying to provoke them into open revolt against him.

During the festival of Pentecost in Jerusalem in c. 4 B.C.E. the resistance and resentment directed toward Sabinus boiled over. The rebellious crowds divided into three units and surrounded the Romans stationed in the temple area. Sabinus assumed the highest point in the area, a tower named for Herod's brother Phasael, and ordered the Romans to attack the Jews (*Ant.* 17.257). A battle continued for a long time around the temple. It was, according to Josephus, a brutal battle, complete with many of the features we have come to expect from a story written by Josephus about a battle between Jews and Romans. The Romans were superior in training and equipment. The Jews were valiant and courageous. Some committed suicide rather than be taken captive by Rome. Many were killed. Some fought increasingly harder as liberty for their country began to emerge as an obtainable goal (*eleutherian tan patrion; Ant.* 17.268). This and other revolts in Galilee and Judea at this time were finally put down through the help of Varus who, when he received word of what was happening, sent additional troops to reclaim the control Sabinus had lost.

Concern about the Passover festival getting out of hand is reflected in the Gospel tradition as well (Matt. 26:5 ‖ Mark 14:2 ‖ Luke 22:2). Matthew records that the chief priests, the elders of the people, and the high priest Caiaphas sought to arrest Jesus and kill him but chose not to do this "during the feast, lest there be a tumult among the people."

However, events in the Gospel narrative move faster than the leaders planned. In 26:6–13 the scene shifts from Jerusalem to a village just outside of the city named Bethany. While in Bethany in the house of Simon (26:6), a woman anoints Jesus with very expensive ointment. The woman pours the ointment on his head. Only in Luke (7:37ff.) and John (12:3) does the woman anoint Jesus' feet and wash them with her hair. In Matthew and Mark the woman simply pours the expensive ointment on his head. In all Gospel versions of this story someone expresses displeasure with what transpires. In John it is Judas Iscariot who protests that the ointment could have been sold for 300 denarii and the money given to the poor (John 12:5). In Luke a Pharisee who has invited Jesus into his home is bothered by the reputation of the woman washing Jesus' feet, not the apparent waste of expensive ointment (Luke 7:39). In Mark only "some" are indignant, claiming the ointment could have been sold and the money given to the poor (Mark 14:5). Matthew explicitly mentions that it is the disciples themselves who are indignant. Like Mark and John they, too, believe that the money from the ointment could have been given to the poor (Matt. 26:9).

But Jesus corrects the disciples' perception in Matthew 26:10–

13. Jesus maintains this woman has done a beautiful thing. "You may always have the poor with you." Mark's verse provides this fuller explanation, "and whenever you will you can do good to them" (Mark 14:7). But, Jesus continues, you will not always have me.

"In pouring this ointment on my body she has prepared me for burial" (26:12). In this sense the scenario designed by the leaders in Jerusalem is not working out. Jesus' death is approaching quickly. The act by the woman, which the disciples do not appreciate, is, in fact, crucial. In Jesus' view it signals a decisive point in the story. Once the body has been anointed, death is only hours away.

Jesus views this act on the part of the anonymous woman as a pivotal event in the Gospel story. "Truly, I say to you, wherever this gospel is preached in the whole world, what she has done will be told in memory of her." This act of preparation, and one assumes understanding and faith on the part of the unnamed woman, is viewed by Jesus as so significant that it is henceforth a fixed part of the gospel story. "Whenever the gospel is preached... what she has done will be told in memory of her."

This is a striking verse. Matthew and Mark (Mark 14:9) both maintain Jesus saw this as a fundamental narrative in the larger story of the whole gospel. Yet this pericope has hardly been viewed thusly in Christian history and preaching. This point has been made forcefully of late by feminist biblical scholars who point to this verse, and a few others, in order to demonstrate that women were part of Jesus' message, if not movement. It is subsequent Christian history and the male-dominated nature of the message and institutions which have neglected this part of the gospel message. E. Schüssler Fiorenza has used this text as a paradigm for looking afresh at the role of women in the Jesus movement, and asking how this new perspective might inform women's roles and responsibilities today. The gospel message, according to Matthew and Mark, must include what this unknown woman has done. But how many times has that been the case in Christian history?

The act by this woman so praised by Jesus becomes the symbolic beginning of Jesus' death. From this verse forward the events take on a life of their own. The narrative moves toward Jesus' death with greater rapidity. We are moments away from the betrayal, the trial, Peter's denial, the death and resurrection scene. The woman's simple act has started a chain of events that cannot or are not supposed to be stopped. Judas is quickly on stage and off again. He is introduced to show that, through his betrayal of Jesus (26:15), the Jerusalem forces are now officially aligned against him through the help of this informant. Judas's betrayal is one more important piece in the narrative's march toward death.

The so-called Lord's Supper, or Last Supper, is another piece that serves to prepare the way for Jesus' death. Matthew 26:17–29 is devoted to the Last Supper; most of it seems to come from Mark 14:12–17. This section is provoked by a question from the disciples: "Where will you have us prepare for you to eat the Passover?" (26:17). The disciples are told to go into the city to a certain person and say, "The Teacher says, My time is at hand; I will keep the passover at your house with my disciples." Mark provides some means of identifying the person (he will be carrying a jar of water; Mark 14:13). Matthew provides no such clues for the disciples. This person will provide a place for Jesus and the twelve to share their last meal together—the Passover meal.

In 26:21–25 Jesus makes public that which the reader already knows. That is, someone from the inside, a member of the group, will betray Jesus to the authorities. All the disciples are deeply disturbed by the news and ask among themselves, "Is it I?" (26:22 ‖ Mark 14:19). Jesus follows this with a Son of man saying or "woe" (26:24). Even though it is necessary and part of the plan, it would be better for the one who betrays him if he had never been born. "Woe to that man by whom the son of man is betrayed!" In 26:25 Judas speaks up, asking, apparently innocently, "Is it I rabbi?" This question is only in Matthew. Mark and Luke provide no parallel to this Matthean question placed in the mouth of Judas. Jesus responds, "You have said so."

This is one distinctly Matthean passage where it seems as though Judas may only be playing his part in a larger cosmic drama. Judas's question has the sound of reluctant resignation.

Is it true? "Is it I?" The power and course of these final events are now spinning out of control and even Judas is caught up in the force and momentum of the imminent confrontation in Jerusalem.

The last meal together is a ritual devoted to Jesus' death. In 26:26–29 Jesus shares the Last Supper with the disciples. The meal pericope reflects a liturgical setting. Jesus' actions at the meal are characterized by four verbs: he took, he blessed, he broke, he gave (26:26). Jesus took the bread, blessed it, broke it up, and gave it to the disciples. "Take, eat; this is my body." Jesus also took a cup and gave it to the disciples and said, "Drink of it, all of you; for this is my blood of the covenant, which is poured out for many for the forgiveness of sins. I shall not drink again of this fruit of the vine until that day when I drink it new with you in my Father's kingdom" (26:29).

This ritual contains aspects of the community's beliefs and hopes, as well as their view of the meaning of Jesus' death. This rite reminds the community of the death of Jesus, and reiterates for the members their beliefs about the purpose of his death. Of course, these beliefs and rationale were developed over time by Matthean Jews. The purposes and theological problems associated with Jesus' death had been part of the reflection of early communities for some time. The formulation of the Eucharist or so-called Lord's Supper represents a fairly developed stage in the community's thinking. The bread represents Jesus' body and the breaking of the bread symbolizes his death. The cup, of course, is his blood of the covenant (*diathekes*), and the community believes Jesus' death was "for many" (*peri pollon*) for the forgiveness of sins (*'amartion*).

It is important to note that, contrary to Luke (Luke 22:20), and Paul (1 Cor. 11:25), this is not a "new" (*kaine*) covenant. Such a thought would be quite foreign to Matthew. There is nothing new in Matthew's thinking or theology; so he maintains. All that has happened is a fulfillment of everything the God of Israel has been saying and doing among God's people through the prophets from the beginning. Jesus' death reminds people of the covenant (i.e., promise) that God has made to God's people.

Why does Jesus' death "forgive sins"? This phrase reminds the reader of the Gospel of the birth narrative. In 1:21 Jesus' name is interpreted by Matthew as meaning "He will save his people from their sins." This function of Jesus' life, and here his death, is reiterated in 26:28. This claim of the purpose of Jesus' life and death nearly starts and nearly finishes the book. What does Matthew have in mind when he says "sins"? There is no indication that Matthew has an ontological state in mind. That is, there is little indication that all people are sinners and must be "saved." These theological formulations come much later in the history of Christianity. But Matthew has been speaking throughout the Gospel of the ills that have corrupted Israel and its leaders. Jesus' message of repentance and reform intends to save Israel from these sins. The so-called sins that Jesus addresses throughout Matthew have been misguided attitudes, broken relationships, distorted leaders, and misinterpretation of the law. These are the sins from which Matthew's Jesus aims to save his people. Matthean Jews believed these were the sins in Judea-Galilee that Jesus lived and died to overcome.

The Last Supper also reminds the Matthean community of their eschatological hopes. The ritual includes the hope of being reunited with Jesus in the kingdom. Jesus and his disciples will prevail over the ills or sins that confront Matthean Jews in their setting. Each time the community shares this ritual they reassert their belief, however fading, that one day they will share this supper with Jesus in the kingdom he promised would come. Jesus will drink this one day with them in that time or place where the hopes of Matthean Jews are fulfilled.

In the context of Matthew's Gospel these passages also serve to prepare Jesus and his disciples for his death. The Last Supper, like the woman who anoints Jesus' head, like the betrayal of Judas, like Jesus' prayer in Gethsemane in 26:36–46 where Jesus prays to do the will of his father rather than be controlled by the fears that face him, all finally prepare Jesus and the twelve for his death. These passages, however, are actually thinly veiled stories that instruct Matthew's community about Jesus' death. Matthew makes plain that he believes Jesus was supposed to die, and die in this fashion. Even those within the group who betray the community fall within God's plan. Matthew has even found some scripture to support this. And he has included, largely thanks to Mark, a body of material that helps the community to remember Jesus' death, as well as point them to a particular interpretation of the meaning and message of that death.

Matthew prepares for, and instructs the community about, Jesus' death in the opening passages of chapter 26. While the reader is well aware that for some time there have been leadership groups planning to do Jesus in, that time is now at hand. As the Jerusalem authorities prepare to act decisively toward Jesus and his followers, Jesus' death looms ever larger. Judas, one of the twelve, is a key player in the drama of Jesus' death. This brief portrait of Judas as informer and perhaps disappointed disciple is crucial to the passion narrative.

## Judas, the Arrest, and Popular Perceptions of Jesus

Judas has a very small but important role in the drama leading to Jesus' death. Judas's importance has grown over time as Christianity has struggled to make theological sense out of Jesus' death. Judas has been characterized in a wide variety of ways in literature, art, and film. He has been portrayed in every manner from poignant and virtuous to the dupe, even demonic. His bit part in the Gospel belies the long shadow his figure has cast over Western cultural history.

Matthew introduces Judas in 26:14–16 as the one among the twelve who will betray Jesus. Matthew shows some indication of wanting to pay some special attention to Judas. As we noted above, only Judas refers to Jesus as "rabbi" in Matthew. This is more than incidental. The most plausible suggestion for this interesting Matthean touch is that this term was starting to be associated with a certain leadership group or coalition, a coalition with which Matthean Judaism was in direct conflict. Judas the betrayer utilizes the forms and terms of authority dominant in the leadership group Matthean Jews oppose.

In 26:14 Matthew describes Judas's decision to go to the chief priest and "deliver" (*paradoso*) Jesus to them. The entire premise here is that the leadership is seeking Jesus and is unable to find him, or find the right time to catch him. Jesus and his followers are holed up outside of Jerusalem but the authorities do not know where. Why else would Judas's offer make any sense? This is what the readers are supposed to understand. Jesus and his disciples have reconnoitered in Bethany, outside of Jerusalem and beyond the reach of those who possess the power to put him away or put him to death. If a historical strategy is embedded in this aspect of the narrative, it would reflect that Jesus is aware that the city contains the people in power who are most opposed to his interpretations and message. This might also help explain why the several, quite significant Galilean cities like Sepphoris or Tiberias are not mentioned in the Gospel tradition — a striking feature of the Gospels for anyone familiar with Galilean history and geography. Jerusalem, too, like these Galilean centers, possessed the personnel and people in power who could act decisively when a person or group looked like they might stir things up again. Given the tendency for such a disruption to take place in Jerusalem at the time of festivals, it is understandable that some Jerusalem authorities might want to nip a problem in the bud.

Matthew alone depicts Judas going to the chief priests and asking, "What will you give me if I deliver him [Jesus] to you?" (26:15). The motive for Judas's betrayal was already an issue by the time of the writing of the Gospels. Both Luke (Luke 22:3) and John (13:27) maintain that Satan entered into Judas. Mark provides little indication of what might have motivated Judas, but does indicate that Judas was paid for his help (Mark 14:11). But Matthew develops Judas's motive further. Only in Matthew does Judas's question to the chief priests begin with "What will you give me if I deliver him up to you?" Matthew makes greed Judas's simple and believable motive. Despite certain modern and popular portrayals of Judas, Matthew provides little indication that Judas was somehow misled about the course the Jesus movement had assumed, or that he believed Jesus had betrayed either the people or his own cause. In Matthew Judas is motivated by the money.

Matthew develops the figure of Judas further than the other

evangelists through his addition of the legend about Judas's remorse at the death of Jesus. In 27:3–10 Matthew records Judas's death. When Judas sees Jesus bound and led away to Pilate the governor, "he changed his mind and brought back the thirty pieces of silver to the chief priests and the elders saying, 'I have sinned in betraying innocent blood.'" The authorities are unmoved and respond, "What is that to us? See to it yourself" (27:4). Matthew then writes that "Judas threw the thirty pieces of silver down in the temple, went out and hung himself" (27:5). Matthew adds the seemingly obscure point that the chief priests take the "blood money" (27:6) and purchase a field in which they can bury foreigners or strangers. To this day the field is called "the Field of Blood" (27:8).

Like many apparently obscure points in Matthew, the detail about the field purchased with thirty pieces of silver serves to connect events in the life and passion of Jesus with scripture. The point about the thirty pieces of silver and the purchasing of the so-called potters' field in 27:7 has to do with Jesus' life and death fulfilling a pattern Matthew discerns in the Hebrew Bible. Not just Jesus' death, but his betrayal by Judas has also been foretold in the scripture. This, too, was a fulfillment of words spoken by the prophets (27:9) and, therefore, confirmation that Jesus was sent and guided by God. Matthew made up this seven-verse narrative about Judas in 27:3–10 based on a loose association with Zechariah 11:12–13 and Jeremiah 19:11, 32:6–15, and 18:2–3. This has nothing to do with what may or may not have happened to the historical Judas. Judas's death is described rather differently in Acts 1:18, where Judas, it is said, fell (perhaps in the field he was to have purchased), burst open, and his insides poured out. There is no mention of his suicide by hanging.

Matthew has utilized the Zechariah passages as yet one more fulfillment citation. He has constructed a legend about Judas for the purposes of employing these verses. The storied thirty pieces of silver for which Judas betrayed Jesus come from Zechariah. This entire section of Zechariah is actually quite instructive. It is about the judgment and destruction of Judah and Israel (Zech. 11:14), the killing of shepherds (11:8), a siege of Jerusalem, the gathering of people against Jerusalem (12:2–3), the "striking of the shepherd and the scattering of the sheep" (13:7), and the redemption of the house of David and the inhabitants of Jerusalem (13:1). The Matthean episode involving Jesus' death in Jerusalem at the hands of false leaders and the betrayal of Jesus by Judas for thirty pieces of silver read like a kind of *midrash*. Midrash is an imaginative form of interpretation that grew out of second-temple and later rabbinic Judaism which is based on a biblical text, but which shapes its own story and interpretation around the verse in an attempt to comment on a more contemporary issue or problem. K. Stendahl has observed that Matthew has a penchant for utilizing scripture and scriptural allusions in this manner. In Matthew's hands the events connected with Judas remind people of these passages from Zechariah, and some passages from Jeremiah. Through these passages the judgment, assault upon, and eventual restoration of Judea and Jerusalem through God's intervention are recalled. Judas, too, plays a part in highlighting the corrupt state of Jerusalem around the time of Jesus, the planned death of the shepherd, and the eventual restitution of the city of David, most likely under the new leadership of Matthean Jews. This brief midrash arguably contains these themes which would not have been lost on Matthew's community.

Does this section of the passion narrative reveal anything about the popular perception of the Jesus movement during Jesus' lifetime? Does the reader gain any insight into what Jesus and his followers were really up to? If the movement was hiding out in Bethany, as we noted above, does that suggest something about the motives and program of the group? Did Jesus have something planned in Jerusalem? The passion narrative depicts Jesus and his followers in and around Jerusalem as a clandestine group. They are hiding out. In Mark and Matthew the authorities seem to rely on Judas to find Jesus and arrest him (Matt. 26:16 ‖ Mark 14:11). It is interesting to note that in the betrayal scene Jesus needs to be identified for the crowd that has come to seize him. This is done through the famous kiss from Judas. "The one I shall kiss is the man; seize him" (26:48). While Jesus and his movement may have been seen as a threat, they were a minor voice in the Jerusalem scene, and Jesus himself was not well enough known to be recognized by the crowd.

Was this popular movement hiding out in preparation for an event during the festival in Jerusalem? Were some members of the Jesus movement around Jerusalem first-century urban terrorists, the so-called Sicarii or "dagger men," whom Josephus mentioned, and to whom R. Horsley and other scholars have recently drawn our attention? Were they hiding out because some were plotting violence on the eve of the festival? Did Jesus and some of his followers simply know the group had attracted enough attention from those in authority to put them all at risk, and therefore kept their distance in Bethany? Or, more simply, did the movement stay in Bethany because that was the closest lodging they could find, and the Gospel writers imagined this small detail as part of a larger strategy on the part of the movement?

The arrest scene would have the readers believe that the authorities viewed Jesus as more than simply a reformer. The Jesus movement was a security risk. In the arrest scene a "great crowd" (*oxlos polus:* Matt. 26:47 ‖ Mark 14:43) comes to arrest Jesus "with swords and clubs." The crowd led by Judas represents a preemptive strike against the popular movement. The local leaders are not present in this narrative, though Matthew and Mark indicate that the crowd is acting with the tacit approval of the Jerusalem authorities. The crowd, too, perhaps through the encouragement of the local authorities, is fearful of the movement. The clubs and swords suggest the anticipation of resistance. They were right. In 26:51 (‖ Mark 14:47 ‖ Luke 22:50) one of the followers strikes the slave of the high priest Caiaphas and cuts his ear off. In the Gospel of John (John 18:10) this follower is identified as Simon Peter. In all the Gospels, except for the earliest account — that is, Mark — Jesus rejects this action explicitly. It was Matthew, not Mark, who penned the famous phrase, "Put your sword back into its place; for all who take the sword will die by the sword" (Matt. 26:52). Jesus responds to the crowd that has come to seize him, saying, "You have come out as against a bandit [*lesten*], with swords and clubs to capture me" (26:55 ‖ Mark 14:48 ‖ Luke 22:52).

As we will see in the trial scene, the crowd has reason to believe they will meet resistance. Even the anachronistic Gospel traditions suggest a modicum of resistance and potential violence. Was Jesus a social reformer or one planning a physical, perhaps armed struggle for the liberty of Israel utilizing the large and emotional crowd of the Passover festival? It is important to remember that there were several Jesus movements in the first century in Palestine. These forms of Judaism that were centered around the life and memory of Jesus exhibited the same diversity as other forms of Judaism. That is, Jesus-centered Judaisms were divided by and debated the same issues as other Judaisms in Palestine in the early Roman period. One of those key issues pertained to one's stance concerning Rome and its local lords. If the various Jesus movements were anything like the other forms of Judaism with which we are familiar, then they too would have been divided, along with other issues, over whether one should submit to unjust leadership and rule, or rebel and call upon God for help.

It is most likely, then, that various Jesus-centered Judaisms would have disagreed with one another on this important point. The short answer to the interesting historical question "was Jesus a revolutionary?" is that some of his followers would have expected a revolution, while others would not have thought that was absolutely necessary to be true to Torah, the God of Israel, and whatever they believed Jesus taught. This issue would have divided certain forms of Judaism centered around Jesus. When one reads the stories about Jesus and the Jesus movements in light of the broader context of colonial Palestine, this is, of course, what we would expect. All colonial contexts divide the indigenous population, and different communities gathered around the memory of Jesus would not have been exempt from this political reality.

The Gospels, especially Mark and Matthew, portray Jesus as hostile to the political climate and the political powers that prevailed in Palestine. He is a vocal opponent of the status quo. Those in power have reason to view Jesus as a threat. Jesus' language of kingship and kingdom, officially saying one does not have to pay taxes (Matthew 17), his apparent threat against the temple (Matt. 27:40), and his fierce attack on those in power make him look as though he plans to get rid of the powers-that-be. Indeed, the apocalyptic traditions associated with Jesus celebrate God destroying those in power. Yes, Jesus seems to have acted like a potential revolutionary. This is what did him in in Jerusalem. While historically Jesus was more of a nuisance than a real political threat, Rome and its clients could not allow such explosive rhetoric to continue. Even this small popular leader needed to be stopped.

Certain scholars, when addressing the question of how Jesus and his movement must have been viewed during his lifetime, conclude that Jesus was a social but not a military revolutionary. This is the position of D. Crossan in his recent, learned book, *Who Killed Jesus?* Yet this is not an easy distinction to maintain. How does one differentiate between social and armed revolutionary? I suggest one of the most important sources concerning this question is the view of Jesus' opponents. The Gospel writers write for so many other reasons than simply to tell us who Jesus was and what he did. And we are unable to say reasonably what Jesus thought. Obtaining Jesus' self-consciousness was a pursuit and fantasy of an earlier generation. The most reasonable source for deciding what Jesus and his first followers were like histori-cally is through the views of their opponents as they come to us in the Gospels. Fair credence must be afforded these views from the outsiders. This view, as it is portrayed to us in the tenden-tious accounts in the Gospel tradition, suggests the enemies of the movement saw Jesus and his followers as bordering on ag-gressive revolutionaries. It is the later Gospel writers who begin to interpret Jesus in light of the events of 70 C.E. and who later try to associate a nonviolent position with Jesus.

Jesus had to have said more, and certainly seemed like more, than just a provocative teacher. Historically, his actions as well as his public proclamations must have made him appear as more of a real revolutionary than a rhetorically gifted sage. Jesus went beyond social reformer and appeared to be more of a vi-olent revolutionary, though he himself stopped short of taking up arms.

This was more than enough cause to be killed in Jesus'

early Roman Palestinian setting. Jesus thought God would destroy the present order. He and his followers were implicated in that scenario. While God would take the lead, no doubt, in Jesus' apocalyptic scenario Jesus and his followers were largely supportive of this cosmic destruction. This, it seems to me, moves them beyond mere social reformers. They envisioned a far more radical narrative for Israel in their day. This view was too revolutionary, and too risky, for those in power.

## Peter and Jesus' Death

Following the so-called Last Supper, once the preparation for Jesus' death is completed, Jesus' arrest and betrayal follows. This section of the story contains the tension surrounding Peter and his denial of Jesus. This feature of the Gospel story is striking because Peter has served as a hero of sorts, and a paradigm in Matthew for discipleship. He is the leader among the twelve, and their spokesperson. Yet, as paradigm for discipleship in Matthew, his denial also reflects the denial that many members or followers may have experienced.

In 26:30 Matthew records that Jesus and the disciples concluded their meal and liturgy together with a hymn. In what follows Matthew follows Mark rather closely (Matt. 26:30–35 ‖ Mark 14:26–31). Outside Jesus says that all of the disciples will fall away "this night because of me" (26:31). Peter protests, saying, "Though they all fall away because of you, I will never fall away" (26:33). "Before the cock crows," says Jesus, "you will deny me three times." Peter maintains that even if he must die with Jesus, he will not deny him (26:35). Reflecting Peter's position as spokesperson for the disciples, Mark and Matthew conclude this section with "And all the disciples [Mark simply says "they"] said the same" (Matt. 26:35 ‖ Mark 14:31).

Jesus tells Peter that "before the cock crows" (i.e., before morning), "you will deny me three times." Mark says that the cock will crow twice (14:30), while Matthew (rather unusually, given his penchant for "doubling") says the cock will crow but once. This may have been an attempt to improve on Mark at this point because in the Mark section where the cock crows (Mark 14:68–72), Mark only records one crow, not two. Matthew sought to fix that oversight by eliminating the prophecy about "two" crows from the cock. Matthew also deleted the passionate denial by Peter (*ekperissos*) in Mark 14:35. This denial is supported through appeal to scripture: "I will strike the shepherd, and the sheep of the flock will be scattered." This is a quotation from Zechariah 13:7. Here Matthew is following Mark (14:27) in quoting this passage from Zechariah. However, this is the same section of Zechariah Matthew used for his midrash on Judas and his betrayal. The connection with the Zechariah text in Matthew continues the theme of the disciples' betrayal of Jesus. Chapter 13 in Zechariah is apocalyptic in substance. It is about the day when Jerusalem will be cleansed. The land will be swept free from idols. And in Zechariah 13:7–9 a people will emerge from "the fire" and God will say, " 'They are my people'; and they will say, 'The Lord is my God.' " The use of Zechariah 13:7 in part of the passion narrative by both Mark and Matthew suggests that in Jesus' death, the writers believe, that day is at hand. Jesus' betrayal by the disciples is interpreted as an event prophesied by Zechariah and associated with the end.

The story about Peter and his denial continues in Matthew 26:58. Jesus is arrested (26:57) and "all the disciples forsook him and fled" (26:56). Peter follows, from a distance, as far as the courtyard and sits with the guards (26:58 ‖ Mark 14:54). Mark records Peter warming himself by the fire, while Matthew reads further into Peter's motives, saying, "He [Peter] sat with guards to see the end [*telos*]." In 26:69–75 ( ‖ Mark 14:66–72) Peter's famous denial is told. Peter is confronted by a maid who says to him, "You were with Jesus the Galilean [Nazarene in Mark 14:67]." In 26:70 Peter says, "I do not know what you are talking about." In Matthew a second maid confronts him outside the courtyard, declaring that Peter was with Jesus of Nazareth. Again, Peter denies this, but this time with an oath (*orkou*; 26:72 — in direct contradiction of 5:33–37), saying he does not know the man. Finally, bystanders claim that Peter is one of them. Peter curses and swears that he does not know the man. At that point the cock crows (26:74), and Peter recalls Jesus' prediction.

It is interesting to note how the bystanders recognize Peter as being with Jesus in Matthew. Only Matthew claims Peter's accent (dialect; *lalia*) betrays him. Mark does not include this detail. Jesus and his followers were known as Galileans (26:70). They were one of several Galilean popular, revolutionary movements who caught some attention in Judea and around Jerusalem in the mid-first century C.E. Peter's Galilean dialect gives him away in the midst of Jerusalem and the events surrounding Jesus' arrest. Recently, there has been a new recognition of the diverse language milieu of Galilee and Judea in the days of Jesus. Graves and grave inscriptions in particular have provided considerable new data concerning the debate over languages in Palestine in the first century. The influence of Greek language in the early Roman period in Israel is more fully appreciated now than even a decade ago. But most scholars would still contend that it was a dialect of Aramaic, not Greek, which gave Peter away. I suspect Jesus and Peter could speak and understand some Greek. Some Jews in Judea or Galilee might even have made Greek their first language by the time of Jesus. But it is most likely that Aramaic was the language of Jesus and his movement — including Peter.

In 26:72 Peter realizes the bitter reality of what has happened to him. What Jesus predicted, and what Peter maintained would never happen, has come to pass. Even he, the apparent leader and spokesman for the followers, fell prey to the threat of association with Jesus and his followers amid the festival and the crackdown on suspect groups in Jerusalem. It is an interesting feature of the development of the Gospel stories that Peter's denial is included by all writers (Matt. 26:69-75 ‖ Mark 14:66-72 ‖ Luke 22:56-62; John 18:25-27). This tradition is not repeated in the Gnostic *Gospel of Thomas*, nor does it appear in what remains of the fragmentary *Gospel of Peter.*

It does not seem likely that the early communities who gathered around the memory of Jesus would create such a story. It is not flattering to them or to one of the early heroes of the movements. Again, while the story focuses on Peter, there is a sense that Peter represents a more general experience within the broader community of first followers. Matthew and Mark note that "all the disciples forsook Jesus and fled" (26:56 ‖ Mark

14:50). Judas also, of course, forsook the movement, and went a step further by turning informant. Peter's experience, developed rather fully in the passages pertaining to his denial, reflects the experience of many early followers of Jesus. Here once again Peter symbolically serves as the spokesperson for many in communities gathered around the memory of Jesus. Peter's denial is not merely, if at all, an anecdotal historical instance that occurred around the death of Jesus. The figure of Peter continues to function as a transparent person in the narrative. Forsaking Jesus as a result of the political pressures and threats involved in being a follower was a reality within the early Jesus-centered Jewish communities. Matthew described earlier in his story the threats and dangers he believed existed locally for his community. The courts in particular emerge in the Sermon on the Mount as a place where the Matthean community felt persecuted. The pressures from local leaders, the unusual legal interpretation practiced by the community, the civic institutions that were turning on Matthean Jews, and more all led some to rethink their involvement in this community centered on Jesus. The story of Peter's denial must be understood as a parable about political pressure and denial within the early Jesus communities.

Even the archetype for leadership and discipleship in Matthew found the pressure of following too much at the end. In this respect the leaders were no different from other followers. All fled and forsook Jesus, including Peter. What is the meaning of this narrative and its teaching? In early Christian literature Peter emerges as a leader and heroic figure. This, of course, includes the Gospels written after 70 C.E., but also Acts of the Apostles and, in certain respects, Paul's letters, though these two apostolic figures were known to have had their disputes (cf. 1 Cor. 1:12; Gal. 2:11). Could this be instructive about forgiveness within these early communities? Peter is rehabilitated in certain respects in the resurrection scenes (Mark 16:7; Luke 24:34; John 21:15–19; 1 Cor. 15:5). It is striking, however, that Peter is not so rehabilitated in Matthew. Although the earlier Marcan tradition on the resurrection explicitly names Peter as one who should receive the news of the resurrection, along with all the other disciples (Mark 16:7), Matthew tellingly deletes this passage. In Mark the women at the tomb are told to "tell the disciples and Peter that he is going before you to Galilee." In Matthew the women are told, "Go quickly and tell his disciples that he has risen from the dead, and, behold, he is going before you to Galilee" (28:7). Matthew has gone out of his way to give Peter special attention and mention throughout the story. When Matthew comes to Mark 16:7, for some reason, he deletes the name of Peter. Peter does not receive the obvious special forgiveness implied in other versions.

This unusual omission by Matthew has led some recent commentators to conclude that Peter forfeited his membership in the group, as well as his salvation. This is a dramatic misunderstanding of Matthew's message. There is no mistaking Matthew's singling out Peter as a model for discipleship. This was discussed in some detail above in chapter 10. Peter's denial in no way changes that. What has been happening to Peter, the questions he has had and the experiences and special teaching he is afforded, are experiences and teaching intended for the entire community. What happens to Peter in the story will or should be happening to many or most Matthean Jews. The same is true for denial. Further, Matthew most likely felt that there was no need to single Peter out in the resurrection scene as Mark does in 16:7. Peter does not deserve special attention and special forgiveness because he denied Jesus. Both Matthew and Mark make clear all the disciples did that (Matt. 26:56 ‖ Mark 14:50). Matthew thought Mark's special mention of Peter obscured this important point. Peter is no different. On the contrary, he is the quintessential disciple. His boast that he would not deny Jesus, the denial scene, and his great remorse are scenes from the life of any disciple. In the Petrine narrative of denial the authors provide in this one archetype the experience of many followers in the volatile and politically unstable context of first-century Palestine. Peter warrants no special mention at the close of the Gospel because he has done nothing different. Again, Peter models the experience, emotion, and response of all would-be disciples who face daily the reality of denial and remorse because of the threats and doubts that surround them. In this important respect Peter's denial has a timeless aspect for most followers.

## The Trial

Matthew 26:57–68 records Matthew's version of Jesus' trial before Caiaphas the high priest. Luke's version states that this impromptu scene took place at the high priest's house (Luke 22:54). Matthew and Mark are not so explicit. The Gospel writers, including Matthew, place other local leaders at the scene, such as elders and scribes. The scene being depicted is a court scene that takes place suddenly, whenever and wherever they found the high priest. In 26:59 the chief priests and "entire council" (*synedrion olon*) seek false testimony against Jesus. This is a direct quote from Mark 14:55, except that Matthew has added the word "false" (*pseudomarturion*) to Mark's "witness" or "testimony" (*marturion*). This confuses the clearer Marcan passage somewhat. Matthew's fuller verse, following Mark now, says, "Now the chief priests and the entire council sought false testimony against Jesus, that they might put him to death, but they found none, though many false witnesses came forward." Mark's original verse is clearer: "Now the chief priests and entire council sought testimony against Jesus to put him to death, but they found none. For many bore false witness against him."

A word should be said here about the meaning of the term "council," or, in Greek, *sanhedrin*. A misunderstanding or anachronism about this term has contributed to many false assumptions about the trial of Jesus. This is a Greek word, not Hebrew. This term was ultimately transliterated into Hebrew and became the technical term for the Jewish official court during the rabbinic period. There is, in fact, an entire tractate in the Mishna concerning the courts and legal proceedings entitled *Sanhedrin*. People have often anachronistically read this more technical meaning back into the earlier Gospel texts. When many readers of the Gospel passion narratives see the term *sanhedrin*, they understand it to mean the official Jewish court like the one discussed in later rabbinic literature. This is a mistake, and a crucial point when trying to understand what might have led to Jesus' death and the events surrounding that death.

This common Greek term for a court or council made its way into Palestinian parlance during the time of Pompey's expansion into Israel and his administrative reorganization of the East. Pompey's General Gabinius reorganized Judea and Galilee according to the usual Roman provincial system between 63 and 55 B.C.E. Josephus tells us that five councils, or *synedria*, were set up in Judea, Galilee, and Jordan for the purposes of Roman regional administration of the newly annexed territory. In *Antiquities* 14.90 Josephus writes, "He [Gabinius] set up five councils [*synedria*] and divided the nation/people [*ethnos*] into as many districts; first Jerusalem, next Gadara, third Amathus, fourth Jericho, and fifth, Sepphoris" (*Ant.* 14.90). Many scholars read the place name Gadara as "Gazara," which was located in northwest Judea. Sepphoris was the only northern city containing a sanhedrin or court. This impressive Greco-Roman city was located in Lower Galilee a few kilometers northwest of Nazareth.

When we read of courts or councils in the Gospels, we should be thinking of this thoroughly Roman judicial institution. The membership of these councils probably included local elites as well as certain Roman officials assigned to the region. The former were usually employed by the Roman colonial powers to facilitate Rome's local rule. The latter were ultimately responsible for decisions, keeping the peace, and collecting the necessary taxes. These *synedria* probably symbolized Roman imperial presence in the region and to many of the indigenous population would have been viewed as a hostile institution. These councils owed their establishment and *raison d'être* in the land to Roman rule. Without Pompey and his successors there would have been no such councils in Israel.

While some of the local Jewish elite may have been involved in the work of these Roman courts, the *synedria* were Roman institutions executing Rome's bidding in the ruled region. At the time of the writing of the Gospels, including Matthew, these councils were not fundamentally Jewish institutions. They were part and parcel of the arm of Rome and its rule in Judea-Galilee. This needs to be understood when deciphering the Gospel trial and passion scenes.

In Jesus' trial the charge that Jesus claimed he would tear down the temple is depicted as carrying some weight. In Matthew 26:61 two witnesses say Jesus claimed, "I am able to destroy

the temple of God and build it in three days." The parallel passage in Mark is less pointed and vague. Mark 14:58 claims Jesus
said, "I will destroy this temple that is made with hands and
in three days I will build another, not made with hands." In
addition, Mark makes it explicit that this charge is also false testimony (Mark 14:57). Matthew seems to exempt this charge from
the category of "false testimony" (cf. Matt. 26:60–61).

According to the narrative, however, it is this final charge
that catches the ear of the high priest Caiaphas, who begins to
ask Jesus questions. For some reason the charge about the temple provokes the following question from Caiaphas: "Have you
no answer to make? What is it that these men testify against
you? . . . I adjure you by the living God, tell us if you are the
Christ, the son of God" (26:62–63). In Mark, Jesus' answer to
this question is quite clear: "I am," (*ego eimi;* 14:62). Matthew's
response to the high priest's question is not nearly as direct. In
Matthew, Jesus answers, "You have said so" (26:64). Here in Matthew Jesus does not answer "yes," or openly proclaim anything
about himself. In both Mark and Matthew Jesus then goes on
to utter another apocalyptic saying about the Son of man. "I
tell you, hereafter, you will see the Son of man seated at the
right hand of power, and coming in the clouds of heaven" (Matt.
26:64 || Mark 14:62).

Jesus' answer, though certainly oblique in Matthew, was apparently enough to warrant the charge of blasphemy from the
high priest, who tore his robes to punctuate symbolically the
notion of blasphemy when he heard Jesus' answer to his question. Caiaphas asks the audience-cum-jury, who were comprised
of local officials and those members of the local council who
were present that evening, " 'You have now heard his blasphemy.
What is your judgement?' And they answered, 'He deserves
death' " (Matt. 26:66).

Once this mini-trial takes place, people begin to mock Jesus.
In both Mark and Matthew some spit in his face and strike him,
and slap him. There is an interesting apparent slip of the pen by
Matthew in this scene which, among other things, clearly demonstrates Matthew's dependence on Mark. In Mark the mockers,
after spitting on him, "cover his face and strike him saying to

him, 'Prophesy!' And the guards started to strike him" (Mark 14:65).

There are two points here when we compare Matthew. First, while the point of the blindfolding followed by the slaps and the cry to "prophesy!" is clear enough in Mark, Matthew makes the point of the mocking explicit. In Mark the mockers yell "Prophesy!" because they are playing a game. They want Jesus to tell them who has hit him. Matthew simply adds the final explanatory phrase, "Prophesy to us, you Christ! Who is it that struck you?" (Matt. 26:68). Matthew paid close enough attention to the Marcan scene to attempt a clarification. However, while — or perhaps as a result of — paying close attention to this detail, Matthew forgot another very important detail, a slip-up pointed out by N. Dahl. The astute reader will notice that while following the Marcan scene closely, Matthew forgot the blindfold over Jesus' eyes! Overlooking this small but important Marcan detail renders the mocking absurd. The joke about "Prophesy to us, you Christ! Who is it that struck you?" only makes sense if Jesus is blindfolded. When one compares Matthew 26:66–67 and Mark 14:64–65 it is evident that somehow Matthew, for all his attention to detail, overlooked this important point. For some of us not so attentive to detail, this Matthean slip of the pen is more of a relief than a troublesome oversight.

The putative trial scene continues in Matthew 27:1–2. In this scene, when morning came, "all the chief priests and the elders of the people took counsel against Jesus to put him to death. They bound him and led him away to Pilate the governor [*hegemoni*]."

In Matthew 27:11 the trial scene continues when Jesus is placed before Pilate the governor and asked by him, "Are you the King of the Jews?" Jesus' answer in all the synoptic Gospels is rather evasive: "You have said so" (Matt. 27:11 ∥ Mark 15:2 ∥ Luke 23:3). The chief priests and elders present continue to accuse him, but Jesus makes no answer (Matt. 27:12). At this point in Luke's narrative there is an extended discussion about whom Jesus is ultimately responsible to — Pilate or Herod. Because Jesus is from Galilee, Pilate sends him to Herod, who just happens to be in Jerusalem at the time. According to Luke,

"Herod and Pilate became friends that day" (Luke 23:12). Mark and Matthew do not have this story from Luke's hand. This Lucan scene depicts a degree of attention to judicial detail and more technical legal issues not present in these first two Gospels.

Matthew 27:15-23 ( ‖ Mark 15:6-14) is the story of the release of Barabbas in place of Jesus. Matthew does not supply any information about Barabbas other than saying he was notorious, while Mark says he was a rebel (*stasiaston*) who had committed murder during the insurrection (Mark 15:7 ‖ Matt. 26:16). Mark does not tell the reader which or what "insurrection." However, this Marcan detail reminds us again of the subtext of violence, resistance, and political brinkmanship that are important (though glossed over) historical features of the life and death of Jesus. Matthew has deleted this seemingly historical background. Mark's version more clearly places Jesus in the category of a Barabbas, that is, a revolutionary and one prone to create or cause violence and instability.

Matthew 27:15 ( ‖ Mark 15:6) claims that Pilate was accustomed, during the feast, to release one prisoner "for the crowd." This is an unusual tradition that possesses no real parallel in the Roman world. This was probably created during the extended period when the recollections and explanations of Jesus' death were being collected by his followers. The point of the exchange between Barabbas and Jesus is intended to heighten the irony of Jesus' death for those who follow him. Jesus, who came to save people, is exchanged for a murderer. This is far less a Roman legal practice and more a product of early church reflection on Jesus' death.

Matthew 27:17-25 implicates Pilate more deeply into the trial, but at the same time tries to expunge any pronounced sense of Pilate's guilt in Jesus' death. Matthew the narrator supplies that Pilate was aware that Jesus was being delivered up "out of envy" (27:18). In addition, only Matthew includes a story about Pilate's wife believing, as a result of a dream, that Jesus was a just (*dikaio*) man (27:19). As in the birth narrative, here again dreams function in the story to let the reader know that God is still at work and controlling the events. Dreams were widely understood as messages or omens from the gods. Matthew also embraced this common Roman belief. Matthew and Mark maintain that the chief priests (and elders in Matthew) persuade the crowd to release Barabbas and destroy Jesus (Matt. 27:21 ‖ Mark 15:11). Pilate maintains that Jesus has done no evil (27:23). Yet the crowd shouts, "Let him be crucified" (27:22–23). Then Pilate, because he sees that a riot (*thorubos*) might start, takes water and washes his hands before the crowd, saying, " 'I am innocent of this man's blood; see to it yourselves.' And all the people answered, 'His blood be upon us and our children!' " (27:24–25). Before commenting on the construction of the trial scene in Matthew and then discussing the crucial verse 25, or "The Cry of the People," let us briefly discuss Pontius Pilate and his place in history and Matthew's narrative.

Pilate is known to us from records outside of the Gospels. He is infamous for several events in the first century involving Jews and Judea. Pilate reportedly brought the standards from a Roman military unit bearing the emperor's image into Jerusalem (*J.W.* 2.169–74; *Ant.* 18.55–59). Josephus also records that he took money from the sacred treasury in the Jerusalem temple (called *corbonas;* cf. Matt. 27:6) to expand an aqueduct. The people were very upset with Pilate about this; they demonstrated their disapproval while in Jerusalem only to have "a large number of Jews perish" (*J.W.* 2.177). Some died from the blows the soldiers delivered, and some died from being trampled by the crowd. Pilate also seems to have brutally put down some trouble among the Samaritans (*Ant.* 18.85–90). Josephus's negative portrayal of Pilate is a bit surprising given his tendency to depict many Roman officials as responsible and pious. Philo of Alexandria also records that Pilate brought shields into Jerusalem bearing the image of the emperor and dedicated them to Tiberius (*Legatio ad Gaium* 299–305). Philo claims Pilate did this not to honor Tiberius but to arouse the multitude. Pilate finally backed down, according to Philo, because he feared reprisal from Tiberius for his failure to keep the peace. Pilate was ultimately recalled to Rome by the governor Vitellius as a result of his handling of the Samaritan uprising (*Ant.* 18.89). Marcellus, a friend of Vitellius's, took over for Pilate in Judea.

Pilate is also mentioned in the so-called *Testimonium Fla-*

*vianum* in Josephus, *Antiquities* 18.63–64. The passage reads as follows:

> About this time there lived Jesus, a wise man, if indeed one ought to call him a man. For he was one who wrought surprising feats and was a teacher of such people as accept the truth gladly. He won over many Jews and many of the Greeks [*hellenikou*]. He was the Messiah. When Pilate, upon hearing him accused by men of the highest standing among us, had condemned him to be crucified, those who had in the first place come to love him did not give up their affection for him. On the third day he appeared to them restored to life, for the prophets of God had prophesied these and countless other marvelous things about him. And the tribe of Christians [*Christianon*], so-called after him, has still to this day not disappeared.

It is an understatement to say this passage from Josephus is a disputed one. Many scholars over the last century have denied its authenticity. The passage has some thorny textual problems that have led some to believe most of it is a later interpolation by Christian scribes. The Latin Vulgate, Arabic, and Greek manuscripts of Josephus are at variance, especially at the crucial phrase, "He was the Christ." The Vulgate version, for example, reads, "He was believed to be the Messiah," a more plausible phrase from the pen of Josephus. There are some clear anachronisms in the text. The name "Christian," for example, was probably not yet extant at the time of Josephus. The theological assertions about the resurrection appearances and the enduring affection of the disciples do not seem to be the sort of issues Josephus tended to take up. These, too, seem like positive assertions concerning Christians by later Christian writers.

The early church figure Origen (185–254) mentions Josephus several times, but claims Josephus did not think Jesus was the Christ (*C. Celsum* 1.47). And again, in his commentary on Matthew, Origen states that Josephus believed Jesus' brother James was a righteous man, though he did not believe that Jesus was the Christ (*Commentarii in Matthaeum* 10.17). However, in Book 2 of his *Ecclesiastical History*, Eusebius cites several passages from this section of Josephus and appears to reflect knowledge of the *Testimonium Flavianum*. This discrepancy between Eusebius and his teacher Origen has been dealt with recently in a learned and critical article by Z. Baras. It is not altogether unlikely that Josephus had heard about Jesus and his followers — especially by the time of the writing of *Antiquities* sometime in the 90s. Some mention of Jesus may be a historical feature of this section of *Antiquities*. It is unlikely that all that is said about Jesus in this section is authentic. This belongs to the theology of later Christian scribes and scholars like Eusebius and others. It is clear, however, that Josephus had heard of Pilate and that he was not well regarded by either Josephus or many of the people living in Judea or Samaria.

In the trial scene Pilate plays a smaller role in Matthew than in John or Luke. In Matthew Pilate is briefly on stage and then off. Pilate is introduced in an attempt to further stress Jesus' innocence. In 27:23–24, Pilate twice rules on Jesus' innocence. "What evil has he done?" Pilate asks. "I am innocent of this man's blood." This is the sum of Pilate's role in the Matthean trial. Matthew wishes only to show that local Roman officials thought Jesus was less a threat than the local leaders of other competing Judaisms. It is the chief priests and other leaders in Matthew who "convince the crowd to ask for Barabbas' release" (27:20). It was a coalition of these leaders who first plotted to capture Jesus on the eve of the festival.

It is quite unlikely that there ever was a formal trial, historically speaking, in the arrest of Jesus. D. Crossan has recently discussed this issue at length. Popular troublemakers like Jesus were rarely afforded the luxury of full, and quite sophisticated, Roman legal processes. These were left for citizens, provincial elites, and other notables. Jesus and other Judean and Galilean popular leaders were dealt with quickly and without the assistance of the legal processes readers of Cicero might expect of trials in the Roman world. Pilate was introduced into the narrative because he was known, or notorious, and as a notable Roman figure could represent Rome's distance from Jesus' predicament and death. Crossan, in fact, points out what E. Bammel had already noted, that a formal trial was probably a literary creation of early oral traditions and later Gospel writers. Direct Roman intervention in the case of Jesus is quite unlikely. What, then, really took place?

Jesus drew the attention of certain leadership groups in Jerusalem. These leaders were worried about the accusations Jesus made about the temple and about the end of history, that is, his apocalyptic pronouncements that celebrated the end of the current order with some relish. To some extent Jesus' claims about himself may have played a role, but here we are on less certain ground because of the interest of the early church in establishing christological claims for Jesus. A small group of leaders, in the interest of order, convinced some local Roman officials to consent to a Roman form of death, or to help in quickly holding a kangaroo court in Jerusalem one evening. As Crossan says, Jesus was killed by a conjunction of local Jewish and Roman authorities. This was done rather quickly, but with the necessary approval of certain officials. In Jerusalem, and in light of the issues shaping Roman Judea at the time, it was an inconspicuous event. Jesus was arrested because of the threats he made. The concern on the part of local Jerusalem leaders who pushed for him to be done away with quickly led to his demise. Otherwise, he might have returned to Galilee to continue his ministry and to draw attention to the plight of people in early Roman colonial Palestine.

The significance of crucifixion should not be overlooked. Bammel showed that crucifixion was predominantly and originally a Roman form of punishment. The form of death reflected the type of crime. This was a crime reserved mostly for robbers and rebels, two groups that of course are not mutually exclusive. Crucifixion made its way to the Greek-speaking East as Roman hegemony and Roman practices took root there from the second century B.C.E. There is some discussion of crucifixion as a form of death in rabbinic literature. "Hanging," probably a euphemism for crucifixion, is mentioned in some rabbinic texts, where for the most part it is viewed as a pagan form of punishment (*Sifre Deut.* 21 [114b]; *b. Sanh.* 46b), and also at Qumran (11QTemple 64.6–13; 4Q 169). That Jesus was crucified suggests Roman involvement in his death at some level. Some local Roman officials most likely gave quick and tacit approval of Jesus' punishment. That Jesus should come to the attention of these people at all is owed, most likely, to local notables who found his group too annoying or dangerous. Yet Jesus was not a figure who would have warranted the full attention and weight of the provincial Roman judicial system. Rather, what happened was a few people with the right amount of influence in and around Jerusalem were able to get some Roman officials to lend their stamp of approval to dealing with Jesus definitively and expeditiously. They enlisted Roman help and personnel to execute him.

Jesus was arrested, or detained, but disappeared in this colonial military setting. As is the case in so many colonial and largely martial environments, people disappear or are tried and killed without anyone's knowledge. This, in fact, is a fear people in such environments must live with on a daily basis. This was also the case in the highly charged and politically precarious setting of imperial Palestine. There was little trace of what happened to Jesus. He, too, disappeared in Jerusalem at festival time. He fell out of favor with a crowd that was able to act quickly and with impunity. There was no formal trial, no representation in a Roman court, and no record of what he may, or may not have done. In this lacuna the early church constructed what it thought happened to Jesus 40–70 years earlier in Roman Palestine. The passion narrative then, including prediction, betrayal, arrest, trial, and death, are anachronistic stories reflecting the animosity the church had for local (mostly Jewish) leaders, and is sprinkled with some historical traditions about Jesus and his followers in Jerusalem during the festival of Passover.

## The Cry of the People

Matthew 27:25 is a crucial verse in the story of Matthew, and in the subsequent interpretation and impact of the Gospel. The so-called Cry of the People has probably contributed more to the Christian charge of Jewish culpability for the death of Jesus than any other verse in the Gospels. It is also this verse that too often

in the history of the West has served to legitimate the suffering
and destruction of Jews.

The passage in question is in response to Pilate washing his
hands of Jesus' blood in 27:24. Pilate says to the crowd, " 'I am
innocent of this man's blood. You [plural] see to it.' And all the
people answered, 'His blood be on us and upon our children.' "
This passage about innocent blood is rooted not only in an important Hebrew Bible theme, but in some specific Hebrew Bible
texts relating to the death of Saul. David, a figure with great
historical and theological significance for early Jesus followers,
in at least two passages from 1 and 2 Samuel (1 Sam. 26:11;
2 Sam. 1:16), warns against "killing the Lord's anointed." In
the Greek translation of the Hebrew Bible, the Septuagint — the
version of the scriptures used by Matthew — this passage would
read "killing the lord's christ" (*kyrios christos*). In 2 Samuel 1:16
David pronounces, "Your blood be upon your head; for your own
mouth has testified against you, saying, 'I have slain the Lord's
anointed.' "

The second-century B.C.E. document 1 Maccabees picks up on
this theme with respect to foreign influences in Jerusalem and
the desolation of the sanctuary or temple: "It became an ambush
against the sanctuary, an evil adversary of Israel continually. On
every side of the sanctuary they shed innocent blood; they even
defiled the sanctuary. Because of them the residents of Jerusalem
fled" (1 Macc. 1:36–38). A passage like this from 1 Maccabees,
utilizing the theme of the shedding of innocent blood and the
corruption and destruction of the sanctuary in Jerusalem, would
have considerable resonance with Matthew and his community
following the destruction of the Jerusalem temple by the Roman
forces in the year 70. As we have noted, in Matthew's thinking
the destruction of the temple and the judgment upon the Jerusalem leadership were tied to Jesus' death. Those responsible for
"shedding innocent blood" were responsible also for the destruction of Jerusalem and the suffering this caused a generation or so
after the death of Jesus. And Judas, prior to his suicide, confesses
that he is guilty of "betraying innocent blood" (27:4).

At the most immediate level, Matthew 27:25 is a kind of
midrash on the themes and passages from 2 Samuel and 1 Mac-

cabees. Matthew believes that once again a great leader in Israel, an anointed agent of God, Jesus, has been killed and his innocent blood has been shed. Just like 2 Samuel, Jesus' innocent blood will be upon the heads of those responsible for killing the Lord's anointed. As in 1 Maccabees, the shedding of this innocent blood by foreigners and corrupt, lawless local leaders who misled many (cf. 1 Macc. 1:11ff.) has led to the destruction of Jerusalem and its sanctuary. For Matthew, steeped in scripture and believing as he did that scripture foretold the story of Jesus, these passages help explicate and interpret what happened to Jesus in Jerusalem and with the foreign and local, native leadership. Once again the Lord's christ has been killed. Innocent blood has been shed and the temple has been laid waste because of it. Matthew mentions this theme of the shedding of innocent blood in the context of Judas's confession (27:5), and in his attack on the local leaders in 23:30.

Matthew's innovation or addition to this scriptural theme in 27:25 is the phrase "and our children." This is a phrase tacked onto the cry of the people that Jesus' innocent blood be upon them. I agree with A. J. Saldarini that this addition is a reference to the destruction of Jerusalem a generation after the death of Jesus. This is Matthew's theodicy for an event that, we know, troubled many faithful Jews in Israel following the first Jewish revolt against Rome. How could it be that we have been overrun, that we have suffered so much and our sanctuary has been destroyed? Matthew, along with several of his contemporaries, tried to offer an explanation for this *grand mal.* His explanation was fashioned for, and perhaps intelligible to, his community of Jesus-centered Jews.

In no way does this passage seek to say all Jews are henceforth responsible for the death of Jesus and should in some cosmic sense pay for it. Nothing could have been further from Matthew's mind. He believed that corrupt local leaders misled the people, these leaders worked poorly with the Roman authorities, and this resulted in the death of Jesus and the destruction of Jerusalem. We saw this theme being developed by Matthew in the parables unique to him in chapters 21 and 22. But, as numerous authors have demonstrated recently, this is not how

Matthew 27:25 has been understood and interpreted in subsequent Christian history. On May 22, 1944, Anne Frank wrote in
her now famous diary an old truth that she had already been
forced to learn at a very tender age: "What one Christian does
is his own responsibility, what one Jew does is thrown back on
all Jews." The ground for such irrationality has historically been
found in the impish misunderstanding and misinterpretation of
Matthew 27:25, and very few other Gospel passages.

## Why Was Jesus Killed, and Who Killed Him?

We will conclude this discussion of the passion narrative in Matthew by asking, "Why was Jesus killed?" and "Who killed him?"
These kinds of historical questions cannot be answered with utter certainty. One must remember that our primary source of
information about this is the Gospels themselves. Of course,
the Gospels are far from objective historical sources — if indeed
such things exist. The Gospels were written to inform and persuade people about certain local, often parochial interests that
were specific to the communities for which the Gospels were
written. Given the nature of the Gospels and their purposes,
deciphering the historical events behind them has never been
easy. This is certainly the case concerning Jesus' death. However,
the death of Jesus, the cause and who was responsible, has had
such powerful repercussions across subsequent Western history
that it is incumbent upon historian and Bible reader alike to attempt to answer these historical questions with precision and
candor. That is to say, because the death of Jesus has too often
served as the ground for Christian acts and attacks against Jews,
an ethical mandate emerges that forces readers of this narrative
to ask these historical questions and to answer them honestly.
One cannot read Matthew's passion in these years following the
holocaust and avoid asking if traditional Christian treatments of
Jesus' death are accurate. As far as we are able to tell, why was
Jesus killed and who, then, killed him?

First, Jesus was a historical figure. One event in the life of
Jesus that historians can be confident actually took place is that

he was killed, probably crucified, in Jerusalem. This aspect of the traditions about Jesus has been challenged by very few since the advent of historical-critical scholarship.

Next, we should recall that the chance of an official trial occurring for the rather obscure group from Galilee and their popular leader Jesus was not very good. Such rabble-rousers were afforded little in the way of conventional legal procedures in the Roman provincial system. Whatever it is people in and around Jerusalem did to Jesus, they did it quickly and with a modicum of official support, if not mere acquiescence.

Third, when we realize that the "council" (*synedrion;* Matt. 26:59) which is said to have tried Jesus was not yet a technical term for the Jewish court, the answer to the question of "who killed Jesus" becomes less clear. Mark, Matthew, Josephus, and other writers acquired this term as a result of Roman dominance and influence in Palestine. In Matthew and Mark *synedrion* is a generic term that suggests a gathering of officials to issue a decision or pass a judgment. In the first century B.C.E. through the first century C.E. this term could be used by native Palestinian writers to describe a gathering of people who intend to "take counsel" together. For Matthew, the Greek term *sumboulion* ("to take counsel together"; cf. Matt. 27:1 ‖ Mark 15:1) would be synonymous with *synedrion.* These are gatherings, more ad hoc than official, of local people who reason or argue together with a view toward coming to a decision. It is likely that these local gatherings were comprised of elites and those with whom they worked, who felt they had the influence and power, if not the prerogative, to maintain order and keep regional imperial figures from getting too involved in local affairs. These gatherings were not Jewish or Roman legal structures empowered by the empire or provincial governors to make decisions. Matthew and Mark use these two terms to describe the local collection of personalities and local powers who contributed to the decision to do away with Jesus.

Matthew's narrative betrays that in all likelihood the decision to get rid of Jesus was arrived at quickly by an impromptu gathering of local elders one evening. Chapter 26 in Matthew records the rather sudden arrest and decision by local leaders.

Chapter 27 attempts to capture the discussions that occurred between local elites and Roman officials. We mentioned earlier that the introduction of Pilate in the narrative was a later creation to symbolize the relationship between local leaders and Roman powers. Pilate was a known, if not infamous name in the Greek East, and the selection of his name to represent the Roman voice in the death of Jesus makes sense in this respect. Local elites would not have possessed the de jure power to do away with Jesus. These leaders would have needed some approval and cooperation from Roman judicial or local military personnel. This meeting of the minds would not have needed to occur very far up the Roman provincial chain of command. Both parties would have seen the wisdom in quickly doing away with the risk Jesus and the group represented. Local leaders were closer to the Jesus movement and were more aware of what his message and movement meant for the safety and order of the region. Jesus probably posed no real, or excessive threat, but it was best not to take any chances. Quickly, and with a modest degree of cooperation between different political and military people, Jesus was killed.

Why was he killed? The Gospels suggest that Jesus was viewed by outsiders and opponents as a rebel. Matthew carries on this tradition in his version of the passion narrative. Jesus himself observes in Matthew that those who come to arrest him come "out as against a bandit" (lestes; 26:55). They come with clubs and swords, apparently expecting resistance or a struggle. Matthew carries on the Marcan tradition that Jesus was crucified along with two other bandits (lestai; Matt. 27:38, 44). As far as local elites and Roman officials were concerned, this was a crucifixion of three lestai, bandits, or rebels. The very fact that Jesus was killed by crucifixion is itself quite suggestive of what outsiders believed he and his group were up to.

Crucifixion was a punishment that said as much about the criminal as it did about Roman order and punishment. Since crucifixion was a Roman form of punishment, we can be confident that local leaders and some Roman officials came together, however briefly, to agree upon what should be done with Jesus. But this Roman form of death was saved for political cases, like those who were understood to be *lestai*, rebels, or bandits. Rebels and bandits are not so easily distinguished. This is particularly the case in a colonial setting where a mixture of local clients and colonial officials work together to keep the region orderly and prosperous for the imperial force. Those who disrupt are threats to security and run the risk of being accused of sedition. In the Roman world robbers and thieves were also crucified as or with political criminals. A famous adage from the Syriac *Sayings of Menander* (no. 50) captures the relationship between robbing and crucifixion: "Stealing is a carpenter of the cross."

Jesus' crucifixion highlights the view of his opponents that he was a threat to the security of the state and should suffer the punishment of rebels and bandits. For this reason the charge (*aitia;* Matt. 27:37) placed over Jesus' head on the cross read, "King of the Jews." For later Gospel writers this title is treated ironically. Historically this charge represented sedition and rebellion. There had been "kings" in Judea for some time. The coins of Herod the Great and Herod Agrippa I both carried the title "King," to name only two. In the provinces kings ruled through the grace of Rome. Judea had a king and Rome believed it did not need another. Claiming to be king is the kind of political crime that would deserve the cross.

What things would have led some people to believe Jesus may have intended to bring down the prevailing order or provoke a rebellion? Several aspects of Matthew's story speak to this question. Jesus is accused in Matthew of saying he would destroy the temple. This, obviously, is the sentiment of a rebel, if not a terrorist. But in Matthew Jesus does not say anything quite as explicit as this. In Matthew 12:2, however, Jesus does say, apparently speaking of himself, "I tell you, something greater than the temple is here." This passage appears only in Matthew. This saying is inserted in the midst of a debate or conflict story concerning sabbath observance. The Matthean implication in this argument is that Jesus is greater than the biblical exception to this sabbath law which involved David and the Bread of the Presence in the temple (1 Sam. 21:1–6). Matthew's Jesus maintains that not only is he more significant than David, he is greater than the temple itself. This Matthean saying would have led some to believe Jesus claimed he would do away with the temple. In the crucifixion scene, and in the context of what Matthew maintains are false testimonies, this comes back in the form of an overt threat against the temple. "You who would destroy the temple and build it in three days, save yourself!" (Matt. 27:40). In Josephus, when something happens to the temple, or the temple is threatened, trouble and revolt are not far behind (cf. *Ant.* 17.251–54; 18.55). Jesus' relationship to and attitude about the temple are suspect, to say the least. This was a highly charged subject in Roman Palestine, and any saying concerning the temple which might have been considered provocative would have led people to view Jesus as a revolutionary.

The Gospel writers maintain that Jesus' assertions about himself, so-called christological claims, played a role in the sentence of crucifixion. If that is so, it would have been because some of the terms and titles that became important in later Christian formulations at the time of Jesus' death carried substantial political overtones. This would have been the case with the titles "son of god" and "christ." "Son of god," for example, was a Roman appellation for the emperor and can be found on the coins of Augustus. "Messiah," or its corresponding Greek term "christ," meaning "anointed one," or "agent," carried strong political overtones in first- and second-century Israel. Several popular messianic movements sprang up at the death of Herod the Great in 4 B.C.E. These popular leaders, or anointed kings, were informed by popular Israelite traditions and caused considerable trouble for local elites and Roman rule. Judas, Ezekias, Athronges, and the famous second-century rebel Bar Kochba are among those who started popular, messianic movements that were hostile to the status quo and to Rome. Bar Kochba coins, stamped during the brief revolt between 133–135 C.E., bear the title "messiah." Mark makes the connection between the term or title "christ" and local Judean politics explicit in 15:32 when he places the phrase in the mouths of those mocking Jesus at the crucifixion: "Let the christ, the King of Israel, come down from the cross that we may see and believe."

Over time the titles "son of god" and "christ" became special terms for believers and followers of Jesus. During most of the first century in Israel these terms carried overt and loaded connotations. These terms were bound up with the political situation in the eastern provinces of the early empire. To lay claim or be associated with these terms was to set oneself against Rome and Rome's clients in Israel. The association of these titles with Jesus was cause enough, from the perspective of those in power, to bring an end to Jesus and his movement. Matthew's passion narrative, though written for a community of followers of Jesus sixty or more years after his death, still reflects the political setting and issues that led to Jesus' death in Jerusalem during the reign of the emperor Tiberius.

Finally, Jesus was an apocalypticist. He spoke of the end of history and the end of the present order in rather powerful terms and images. Jesus was by no means alone in this way. Apocalypticism is a usual development in colonial settings and environments where the subjects feel as though their world and their lives are out of control. Many of Jesus' contemporaries shared this sentiment and worldview. At the beginning of Matthew's apocalyptic discourse in 24:2, Jesus announces what will happen, soon, because the end is near. "Jesus left the temple and was going away, when his disciples came to point out to him the buildings of the temple. But he answered them, 'You see all these do you not? Truly, I say to you, there will not be left here one stone upon another, that will not be thrown down'" (24:1–2). Matthew took this passage over from Mark. However, Matthew obscured the praise the Marcan disciples offer the temple building. The Matthean version punctuates the impending destruction of the temple, because of the end, and the divine judgment, for which Jesus is messenger and agent.

While most apocalypticists stress that God will soon be acting, and that God will do the judging and destroying, the manner in which apocalyptic itself is set against the present order makes the messenger highly suspect. Although Jesus claims God will do the destroying, as messenger of this apocalyptic doom he, too, must be viewed as an enemy of the state. From the perspective of those in power, there exists too fine a line between a war in heaven and a war on earth. If those in power allowed people to continually predict the former, they would eventually have the latter. Jesus, like many of his contemporaries, gave expression to his deep distrust of and frustration with the prevailing powers through apocalyptic language and images. The anger many people felt toward Rome and the people Rome chose to work with in Galilee-Judea was often captured in the language of imminent destruction, divine judgment, and vindication of the beleaguered in Israel. For those in power, Jesus' apocalypticism, even if fantastic and a pipe dream, could not be permitted to fester. This view of the world, and how God would eventually act in history, was not tolerated by Rome and its clients. Apocalypticism has always been destabilizing, frightening to those in power and an anomic force that could, at any time, erupt into overt resistance. Jesus' sayings about the end contributed to his own demise.

In summary, who killed Jesus, and why? Jesus was killed by an informal coalition of local leaders and Roman officials or soldiers. They came together quickly, probably during a busy festival in Jerusalem, and felt they needed to do something about a potential troublemaker named Jesus. He was viewed as a threat or problem because of the things we noted above. In the name of order and security he was apprehended, the charges were discussed summarily, and he was executed. He was like a number of others in Roman Palestine who came up against this conjunction of local and imperial powers.

They killed Jesus because he was associated with several things that were interpreted as ultimately hostile to Rome and its rule. Certain sayings about the temple sounded too revolutionary, or were too easily interpreted as potential terrorist attacks on this crucial civic institution. Jesus' position on taxes would have contributed to various leaders' concern about him. In Matthew in particular, Jesus is remembered as saying "the sons" need not pay taxes; they are free (17:26). And Jesus predicted the end, and God's judgment of the present order, in a way that made no secret of his opposition to those in power. When these things were brought to the attention of those who possessed the modest amount of authority necessary to execute rebels, they found it expedient to kill him. He was given the form of execution consistent with their perception of him. He suffered the death of bandits and rebels.

After Jesus' death, his followers tried to make sense of what happened to him and why. Matthew's passion narrative is an example of what his followers tried to do with respect to the problem and profound disappointment of his death. As D. Crossan has pointed out, one of the first places Gospel writers like Matthew looked for direction and insight was the Bible, the scriptures. Matthew uses scripture throughout his Gospel to support his interpretation and understanding of Jesus. This is also the case with Jesus' death (cf. 26:14, 58, 59). A number of the events and personalities in the Gospel of Matthew relating to Jesus' death are informed by Matthew's rereading of scripture in light of that death. There is a great deal of "prophecy historicized" and far less "history remembered" than the traditional treatment of Jesus' death in Western Christendom usually has recognized.

One cannot say "the Jews killed Jesus," though Matthew's Gospel has served as a classic location for that Western, predominantly Christian formulation. Jesus was killed for appearing and, in many respects, in fact being a revolutionary. Jesus' words were suspect, and at many points the apocalyptic images he employed were far too violent. Jesus' message at too many points seemed to cultivate the hope of the demise of the system that had been in place in Israel for over 100 years. An ad hoc collection of local and imperial officials — Jews, Gentiles, and Roman personnel — made a quick decision to execute Jesus the next morning along with some other bandits who had come up against the same group and who appeared to pose the same threat. The elaborate formulations about the culpability and guilt for Jesus' death are part of subsequent formulations within Christian history which cannot reasonably be grounded in the history of Roman Palestine or a judicious reading of Matthew.

# Further Reading

Bammel, E. "Crucifixion as a Punishment in Palestine." In *The Trial of Jesus: Cambridge Studies in Honor of C.F.D. Moule*, ed. E. Bammel, 162–66. Naperville, Ill.: A. R. Allenson, 1970.

———. "Ex illa itaque die consilium fecerant. . . ." In *The Trial of Jesus: Cambridge Studies in Honor of C. F. D. Moule*, ed. E. Bammel, 11–40. Naperville, Ill.: A. R. Allenson, 1970.

Baras, Z. "The *Testimonium Flavianum* and the Martyrdom of James." In *Josephus, Judaism, and Christianity*, ed. L. Feldman and G. Hata, 338–48. Detroit: Wayne State Press, 1987.

Brown, R. E. *The Death of the Messiah: From Gethsemane to the Grave — A Commentary on the Passion Narratives in the Four Gospels.* Garden City, N.Y.: Doubleday, 1994.

Crossan, J. D. *Who Killed Jesus? Exposing the Roots of Anti-Semitism in the Gospel Story of the Death of Jesus.* San Francisco: Harper, 1995.

Dahl, N. A. "The Passion Narrative in Matthew." In *The Interpretation of Matthew*, ed. G. Stanton, 42–55. Philadelphia: Fortress, 1983.

Fitzmyer, J. A. "Anti-Semitism and the Cry of 'All the People' (Mt 27:25)." *TS* 26 (1965): 667–71.

Horsley, R. H., and J. S. Hanson, *Bandits, Prophets, and Messiahs: Popular Movements at the Time of Jesus.* Minneapolis: Winston, 1985.

Horst, P. van der, "Das Neue Testament und die jüdischen Grabinschriften aus hellenistisch-römischer Zeit." *BZ* 36 (1992): 161–78.

Kampling, R. *Das Blut Christi und die Juden. Mt.27, 25 bei den lateinischsprachigen christlichen Autoren bis zu Leo dem Grossen.* Münster: Aschendorff, 1984.

Mora, V. *Le refus d'Israël. Matthieu 27, 25.* Paris: Cerf, 1986.

Overman, J. A. "Heroes and Villains in Palestinian Lore: Matthew's Use of Traditional Jewish Polemic in the Passion Narrative." SBLSP (1990): 597–601.

Porton, G. *Understanding Rabbinic Midrash.* New York: KTAV, 1985.

Rivkin, E. *What Crucified Jesus?* Nashville: Abingdon, 1984.

Saldarini, A. J. *Matthew's Christian-Jewish Community.* Chicago: University of Chicago Press, 1992.

Schüssler Fiorenza, E. *In Memory of Her: A Feminist Theological Reconstruction of Christian Origins.* New York: Crossroad, 1983.

Senior, D. *The Passion of Jesus in the Gospel of Matthew.* Wilmington, Del.: Michael Glazier, 1985.

Stendahl, K. *The School of St. Matthew and Its Use of the Old Testament.* Philadelphia: Fortress, 1968.

*Chapter Fifteen* _____

# Resurrection and Appearance —
# 28:1–20

_____

## The Women and the Resurrection

The final chapter of Matthew is devoted to the resurrection of Jesus and the so-called final commission. The resurrection scene begins "after the sabbath" (Matt. 28:1). In all the Gospel accounts women are the first to come to the tomb. In Matthew and Mark it is Mary Magdalene and another Mary who come to see the sepulcher. In Luke the women are unnamed (Luke 24:1). In John it is only Mary Magdalene who comes to the tomb (John 20:1).

According to Matthew, when Mary Magdalene and the other Mary come to the tomb an earthquake (*seismos*) occurs. An angel descends from heaven and rolls the stone back and sits upon it (Matt. 28:2; Mark 16:5 describes the figure somewhat cryptically as simply "a young man"). In all other Gospel accounts the witnesses see that the stone sealing the tomb has been rolled away (Mark 16:4 ‖ Luke 24:2; John 20:1). Only Matthew explains how the stone was ever moved. Again Matthew uses the notion of a phenomenon from nature to signal the action of God or God's messengers. Matthew utilizes this theme in the passion narrative (27:51ff.) and in his account of the birth of Jesus when the star and dreams serve to guide people and signal God's plans and will for people. A *seismos* is also noted by Matthew in the stilling of the storm (8:24) and in the apocalyptic discourse (24:7). This Matthean insertion helps answer an obvious question concerning the women and how they ever would have been able to look inside the tomb and see that Jesus was not there. The *seismos*, the rolling stone, and the angel as messenger all attempt to address the questions and doubts people would understandably have about this account. Also, related to this, only Matthew supplies the information that the soldiers guarding the tomb "become like dead men" (28:4) when they see the heavenly figure sitting upon the moved stone. This, too, attempts to respond to a question concerning whatever happened to the usually trustworthy, if not zealous, guards who had been ordered to watch the tomb. Matthew alone supplies the notion that the trauma and terror of the events send the soldiers into shock.

In 28:5ff. Matthew follows Mark in having the angel address the women. "Do not be afraid ["amazed" in Mark 16:6]; for I know that you seek Jesus who was crucified. He is not here; for he has been raised, as he said. Come see the place where he lay." Matthew supplies the little phrase, "as he said," as an addition to the Marcan version. This is the start of a process, not quite as evident in Mark, where early followers tried to make sense out of the events of the Passover week through a reconstruction of the words and actions of Jesus. The collective memories of the communities gathered around Jesus tried to remember or recover whatever he said that might throw light on the events of his death and resurrection. Matthew's little addition reminds the reader that Jesus had spoken about this, said it would happen, and that this was all in the plan. This, too, had to happen "in order to fulfill all things." Luke expands on this theme even further in 24:6 when he recites a Son of man saying of Jesus' spoken about his death "while he was still in Galilee." Jesus's death was a shock and conundrum for the early communities gathered around him. The narratives about his death and resurrection also aim at responding to the hard and crucial questions about his life and death which the first generation of followers had.

The women coming first to the tomb was a standard and significant feature of the resurrection story for the Gospel writers. In Matthew the two women are the witnesses to the evidence for the event (i.e., the earthquake, the stone rolled away, the soldiers becoming like dead men, and the angel of God), and they are the messengers to the community about what has happened and what the angel said to them. The women are the ones who carry the news about Jesus reuniting with his followers up north, in Galilee. This feature of the Gospel story makes the women who followed Jesus absolutely indispensable figures in the drama. According to Jesus, the woman who anointed his body for burial is henceforth a vital part of the Gospel (26:13), and the women at the tomb in 28:6–8 now also become pivotal players in the story. Without the women and their visit to the tomb, and without their bearing the message to the community, there would be no continuation of the movement and, presumably, no Matthean community.

The women may have come to the tomb in accordance with a custom where people frequently watched the tomb of a loved one until the third day after death. Whatever the reason may have been historically or traditionally, the presence of the women in Matthew's story fill out some questions that remain from Mark's account. How did the stone get moved? Who was at the tomb to give the message to the women? How does this accord with what Jesus said while he was alive? These and other understandable and, at times, mundane questions have frequently informed Matthew's narrative. Matthean Jews had some questions about the life of Jesus, his death, and his message to the community. Earlier accounts that they had received from others left these questions unanswered. Matthew's own version of the scene at the sepulcher addresses some of these questions. The actions and role of the women in the narrative carry Matthew's answers to these questions. Consequently, the women are critical figures in Matthew's drama. They carry answers to the critical questions that had developed over time in the community. Above all, the women in the narrative bear the message they received from the angel that Jesus remains with the community and will gather with them again in Galilee.

The women are told by the angel that Jesus has "been raised" (*egerthe;* 28:6). The idea of a resurrection was relatively new in the second-temple period and among Matthew's contemporaries. This notion does not refer to someone being resuscitated or coming back to life. And resurrection is not immortality of the soul, which was a common notion in the broader Greek world. The resurrection was considered a time as well as an event. Resurrection symbolized the time when God would act decisively, break into history, and restore life in its fullness. At that time the just would be raised to life and the wicked would be condemned, and God's kingdom, as it had been imagined and anticipated, would be revealed. In Matthew's view, Jesus being raised signals that resurrection time.

This idea of a resurrection emerges rather faintly late in the second-temple period. Daniel 12:1–3 and 2 Maccabees 7 contain some of the earliest reflections of the hope of a vindication and resurrection for the righteous. This hope may well have had its ground in the older hope about the restoration of Israel in the days to come (Ezek. 37:1–14; Hos. 6:1–2). In Jesus' day the resurrection was the source of some debate and conflict between different Jewish groups. The resurrection was a point of distinction, if not a bone of contention, between Pharisees and Sadducees (Acts 23:6–8; Matt. 22:23). Josephus also mentions that the Pharisees and Sadducees differ on what happens at death and the fate of the soul (*J.W.* 2.162–66; *Ant.* 18.12–17). Daniel (12:2) provides the classic statement of the hope of a resurrection as it emerged 150–200 years before the birth of Jesus: "And many of those who sleep in the dust of the earth shall awake, some to everlasting life, and some to shame and everlasting contempt." This eschatological hope informed most of the early Jesus movements and Matthew's community was no exception. They believed in a fulfillment of Israel's history, a vindication of the righteous, and a judgment for the wicked. Jesus' death and resurrection, they believed, were very important stages or steps in the unfolding of that cosmic drama driven by Israel's God.

A resurrection involves corporeality; it includes the body. This notion of the afterlife is not concerned only or just with the soul. While Jesus' resurrection body in the Gospel resurrection narratives is depicted as somewhere between human and heavenly, he does, nonetheless, have a body and he apparently took both soul and body into the resurrection age. The body is recognized and accounted for in this belief system. Aside from Jesus, whose resurrection is necessarily special and proto-typical, resurrection is also a corporate or collective event. The just are raised together in the Gospels' view. Earlier the Apostle Paul gave expression to the same collective hope: "The trumpet shall sound and the dead shall be raised" (1 Cor. 15:52). A resurrection is something that happens to the faithful together, at once, in a moment. It is not only an individual or existential event. The resurrection is an event in the life of the community.

The New Testament does not supply a description of Jesus' resurrection. What it does supply is a description of the empty tomb and an accounting of Jesus appearing to his followers. The only exception to this is Mark's Gospel which, in keeping with the profound significance that author places on mystery, records at the close of the Gospel that after hearing from the young man at the tomb that Jesus had been raised, and seeing where they laid him, the women "said nothing to anyone for they were afraid" (Mark 16:8). The original ending of Mark's Gospel does not include accounts of resurrection appearances. Later scribes who penned verses 16:9–20 had to supply those appearances.

The earliest account of Jesus' resurrection and ensuing appearances comes from the Apostle Paul in 1 Corinthians 15:3–8, written in the early 50s C.E.

He [Jesus] was buried, he was raised in accordance with the scriptures, and he appeared to Cephas, then to the twelve. Then he appeared to more than five hundred brethren at one time, most of whom are still alive, though some have fallen asleep. Then he appeared to James, then to all the apostles. Last of all, as to one untimely born, he appeared also to me.

Paul's account, dating to about twenty years after the events, focuses on the appearances as his evidence that Jesus has in fact been raised. You will notice that Paul's version makes no mention of the women, though they may be counted among the "five hundred." Early followers of Jesus maintained that the

evidence for his resurrection was found in the accounts other believers gave of their experience of seeing and "being with" Jesus
after his death. This is why the appearances are so important
to most of the writers who try to explain the early communities' hope of Jesus' ongoing presence among them following
his death.

In 28:7 the women are told by the angel to "go quickly and
tell his disciples that he has risen from the dead and behold,
he is going before you to Galilee; there you will see him. Behold, I have told you." The instruction to assemble again in
Galilee follows the Marcan version, except for two important
Matthean changes. First, the Marcan version stresses that Peter
should receive special word that Jesus is alive and preceding the
disciples back to Galilee. Despite the emphasis placed on Peter in
Matthew's Gospel, in Matthew's version of the resurrection narrative Peter does not warrant particular mention. As we noted
in our discussion of the passion narrative, in his role as spokesperson for and paradigm of discipleship Peter symbolizes the
denial of many followers of Jesus in the wake of the struggles and
fears of discipleship. Speaking to the disciples Matthew's Jesus
says, "You will all fall away because of me this night" (26:31). As
prototype for the disciples in Matthew, the story of Peter's denial symbolizes what many disciples go through. The experience
of denial was not unique to Peter. On the contrary, he captured a
common aspect of following in the story of his denial and falling
away. This is not necessarily Mark's view. In Mark 16:7 Peter deserves an extra mention. But for Matthew and his narrative all
disciples are met in Peter, and he represents all of them. There
was, therefore, no need in Matthew's view to single out Peter in
the resurrection scene.

Also, and significantly, Matthew recognizes an important
piece missing in the earlier Marcan version. The women in Mark,
as mentioned above, do not tell anyone what the messenger at
the tomb says. This is a fitting ending for the author of the oldest
Gospel. The themes of mystery and the fear that characterize his
resurrection scene run throughout the Gospel of Mark. But this
is not Matthew's approach to the resurrection story. His disciples
and followers have never been in the dark, lacking in under-

standing, nor do they fail to fulfill their charge. Consequently, in 28:8 Matthew adds that the women "departed quickly from the tomb with fear and great joy, and ran to tell his disciples." Matthew could not abide the silence of the Marcan women. This left too many questions. Matthew supplemented the "fear" the Marcan women were feeling with "great joy," and the Matthean women faithfully went straight away to the disciples to tell them what had happened.

In Matthew Jesus does appear to meet his followers while in the Jerusalem area. His followers came to him and took hold of his feet "and worshiped him" (28:9). This is the first of two resurrection appearances in Matthew. The instruction to gather in Galilee is given again, only this time by the risen Jesus, not an angel. The reader is aware that this is a post-resurrection appearance, and belongs to the memory and liturgical life of the Matthean community because of the mention of the group's worship (*prosekunesan*) of Jesus. While there are several places in Matthew's Gospel where people worship or attempt to worship Jesus (cf. 8:2; 9:18), the reader recalls most vividly the wise men in the birth narrative at the start of the Gospel who "saw his star in the east and came to worship him." This act of the disciples in 28:9 points back toward the act of the *magi* in 2:11 who "fell down and worshiped" the child Jesus. In the birth and in the resurrection Jesus is worshiped in Matthew.

In 28:10 Jesus reiterates the command to gather in Galilee. The disciples are commanded to tell all the other "brethren" to go to Galilee. They will see Jesus there. This twice-given command to return to Galilee reminds the reader that this group is a Galilean movement. Galilee was their home and the place where it all began. It was also the place where they could begin again. Jerusalem was not the place where Mark or Matthew envisioned a future for their communities. Perhaps that would work for the author of the Gospel of Luke. But the place where the powers-that-be and the local leaders gathered was not the place for Matthean Jews or Marcan charismatics. They returned north, back to where the popular movement had its start, and back to where the movements could begin the hard and real work of rebuilding, recalling, and renewing.

## The Guards and the Rumor

Matthew's insertion about the guards and the rumor that someone stole the body in 28:11–15 is a distinctive part of his
resurrection narrative. In 28:11 Matthew records that some of
the guards went into the city to report what had taken place. The
term for the guards (*tas koustodias*) is a latinism that oddly has
made its way into the Matthean text. This appears also in 27:65
where Pilate assigns a guard (*koustodias*) to the tomb because of
what the Pharisees and chief priests tell him about Jesus' words
that he would rise from the dead after three days. This lone Latin
word is suggestive of the involvement of Roman officials and
soldiers along with certain local elite and leaders in the death
of Jesus. The guards assemble with the elders and, after taking
counsel (*sumboulion*), the guards are given a sum of money to
tell the story that the body had been stolen by Jesus' disciples.

The story put out by the elders is that the disciples came by
night and stole Jesus away while the guards were asleep. But
the story puts the guards in jeopardy because they had failed
at their post. This is dealt with in 28:14 where the elders promise to prevail upon Pilate on behalf of the guards should Pilate
ever come to hear about this episode. "If this comes to the
governor's ears," the chief priests and elders assure the guard,
"we will satisfy him and keep you out of trouble." The promise
of intervening on behalf of the guard with Pilate captures the
relationship of convenience that must exist between colonial officials and local clients. Both parties need one another and can
expect favors and a turn of the head from each other from time
to time. This probably never became an issue with Pilate. Even
28:14 seems to suggest it is improbable that Pilate should come
to hear about the incident. This, again, indicates a distance between high-ranking Roman and imperial officials and the death
of Jesus. This all took place on a local, probably ad hoc, and
rather low administrative level. Should this issue ever reach the
higher echelons of political power, the local clients and leaders
will take care of it for the guards, or so they say.

Matthew 28:11–15 is clearly a story common within Matthew's milieu. This is the most widespread explanation Mat-

thew's contemporaries provide for the unusual story spread by Matthean Jews that Jesus of Nazareth rose from the dead. The body must have been stolen. The guards must have dozed off. His followers stealthily took the body to see it buried as they wished, not as a crucified bandit or rebel. Matthew even includes the explanation in 28:15 that "this story has been spread among the Jews to this day." Matthew knows, and his community knows, that this is the most obvious and common explanation for the curious belief on the part of his community that Jesus indeed rose from the dead. The author acknowledges this explicitly in 28:15.

Matthew 28:15 also includes Matthew's lone use of the *Ioudaioi*, or "Jews." Does this suggest that the author must be a Gentile because he speaks about Jews in this manner? Does this mean that Matthew is not one of them? Not at all. In fact, R. Kraemer, among others, has shown that the Greek term *Ioudaios* was a common title or term applied to Jews by other Jews in Greco-Roman inscriptions. Also, Josephus, for example, will often refer to *Ioudaioi* when describing the Jews as they gathered to fight, deliberate, or rebel. Josephus was certainly a Jew and thought of himself as part of the Jewish people. While the meaning of this term is far from absolute, it does not suggest that Matthew was a Gentile and is here slandering the Jews. Rather, this term is used here, as in many inscriptions and in Josephus, as a circumlocution for all Jews, or, more precisely, themselves. That is, Matthew's use of the term "Jews" here in 28:15 really says something like "This rumor has circulated among all of us [*Ioudaiois*] to this day."

Matthew recognizes the currency of this rumor, which seeks to explain and discredit his resurrection story. Matthew responds to the rumor by doing the same. He tells a story that accounts for the origin and purpose of the popular explanation about the resurrection story. Where did this explanation for the resurrection that Jesus' body was stolen come from? The Matthean community has heard this rumor for some time, and the question has arisen: where did this story come from? And could it be true? Matthew quite openly acknowledges this story and tries to put it to rest. This story, or from his vantage point scurrilous rumor, goes back to the bribe offered the soldiers the morning of Jesus' resurrection. Even in his account of the resurrection Matthew has an ear toward what those outside his community — perhaps his rivals and competitors — are thinking and saying about Matthean Judaism. As he tells this aspect of the story of Jesus, here too Matthew addresses the voices and perspectives that contest the beliefs and behavior of the Matthean community.

## Jesus' Final Teaching: "Go to all people..."

Matthew's Gospel concludes with what is usually referred to as the "Final Commissioning" in 28:16–20. In this final dramatic scene in the Gospel the eleven remaining disciples go forward to Galilee. There they see the resurrected Jesus. In 28:17, as in 28:11, they worship him (*prosekunesan*). Rather strikingly, however, according to Matthew, some of the eleven doubt or hesitate (*distazo*). Even in the resurrection scene and at the closing scene of his story Matthew maintains the premise that the community is not ultimately involved in sorting out the wheat from the chaff, or deciding who passes muster as a member of the group. The only possible exception to this Matthean corollary is in Matthew 18. But even there, as we discussed above, the disciplining of any member is carefully couched within the broader context of community forgiveness and instruction. There are those among the remaining eleven who doubt, even after experiencing the appearance of Jesus, and still they are counted among the disciples and deserve mention in the story. This curious exception in the belief and conviction of some disciples does not warrant their exclusion from the narrative or, we can assume therefore, from the Matthean community. In Matthew's view, this also leaves open the possibility of continued learning and the acquisition of knowledge, which for him is a pronounced feature of discipleship. Some do hesitate and doubt in the context of Matthean Judaism. This is skillfully acknowledged by the author, and this contemporary reality is built into Matthew's story of the life of his community.

In 28:18 Jesus returns to a theme that has been of considerable interest to Matthew. Jesus reiterates that all authority (*pasa exousia*) has been granted to him from God. "All authority has been given to me in heaven and on earth," Jesus tells the eleven. This authority is not just restricted to or about heaven or the hereafter. Jesus' authority from God is putatively operative in the here and now, as far as the Matthean community is concerned. This belief was expressed in chapter 16 in the so-called Petrine Confession and again in chapter 18 when discussing community discipline. Matthew concludes by returning to this theme of authority. Jesus is the most authoritative figure Matthean Jews have known. This authority has been passed on to them. They are not to follow or trust in other voices. Other political authorities are not persuasive where the belief system of Matthew's church is concerned. All authority in heaven and on earth has been granted to the group. They are charged with exercising that authority. It is difficult not to view this distinctively Matthean conclusion as one more expression of Matthew's rivalry with other local authorities and Judaisms. All authority resides with the anointed leader and divine agent of the Matthean community, Jesus. Jesus has passed this authority on to his followers in the community, who should now, in this post-resurrection period, act out this authority.

The issues of who makes the decisions, who is in charge, who interprets, and who will fill the political and religious vacuum in Palestine following the trauma of the first revolt have guided and defined Matthew's Gospel. These issues were alive and timely within Matthew's church. He devoted considerable time and space to these questions. The questions of leadership, authority, and direction may well have provoked the writing of this Gospel in the first place. These are crucial issues for Matthean Jews, and many other Judaisms in Palestine in the post-70 period as well. Matthew's portrait of Jesus, in many respects, constitutes a response to these vital Matthean questions about leadership, authority, and the future. Matthew's shaping of the last scene of the story is intended once again to reiterate and assure the community that they do possess authority, sound leadership, and are headed into the future in the right manner and direction.

This authority is intended to inform the actions in which the community is supposed to be engaged. In 28:19 Jesus gives his instructions to the community. "Go therefore and make disciples of all people, baptizing them in the name of the Father, and of the son, and of the holy spirit, teaching them to observe all that I have commanded you; and lo, I am with you always, to the close of the age."

The paramount activity of the church, based on this commission, is the act or process of "making disciples." What might this mean? For Matthew, this process is an educational one. That is, making disciples is about helping people learn the things Jesus taught them. Matthew has been careful to highlight this throughout the book. Matthew's disciples understand. They know. They learn, through the course of the story, to fulfill their charge from Jesus. This portrait of the disciples stands in rather stark contrast to the Marcan portrait of Jesus' followers. Faith in Mark affords a great occasion for misunderstanding, being in the dark, fear and miscues. Matthew has toned down this feature of Marcan discipleship considerably. In Matthew's final commission we see Jesus' own process of disciple-making come to fulfillment. In the final commission the disciples have clearly become teachers. They now, like Jesus before them, will "make disciples." They now have become teachers. In the final commission Matthew makes explicit that this is now their task. They are teachers. "Teach them," says the Matthean Jesus, "to observe all that I have commanded you." The followers of Jesus now are called to engage in *didaskontes;* they are charged by Jesus to foster the educational process of *teaching* people the things Jesus taught them. In the closing scene of the book the students have become teachers.

One of the most interesting phrases in the final commissioning is the phrase from 28:19a, *panta ta ethne,* usually rendered "go to all the nations." This phrase has been the subject of considerable debate. D. Hare and D. Harrington, and J. P. Meier have written articles on how this phrase should be translated. And more recently A. J. Levine's monograph has focused on

Matthew 10:6, but devoted considerable analysis to 28:19. This phrase has often been understood as a turning from Israel to the wider Roman world. In particular, many translators have seen in this phrase a turning from Israel and a rejection of the Jews, and an embrace of the gentile world. This ethnic shift in Matthew prefigures, in a thinly veiled way, the rejection of the Jews by God and the elevation of the church as God's new chosen people.

This interpretation owes a great deal to the predilections of twentieth-century biblical scholarship, particularly scholarship from the middle part of this century. In fact, W. D. Davies has noted that it was not until the mid part of this century that a scholar even asserted that the author of Matthew was not a Jew. Davies has in mind K. Clark's article on Matthew's "Gentile bias" which was published in 1947. This view was followed by some Matthean scholars through the 1980s, but this view is clearly now a small minority. But in the midpoint of the twentieth century many New Testament interpreters saw in verses like Matthew 28:19 an affirmation of what was being said in more popular and destructive terms in more than a few cultural and political venues, that is, that the Jews had been rejected and the favor of God had turned toward the Gentiles — that is, the church. There God's people would flourish. This is an instance of scholarship following the more popular cultural currents of the period.

This point of view is present in nuanced and modified forms in the so-called salvation history scheme of reading the Gospels. This was a very popular approach for a good part of the twentieth century. This scheme, referred to by German scholars as *heilsgeschichte*, purports that God acted in Jesus. God sent Jesus first to the Jews. The Jews rejected Jesus so God turned then to the nations, the Gentiles or non-Jews. D. B. Howell recently summarized this approach to reading Matthew in his *Matthew's Inclusive Story.* If one approaches Matthew with this ideological presupposition, Matthew 10:6 contrasts nicely with 28:19. By selecting only these two verses and lifting them out of the larger Gospel story one can find some ground for saying early in the story Jesus goes only to the "house of Israel." With this mission an apparent failure, at the close of the story Jesus sends the disciples "to the Gentiles," and not, therefore, to the Jews.

We have seen that rejecting the Jews, or the eclipse of Israel, could hardly be further from Matthew's mind. The author has many questions and problems within his setting and with the current leadership in that setting. But Matthew understands his church as fulfilling and incorporating Torah and God's will as it has always been understood by faithful Israel. His community is a continuation of that faithful body. What, then, could Matthew mean in this phrase, *panta ta ethne?*

Matthew has used this phrase before, though many interpreters have failed to take sufficient note of this. In 24:9, 14, Matthew uses this phrase to describe Matthean Judaism's reach out into the rest of the world. Matthew 24:14 is particularly instructive here. "And this gospel will be preached throughout the whole world [*oikoumene*] as a testimony to all nations [*pasin tois ethnesin*]; then the end will come." Matthew's apocalypticism and view of the end of history involve all the people or races of the world. The message that Matthew believes God has promoted through Jesus is intended for all people. At least in his view all people should hear the message before the end comes. The consummation of the end is indeed tied to *all the world.* In this passage from chapter 24 the phrase *pasin tois ethnesin* is roughly synonymous with the more common Greek term *oikoumene.* Both this one term and the one phrase simply mean the rest of the world.

While chapter 24 of Matthew contains a considerable amount of Marcan material, 24:13-14 contains no Marcan parallel. This is distinctly Matthean. The language connecting the end and the rest of the world is a product of Matthew's own hand. The idea may not be distinctly his, almost certainly not, but the language is his. He consciously shaped these passages. Matthew inserted his belief that the end cannot come without the rest of the world hearing Matthean Judaism's message into earlier Marcan material. The teaching and mission announced in 28:16ff. are also features of Matthew's rather tame, but nevertheless resilient, apocalypticism.

Does Matthew mean that other Jews in the diaspora need to

hear about Jesus-centered Judaism? Probably. Matthew almost certainly would have known about Jewish communities outside of Palestine and he would have believed that they, too, needed to embrace Matthean Judaism in order to "fulfill all righteousness." But Matthew is not hostile to Gentiles. They would be included as well in this Matthean charge in 28:19. Most forms of Judaism in this period regularly attracted Gentiles to their gatherings. So-called God-fearers, mentioned only in the Acts of the Apostles, have become a symbol and *cause célèbre* in certain scholarly circles because they represent or symbolize certain groups of Gentiles sympathetic to various forms of Judaism in the Roman period. Such a phenomenon would not have been unknown to Matthew, and could have very likely been part of his own community's experience. Gentiles, too, were part of the Jewish experience in the Roman world. Matthew knew that and even thought that they figured into the Gospel message as well. They may have been an afterthought, but Gentiles, along with diaspora Jews, should hear the message of the Gospel. When this has happened, then the end will come.

This passage helps to explain any existing doubts about the end. After all, Jesus had been killed some time ago, and that was to have ushered in the kingdom of heaven. A close reading of Matthew reveals he believed Jesus' death was the beginning of the end. The first revolt against Rome and the destruction of the temple served as further confirmation that the end was near. Now the plight and struggle of the Matthean community was yet more proof of the imminent end of this age and the judgment that was due the wicked leaders in Matthew's setting. A Matthean Jew might ask then, what is the delay? Matthew's partial answer to that question is that the message must go everywhere and to everyone before the end, which is swiftly approaching, comes.

This is the primary thrust of 28:19. It is related to Matthew's distinctive apocalypticism. What does this important phrase mean? It simply means that Matthean Jews were supposed to go everywhere, to all people (*panta ta ethne*), and teach what Jesus taught them, and develop members and people who lived out Matthean Judaism in its fullest sense. Between 24:14 and

28:19 there is no reason to think that this phrase is about a race's rejection and the divine embrace of yet another race. On the contrary, this phrase denotes everyone everywhere. This is, of course, an unrealistic goal, but one Matthew theoretically affirmed. Matthean Judaism's view of the world, their legal interpretation and their priorities should prevail for everyone. That is what God announced in Jesus.

Matthew believed that all people should be able to understand and live out Matthean Judaism. He believed it was for all people. The Matthean community, as we noted, appears to be lacking in enthusiastic missionaries. This Matthean conclusion to the Gospel might provoke more members to take the rest of the world seriously. This mission gave Matthean Jews a chance to teach and to enforce their view of the prevailing order, which they believed they received from Jesus. The community had become teachers to the world, theoretically. They were encouraged through this commission to teach all others, in whatever setting and in any place, all they understood about being complete disciples.

The reader may recall that one of Matthew's charges against the scribes and Pharisees was their commitment to proselytization. "Woe to you scribes and Pharisees, hypocrites! For you traverse sea and land to make a single proselyte, and when he becomes a proselyte, you make him twice the child of hell as yourself" (23:15). Matthew believed that his opponents were actively attracting people to their form of Judaism, if not their very own gathering place. Matthew, too, believed his community could attract people to their Judaism. However, in light of 9:35ff., this might have been wishful thinking on Matthew's part. You may remember, "The harvest is plentiful but the laborers are few." Perhaps 28:19 will help remedy that Matthean shortfall?

An obvious and striking feature of the Matthean commission is the invocation of the triadic formula, "the Father, the son, and the holy spirit," in 28:19. This same triadic formula appears also in *Didache* 7:1–3. J. Schaberg and O. Michel suggest that this formula comes not from an early baptismal liturgy but from an early reworking of Daniel 7. "There came one like a son of man, and he came to the Ancient of Days and was presented before him. And to him was given dominion and glory and kingdom, that all peoples, nations, and languages should serve him."

This apocalyptic passage from Daniel that was so very formative for early Jesus movements may very likely have informed even this final passage from Matthew. The apocalyptic connection between the nations and God's future is present in this Daniel passage. Matthew would have recognized this and appreciated it.

And, of course, it was Daniel's Son of man from chapter 7 that the Gospel writers — including Matthew — saw in Jesus. Matthew's final commission reiterates that once more. For Matthew Jesus the Son of man is also an authoritative earthly figure, not just a heavenly figure. So 28:18 says, like Daniel 7:14, that all authority has been given to Jesus — all authority over the inhabited world. Daniel's vision includes "all people of the earth, nations, and languages." Here the LXX version of Daniel is even more analogous to Matthew's commission in that Daniel, like Matthew, also includes the phrase *panta ta ethne*. Daniel's vision is continued and fulfilled in Jesus, according to Matthew. So the final commission, like Daniel's commission, includes a charge for the rest of the world, for all people. Jesus' authority, and thereby the authority of the Matthean community, extends to the rest of the world.

Matthew saw Jesus as Daniel's Son of man, and God as Daniel's "Ancient of Days." But the notion of the holy spirit (*hagiou pneumatos*) in 28:19b surprises the reader. Where did this come from? Only John at the start of the Gospel and prior to Jesus' ministry, mentions the notion of the holy spirit (3:11). Jesus, John says, will baptize in the holy spirit. This is a distinguishing mark between Jesus and John. John's baptism is with water, Jesus' is with "the holy spirit and with fire" (3:11).

This promise from John is still unfulfilled in the story until the final commission. Jesus, through the fully trained Matthean disciples, will "baptize" all the people in the "name of the father, and the son, and the holy spirit." In this final commission John's words about Jesus are fulfilled.

This term must mean that the community believed that they enjoyed the continued presence and the continued power and authority of Jesus through this spirit. How else would the work Jesus commanded be fulfilled, and how else would the community possess the requisite authority to manage their affairs, survive their struggles, and assert their interpretations and perspectives in their setting, much less prevail in that setting? These things can be accomplished because of the presence of Jesus which, Matthew believes, the spirit can effect within the community.

Indeed, this ongoing presence forms the conclusion of the pericope. The final commission ends with a promise that must have been meaningful to this community in crisis. "Lo, I am with you, even to the close of the age." Matthew's Jesus promises his presence with the struggling community. And the conclusion punctuates the eschatological thrust of the commission. He will be with the church, *even to the end of the age.* The promise of Jesus' presence is reminiscent of a scene at the start of the book. Jesus' name, Emmanuel in 1:23, is the first promise of presence. The second is in 18:20 where Jesus says, in a passage that obviously represents the situation of Matthew's church and not the historical Jesus, "where two or three are gathered in my name, there I am in the midst of them." The third promise of presence is in the final commission. This presence, the church asserts, is accomplished through the spirit.

There are two important features to this final commission. One is educational, the other eschatological. For Matthew, the two are by no means unrelated. Matthew's community is theoretically open to the world. All people and races can be part of the kingdom of heaven. Matthew saw this in certain LXX passages, and his community carried on that tradition. It should be noted up front, though, that those are Matthean members in good standing who follow the laws and traditions and "fulfill all righteousness," whether Jew or Gentile, in the diaspora or homeland.

Matthew's interpretation of the law and of current events may not have resulted in an increase in interest or membership. It is difficult to know certainly. Matthew wished his community would engage in more missionary-like activity, but the reaction to his pleas seem to have been less than enthusiastic. By the time of the writing of the Gospel Matthew could sense certain realities for his community taking shape. They were not in charge in their setting and their future was not terribly bright.

Matthew's position of Matthean Judaism being open to other people and races is related to his view of the end. If others hear about the message of Matthean Judaism, then the end will come. Both 24:14 and 28:20 suggest that. Mission, despite the modest interest in it in Matthew's church, is related to Matthew's view of history. This era or age will draw to a close and the age that promises a better life for Matthean Jews will draw near if the mission to the rest of the world is engaged.

Second, Matthew's commission highlights teaching. Matthean Jews are fully trained teachers and scribes. They have been good learners, they command the material and the arguments that have been presented to them, and they are now teachers of the things Jesus taught them through the author Matthew. Matthew's educational and pedagogical thrust has not waned throughout the course of the book. And it is still evident in the final scene. Jesus teaches and he implores Matthean Jews to, in turn, become teachers to the people and races of the world. This is counsel and a strategy that ultimately worked for Christianity in another setting and with other messages. This, though, did not finally result in the flourishing of Matthean Judaism. The instruction and reiteration of the principles of Matthean Judaism probably sustained and confirmed the group in the face of crises, but did not result in any substantial growth of the movement.

## Further Reading

Clark, K. W. "The Gentile Bias in Matthew." *JBL* 66 (1947): 165–72.

Davies, W. D., and D. Allison. *A Critical and Exegetical Commentary on the Gospel According to Saint Matthew*, vol. 1. Edinburgh: T. & T. Clark, 1988.

Hare, D., and D. Harrington. "Make Disciples of All the Gentiles (Matthew 28:19)." *CBQ* 37 (1975): 359–69.

Harrington, D. *The Gospel of Matthew*. Sacra Pagina 1. Collegeville, Minn.: Michael Glazier/Liturgical Press, 1991.

Howell, D. B. *Matthew's Inclusive Story: A Study in the Narrative Rhetoric of the First Gospel.* JSNT 42. Sheffield: JSOT Press, 1990.

Hubbard, B. J. *The Matthean Redaction of a Primitive Apostolic Commissioning: An Exegesis of Matthew 28:16–20.* SBLDS 19. Missoula, Mont.: Scholars Press, 1974.

Kraemer, R. "On the Meaning of the Term 'Jew' in Greco-Roman Inscriptions." *HTR* 82 (1989): 35–54.

Levine, A. J. *The Social and Ethnic Dimensions of Matthean Social History. "Go nowhere among the Gentiles..." (Matt. 10.5b).* Lewiston, N.Y.: Mellen, 1988.

Longstaff, T. R. W. "The Women at the Tomb: Matthew 28:1 Reexamined." *NTS* 27 (1981): 277–82.

Meier, J. P. "*Nations* or *Gentiles* in Matthew 28:19?" *CBQ* 39 (1977): 94–102.

Michel, O. "The Conclusion of Matthew's Gospel: A Contribution to the History of the Easter Message." Trans. R. Morgan. In *The Interpretation of Matthew,* ed. G. Stanton, 30–41. Philadelphia: Fortress, 1983.

Schaberg, J. *The Father, the Son and the Holy Spirit. The Triadic Phrase in Matthew 28:19b.* SBLDS 61. Chico, Calif.: Scholars Press, 1982.

# The Messages of Matthew's Gospel and the Fate of Matthew's Church

Matthew's Gospel was written for the purpose of responding to the crises his community faced toward the end of the first century in Roman Palestine. As a follower of Jesus, and one who held that Israel had met its fulfillment in Jesus, Matthew believed that Jesus, properly understood and interpreted, could effectively address the situation of Matthean Jews and the conflicts and tensions that characterized his church. He intended to have his story of Jesus remind his congregation of the things that mattered most in this time of transition and upheaval in Israel.

It is too easy to misunderstand and misconstrue Matthew when his context and setting are not fully appreciated. The history of interpretation of Matthew's Gospel provides ample and too often sad evidence of that. To understand Matthew's messages one must also understand the context in which he wrote, and the issues and questions that shaped that context. Matthew's church lived in a time of profound change. Questions of authority, of empire and colonial realms, of interpretation, competition and contention, questions about the future: these are the forces and fears that conformed Matthew's message and his church. In the wake of the first revolt against Rome and the vacuum that created in Galilee and Judea, many forms of Judaism found that their future was in doubt. For most forms of Judaism in this post-70 period, their fears were well founded. Many of the types of Judaism we know about from this period did disappear.

And they happen to drop off the pages of history right around the time Matthew was writing his Gospel.

Matthew's messages seemed to receive some play and enjoy some resonance for a time in the early second century. The *Didache*, 5 Ezra, perhaps the *Gospel of Peter*, and some other fragments indicate a positive reception for Matthew's Gospel soon after its writing. For those groups gathered around Jesus in the early second century who could not imagine a faithful life outside of Judaism, this was a meaningful Gospel. One of the paramount messages of this story is that Judaism as God intended it to be lived out is realized through the Matthean Jesus. For the communities of the second century who shared this presupposition, Matthew's Gospel was a helpful and instructive text.

It is the case, however, that followers of Jesus separated from Judaism, which was something Matthew could not have imagined. A new religion and a new term emerged in the second century. This new religion and identity was Christianity. This new group was related to Judaism but, over time, understood itself as distinct from Judaism. By the end of the second century some of these Christian writers even understood themselves as over against Jews and Judaism. These were the so-called *Adversus Ioudaios* authors and preachers of the second through fourth centuries. Several of these writers employed passages from Matthew to support their anti-Jewish views and to promote the church's usurpation of Israel. Matthew became a Christian book when it made its way into the New Testament canon in the late second century. By this time, painfully to Matthew certainly and to others as well, to be Christian meant to be not Jewish. As G. Strecker demonstrated in his appendix to Bauer's *Orthodoxy and Heresy*, Matthew's type of Jesus-centered Judaism, or Matthean Judaism, by roughly the third century, save a few odd and isolated pockets, died out. Matthew's story became a text aligned with the church and very often set against Jews and Israel.

Few things could be further from Matthew's message and initial setting. Matthew's original intent was to instruct his congregation about the direction, nature, and identity of Israel in a time when many things were up for grabs. Matthew wrote a story that presented Jesus as the teacher who lectured on how one should live. Much of the Sermon on the Mount is Matthew's compilation of Jesus' teaching on that subject, though it is by no means isolated to the Sermon. Relationships, the religious life, and the nature of community are themes that shaped the Sermon. Law and order, civic life, and ethics within the group and the broader society are aspects of the Matthean Jesus' teaching. Matthew stresses the importance and validity of the law. Yet he also teaches the congregation how to interpret and prioritize the law. The Golden Rule and the so-called Great Commandment are rightfully considered distillations of Matthean instruction about the law and relationships. And Matthew meant to teach his church about living with tension and discord on a daily basis.

Matthew's conflict and contention with local leaders, called "the scribes and Pharisees," casts a shadow over the entire Gospel. The tenor of this debate from the Matthean side is rancorous, even embittered. The congregation is repeatedly told about the ills of and the dangers associated with these other local leaders. They are taught how to live with this reality. They are taught how to discern between the things the Matthean Jesus insists are true, righteousness or justice (*dikaiosyne*), things that "bear fruit," and those things that are misguided and usually associated with the false leaders in his setting. There is little mistaking that Matthew felt on the short end of his competition with the leadership group represented by the scribes and Pharisees. This was a reality in the Matthean setting which repeatedly informed the author's thinking and writing. This group, which I have referred to as Formative Judaism following the lead of J. Neusner and others, had the upper hand in Matthew's setting. This was a local political reality Matthean Jews had to face regularly and with which they had to contend.

Matthew's Gospel has enjoyed a very long shelf life. It is still read and informs the beliefs and behavior of many people. This is what Matthew intended. That this is still the case is a testimony to the power of Matthew's story and its effectiveness. Matthew's story, however, is not read by Israel or by Jews. At least it does not enjoy the authority it putatively does within the church and largely Christian West. This is an odd turn and not one anticipated by Matthew. The advice and messages of Matthew's Gospel can help any congregation and its adherents confronting any set of problems roughly analogous to Matthew's church. But Christian interpreters should recall that Matthew meant to speak about Israel. Of course, no one can change the last 2,000 years, but this insight alone should inform with new sensitivities and awareness the interpretation and application of Matthew's Gospel.

Matthew's advice to his community in crisis was to take their stand in the midst of the troubles in Galilee in the late first century and make their case. Matthew believed that his congregation possessed the way out of the malaise that characterized Palestinian society at the close of the century. Matthew's story takes on the competition and lays out the Matthean case for their role in the future of Israel. Matthew believed that Jesus helped his community truly understand and fulfill the law. Other Judaisms and other leaders failed at this. He believed that Matthean Judaism could serve as the "faithful tenants" and negotiate the space and the difference between the Roman imperial powers and the local traditions and practices in Israel. The kingdom should or will be given to the Matthean community and taken away from false leaders and voices, because the former has been faithful and borne fruit, while the latter has led the people astray. These false leaders were in large measure responsible for the destruction and dislocation that had occurred in Israel.

Matthew shows no indication of wanting to negotiate or work things out with the local leaders. He believed that there was little to be gained through such an engagement. Matthean Jews would be the leaders in Israel and they, when their time came, would be good and faithful leaders and teachers. This posture by Matthew put local people in the position of having to choose. The Gospel leaves one with the sense that there is little chance of a reconciliation or a negotiated settlement. These two competing leadership groups represent different decisions and different priorities for Israel's future. People had to choose. Amid all the strengths of Matthew's advice to his community, and given the impact of his instruction that still informs values and behavior in many settings, this was probably the message that contributed most to Matthean Judaism's demise.

One may applaud the resolute manner in which Matthew laid out his position overagainst the scribes and Pharisees. The priorities and the positions of the Matthean church are clear. He fashioned a distinct identity for fellow members in his setting. The contrast with the opposing leaders is stark. But merely from the perspective of what survived and what did not, it was the forms of Judaism which worked and negotiated, which built bridges and formed coalitions that seemed to emerge from the smoke of the transition in Israel around the year 200 C.E. The Judaism that survived and finally flourished in Palestine was a Judaism that reflected several elements and aspects. So-called rabbinic Judaism seems to have been able to take in various forms of Judaism and Jewish perspectives on a range of topics and fashion these into a viable and enduring Judaism in the middle and late Roman period. Because of the strong and at points strident position Matthew staked out, his Judaism did not emerge as an obvious player in that later coalition. His voice is not in evidence.

Yet because of the odd turn that Matthew could not have anticipated or imagined, that is, the rise of another new religion, Matthew's Gospel did obtain an enduring voice. As we have noted, because of this development after the writing of the Gospel, Matthew's messages have often been misappropriated by the church to denounce the very things Matthew meant to uphold: the Torah, God's people, and the future of Israel. A reading of Matthew better informed about his context may help overcome such misreadings. But Matthew's Gospel became the church's first Gospel because it did speak to congregations in crisis and to people who faced some of the very uncertainties we have charted in Matthew's church. The author's insight and the power of his rhetoric justifiably claim an unusual legacy. Matthew's counsel and advice at a particularly crucial time in the life of one single congregation continue to guide and inform similar communities and individuals in analogous situations. In our treatment of the Sermon on the Mount we noted the many inspired religious and political figures who took their lead from

Matthew. This continues to be the case. And there are many communities in many different settings, in various cultures, speaking many different languages, who find in Matthew's advice to his church and community in crisis guidance for their own congregations. This commentary has encouraged people to take Matthew's messages and counsel seriously. This includes hearing his messages in the context in which they were developed and delivered. This also includes critically listening to his advice and, with the advantage of hindsight, recognizing and assessing the ramifications of that advice. Matthew would expect his followers to be an informed and critical audience. This is what he means when he says, "Every scribe who has been trained for the kingdom of heaven is like a householder who brings out of his treasure what is new and what is old" (13:52). The treasure Matthew believed his congregation possessed was a combination of the history and promises of his people interpreted in light of the current events in his setting. Matthew's story of Jesus offers his position on who Matthean Jews are, and where they should be headed. A thoughtful and thorough assessment of the history and traditions of his people, as well as an appreciation and apprehension of the new things that have occurred to his community because of that history, will enable the careful scribe and disciple to make informed choices within and sound interpretations of their situation.

"Teaching people to observe all that [Jesus] commanded" means teaching people how to understand their place and their role in Israel as well as how to survive in the precarious period of 70–135 C.E. Matthew's story of Jesus intends to instruct and train his community in this manner. Followers are to become active players in a political and religious drama in Palestine. And they are people who can offer a position and an argument about identity, direction, and leadership in a time of transition and tension. Whether or not this position should prevail does not seem to be an obvious concern for Matthew. What is clearly a concern, however, is that his disciples "trained for the kingdom of heaven" understand who they are and where they are going, and why they are not going in another direction, namely the position offered by the competing local leaders. And Matthean disciples are trained to offer reasons and arguments for why their position, and their interpretation of the current state of affairs, is accurate. The informed and critical voice of Matthean disciples carried into the second century. Matthew's Gospel represents a voice and a claim about one community's identity and future amid the crises and concerns that confronted many Jewish communities. Matthew's Gospel adds considerable information and insight into the rich variety of voices in one of the most important and formative periods in both Jewish and Christian history.

## Further Reading

MacLennan, R. S. *Early Christian Texts on Jews and Judaism*. Atlanta: Scholars Press, 1990.

Massaux, E. *Influence de L'Évangile de saint Matthieu sur la littérature chrétienne avant saint Irénée*. Leuven: Publications Universitaires, 1950.

Overman, J. A. *Matthew's Gospel and Formative Judaism: The Social World of the Matthean Community*. Minneapolis: Fortress, 1990.

Saldarini, A. J. *Matthew's Christian-Jewish Community*. Chicago: University of Chicago, 1994.

Strecker, G. Foreword to the second German edition of W. Bauer, *Orthodoxy and Heresy in Earliest Christianity*, ed. R. Kraft and G. Krodel. Philadelphia: Minneapolis, 1971.

# References

Bacon, B. W. "Pharisees and Herodians in Mark." *JBL* 39 (1920): 102–11.

Balch, D., ed. *Social History of the Matthean Community: Cross-Disciplinary Approaches.* Minneapolis: Fortress, 1991.

Bammel, E. "Crucifixion as a Punishment in Palestine." In *The Trial of Jesus: Cambridge Studies in Honor of C. F. D. Moule,* ed. E. Bammel, 162–66. Naperville, Ill.: A. R. Allenson, 1970.

———. "Ex illa itaque die consilium fecerant. . . . " In *The Trial of Jesus: Cambridge Studies in Honor of C. F. D. Moule,* ed. E. Bammel, 11–40. Naperville, Ill.: A. R. Allenson, 1970.

Bammel, E., and C. F. D. Moule, eds. *Jesus and the Politics of His Day.* Cambridge: Cambridge University Press, 1984.

Baras, Z. "The *Testimonium Flavianum* and the Martyrdom of James." In *Josephus, Judaism, and Christianity,* ed. L. Feldman and G. Hata, 338–48. Detroit: Wayne State Press, 1987.

Baumgarten, A. I. "The Pharisaic *Paradosis.*" *HTR* 80 (1987): 63–78.

Baumgarten, J. M. "The Pharisaic-Sadducean Controversies about Purity and the Qumran Texts." *JJS* 31 (1980): 157–70.

Berger, P. L. *The Sacred Canopy: Elements of a Sociological Theory of Religion.* Garden City, N.Y.: Doubleday, 1969.

Berger, P., and T. Luckmann. *The Social Construction of Reality.* Garden City, N.Y.: Doubleday, 1967.

Betz, H. D. *Nachfolge und Nachahmung Jesu Christi im Neuen Testament.* BHTh 37. Tübingen: J. C. B. Mohr (Paul Siebeck), 1967.

Betz, O. "Felsenmann und Felsengemeinde." *ZNW* 48 (1957): 49–77.

Bornkamm, G. "The Authority to Bind and to Loose in the Church in Matthew's Gospel." In *Jesus and Man's Hope,* ed. D. G. Miller, 1:37–50. Pittsburgh: Pittsburgh Theological Seminary, 1970.

———. "The Authority to 'Bind' and to 'Loose' in the Church of Matthew's Gospel: The Problem of Sources in Matthew's Gospel." In *The Interpretation of Matthew,* ed. G. Stanton, 85–97. Philadelphia: Fortress, 1983.

———. *Jesus of Nazareth.* New York: Harper, 1960.

420

———. "The Stilling of the Storm." In *Tradition and Interpretation in Matthew*, ed. G. Bornkamm, G. Barth, and H. Held, 52–57. Philadelphia: Westminster, 1963.

Bornkamm, G., G. Barth, and H. Held. *Tradition and Interpretation in Matthew*. Philadelphia: Westminster, 1963.

Brooten, B. *Women Leaders in the Ancient Synagogue: Inscriptional Evidence and Background Issues*. Brown Judaic Studies 36. Chico, Calif.: Scholars Press, 1982.

Brown, R. E. *The Birth of the Messiah*. Garden City, N.Y.: Doubleday, 1977.

———. *The Death of the Messiah: From Gethsemane to the Grave — A Commentary on the Passion Narratives in the Four Gospels*. Garden City, N.Y.: Doubleday, 1994.

Bultmann, R. *The History of the Synoptic Tradition*. Rev. ed. Trans. J. Marsh. San Francisco: Harper and Row, 1963.

Burnett, F. W. *The Testimony of Jesus-Sophia: A Redactional-Critical Study of the Eschatological Discourse in Matthew*. Washington, D.C.: University Press of America, 1981.

Clark, K. W. "The Gentile Bias in Matthew." *JBL* 66 (1947): 165–72.

Cohen, S. *Josephus in Galilee and Rome: His Vita and Development as a Historian*. Leiden: Brill, 1979.

———. "Respect for Judaism by Gentiles According to Josephus." *HTR* 80 (1987): 409–30.

Cope, L. "The Death of John the Baptist in the Gospel of Matthew." *CBQ* 38 (1976): 515–19.

———. *Matthew: A Scribe Trained for the Kingdom of Heaven*. Washington, D.C.: Catholic Biblical Association, 1976.

Crossan, D. *Finding Is the First Act: Trove Folktales and Jesus' Treasure Parable*. Semeia Supplements 9. Missoula, Mont.: Scholars Press, 1979.

———. *In Parables: The Challenge of the Historical Jesus*. New York: Harper and Row, 1973.

———. *Who Killed Jesus? Exposing the Roots of Anti-Semitism in the Gospel Story of the Death of Jesus*. San Francisco: Harper, 1995.

Dahl, N. A. "The Passion Narrative in Matthew." In *The Interpretation of Matthew*, ed. G. Stanton, 42–55. Philadelphia: Fortress, 1983.

Danker, F. *Benefactor: Epigraphic Study of a Greco-Roman and New Testament Semantic Field*. St. Louis: Clayton, 1982.

Daube, D. "*Kerdano* as a Missionary Term." *HTR* 40 (1947): 109–20.

Davies, W. D. *The Setting of the Sermon on the Mount*. Cambridge: Cambridge University Press, 1964.

Davies, W. D., and D. C. Allison. *A Critical and Exegetical Commentary on the Gospel According to Saint Matthew*, 2 vols. International Critical Commentary Series. Edinburgh: T. & T. Clark, 1988–91.

———. *Matthew 8–17: An Exegetical and Critical Commentary*. Edinburgh: T. & T. Clark, 1992.

Deutsch, C. *Hidden Wisdom and the Easy Yoke: Wisdom, Torah and Discipleship in Matthew 11:25-30.* Sheffield: JSOT, 1987.

Dodd, C. H. *The Parables of the Kingdom.* London: Fontana, 1961.

Donahue, J. R. "The 'Parable' of the Sheep and the Goats: A Challenge to Christian Ethics." *TS* 47 (1986): 3–31.

———. "Tax Collectors and Sinners." *CBQ* 33 (1971): 39–61.

Donaldson, T. L. "Moses Typology and the Sectarian Nature of Early Christian Anti-Judaism." *JSNT* 12 (1981): 27–52.

Duling, D. "The Therapeutic Son of David: An Element in Matthew's Christological Apologetic." *NTS* 24 (1978): 392–410.

Dupont, J. *Les Béatitudes: Le probléme littéraire. Les deux versions du Sermon sur la Montagne et des Béatitudes.* Bruges: Abbaye de Saint-André, 1958.

Edwards, D. "Religion, Power and Politics: Jewish Defeats by the Romans in Iconography and Josephus." In *Diaspora Jews and Judaism: Essays in Honor of, and in Dialogue with A. Thomas Kraabel,* ed. J. A. Overman and R. S. MacLennan, 293–309. Atlanta: Scholars Press, 1992.

Edwards, R. A. *The Sign of Jonah in the Theology of the Evangelists and Q.* Naperville, Ill.: Allenson, 1971.

*The Fathers According to Rabbi Nathan.* Trans. with introduction and commentary by J. Goldin. New Haven: Yale University Press, 1955.

Feldman, L. *Josephus and Modern Scholarship.* New York: de Gruyter, 1984.

Fischer, L. *Gandhi: His Life and Message.* New York: Mentor, 1954.

Fitzmyer, J. A. "Anti-Semitism and the Cry of 'All the People' (Mt 27:25)." *TS* 26 (1965): 667–71.

———. "The Use of Explicit Old Testament Quotations in the Qumran Literature and in the New Testament." In *Essays in the Semitic Background of the New Testament,* 3–58. Missoula, Mont.: Scholars Press, 1974.

Forkman, G. *The Limits of Religious Community: Expulsion from the Religious Community within the Qumran Sect, within Rabbinic Judaism, and within Primitive Christianity.* Lund: Gleerup, 1972.

Fowler, R. M. *Loaves and Fishes: The Function of the Feeding Stories in the Gospel of Mark.* SBLDS 54. Chico, Calif.: Scholars Press, 1981.

Frankemölle, H. *Jahwebund und Kirche Christi.* Münster: Aschendorff, 1974.

Garland, D. *The Intention of Matthew 23.* NovTSup 52. Leiden: Brill, 1979.

Gerhardsson, B. "'An ihren Früchten sollt ihr sie erkennen': Die Legitimitätsfrage in der matthäischen Christologie." *EvTh* 42 (1982): 113–26.

Gnilka, J. *Das Evangelium Nach Markus (Mk. 1–8, 26).* EKKNT 2.1. Zürich: Benziger, 1978.

———. "Matthäusgemeinde und Qumran." *BZ* 7 (1963): 43–63.

Goldammer, K. "Navis Ecclesiae." *ZNW* 40 (1941): 76–91.

Goodman, M. "The First Jewish Revolt: Social Conflict and the Problem of Debt." *JJS* 33 (1982): 418–27.

———. "Nerva, the *Fiscus Judaicus* and Jewish Identity." *JRS* 79 (1989): 40–44.

———. *The Ruling Class of Judea: The Origins of the Jewish Revolt against Rome A.D. 66–70*. Cambridge: Cambridge University Press, 1987.

Gray, S. W. *The Least of My Brothers: Matthew 25:31–46 — A History of Interpretation*. SBL Dissertation Series 114. Atlanta: Scholars Press, 1989.

Green, W. S., J. Neusner, and E. Frerichs, eds. *Judaisms and Their Messiahs at the Turn of the Christian Era*. Cambridge: Cambridge University Press, 1987.

Guelich, R. "Interpreting the Sermon on the Mount." *Interpretation* 41 (1987): 117–30.

———. *Mark 1–8:26*. Word Biblical Commentary 34a. Waco, Tex.: Word, 1989.

———. *The Sermon on the Mount: A Foundation for Understanding*. Waco, Tex.: Word, 1982.

Haenchen, E. *The Acts of the Apostles: A Commentary*. Philadelphia: Westminster, 1971.

Hare, D., and D. Harrington. "Make Disciples of All the Gentiles (Matthew 28:19)." *CBQ* 37 (1975): 359–69.

Harrington, D. *The Gospel of Matthew*. Sacra Pagina 1. Collegeville, Minn.: Michael Glazier/Liturgical Press, 1991.

———. "Matthean Studies since Joachim Rohde." *Heythrop Journal* 16 (1975): 375–88.

Hengel, M. *The Charismatic Leader and His Followers*. Trans. J. Greig. New York: Crossroad, 1981.

———. *Judaism and Hellenism*. Philadelphia: Fortress, 1974.

Horbury, W. "The Temple Tax." In *Jesus and the Politics of His Day*, ed. E. Bammel and C. F. D. Moule, 266–73. Cambridge: Cambridge University Press, 1986.

Horsley, R. "Ancient Jewish Banditry and the Revolt against Rome, A.D. 66–70." *CBQ* 43 (1981): 409–32.

———. "Ethics and Exegesis: 'Love Your Enemies' and the Doctrine of Non-Retaliation." *JAAR* 54 (1986): 3–31.

———. *Jesus and the Spiral of Violence*. San Francisco: Harper and Row, 1987.

Horsley, R. H., and J. S. Hanson. *Bandits, Prophets, and Messiahs: Popular Movements at the Time of Jesus*. Minneapolis: Winston, 1985.

Horst, P. van der, "Das Neue Testament und die jüdischen Grabinschriften aus hellenistisch-römischer Zeit." *BZ* 36 (1992): 161–78.

Howell, D. B. *Matthew's Inclusive Story: A Study in the Narrative Rhetoric of the First Gospel*. JSNT 42. Sheffield: JSOT Press, 1990.

Hubbard, B. J. *The Matthean Redaction of a Primitive Apostolic Commissioning: An Exegesis of Matthew 28:16-20.* SBLDS 19. Missoula, Mont.: Scholars Press, 1974.

Hultgren, A. *Jesus and His Adversaries: The Form and Function of the Conflict Stories in the Synoptic Gospels.* Minneapolis: Augsburg, 1979.

Hummel, R. *Die Auseinandersetzung zwischen Kirche und Judentum im Matthäusevangelium.* Munich: Chr. Kaiser, 1963.

Isler, S. *The Dositheans: A Samaritan Sect in Late Antiquity.* Leiden: Brill, 1976.

Jellicoe, S. *The Septuagint and Modern Study.* Oxford: Clarendon, 1968.

Jeremias, J. *The Parables of Jesus.* 2nd rev. ed. Trans. S. H. Hooke. New York: Scribner's, 1972.

Johnson, L. T. *The Gospel of Luke.* Sacra Pagina 3. Collegeville, Minn.: Michael Glazier/Liturgical Press, 1991.

Kampen, J. "The Matthean Divorce Texts Reexamined." In *New Qumran Texts and Studies,* ed. G. Brooke, 149–67. Leiden: Brill, 1994.

Kampling, R. *Das Blut Christi und die Juden. Mt. 27, 25 bei den lateinischsprachigen christlichen Autoren bis zu Leo dem Grossen.* Münster: Aschendorff, 1984.

Käsemann, E. "Die Anfange christlichen Theologie." *ZTK* 57 (1960): 158–79.

Kee, H. C. *Community of the New Age: Studies in Mark's Gospel.* London: SCM Press, 1977.

———. "The Terminology of Mark's Exorcism Stories." *NTS* 14 (1967–68): 232–46.

Kelber, W. *Mark's Story of Jesus.* Philadelphia: Fortress, 1979.

Kilpatrick, J. *The Origins of the Gospel According to St. Matthew.* Oxford: Clarendon, 1946.

Kimelman, R. "*Birkat Ha-Minim* and the Lack of Evidence for an Anti-Christian Jewish Prayer in Antiquity." In *Jewish and Christian Self-Definition,* ed. E. P. Sanders, 2:226–44. Philadelphia: Fortress, 1981.

King, M. L., Jr. *A Stride toward Freedom: The Montgomery Story.* New York: Harper, 1958.

Kingsbury, J. D. "The Figure of Peter in Matthew's Gospel as a Theological Problem." *JBL* 98 (1979): 67–87.

———. *Matthew as Story.* Philadelphia: Fortress, 1987.

———. "Observations on the 'Miracle Chapters' of Matthew 8-9." *CBQ* 40 (1978): 559–73.

———. "The Parable of the Wicked Husbandmen and the Secret of Jesus' Divine Sonship in Matthew: Some Literary-Critical Observations." *JBL* 105 (1986): 643–55.

———. *The Parables of Jesus in Matthew 13.* Richmond, Va.: John Knox, 1969.

———. "The Verb 'Akoluthein' as an Index of Matthew's View of His Community." *JBL* 97 (1978): 67–87.

Kissinger, W. S. *The Sermon on the Mount: A History of Interpretation and Bibliography.* Metuchen, N.J.: Scarecrow, 1975.

Kloppenborg, J. *The Formation of Q: Trajectories in Ancient Wisdom Collections.* Philadelphia: Fortress, 1987.

Kohler, K. "The Origin and Composition of the Eighteen Benedictions." In *Contributions to the Scientific Study of the Jewish Liturgy,* ed. J. Petuchowski. New York: KTAV, 1970.

Kraabel, A. T. "The Disappearance of the God-Fearers." *Numen* 28 (1981): 113–26.

———. "Immigrants, Exiles, Expatriates, and Missionaries." In *Religious Propaganda and Missionary Competition in the New Testament World: Essays Honoring Dieter Georgi,* ed. L. Bormann, K. Del Tredici, and A. Standhartinger, 71–88. Leiden: Brill, 1994.

Kraemer, R. "On the Meaning of the Term 'Jew' in Greco-Roman Inscriptions." *HTR* 82 (1989): 35–54.

Kriesburg, L. *The Sociology of Social Conflict.* Englewood Cliffs, N.J.: Prentice-Hall, 1973.

Légasse, S. "Le refroidissement de l'amour avant la fin (Mt 24.12)." *SNTU* 8 (1983): 91–102.

Levine, A. J. *The Social and Ethnic Dimensions of Matthean Social History. "Go nowhere among the Gentiles... " (Matt. 10.5b).* Lewiston, N.Y.: Mellen, 1988.

Levine, L., ed. *Ancient Synagogues Revealed.* Detroit: Wayne State University, 1982.

———, ed. *The Galilee in Late Antiquity.* Cambridge: Harvard University Press; New York: KTAV, 1992.

Lona, H. "In meinem Namen versammelt. Mt. 18, 20 und liturgisches Handeln." *Archiv für Liturgiewissenschaft* 27 (1985): 373–404.

Longstaff, T. R. W. "The Women at the Tomb: Matthew 28:1 Reexamined." *NTS* 27 (1981): 277–82.

Luz, U. "The Disciples in the Gospel According to Matthew." In *The Interpretation of Matthew,* ed. G. Stanton, 98–128. Philadelphia: Fortress, 1983.

———. *Matthew in History: Interpretation, Influence, and Effects.* Minneapolis: Fortress, 1994.

Ma'oz, Z. "Banias Excavation Project — 1988." *Exploration and Surveys in Israel* 7.8 (1989): 10–11.

MacLennan, R. S. *Early Christian Texts on Jews and Judaism.* Atlanta: Scholars Press, 1990.

Malherbe, A. J. *Paul and the Popular Philosophers.* Minneapolis: Fortress, 1989.

Malina, B. "Does *Porneia* Mean Fornication?" *NovT* 14 (1972): 10–17.

———. "The Individual and the Community — Personality in the Social World of Early Christianity." *BTB* 9 (1979): 126–38.

Manns, F. "Un centre judeo-chretian important: Sepphoris." In *Essais sur le Judeo-Christianisme*, 165–90. Jerusalem: Franciscan Press, 1977.

Massaux, E. *Influence de L'Évangile de saint Matthieu sur la littérature chrétienne avant saint Irénée.* Leuven: Publications Universitaires, 1950.

Meier, J. P. "*Nations* or *Gentiles* in Matthew 28:19?" *CBQ* 39 (1977): 94–102.

Meshorer, Y. *The Coins of Eretz Israel and the Decapolis in the Roman Period.* Jerusalem: Israel Museum, 1985.

Meyer, M. *The Gospel of Thomas: The Hidden Sayings of Jesus.* San Francisco: HarperCollins, 1992.

Meyers, E. "The Cultural Setting of Galilee: The Case of Regionalism in Early Judaism." *ANRW* II.19.1 (1979): 686–702.

Meyers, E. M., and A. T. Kraabel. "Archaeology, Iconography, and Non-literary Remains." In *Early Judaism and Its Modern Interpreters*, ed. R. Kraft and G. Nickelsburg, 175–210. Atlanta: Scholars Press, 1986.

Michel, O. "The Conclusion of Matthew's Gospel: A Contribution to the History of the Easter Message." Trans. R. Morgan. In *The Interpretation of Matthew*, ed. G. Stanton, 30–41. Philadelphia: Fortress, 1983.

Miller, S. *Studies in the History and Traditions of Sepphoris.* Leiden: Brill, 1984.

Minear, P. "The Disciples and the Crowds in the Gospel of Matthew." In *Gospel Studies in Honor of S. E. Johnson*, ed. M. Shepherd and E. Hobbs. ATR Suppl. Series 3 (1974): 28–44.

Mora, V. *Le refus d'Israël. Matthieu 27, 25.* Paris: Cerf, 1986.

Murphy, F. *The Structure and Meaning of Second Baruch.* SBLDS 78. Atlanta: Scholars Press, 1985.

Nau, A. J. *Peter in Matthew: Discipleship, Diplomacy, and Dispraise.* Collegeville, Minn.: Michael Glazier/Liturgical Press, 1992.

Neusner, J. "First Cleanse the Inside." *NTS* 22 (1976): 486–95.

———. "The Formation of Rabbinic Judaism: Yavneh from A.D. 70–100." *ANRW* II.19.2 (1979): 3–42.

———. *From Politics to Piety: The Emergence of Pharisaic Judaism.* Englewood Cliffs: Prentice-Hall, 1973.

———. "The Idea of Purity in Ancient Judaism." *JAAR* 43 (1975): 15–26.

———. *The Mishna: A New Translation.* New Haven, Conn.: Yale University Press, 1988.

———. "Two Pictures of the Pharisees: Philosophical Circle and Eating Club." *ATR* 64 (1982): 525–38.

Nickelsburg, G., Jr. *Resurrection, Immortality, and Eternal Life in Intertestamental Judaism.* Harvard Theological Studies 26. Cambridge: Harvard University Press, 1972.

Overman, J. A. "The Diaspora in the Modern Study of Ancient Judaism." In *Diaspora Jews and Judaism: Essays in Honor of, and in Dialogue with, A. Thomas Kraabel,* ed. J. A. Overman and R. S. MacLennan, 63–78. Atlanta: Scholars Press, 1992.

———. "The God-Fearers: Some Neglected Features." *JSNT* 32 (1988): 17–26.

———. "Heroes and Villains in Palestinian Lore: Matthew's Use of Traditional Jewish Polemic in the Passion Narrative." SBLSP 29 (1990): 585–96.

———. *Matthew's Gospel and Formative Judaism: The Social World of the Matthean Community.* Minneapolis: Fortress, 1990.

———. "Recent Advances in the Archaeology of the Galilee in the Roman Period." *Currents in Research: Biblical Studies* 1 (1993): 35–58.

———. "Who Were the First Urban Christians? Urbanization in Galilee in the First Century." SBLSP 27 (1988): 160–68.

Overman, J. A., and R. S. MacLennan. *Diaspora Jews and Judaism: Essays in Honor of, and in Dialogue with, A. Thomas Kraabel.* University of South Florida Studies in the History of Judaism 41. Atlanta: Scholars Press, 1992.

Perkins, P. *Love Commands in the New Testament.* New York: Paulist, 1982.

Pesch, R. *Das Markusevangelium.* HTKNT. Freiburg: Herder, 1977.

Pesch, W. *Matthäus als Seelsorger.* Stuttgart: Katholisches Bibelwerk, 1966.

Porton, G. *Goyim: Gentiles and Israelites in Mishna-Tosefta.* Atlanta: Scholars Press, 1988.

———. *Understanding Rabbinic Midrash.* New York: KTAV, 1985.

Przybylski, B. *Righteousness in Matthew and His World of Thought.* Cambridge: Cambridge University Press, 1980.

———. "The Role of Matt. 3:13–4:11 in the Structure and Theology of the Gospel of Matthew." *BTB* 4 (1974): 222–35.

Quesnell, Q. "Made Themselves Eunuchs for the Kingdom of Heaven." *CBQ* 30 (1968): 335–58.

Reynolds, J., and R. Tannenbaum. *Jews and Godfearers at Aphrodisias.* Cambridge: Cambridge Philological Society, 1987.

Rivkin, E. *What Crucified Jesus?* Nashville: Abingdon, 1984.

Robertson, A. T. *A Grammar of the Greek New Testament in the Light of Historical Research.* Nashville: Broadman Press, 1934.

Rothfuchs, W. *Die Erfüllungszitate des Matthäus-Evangeliums.* Stuttgart: Kohlhammer, 1969.

Rowley, H. H. "The Herodians in the Gospels." *JTS* 41 (1940): 14–27.

Saldarini, A. J. "Apocalyptic and Rabbinic Literature." *CBQ* 37 (1975): 348–58.

———. "Delegitimation of Leaders in Matthew 23." *CBQ* 54 (1992): 659–80.

————. *Matthew's Christian-Jewish Community.* Chicago Studies in the History of Judaism. Chicago: University of Chicago Press, 1994.

————. *Pharisees, Scribes, and Sadducees in Palestinian Society: A Sociological Approach.* Wilmington, Del.: Michael Glazier, 1988.

Sanders, E. P. *Jesus and Judaism.* Philadelphia: Fortress, 1985.

————. *Judaism: Practice and Belief 63 B.C.E.-66 C.E.* Philadelphia: Trinity Press International, 1992.

Schaberg, J. *The Father, the Son and the Holy Spirit. The Triadic Phrase in Matthew 28:19b.* SBLDS 61. Chico, Calif.: Scholars Press, 1982.

Schäfer, P. "Die sogenannte Synode von Jabne." In *Studien zur Geschichte und Theologie des rabbinischen Judentums,* 45–64. Leiden: Brill, 1978.

Schiffman, L. *The Eschatological Community of the Dead Sea Scrolls.* SBL Monograph Series 28. Atlanta: Scholars Press, 1989.

————. "The New Halakhic Letter (4QMMT) and the Origins of the Dead Sea Sect." *BA* 53 (1990): 64–73.

Schlatter, A. *Der Evangelist Matthäus.* Stuttgart: Calwer, 1948.

Schoedel, W. R. "Ignatius and the Reception of the Gospel of Matthew in Antioch." In *Social History of the Matthean Community,* ed. Balch, 129–77.

Schüssler Fiorenza, E. *In Memory of Her: A Feminist Theological Reconstruction of Christian Origins.* New York: Crossroad, 1983.

Schweitzer, A. *The Quest for the Historical Jesus.* 3rd ed. New York: Macmillan, 1968.

Schweizer, E. "Matthew's Church." In *The Interpretation of Matthew,* ed. G. Stanton, 129–55. Philadelphia: Fortress, 1983.

————. "Observance of the Law and Charismatic Activity in Matthew." *NTS* 16 (1970): 213–30.

Scott, B. "The King's Accounting. Matthew 18:23–34." *JBL* 104 (1985): 429–42.

Segal, A. "Matthew's Jewish Voice." In *Social History of the Matthean Community,* ed. Balch, 3–37.

Senior, D. *The Passion of Jesus in the Gospel of Matthew.* Wilmington, Del.: Michael Glazier, 1985.

Slingerland, H. D. "The Transjordan Origin of St. Matthew's Gospel." *JSNT* 3 (1979): 18–28.

Smith, M. *Jesus the Magician.* San Francisco: Harper and Row, 1978.

Smith, R. R. "*Simulacra Gentium:* The *Ethne* from the Sebasteion at Aphrodisias." *JRS* 78 (1988): 50–77.

Stanton, G. *A Gospel for a New People: Studies in Matthew.* Edinburgh: T. & T. Clark, 1992.

————. "The Origin and Purpose of Matthew's Gospel: Matthean Scholarship from 1945–1980." *ANRW* II.25.3 (1889–1951).

Stendahl, K. "Quis et Unde? An Analysis of Matthew 1–2." In *The Interpretation of Matthew,* ed. G. Stanton. Philadelphia: Fortress, 1983.

———. *The School of St. Matthew and Its Use of the Old Testament.* 2nd ed. Philadelphia: Fortress, 1968.

Strange, J. "Archaeology and the Religion of Judaism in Palestine." *ANRW* II.19.1 (1979): 646–85.

———. "Review Article: The Capernaum and Herodium Publications." *BASOR* 226 (1977): 65–73.

Strecker, G. *Der Weg der Gerechtigkeit: Untersuchung zur Theologie des Matthäus.* Göttingen: Vandenhoeck and Ruprecht, 1962.

Strecker, G. Foreword to the second German edition of W. Bauer, *Orthodoxy and Heresy in Earliest Christianity*, ed. R. Kraft and G. Krodel. Philadelphia: Minneapolis, 1971.

Theissen, G. "Das 'schwankende Rohr' im Mt. 11, 7 und die Gründungsmünzen von Tiberias. Ein Beitrag zur Lokalkoloritforschung in den synoptischen Evangelien." *ZDPV* 101 (1985): 43–55.

———. *Sociology of Early Palestinian Christianity.* Philadelphia: Fortress, 1978.

Thompson, W. *Matthew's Advice to a Divided Community: Mt. 17:22–18:35.* Rome: Biblical Institute, 1970.

Tilborg, S. van. *The Jewish Leaders in Matthew.* Leiden: Brill, 1972.

Trilling, W. "Amt und Amtsverständnis bei Matthäus." In *Mélanges Bibliques: Festschrift for B. Rigaux*, ed. A. Descamps, 29–44. Gembloux: Duculot, 1969.

———. *Das Wahre Israel: Studien zur Theologie des Matthäus-Evangeliums.* Munich: Kösel, 1964.

Vaage, L. *Galilean Upstarts: Jesus' First Followers According to Q.* Valley Forge, Pa.: Trinity Press International, 1994.

Van Segbroeck, F. "Jésus rejeté par sa patrie (Mt 13, 54–58)." *Biblica* 49 (1968): 167–98.

Vawter, B. "Divorce and the New Testament." *CBQ* 39 (1977): 528–42.

Vermes, G. *The Dead Sea Scrolls in English.* 3rd ed. London: Penguin, 1987.

———. *Jesus and the World of Judaism.* London: SCM, 1983.

Viviano, B. T. "Where Was the Gospel of Matthew Written?" *CBQ* 41 (1979): 533–46.

Weber, M. *Economy and Society.* Ed. G. Roth and C. Wittich. Berkeley: University of California Press, 1978.

Wilder, A. N. *Early Christian Rhetoric: The Language of the Gospel.* Cambridge: Harvard University Press, 1971.

———. *Jesus' Parables and the War of Myths.* Philadelphia: Fortress, 1982.

Wink, W. *John the Baptist in the Gospel Tradition.* SNTSMS 7. Cambridge: Cambridge University Press, 1968.

Witherington, B. "Jesus and the Baptist — Two of a Kind?" SBLSP 27 (1988): 225–44.

Wuellner, W. *The Meaning of "Fishers of Men."* Philadelphia: Fortress, 1968.

# Index of Texts

430

**JOSEPHUS**

# Index of Names

J. Andrew Overman is Associate Professor and Chair of the Classics Department at Macalester College, Saint Paul, Minnesota, and is the author of *Matthew's Gospel and Formative Judaism: The*